Fodor's 96

Santa Fe, Taos, Albuquerque

Ron Butler

"Fodor's guides . . . are an admirable blend of the cultural and the practical."

—*The Washington Post*

"Researched by people chosen because they live or have lived in the country, well-written, and with good historical sections . . . Obligatory reading for millions of tourists."

—*The Independent, London*

"Usable, sophisticated restaurant coverage, with an emphasis on good value."

—*Andy Birsh, Gourmet restaurant columnist, quoted by Gannett News Service*

"Packed with dependable information."

—*Atlanta Journal-Constitution*

"Fodor's always delivers high quality . . . thoughtfully presented . . . thorough."

—*Houston Post*

"Valuable because of their comprehensiveness."

—*Minneapolis Star-Tribune*

Fodor's Travel Publications, Inc.
New York • Toronto • London • Sydney • Auckland

Fodor's Santa Fe, Taos, Albuquerque

Editor: David Low

Editorial Contributors: Steven Amsterdam, Ron Butler, Carmella Padilla, Alexander Parsons, M.T. Schwartzman (Gold Guide editor), Dinah A. Spritzer.

Creative Director: Fabrizio La Rocca

Cartographer: David Lindroth

Illustrator: Karl Tanner

Cover Photograph: Scott Lynn Riley

Text Design: Between the Covers

Copyright © 1996 by Fodor's Travel Publications, Inc.

ISBN 0–679–03067–0

Acknowledgment

To my daughter, Alexandra. They'll love you in Santa Fe.

Special Sales

Fodor's Travel Publications are available at special discounts for sales promotions or premiums. Special editions, including personalized covers, excerpts of existing guides, and corporate imprints, can be created in large quantities for special needs. For more information, write to Special Marketing, Fodor's Travel Publications, 201 E. 50th St., New York, NY 10022, or call 800/800–3246. In the U.K., write to Fodor's Travel Publications, 20 Vauxhall Bridge Rd. London, England SW1V 2SA.

CONTENTS

Maps

ON THE ROAD WITH FODOR'S

GOOD TRAVEL GUIDE is like a wonderful traveling companion. It's charming, it's brimming with sound recommendations and solid ideas, it pulls no punches in describing lodging and dining establishments, and it's consistently full of fascinating facts that make you view what you've traveled to see in a rich new light. In the creation of *Santa Fe, Taos, Albuquerque '96*, we at Fodor's have gone to great lengths to provide you with the very best of all possible traveling companions—and to make your trip the best of all possible vacations.

About Our Writers

The information in these pages is a collaboration of a few extraordinary writers.

Ron Butler, who wrote earlier editions of this guidebook, has traveled extensively around the Southwest. His books include *Esquire's Guide to Modern Etiquette* and *The Best of the Old West*, and his articles have appeared in *Travel & Leisure*, *Travel Holiday*, and *Ladies' Home Journal*.

Carmella Padilla, who revised the chapters on Santa Fe, Albuquerque, and the Pueblos of the Rio Grande, is a Sante Fe native and has been based there as a freelance writer since 1989. Before that, she lived in Albuquerque for seven years and worked as newspaper reporter. Her features for various local and national publications lend a unique insider's perspective on New Mexico's cultural landscape. Carmella's healthy appetite for chile, margaritas, and other native delights has made her a reliable culinary consultant for visitors to the state.

Based in Santa Fe, **Alexander Parsons,** who updated the chapters on Taos, Carlsbad, and southern New Mexico, has worked in the editorial department at Random House. He currently writes for Associated Press and *Santa Fean Magazine*.

What's New

A New Design
If this is not the first Fodor's guide you've purchased, you'll immediately notice our new look. More readable and easier to use than ever? We think so—and we hope you do, too.

Let Us Do Your Booking
Our writers have scoured Santa Fe, Taos, an Albuquerque and Southern New Mexico to come up with an extensive and well-balanced list of the best B&Bs, inns, and hotels, both small and large, new and old. But you don't have to beat the bushes to come up with a reservation. Now we've teamed up with an established hotel-booking service to make it easy for you to secure a room at the property of your choice. It's fast, it's free, and confirmation is guaranteed. If your first choice is booked, the operators can line up your second right away. Just call 800/FODORS-1 or 800/363-6771 (0800/89–1030 when in Great Britain; 0014/800–12–8271 when in Australia; 1800/55–9101 when in Ireland).

Travel Updates
In addition, just before your trip, you may want to order a Fodor's Worldview Travel Update. From local publications all over Santa Fe, Taos, Albuquerque, and Southern New Mexico, the lively, cosmopolitan editors at Worldview gather information on concerts, plays, opera, dance performances, gallery and museum shows, sports competitions, and other special events that coincide with your visit. See the order blank at the back of this book, call 800/799–9609, or fax 800/799–9619.

And in Santa Fe, Taos, Albuquerque
Accolades for New Mexico are coming from everywhere. The **Mabel Dodge Luhan House,** now a bed-and-breakfast inn in Taos, was recently named a National Historic Landmark by the U.S. Department of the Interior. Mabel Dodge Luhan was an heiress, a longtime Taos resident, and a collector of famous artists and writers. She brought D. H. Lawrence to Taos with his wife, Frieda. Lawrence lived in Taos for 22 months over a three-year period, writing several important works during that time, and although Taos has long attracted artists and writers, none has had a more profound impact on the community.

"I won't say we can't keep them on the shelves," says Susanna Tvede, manager of the **Taos Book Shop,** the oldest bookstore in New Mexico, "but Lawrence has always been a big seller here. We move hundreds of copies each year—*Lady Chatterly's Lover, The Virgin and the Gypsy, The Plumed Serpent,* and of course the short stories. The out-of-print books are in particularly big demand—*Mornings in Mexico,* for instance, which he wrote here."

The 1,000-year-old **Taos Pueblo** was recently designated a World Heritage Site—the United Nations' equivalent of a National Historic Landmark. It is New Mexico's second (the other is **Chaco Canyon**), and one of only 17 in the entire United States. The news delights opponents of the long-discussed and much-disputed plan to build a commercial airport in Taos. Jets landing and taking off in proximity to the Taos Pueblo would surely rattle its fragile adobe walls into a pile of rubble. Therefore, no airport.

A recent U.S. Department of Commerce study ranked both Albuquerque and Santa Fe second nationally (behind Philadelphia) as historical, cultural, and minority centers, praising them for "capitalizing on their Hispanic and Native American heritage by devising events that enhance their appeal."

But Santa Fe's good press has its down side as well. The median price of a single-family home in Santa Fe has climbed to $173,750—comparable to the price of a similar abode in Los Angeles. Real-estate taxes are soaring. Many people born in the former Spanish colonial capital can no longer afford to live there.

New hotels continue to blossom (including three moderately priced properties on Santa Fe's Cerrillos Road: a 59-room Comfort Inn, a 78-room Travelodge, and a 56-room Fairfield), while others are revered in the warm wrap of nostalgia. **La Posada de Albuquerque** was the Albuquerque Hilton when it opened in 1939, one of the very first in the worldwide Hilton chain. Conrad Hilton honeymooned there with his bride, Zsa Zsa Gabor. Albuquerque's **Best Western Fred Harvey Hotel** also harks back to a time when the West was young and Fred Harvey's name meant good food and hot coffee and his chain of Harvey House restaurants inspired books, collectors, and

an MGM musical—*The Harvey Girls,* starring Judy Garland. You won't find Harvey Houses at every Western crossroads and whistle stop anymore. But at least that bit of nostalgia remains at the modern Fred Harvey high rise in Albuquerque. **Woolworth's** exercised a final renewal option on the lease of its store on the Santa Fe Plaza, ensuring **Frito Pies** for hungry customers at least through 1998.

Ottmar Liebert, whose classical guitar is flavored with jazz and pop influences, sold over a half-million copies of his *Nouveau Flamenco,* much of its appeal riding on the popularity of his song "Santa Fe." Born in Cologne, Germany, to a Chinese-German father and a Hungarian mother, Liebert is a longtime Santa Fe resident who often appears in local clubs. **R. C. Gorman,** the globe-trotting Navajo artist who lives in Taos—he virtually commutes between there and Japan, where his work is in great demand—continues as a larger-than-life goodwill ambassador for New Mexico. **Allan Houser,** a Chiricahua Apache and one of America's premier sculptors, died in 1994. His artistic legacy is remembered at the **Allan Houser Sculpture Garden,** part of the new Museum of the Institute of American Indian Arts, just east of the Santa Fe Plaza in the renovated former Federal Post Office. Santa Clara pueblo painter **Pablita Velarde,** one of the state's first Native American women to be widely recognized as an accomplished painter, was selected as *New Mexico Magazine*'s 1996 Distinguished Calendar Artist. The state-owned magazine's 1996 calendar offers a diverse collection of Velarde's bright, somewhat contemporary depictions of pueblo Indian traditions. Meanwhile, Georgia O'Keeffe, who died in Santa Fe in 1986 at the age of 98, remains the state's favorite pinup lady. A photo of her hands, taken by her late husband, Alfred Stieglitz, in 1920, was sold at a New York auction to an anonymous bidder for $398,500—the highest sum ever paid at an auction for a photograph.

How to Use This Book

Organization

Up front is the **Gold Guide**, comprising two sections on gold paper that are chock-full of information about traveling within your destination and traveling in general. Both are in alphabetical order by topic.

Important Contacts A to Z gives addresses and telephone numbers of organizations and companies that offer destination-related services and detailed information or publications. Here's where you'll find information about how to get to Santa Fe, Taos, and Albuquerque from wherever you are. **Smart Travel Tips A to Z**, the Gold Guide's second section, gives specific tips on how to get the most out of your travels, as well as information on how to accomplish what you need to in Santa Fe, Taos, and Albuquerque.

In this guide, chapters are devoted to Santa Fe and Vicinity, Taos, Albuquerque, Carlsbad and Southern New Mexico, and the Pueblos of the Rio Grande. Each chapter (except for the one on the Pueblos of the Rio Grande) covers exploring, shopping, sports, dining, lodging, and arts and nightlife, and ends with a section called Essentials, which tells you how to get there and get around and gives you important local addresses and telephone numbers.

At the end of the book you'll find Portraits, with a wonderful essay about New Mexico by D.H. Lawrence, followed by suggestions for pretrip reading, both fiction and nonfiction. Here we also recommend movies you can rent on videotape to get you in the mood for your travels.

Stars

Stars in the margin are used to denote highly recommended sights, attractions, hotels, and restaurants.

Credit Cards

The following abbreviations are used: **AE,** American Express; **D,** Discover; **DC,** Diners Club; **MC,** MasterCard; and **V,** Visa.

Please Write to Us

Everyone who has contributed to Fodor's *Santa Fe, Taos, Albuquerque '96* has worked hard to make the text accurate. All prices and opening times are based on information supplied to us at press time, and the publisher cannot accept responsibility for any errors that may have occurred. The passage of time will bring changes, so it's always a good idea to call ahead and confirm information when it matters—particularly if you're making a detour to visit specific sights or attractions. When making reservations at a hotel or inn, be sure to mention if you have a disability or are traveling with children, if you prefer a private bath or a certain type of bed, or if you have specific dietary needs or any other concerns.

Were the restaurants we recommended as described? Did our hotel picks exceed your expectations? Did you find a museum we recommended a waste of time? We would love your feedback, positive and negative. If you have complaints, we'll look into them and revise our entries when the facts warrant it. If you've happened upon a special place that we haven't included, we'll pass the information along to the writers so they can check it out. So please send us a letter or postcard (we're at 201 East 50th Street, New York, New York 10022.) We'll look forward to hearing from you. And in the meantime, have a wonderful trip!

Karen Cure

Karen Cure
Editorial Director

New Mexico

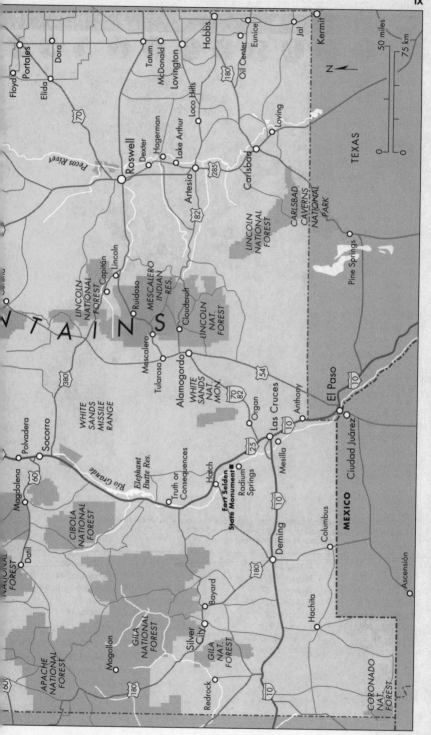

x

Numbers below vertical bands relate each zone to Greenwich Mean Time (0 hrs.).
Local times frequently differ from these general indications,
as indicated by light-face numbers on map.

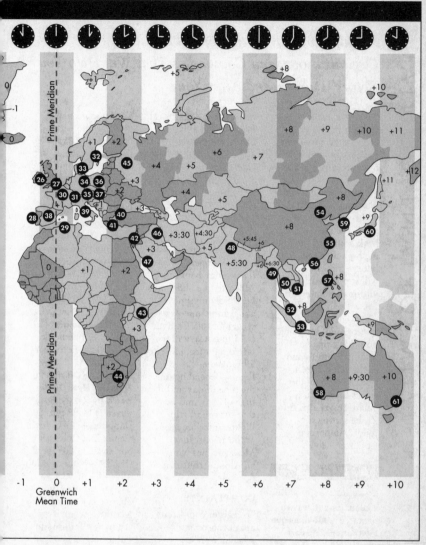

IMPORTANT CONTACTS A TO Z

An Alphabetical Listing of Publications, Organizations, and Companies That Will Help You Before, During, and After Your Trip

No single travel resource can give you every detail about every topic that might interest or concern you at the various stages of your journey—when you're planning your trip, while you're on the road, and after you get back home. The following organizations, books, and brochures will supplement the information in *Fodor's Santa Fe, Taos, Albuquerque '96.* For related information, including both basic tips on visiting Santa Fe and background information on many of the topics below, study Smart Travel Tips A to Z, the section that follows Important Contacts A to Z.

A

AIR TRAVEL

The major gateway to Santa Fe is **Albuquerque International Airport** (☎ 505/842–4366), 65 miles southwest of Santa Fe and 130 miles south of Taos. Flying time is 5 hours from New York, 1 1½ hours from Chicago, and 1 hour from Los Angeles.

CARRIERS

Carriers serving Albuquerque International include **America West** (☎ 800/235–9292), **American** (☎ 800/433–7300), **Continental** (☎ 800/525–0280), **Delta**

(☎ 800/221–1212), **Mesa Air** (☎ 800/637–2247), **Northwest** (☎ 800/692–7000), **Southwest** (☎ 800/444–5660), **TWA** (☎ 800/221–2000), **United** (☎ 800/241–6522), and **USAir** (☎ 800/428–4322).

Air-shuttle service via Mesa Air operates four times a day between Albuquerque and Santa Fe; the flying time aboard the nine-passenger Cessna Caravan is 25 minutes, and the fare ranges from $49 to $99 for one-way flights, depending on the time of day and the time of year, and twice that for round-trip flights. Interline buses at the airport link Mesa Airlines with all Albuquerque connections.

COMPLAINTS

To register complaints about charter and scheduled airlines, contact the U.S. Department of Transportation's **Office of Consumer Affairs** (400 7th St. NW, Washington, DC 20590, ☎ 202/366–2220 or 800/322–7873).

PUBLICATIONS

For general information about charter carriers, ask for the Office of Consumer Affairs' brochure **"Plane Talk: Public Charter Flights."** The Department of

Transportation also publishes a 58-page booklet, **"Fly Rights"** ($1.75; Consumer Information Center, Dept. 133B, Pueblo, CO 81009).

For other tips and hints, consult the Consumers Union's monthly **"Consumer Reports Travel Letter"** ($39 a year; Box 53629, Boulder, CO 80322, ☎ 800/234–1970) and the newsletter **"Travel Smart"** ($37 a year; 40 Beechdale Rd., Dobbs Ferry, NY 10522, ☎ 800/327–3633); *The Official Frequent Flyer Guidebook,* by Randy Petersen ($14.99 plus $3 shipping; 4715-C Town Center Dr., Colorado Springs, CO 80916, ☎ 719/597–8899 or 800/487–8893); *Airfare Secrets Exposed,* by Sharon Tyler and Matthew Wonder (Universal Information Publishing; $16.95 plus $3.75 shipping from Sandcastle Publishing, Box 3070-A, South Pasadena, CA 91031, ☎ 213/255–3616 or 800/655–0053); and *202 Tips Even the Best Business Travelers May Not Know,* by Christopher McGinnis ($10 plus $3 shipping; Irwin Professional Publishing, 1333 Burr Ridge Pkwy., Burr Ridge, IL 60521, ☎ 800/634–3966).

B

BETTER BUSINESS BUREAU

For local contacts, consult the **Council of Better Business Bureaus** (4200 Wilson Blvd., Arlington, VA 22203, ☎ 703/276-0100).

BUS TRAVEL

Frequent ground-shuttle service between Albuquerque and Santa Fe is available via **Greyhound/Trailways** (☎ 800/231-2222); the cost is $10.50. Continuing on to Taos costs $9.94 more. **Shuttlejack** (☎ 800/452-2665) also offers bus service between Albuquerque and Santa Fe, $20 one-way, but doesn't go to Taos.

C

CAR RENTAL

Major car-rental companies represented in Santa Fe include **Alamo** (☎ 800/327-9633, 0800/272-2000 in the U.K.), **Avis** (☎ 800/331-1212, 800/879-2847 in Canada), **Budget** (☎ 800/527-0700, 0800/181-181 in the U.K.), **Dollar** (known as Eurodollar outside North America, ☎ 800/800-4000, 0181/952-6565 in the U.K.), **Hertz** (☎ 800/654-3131, 800/263-0600 in Canada, 0181/679-1799 in the U.K.), and **National** (☎ 800/227-7368, 0181/950-5050 in the U.K., where it is known as Europcar). Rates in Santa Fe begin at $32 a day and $185 a week for an economy car with unlimited mileage. This does not include taxes, which are 10.82% on car rentals. If you rent at the airport, there is an additional 2% tax.

Other rental agencies in New Mexico include **General** (☎ 800/327-7607), **PayLess** (☎ 800/541-1566), **Rent Rite** (☎ 800/554-7483), **Rich Ford** (☎ 800/331-3271), and **Thrifty** (☎ 800/367-2277).

CHILDREN AND TRAVEL

BABY-SITTING

In Santa Fe, **The Kid Connection** (☎ 505/471-3100) offers reputable services. **Trudy's Discovery House** (☎ 505/758-1659) in Taos provides drop-in day care for visiting families.

FLYING

Look into **"Flying with Baby"** ($5.95 plus $1 shipping; Third Street Press, Box 261250, Littleton, CO 80126, ☎ 303/595-5959), cowritten by a flight attendant. **"Kids and Teens in Flight,"** free from the U.S. Department of Transportation's Office of Consumer Affairs, offers tips for children flying alone. Every two years the February issue of **Family Travel Times** (*see* Know-How, *below*) details children's services on three dozen airlines.

GAMES

The gamemeister, Milton Bradley, has games to help keep little (and not so little) children from getting fidgety while riding in planes, trains, and automobiles. Try packing the *Travel Battleship* sea battle game ($7); *Travel Connect Four,* a vertical strategy game ($8); the *Travel Yahtzee* dice game ($6); the *Travel Trouble* dice and board game ($7); and the *Travel Guess Who* mystery game ($8).

KNOW-HOW

Family Travel Times, published four times a year by Travel with Your Children (TWYCH, 45 W. 18th St., New York, NY 10011, ☎ 212/206-0688; annual subscription $40), covers destinations, types of vacations, and modes of travel.

The **Family Travel Guides** catalogue ($1 postage; ☎ 510/527-5849) lists about 200 books and articles on family travel. **Great Vacations with Your Kids,** by Dorothy Jordon and Marjorie Cohen ($13; Penguin USA, 120 Woodbine St., Bergenfield, NJ 07621, ☎ 201/387-0600 or 800/253-6476), and **Traveling with Children—And Enjoying It,** by Arlene K. Butler ($11.95 plus $3 shipping; Globe Pequot Press, Box 833, 6 Business Park Rd., Old Saybrook, CT 06475, ☎ 203/395-0440 or 800/243-0495, 800/962-0973 in CT) help plan your trip with children, from toddlers to teens. Also check **Take Your Baby and Go! A Guide for Traveling with Babies, Toddlers and Young Children,** by Sheri Andrews, Judy Bordeaux, and Vivian Vasquez ($5.95 plus $1.50 shipping; Bear Creek Publications, 2507 Minor Ave.,

Seattle, WA 98102, ☎ 206/322–7604 or 800/326–6566).

LODGING

HOTELS➣ At the **Best Western Hotels** (☎ 800/528–1234) in Albuquerque and Santa Fe, children under 12 stay free. All **Holiday Inns** (☎ 800/465–4329) allow children under 19 to stay free. **Bishop's Lodge** (☎ 505/983–6377) in Santa Fe has a summer activities schedule for children, including a riding and horsemanship program.

CONDOMINIUMS AND RESORTS➣ **Campanilla Compound** (334 Otero St., Santa Fe 87501, ☎ 505/988–7585) offers excellent facilities for families with children. In many cases, especially for larger families, resort accommodations work out to be much cheaper than hotels.

ADVENTURE HOLIDAYS➣ In the Southwest region, adventure holidays for children and families abound. **Southwest Adventure Group, Inc.** (142 Lincoln Ave. #103, Santa Fe 87501, ☎ 505/984–2080 or 800/723–9815) provides educational trips and activities for groups of 10 or more children and teens, leaving parents free to relax and explore. A separate Family Adventure Group offers hot-air ballooning, animal tracking, and overnight family backpacking trips. **Santa Fe Detours** (La Fonda Hotel, 100 E. San Francisco St., Santa Fe 87501, ☎ 800/338–6877) organizes wagon rides and safaris for children.

TOUR OPERATORS

Contact **Grandtravel** (6900 Wisconsin Ave., Suite 706, Chevy Chase, MD 20815, ☎ 301/986–0790 or 800/247–7651), which has tours for people traveling with grandchildren ages 7–17.

CUSTOMS

CANADIANS

Contact **Revenue Canada** (2265 St. Laurent Blvd. S, Ottawa, Ontario K1G 4K3, ☎ 613/993–0534) for a copy of the free brochure **"I Declare/Je Déclare"** and for details on imports that exceed the standard duty-free limit.

U.K. CITIZENS

HM Customs and Excise (Dorset House, Stamford St., London SE1 9NG, ☎ 0171/202–4227) can answer questions about U.K. customs regulations and publishes **"A Guide for Travellers,"** detailing standard procedures and import rules.

D
FOR TRAVELERS WITH DISABILITIES

COMPLAINTS

To register complaints under the provisions of the Americans with Disabilities Act, contact the U.S. Department of Justice's **Public Access Section** (Box 66738, Washington, DC 20035, ☎ 202/514–0301, TTY 202/514–0383, FAX 202/307–1198).

LOCAL INFO

Most of the region's national parks and recreational areas have accessible visitor centers, rest rooms, campsites, and trails, and more are being added every year. For information on accessible facilities at specific parks and sites in New Mexico, contact the **National Park Service, Southwest Region** (Box 728, Santa Fe 87504, ☎ 505/988–6375).

ORGANIZATIONS

FOR TRAVELERS WITH HEARING IMPAIRMENTS.➣ Contact the **American Academy of Otolaryngology** (1 Prince St., Alexandria, VA 22314, ☎ 703/836–4444, FAX 703/683–5100, TTY 703/519–1585).

FOR TRAVELERS WITH MOBILITY PROBLEMS.➣ Contact the **Information Center for Individuals with Disabilities** (Fort Point Pl., 27–43 Wormwood St., Boston, MA 02210, ☎ 617/727–5540, 800/462–5015 in MA, TTY 617/345–9743); **Mobility International USA** (Box 10767, Eugene, OR 97440, ☎ and TTY 503/343–1284, FAX 503/343–6812), the U.S. branch of an international organization based in Belgium (*see below*) that has affiliates in 30 countries; **MossRehab Hospital Travel Information Service** (1200 W. Tabor Rd., Philadelphia, PA 19141, ☎ 215/456–9603, TTY 215/456–9602); the **Society for the Advancement of Travel for the Handicapped** (347 5th Ave., Suite 610, New York, NY 10016, ☎ 212/447–7284, FAX 212/725–8253); the **Travel Industry and Disabled Exchange** (TIDE, 5435

Donna Ave., Tarzana, CA 91356, ☎ 818/344–3640, FAX 818/344–0078); and **Travelin' Talk** (Box 3534, Clarksville, TN 37043, ☎ 615/552–6670, FAX 615/552–1182).

FOR TRAVELERS WITH VISION IMPAIRMENTS.➤ Contact the **American Council of the Blind** (1155 15th St. NW, Suite 720, Washington, DC 20005, ☎ 202/467–5081, FAX 202/467–5085) or the **American Foundation for the Blind** (15 W. 16th St., New York, NY 10011, ☎ 212/620–2000, TTY 212/620–2158).

IN THE U.K.

Contact the **Royal Association for Disability and Rehabilitation** (RADAR, 12 City Forum, 250 City Rd., London EC1V 8AF, ☎ 0171/250–3222) or **Mobility International** (rue de Manchester 25, B–1070 Brussels, Belgium, ☎ 00–322–410–6297), an international clearinghouse of travel information for people with disabilities.

PUBLICATIONS

Several free publications are available from the U.S. Information Center (Box 100, Pueblo, CO 81009, ☎ 719/948–3334): **"New Horizons for the Air Traveler with a Disability"** (address to Dept. 355A), describing legally mandated changes; the pocket-size **"Fly Smart"** (Dept. 575B), good on flight safety; and the Airport Operators Council's worldwide **"Access Travel: Airports"** (Dept. 575A).

Fodor's **Great American Vacations for Travelers with Disabilities** ($18; available in bookstores, or call 800/533–6478) details accessible attractions, restaurants, and hotels in U.S. destinations. The 500-page **Travelin' Talk Directory** ($35; Box 3534, Clarksville, TN 37043, ☎ 615/552–6670) lists people and organizations that help travelers with disabilities. For specialist travel agents worldwide, consult the **Directory of Travel Agencies for the Disabled** ($19.95 plus $2 shipping; Twin Peaks Press, Box 129, Vancouver, WA 98666, ☎ 206/694–2462 or 800/637–2256). The Sierra Club publishes **Easy Access to National Parks** ($16 plus $3 shipping; 730 Polk St., San Francisco, CA 94109, ☎ 415/776–2211 or 800/935–1056).

TRAVEL AGENCIES AND TOUR OPERATORS

The Americans with Disabilities Act requires that travel firms serve the needs of all travelers. However, some agencies and operators specialize in making group and individual arrangements for travelers with disabilities, among them **Access Adventures** (206 Chestnut Ridge Rd., Rochester, NY 14624, ☎ 716/889–9096), run by a former physical-rehab counselor. In addition, many general-interest operators and agencies (*see* Tour Operators, *below*) can also arrange vacations for travelers with disabilities.

FOR TRAVELERS WITH HEARING IMPAIRMENTS➤ One agency is **International Express** (7319-B Baltimore Ave., College Park, MD 20740, ☎ TTY 301/699–8836, FAX 301/699–8836), which arranges group and independent trips.

FOR TRAVELERS WITH MOBILITY PROBLEMS➤ A number of operators specialize in working with travelers with mobility impairments, including **Hinsdale Travel Service** (201 E. Ogden Ave., Suite 100, Hinsdale, IL 60521, ☎ 708/325–1335 or 800/303–5521), a travel agency that will give you access to the services of wheelchair traveler Janice Perkins; and **Wheelchair Journeys** (16979 Redmond Way, Redmond, WA 98052, ☎ 206/885–2210), which can handle arrangements worldwide.

FOR TRAVELERS WITH DEVELOPMENTAL DISABILITIES➤ Contact the nonprofit **New Directions** (5276 Hollister Ave., Suite 207, Santa Barbara, CA 93111, ☎ 805/967–2841), as well as the general-interest operators above.

Options include **Entertainment Travel Editions** (fee $28–$53, depending on destination; Box 1068, Trumbull, CT 06611, ☎ 800/445–4137); **Great American Traveler** ($49.95 annually; Box 27965, Salt Lake City, UT 84127, ☎ 800/548–2812); **Moment's Notice Discount Travel Club** ($25 annually, single or family; 163 Amsterdam

Ave., Suite 137, New York, NY 10023, ☎ 212/486–0500); **Privilege Card** ($74.95 annually; 3391 Peachtree Rd. NE, Suite 110, Atlanta, GA 30326, ☎ 404/262–0222 or 800/236–9732); **Travelers Advantage** ($49 annually, single or family; CUC Travel Service, 49 Music Sq. W, Nashville, TN 37203, ☎ 800/548–1116 or 800/648–4037); and **Worldwide Discount Travel Club** ($50 annually for family, $40 single; 1674 Meridian Ave., Miami Beach, FL 33139, ☎ 305/534–2082).

G

GAY AND LESBIAN TRAVEL

ORGANIZATIONS

The **International Gay Travel Association** (Box 4974, Key West, FL 33041, ☎ 800/448–8550), a consortium of 800 businesses, can supply names of travel agents and tour operators.

PUBLICATIONS

The premier international travel magazine for gays and lesbians is **Our World** ($35 for 10 issues; 1104 N. Nova Rd., Suite 251, Daytona Beach, FL 32117, ☎ 904/441–5367). The 16-page monthly **"Out & About"** ($49 for 10 issues; ☎ 212/645–6922 or 800/929–2268) covers gay-friendly resorts, hotels, cruise lines, and airlines.

TOUR OPERATORS

Toto Tours (1326 W. Albion, Suite 3W, Chicago, IL 60626, ☎ 312/274–8686 or 800/565–1241) offers group tours worldwide.

TRAVEL AGENCIES

The largest agencies serving gay travelers are **Advance Travel** (10700 Northwest Freeway, Suite 160, Houston, TX 77092, ☎ 713/682–2002 or 800/695–0880); **Islanders/ Kennedy Travel** (183 W. 10th St., New York, NY 10014, ☎ 212/242–3222 or 800/988–1181); **Now Voyager** (4406 18th St., San Francisco, CA 94114, ☎ 415/626–1169 or 800/255–6951); and **Yellowbrick Road** (1500 W. Balmoral Ave., Chicago, IL 60640, ☎ 312/561–1800 or 800/642–2488). **Skylink Women's Travel** (746 Ashland Ave., Santa Monica, CA 90405, ☎ 310/452–0506 or 800/225–5759) works with lesbians.

I

INSURANCE

Travel insurance covering baggage, health, and trip cancellation or interruptions is available from **Access America** (Box 90315, Richmond, VA 23286, ☎ 804/285–3300 or 800/284–8300); **Carefree Travel Insurance** (Box 9366, 100 Garden City Plaza, Garden City, NY 11530, ☎ 516/294–0220 or 800/323–3149); **Near Services** (Box 1339, Calumet City, IL 60409, ☎ 708/868–6700 or 800/654–6700); **Tele-Trip** (Mutual of Omaha Plaza, Box 31716, Omaha, NE 68131, ☎ 800/228–9792); **Travel Insured International** (Box 280568, East Hartford, CT 06128–0568, ☎ 203/528–7663 or 800/243–3174); **Travel Guard International** (1145 Clark St., Stevens Point, WI 54481, ☎ 715/345–0505 or 800/826–1300); and **Wallach & Company** (107 W. Federal St., Box 480, Middleburg, VA 22117, ☎ 703/687–3166 or 800/237–6615).

IN THE U.K.

The **Association of British Insurers** (51 Gresham St., London EC2V 7HQ, ☎ 0171/600–3333; 30 Gordon St., Glasgow G1 3PU, ☎ 0141/226–3905; Scottish Provident Bldg., Donegall Sq. W, Belfast BT1 6JE, ☎ 01232/249176; and other locations) gives advice by phone and publishes the free **"Holiday Insurance,"** which sets out typical policy provisions and costs.

L

LODGING

APARTMENT AND VILLA RENTAL

Among the companies to contact is **Vacation Home Rentals Worldwide** (235 Kensington Ave., Norwood, NJ 07648, ☎ 201/767–9393 or 800/633–3284).

HOME EXCHANGE

Principal clearinghouses include **Intervac International** ($65 annually; Box 590504, San Francisco, CA 94159, ☎ 415/435–3497), which has three annual directories; and **Loan-a-Home** ($35–$45 annually; 2 Park La., Apt. 6E, Mount Vernon, NY 10552-3443, ☎ 914/664–7640), which specializes in long-term exchanges.

M
MONEY MATTERS

ATMS

For specific **Cirrus** locations in the United States and Canada, call 800/424–7787. For U.S. **Plus** locations, call 800/843–7587 and enter the area code and first three digits of the number you're calling from (or of the calling area where you want an ATM).

WIRING FUNDS

Funds can be wired via **American Express MoneyGram**^{SM} (☎ 800/926–9400 from the U.S. and Canada for locations and information) or **Western Union** (☎ 800/325–6000 for agent locations or to send using MasterCard or Visa, 800/321–2923 in Canada).

N
NATIONAL MONUMENTS

There are 12 national monuments in New Mexico: **Aztec Ruins National Monument** (Box 640, Aztec 87410, ☎ 505/334–6174); **Bandelier National Monument** (HCR 1, Box 1, Suite 15, Los Alamos 87544, ☎ 505/672–3861); **Capulin Volcano National Monument** (Box 40, Capulin 88414, ☎ 505/278–2201); **Chaco Culture National Historic Park** (Star Rte. 4, Box 6500, Bloomfield 87413, ☎ 505/988–6716 or 505/988–6727); **El Malpais National Monument and Conservation Area** (Box

939, Grants 87020, ☎ 505/285–4641); **El Morro National Monument** (Rte. 2, Box 43, Ramah 87321-9603, ☎ 505/783–4226); **Fort Union National Monument** (Box 127, Watrous 87753, ☎ 505/425–8025); **Gila Cliff Dwellings National Monument** (Rte. 11, Box 100, Silver City 88061, ☎ 505/536–9461 or 505/757–6032); **Pecos National Historical Park** (Drawer 418, Pecos 87552, ☎ 505/757–6414); **Petroglyph National Monument** (6900 Unser Blvd. NW, Albuquerque 87120, ☎ 505/897–8814); **Salinas Pueblo Missions National Monument** (Box 496, Mountainair 87036, ☎ 505/847–2290); and **White Sands National Monument** (Box 458, Alamogordo 88310, ☎ 505/479–6124). For more information, contact the **National Parks Service** (Box 728, Santa Fe 87504, ☎ 505/988–6012).

NATIONAL PARKS

Carlsbad Caverns National Park (3225 National Parks Hwy., Carlsbad 88220, ☎ 505/785–2232 or 505/785–2107 for 24-hr recorded information), in the southeastern part of the state (27 mi southwest of Carlsbad on U.S. 62/180), contains one of the largest and most spectacular cave systems in the world.

A variety of passes for senior citizens, travelers with disabilities, and frequent visitors are available. They can be purchased at any park

charging admission or by mail from the **National Park Service** (Dept. of the Interior, Washington, DC 20240).

P
PASSPORTS AND VISAS

U.K. CITIZENS

For fees, documentation requirements, and to get an emergency passport, call the **London Passport Office** (☎ 0171/271–3000). For visa information, call the **U.S. Embassy Visa Information Line** (☎ 0891/200–290; calls cost 49p per minute or 39p per minute cheap rate) or write the **U.S. Embassy Visa Branch** (5 Upper Grosvenor St., London W1A 4JB). If you live in Northern Ireland, write the **U.S. Consulate General** (Queen's House, Queen St., Belfast BTI 6EQ).

PHOTO HELP

The **Kodak Information Center** (☎ 800/242–2424) answers consumer questions about film and photography.

S
SENIOR CITIZENS

EDUCATIONAL TRAVEL

The nonprofit **Elderhostel** (75 Federal St., 3rd Floor, Boston, MA 02110, ☎ 617/426–7788), for people 60 and older, has offered inexpensive study programs since 1975. The nearly 2,000 courses cover everything from marine science to Greek myths and cowboy poetry. Fees for programs in the United States and Canada, which usually last one week, run about $300, not including transportation.

ORGANIZATIONS

Contact the **American Association of Retired Persons** (AARP, 601 E St. NW, Washington, DC 20049, ☎ 202/434–2277; $8 per person or couple annually). Its Purchase Privilege Program gets members discounts on lodging, car rentals, and sightseeing, and the AARP Motoring Plan furnishes domestic trip-routing information and emergency road-service aid for an annual fee of $39.95 per person or couple ($59.95 for a premium version).

For other discounts on lodgings, car rentals, and other travel products, along with magazines and newsletters, contact the **National Council of Senior Citizens** (membership $12 annually; 1331 F St. NW, Washington, DC 20004, ☎ 202/347–8800) and *Mature Outlook* (subscription $9.95 annually; 6001 N. Clark St., Chicago, IL 60660, ☎ 312/465–6466 or 800/336–6330).

PUBLICATIONS

The 50+ Traveler's Guidebook: Where to Go, Where to Stay, What to Do, by Anita Williams and Merrimac Dillon ($12.95; St. Martin's Press, 175 5th Ave., New York, NY 10010, ☎ 212/674–5151 or 800/288–2131), offers many useful tips. **"The Mature Traveler"** ($29.95; Box 50400,

Reno, NV 89513, ☎ 702/786–7419), a monthly newsletter, covers travel deals.

SPORTS

BICYCLING

For information on New Mexico cycling events, call the **New Mexico Touring Society** (☎ 505/298–0085).

BIRD-WATCHING

The **Bosque del Apache National Wildlife Refuge** (Box 1246, Socorro 87801, ☎ 505/835–1828), 90 miles south of Albuquerque, is the winter home of thousands of migrating birds, including one of only two wild flocks of the rare whooping crane.

CAMPING

For information on New Mexico's five national forests and the Kiowa National Grasslands (part of the Cibola National Forest), contact the **USDA Forest Service** (*see* Visitor Info, *below*); **Carson National Forest** (Forest Service Bldg., 208 Cruz Alta Rd., Box 558, Taos 87571, ☎ 505/758–6200); **Cibola National Forest** (2113 Osuna Rd. NE, Suite A, Albuquerque 87113, ☎ 505/275–5207); **Gila National Forest** (3005 E. Camino del Bosque, Silver City 88061, ☎ 505/388–8201); **Lincoln National Forest** (Federal Bldg., 1101 New York Ave., Alamogordo 88310, ☎ 505/437–6030); and **Santa Fe National Forest** (1220 South St. Francis Dr., Box 1689, Santa Fe 87504, ☎ 505/988–6940).

CANOEING, KAYAKING, AND RIVER RAFTING

Most of the hard-core river rafting is done in the Taos area; the **Taos County Chamber of Commerce** (1139 Paseo del Pueblo Sur, Drawer 1, Taos 87571, ☎ 505/758–3873 or 800/732–8267) can supply a list of local outfitters. For statewide information concerning river recreational activities, contact the **New Mexico Department of Tourism** (*see* Visitor Info, *below*).

FISHING

For information or to obtain copies of state fishing regulations and maps, contact the **New Mexico Game and Fish Department** (Villagra Bldg., 408 Galisteo St., Box 25112 Santa Fe 87503, ☎ 505/827–7899). The **Sport Fishing Promotions Council**'s toll-free hot line (☎ 800/275–3474) provides anglers with 24-hour up-to-date information on fishing conditions, regulations, and boat-launch sites.

Fishing on Native American reservations is not subject to regulations but may require special permits; the **Indian Pueblo Cultural Center** (*see* Visitor Info, *below*) can provide further information.

GOLFING

The **Sun Country Amateur Golf Association** (10035 Country Club La. NW, No. 5, Albuquerque 87114, ☎ 505/897–0864) can provide a list of courses, along with details on the greens fees and hours for each club.

HIKING

The **State Parks and Recreation Division** (Energy, Minerals, and Natural Resources Dept., 408 Galisteo St., Box 1147, Santa Fe 87504, ☎ 505/827–7465 or 800/451–2451) can provide hiking information and maps.

HORSE RACING

The state's tracks include **Downs at Santa Fe** (5 mi south of Santa Fe, ☎ 505/471–3311; open early June–Labor Day, Wed., Fri.–Sun., holidays); **Downs at Albuquerque** (New Mexico State Fairgrounds, E. Central Ave., ☎ 505/262–1188; open Jan.–June 15, Wed., Fri.–Sun., holiday Mon.); **Ruidoso Downs Racetrack** (☎ 505/378–4431; open early May–Labor Day, Thurs.–Mon., holidays); **San Juan Downs** (7 mi east of Farmington, ☎ 505/326–4551; open last weekend in Apr.–Labor Day, weekends and holidays); and **Sunland Park Racetrack** (5 mi north of El Paso, Texas, ☎ 505/589–1131; open mid-Oct.–mid-May, Wed., Fri.–Sun., holidays).

HUNTING

Out-of-state hunters must check with the New Mexico Game and Fish Department for hunting dates in the area they plan to visit. General big-game hunting licenses are not available to nonresidents, but separate licenses may be bought for turkey and all big game. A general license for small game (squirrels and birds other than turkey) is available to nonresidents for $51. Native American tribes have their own fee schedules. For more information, contact the New Mexico Game and Fish Department (*see* Fishing, *above*).

SKIING

Check with the **Bureau of Land Management** (1474 Rodeo Rd., Santa Fe 87501, ☎ 505/438–7400) and state park officials for local snow and trail conditions and weather updates.

The major downhill ski areas in New Mexico include **Angel Fire Resort** (Drawer B, Angel Fire 87710, ☎ 505/377–6401 or 800/633–7463); **Pajarito Mountain Ski Area** (Box 155, Los Alamos 87544, ☎ 505/662–7669 or 505/662–5725); **Red River Ski Area** (Box 900, Red River 87558, ☎ 505/754–2223); **Sandia Peak Ski Area** (10 Tramway Loop NE, Albuquerque 87122, ☎ 505/242–9133 or 505/242–9052); **Santa Fe Ski Area** (1210 Louisa St., Suite 10, Santa Fe 87505, ☎ 505/982–4429); **Sipapu Lodge and Ski Area** (Rte. Box 29, Vadito 87579, ☎ 505/587–2240); **Ski Apache** (Box 220, Ruidoso 88345, ☎ 505/336–4356 or 505/336–4357); **Snow Canyon** (Box 498, Cloudcroft 88317, ☎ 505/682–2333 or 800/333–7542); and **Taos Ski Valley** (Box 90, Taos Ski Valley 87525, ☎ 505/776–2291). For information about the state's ski areas or to order a free 48-page *Skier's Guide,* call **Ski New Mexico** (☎ 800/755–7669).

New Mexico's state monuments include **Coronado State Monument** (NM 44, off I–25, Box 95, Bernalillo 87004, ☎ 505/867–5351), 18 miles north of Albuquerque, which preserves ruins of a prehistoric Native American pueblo; it has self-guided trails, a visitor center, and a museum. **Jemez State Monument** (NM 4, 1 mi north of Jemez Springs, Box 143, Jemez Springs 87025, ☎ 505/829–3530) has ruins of a 17th-century mission church and pueblo. **Lincoln State Monument** (U.S. 380, 12 mi east of Capitan, Courthouse Museum, Lincoln 88338, ☎ 505/653–4372), **Fort Selden** (Radium Springs exit off I–25, 13 mi north of Las Crucas, Box 58, Radium 88054, ☎ 505/526–8911), and **Fort Sumner** (2 mi east of the town Fort Sumner, on Billy the Kid Rd., Rte. 1, Box 356, Fort Sumner 88119, ☎ 505/355–2573) all give insight into the 19th-century territorial period of New Mexico. For more information, contact the **Monument Division, Museum of New Mexico** (Box 2087, Santa Fe 87504, ☎ 505/827–6334).

STATE PARKS

Established in the 1930s, New Mexico's state park system is composed of 45 parks throughout the state, ranging from high mountain lakes and pine forests in the north to the Chihuahuan Desert lowlands of the south. Pristine and unspoiled, they offer all outdoor recreational facilities. For maps and brochures, contact the **State Parks and Recreational Division** (Energy, Minerals, and Natural Resources Dept., 408 Galisteo St., Box 1147, Santa Fe 87504, ☎ 505/827–7465 or 800/451–2451).

STUDENTS

HOSTELING

Contact **Hostelling International–American Youth Hostels** (733 15th St. NW, Suite 840, Washington, DC 20005, ☎ 202/783–6161) in the United States, **Hostelling International–Canada** (205 Catherine St., Suite 400, Ottawa, Ontario K2P 1C3, ☎ 613/237–7884) in Canada, and the **Youth Hostel Association of England and Wales** (Trevelyan House, 8 St. Stephen's Hill, St. Albans, Hertfordshire AL1 2DY, ☎ 01727/855215 or 01727/845047) in the United Kingdom. Membership ($25 in the United States, C$26.75 in Canada, and £9 in the United Kingdom) gets you access to 5,000 hostels worldwide that charge $7–$20 nightly per person.

I.D. CARDS

To be eligible for discounts on transportation and admissions, get the **International Student Identity Card** (ISIC) if you're a bona fide student or the **International Youth Card** (IYC)

if you're under 26. In the United States, the ISIC and IYC cards cost $16 each and include basic travel accident and illness coverage, plus a toll-free travel hot line. Apply through the Council on International Educational Exchange (*see* Organizations, *below*). Cards are available for $15 each in Canada from **Travel Cuts** (187 College St., Toronto, Ontario M5T 1P7, ☎ 416/979–2406 or 800/667–2887) and in the United Kingdom for £5 each at student unions and student travel companies.

ORGANIZATIONS

A major contact is the **Council on International Educational Exchange** (CIEE, 205 E. 42nd St., 16th Floor, New York, NY 10017, ☎ 212/661–1450) with locations in Boston (729 Boylston St., Boston, MA 02116, ☎ 617/266–1926), Miami (9100 S. Dadeland Blvd., Miami, FL 33156, ☎ 305/670–9261), Los Angeles (1093 Broxton Ave., Los Angeles, CA 90024, ☎ 310/208–3551), 43 other college towns nationwide, and the United Kingdom (28A Poland St., London W1V 3DB, ☎ 0171/437–7767). Twice a year, it publishes *Student Travels* magazine. The CIEE's Council Travel Service offers domestic air passes for bargain travel within the United States and is the exclusive U.S. agent for several student-discount cards.

Campus Connections (325 Chestnut St., Suite 1101, Philadelphia, PA

19106, ☎ 215/625–8585 or 800/428–3235) specializes in discounted accommodations and airfares for students. The **Educational Travel Centre** (438 N. Frances St., Madison, WI 53703, ☎ 608/256–5551) offers rail passes and low-cost airline tickets, mostly for flights departing from Chicago.

In Canada, also contact **Travel Cuts** (*see above*).

T

TOUR OPERATORS

Among the companies selling tours and packages to Santa Fe, the following have a proven reputation, are nationally known, and offer plenty of options.

GROUP TOURS

Deluxe escorted tours to Santa Fe are available from **Maupintour** (Box 807, Lawrence, KS 66044, ☎ 913/843–1211 or 800/255–4266) and **Tauck Tours** (11 Wilton Rd., Westport, CT 06880, ☎ 203/226–6911 or 800/468–2825). Another operator falling between deluxe and first-class is **Globus** (5301 S. Federal Circle, Littleton, CO 80123, ☎ 303/797–2800 or 800/221–0090). In the first-class and tourist range, try **Collette Tours** (162 Middle St., Pawtucket, RI 02860, ☎ 401/728–3805 or 800/832–4656), **Domenico Tours** (750 Broadway, Bayonne, NJ 07002, ☎ 201/823–8687 or 800/554–8687), and **Mayflower Tours** (1225 Warren Ave., Downers Grove, IL

60515, ☎ 708/960–3430 or 800/323–7604). For budget and tourist class programs, try **Cosmos** (*see* Globus, *above*).

Also look into **Recursos de Santa Fe** (826 Camino de Monte Rey, Santa Fe, NM 87501, ☎ 505/982–9301, FAX 505/989–8608), which can arrange customized trips and itineraries built around a specific theme, including cooking, gardening, Navajo weaving, and pottery in the Western pueblos.

PACKAGES

Independent vacation packages are available from major airlines and tour operators. Contact **American Airlines Fly AAway Vacations** (☎ 800/321–2121), **Continental Airlines' Grand Destinations** (☎ 800/634–5555), **Delta Dream Vacations** (☎ 800/872–7786), **Certified Vacations** (Box 1525, Ft. Lauderdale, FL 33302, ☎ 305/522–1414 or 800/233–7260), **Globetrotters** (139 Main St., Cambridge, MA 02142, ☎ 617/621–9911 or 800/999–9696), **Kingdom Tours** (300 Market St., Kingston, PA 18704, ☎ 717/283–4241 or 800/872–8857), **United Vacations** (☎ 800/328–6877), and **USAir Vacations** (☎ 800/455–0123).

For customized independent packages, contact **Recursos de Santa Fe** (*see* Group Tours, *above*).

FROM THE U.K.

Several companies, such as **British Airways**

Holidays (Astral Towers, Betts Way, London Rd., Crawley, West Sussex RH10 2XA, ☎ 01293/518–022), **Jetsave** (Sussex House, London Rd., East Grinstead, W. Sussex RH19 1LD, ☎ 01342/312033), and **Trailfinders** (42–50 Earls Court Rd., London W8 7RG, ☎ 0171/937–5400; 58 Deansgate, Manchester M3 2FF, ☎ 0161/839–6969), can arrange fly/drive tours of the region.

Travel agencies that offer cheap fares to Santa Fe include **Trailfinders, Flightfile** (49 Tottenham Court Rd., London W1P 9RE, ☎ 0171/700–2722), and **Travel Cuts** (295a Regent St., London W1R 7YA, ☎ 0171/637–3161; *see* Students, *above*).

THEME TRIPS

ARCHAEOLOGY➣ For archaeologist-guided tours of prehistoric sites and contemporary Indian villages in New Mexico, contact the **Archaeological Conservancy** (5301 Central Ave. NE, Suite 1218, Albuquerque 87108, ☎ 505/266–1540). Also check with **American Southwest Tours** (Box 4300, Durango, CO 81302, ☎ 303/247–2955 or 800/644–5755) for tours that explore native history and culture and visit significant archaeological sites.

ART/PHOTOGRAPHY➣ Artists and photographers looking to capture the images of the Southwest should contact **Atwell Fine Art**

(5741 Cerrillos Rd., Santa Fe 87505, ☎ 800/235-8412) and **Pueblo Arts** (5555 Zuni SE, #515, Albuquerque 87108, ☎ 505/766–6950).

BICYCLING➣ Bike trips from **Backroads** (1516 5th St., Suite Q333, Berkeley, CA 94710–1740, ☎ 510/527–1555 or 800/245–3874) stop at Indian pueblos, Spanish colonial villages, art galleries, and fine crafts studios during an inn-to-inn tour of northern New Mexico. The tour also includes a river-rafting trip on the Rio Grande.

FOOD AND WINE➣ For a gourmet tour of the Southwest, contact **Destination Southwest** (121 Tijeras NE, Suite 1100, Albuquerque 87102, ☎ 505/766–9068 or 800/999–3109).

HIKING/WALKING➣ Contact **TrekAmerica** (Box 189 Rockaway, NJ 07866, ☎ 201/983–1144 or 800/221–0596) for a tour that combines hiking and camping with hotel stays in and around Santa Fe. **Native Sons Adventures** (Box 6144, Taos 87571, ☎ 505/758–9342 or 800/753–7559) offers custom hiking, mountain biking, and rafting for nature lovers.

LEARNING VACATIONS➣ **Earthwatch** (680 Mount Auburn, Box 403N, Watertown, MA 02272, ☎ 617/926–8200 or 800/776–0188) sometimes sponsors scientific expeditions in the Santa Fe area. The **National Audubon Society** (950

3rd Ave., New York, NY 10022, ☎ 212/546–9140) also runs programs to New Mexico on occasion. **Victor Emanual Nature Tours** (Box 33008, Austin, TX 78764, ☎ 512/328–5221) specializes in bird-watching and natural history trips.

RIVER RAFTING➤ For day trips and overnight adventures on the Rio Grande or Rio Charma, contact **Whitewater Information and Reservations** (100 E. San Francisco St., Santa Fe 87501, ☎ 505/983–6565 or 800/338–6877), **Far Flung Adventures** (Box 707, El Prado 87529, ☎ 505/758–2628 or 800/359–2627), and **New Wave Rafting Company** (Rte. 5, Box 302A, Santa Fe 87501, ☎ 505/984–1444 or 800/984–1444).

ORGANIZATIONS

The **National Tour Association** (546 E. Main St., Lexington, KY 40508, ☎ 606/226–4444 or 800/755–8687) and **United States Tour Operators Association** (USTOA, 211 E. 51st St., Suite 12B, New York, NY 10022, ☎ 212/750–7371) provide lists of member operators and information on booking tours.

PUBLICATIONS

Consult the brochure *"On Tour"* and ask for a current list of member operators from the National Tour Association (*see* Organizations, *above*). Also get a copy of the **"Worldwide Tour & Vacation Package Finder"** from the USTOA (*see* Organizations, *above*) and the Better Business Bureau's **"Tips on Travel Packages"** (publication No. 24-195, $2; 4200 Wilson Blvd., Arlington, VA 22203).

TRAVEL AGENCIES

For names of reputable agencies in your area, contact the **American Society of Travel Agents** (1101 King St., Suite 200, Alexandria, VA 22314, ☎ 703/739–2782).

V

VISITOR INFO

Helpful information sources in New Mexico are: **New Mexico Department of Tourism** (Lamy Bldg., 491 Old Santa Fe Trail, Santa Fe 87503, ☎ 505/827–7400 or 800/545–2070, FAX 505/827–7402), **Albuquerque Convention & Visitors Bureau** (121 Tijeras NE, Box 26866, Albuquerque 87125, ☎ 505/243–3696 or 800/733–9918, FAX 505/247–9101), **Santa Fe**

Convention & Visitors Bureau (201 W. Marcy St., Box 909, Santa Fe 87504, ☎ 505/984–6760 or 800/777–2489, FAX 505/984–6679), **Taos County Chamber of Commerce** (Drawer I, Taos 87571, ☎ 505/758–3873 or 800/732–8267, FAX 505/758–3872), **USDA Forest Service, Southwestern Region** (Public Affairs Office, 517 Gold Ave. SW, Albuquerque 87102, ☎ 505/842–3292), **Indian Pueblo Cultural Center** (2401 12th St. NW, Albuquerque 87102, ☎ 505/843–7270 or 800/766–4405 outside NM).

In the United Kingdom, also contact the **United States Travel and Tourism Administration** (Box 1EN, London W1A 1EN, ☎ 0171/495–4466). For a free USA pack, write the USTTA at Box 170, Ashford, Kent TN24 0ZX. Enclose stamps worth £1.50.

W

WEATHER

For current conditions and forecasts, plus the local time and helpful travel tips, call the **Weather Channel Connection** (☎ 900/932–8437; 95¢ per minute) from a touch-tone phone.

SMART TRAVEL TIPS A TO Z

Basic Information on Traveling in Santa Fe and Savvy Tips to Make Your Trip a Breeze

The more you travel, the more you know about how to make trips run like clockwork. To help make your travels hassle-free, Fodor's editors have rounded up dozens of tips from our contributors and travel experts all over the world, as well as basic information on visiting Santa Fe. For names of organizations to contact and publications that can give you more information, see Important Contacts A to Z, *above*.

A
AIR TRAVEL

If time is an issue, **always look for nonstop flights,** which require no change of plane. If possible, **avoid connecting flights,** which stop at least once and can involve a change of plane, although the flight number remains the same; if the first leg is late, the second waits.

CUTTING COSTS

The Sunday travel section of most newspapers is a good source of deals.

MAJOR AIRLINES➤ The least-expensive airfares from the major airlines are priced for round-trip travel and are subject to restrictions. You must usually **book in advance and buy the ticket within 24 hours** to get cheaper fares, and you may have to **stay over a Saturday night.**

The lowest fare is subject to availability, and only a small percentage of the plane's total seats are sold at that price. It's good to **call a number of airlines, and when you are quoted a good price, book it on the spot**—the same fare on the same flight may not be available the next day. Airlines generally allow you to change your return date for a $25–$50 fee, but most low-fare tickets are nonrefundable. However, if you don't use it, you can apply the cost toward the purchase price of a new ticket, again for a small charge.

CONSOLIDATORS➤ Consolidators, who buy tickets at reduced rates from scheduled airlines, sell them at prices below the lowest available from the airlines directly—usually without advance restrictions. Sometimes you can even get your money back if you need to return the ticket. Carefully read the fine print detailing penalties for changes and cancellations. If you doubt the reliability of a consolidator, **confirm your reservation with the airline.**

ALOFT

AIRLINE FOOD➤ If you hate airline food, **ask for special meals when booking.** These can be vegetarian, low-choles-

terol, or kosher, for example; commonly prepared to order in smaller quantities than standard catered fare, they can be tastier.

SMOKING➤ Smoking is banned on all flights within the United States of less than six hours' duration and on all Canadian flights; the ban also applies to domestic segments of international flights aboard U.S. and foreign carriers.

C
CAMERAS, CAMCORDERS, AND COMPUTERS

LAPTOPS

Before you depart, **check your portable computer's battery,** because you may be asked at security to turn on the computer to prove that it is what it appears to be. At the airport, you may prefer to **request a manual inspection,** although security X-rays do not harm hard-disk or floppy-disk storage. You may want to **find out about repair facilities at your destination** in case you need them.

PHOTOGRAPHY

If your camera is new or if you haven't used it for a while, **shoot and develop a few rolls of film** before you leave. Always **store film in a cool, dry place**—never in the car's glove com-

THE GOLD GUIDE / SMART TRAVEL TIPS

partment or on the shelf under the rear window.

Every pass through an X-ray machine increases film's chance of clouding. To protect it, carry it in a clear plastic bag and **ask for hand inspection at security.** Such requests are virtually always honored at U.S. airports. Don't depend on a lead-lined bag to protect film in checked luggage—the airline may increase the radiation to see what's inside.

VIDEO

Before your trip, **test your camcorder, invest in a skylight filter to protect the lens, and charge the batteries.** (Airport security personnel may ask you to turn on the camcorder to prove that it's what it appears to be.)

Videotape is not damaged by X-rays, but it may be harmed by the magnetic field of a walk-through metal detector, so **ask that videotapes be hand-checked.**

CHILDREN AND TRAVEL

BABY-SITTING

For recommended local sitters, **check with your hotel desk.** *See also* Children and Travel *in* Important Contacts A to Z, *above.*

DRIVING

If you are renting a car, **arrange for a car seat when you reserve.** Sometimes they're free.

FLYING

On domestic flights, children under 2 not occupying a seat travel free, and older children currently travel on the

lowest applicable adult fare.

BAGGAGE➤ In general, the adult baggage allowance applies for children paying half or more of the adult fare.

SAFETY SEATS➤ According to the Federal Aviation Administration (FAA), it's a good idea to **use safety seats aloft.** Airline policy varies. U.S. carriers allow FAA-approved models, but airlines usually require that you buy a ticket, even if your child would otherwise ride free, because the seats must be strapped into regular passenger seats.

FACILITIES➤ When making your reservation, **ask for children's meals or freestanding bassinets** if you need them; the latter are available only to those with seats at the bulkhead, where there's enough legroom. If you don't need a bassinet, **think twice before requesting bulkhead seats**—the only storage for in-flight necessities is in the inconveniently distant overhead bins.

LODGING

Most hotels allow children under a certain age to stay in their parents' room at no extra charge, while others charge them as extra adults; be sure to **ask about the cut-off age.**

CUSTOMS AND DUTIES

IN SANTA FE

British visitors age 21 or over may import the following into the United States: 200

cigarettes or 50 cigars or 2 kilograms of tobacco; one U.S. liter of alcohol; gifts to the value of $100. Restricted items include meat products, seeds, plants, and fruits. Never carry illegal drugs.

BACK HOME

IN CANADA➤ Once per calendar year, when you've been out of Canada for at least seven days, you may bring in C$300 worth of goods duty-free. If you've been away less than seven days but more than 48 hours, the duty-free exemption drops to C$100 but can be claimed any number of times (as can a C$20 duty-free exemption for absences of 24 hours or more). You cannot combine the yearly and 48-hour exemptions, use the C$300 exemption only partially (to save the balance for a later trip), or pool exemptions with family members. Goods claimed under the C$300 exemption may follow you by mail; those claimed under the lesser exemptions must accompany you.

Alcohol and tobacco products may be included in the yearly and 48-hour exemptions but not in the 24-hour exemption. If you meet the age requirements of the province through which you reenter Canada, you may bring in, duty-free, 1.14 liters (40 imperial ounces) of wine or liquor *or* 24 12-ounce cans or bottles of beer or ale. If you are 16 or older, you may bring in, duty-free, 200 cigarettes, 50 cigars or cigarillos, and 400 tobacco sticks or 400 grams of manufactured tobacco. Alcohol and tobacco must accompany you on your return.

An unlimited number of gifts valued up to C$60 each may be mailed to Canada duty-free. These do not count as part of your exemption. Label the package "Unsolicited Gift—Value under $60." Alcohol and tobacco are excluded.

IN THE U.K.➣ From countries outside the EU, including the United States, you may import duty-free 200 cigarettes, 100 cigarillos, 50 cigars or 250 grams of tobacco; 1 liter of spirits or 2 liters of fortified or sparkling wine; 2 liters of still table wine; 60 milliliters of perfume; 250 milliliters of toilet water; plus £136 worth of other goods, including gifts and souvenirs.

D

FOR TRAVELERS WITH DISABILITIES

When discussing accessibility with an operator or reservationist, **ask hard questions.** Are there any stairs, inside *or* out? Are there grab bars next to the toilet *and* in the shower/tub? How wide is the doorway to the room? To the bathroom? For the most extensive facilities, meeting the latest legal specifications, **opt for newer accommodations,** which more often have been designed with access in mind. Older properties or ships must

usually be retrofitted and may offer more limited facilities as a result. Be sure to **discuss your needs before booking.**

DISCOUNT CLUBS

Travel clubs offer members unsold space on airplanes, cruise ships, and package tours at as much as 50% below regular prices. Membership may include a regular bulletin or access to a toll-free hot line giving details of available trips departing from three or four days to several months in the future. Most also offer 50% discounts off hotel rack rates. Before booking with a club, **make sure the hotel or other supplier isn't offering a better deal.**

DRIVING

I–40 runs east–west across the middle of the state; I–10 cuts across the southern part of the state from the Texas border at El Paso to the Arizona line, through Las Cruces, Deming, and Lordsburg; I–25 runs north from the state line at El Paso through Albuquerque and Santa Fe, then angles northeast to the Colorado line near Raton.

U.S. highways connect all major cities and towns with a good network of paved roads. State roads go to the smaller towns; most of them are paved, two-lane thoroughfares. Roads on Native American lands are designated by wooden, arrow-shape signs; these, like roads in

national forests, are usually not paved.

Technically, there may not be a lot of true desert in New Mexico, but there is a lot of high, dry, lonesome country. For a safe trip, **keep your gas tank full and abide by the signs**—you shouldn't have any trouble.

Arroyos, dry washes or gullies, are bridged on major roads, but lesser roads often dip down through them. These can be a hazard during the rainy season of July, August, and September. Even if it looks shallow, **don't try to cross an arroyo filled with water**—it may have an axle-breaking hole in the middle. Just wait a little while, and it will drain off almost as quickly as it filled. If you stall in a running arroyo, get out of the car and onto high ground if possible. If you are in backcountry, never drive (or walk) in a dry arroyo bed if the sky is dark anywhere upstream. A sudden thunderstorm 15 miles away could send a raging flash flood down a wash that was perfectly dry a few minutes earlier.

Avoid unpaved roads in New Mexico—unless they are well graded and graveled—when they are wet. The soil has a lot of *caliche,* or clay, in it that gets very slick when mixed with water.

F

FISHING

Anyone over 12 who wishes to fish must **buy**

a New Mexico fishing license. Including a trout-validation stamp, the license costs out-of-state visitors $9 per day or $17 for 5 days. Temporary licenses are also available. Nearly 300 stores, in addition to game-and-fish offices, sell fishing and hunting licenses.

I
INSURANCE

BAGGAGE

Airline liability for your baggage is limited to $1,250 per person on domestic flights. On international flights, the airlines' liability is $9.07 per pound or $20 per kilogram for checked baggage (roughly $640 per 70-pound bag) and $400 per passenger for unchecked baggage. Insurance for losses exceeding the terms of your airline ticket can be bought directly from the airline at check-in for about $10 per $1,000 of coverage; note that it excludes a rather extensive list of items, shown on your airline ticket.

FLIGHT

You should **think twice before buying flight insurance.** Often purchased as a last-minute impulse at the airport, it pays a lump sum when a plane crashes, either to a beneficiary if the insured dies or sometimes to a surviving passenger who loses eyesight or a limb. Supplementing the airlines' coverage described in the limits-of-liability paragraphs on your ticket, it's expensive and basically

unnecessary. Charging an airline ticket to a major credit card often automatically entitles you to coverage and may also embrace travel by bus, train, and ship.

FOR U.K. TRAVELERS

According to the Association of British Insurers, a trade association representing 450 insurance companies, it's wise to **buy extra medical coverage when you visit the United States.** You can buy an annual travel-insurance policy valid for most vacations during the year in which it's purchased. If you go this route, make sure it covers you if you have a preexisting medical condition or are pregnant.

TRIP

Without insurance, you will lose all or most of your money if you must cancel your trip because of illness or any other reason. Especially if your airline ticket, cruise, or package tour is nonrefundable and cannot be changed, it's essential that you **buy trip-cancellation-and-interruption insurance.** When considering how much coverage you need, look for a policy that will cover the cost of your trip plus the nondiscounted price of a one-way airline ticket should you need to return home early. Read the fine print carefully, especially sections defining "family member" and "preexisting medical conditions." Also **consider default or bankruptcy insurance,**

which protects you against a supplier's failure to deliver. However, such policies often do not cover default by a travel agency, tour operator, airline, or cruise line if you bought your tour and the coverage directly from the firm in question.

L
LODGING

In addition to hotels, New Mexico offers a broad range of alternative accommodations, from charming bed-and-breakfasts in quaint residential areas to small alpine lodges near the primary ski resorts. Of course, you'll also find major-chain hotels. Low-season rates, which fluctuate, tend to be 20% lower than during the peak tourist months of July and August. Reservations are also easier to obtain during low season (*see* When to Go, *below*).

APARTMENT AND VILLA RENTALS

If you want a home base that's roomy enough for a family and comes with cooking facilities, **consider a furnished rental.** It's generally cost-wise, too, although not always—some rentals are luxury properties (economical only when your party is large). Home-exchange directories list rentals—often second homes owned by prospective house swappers—and some services search for a house or apartment for you (even a castle if that's your fancy) and handle the paperwork.

Some send an illustrated catalogue and others send photographs of specific properties, sometimes at a charge; up-front registration fees may apply.

HOME EXCHANGE

If you would like to find a house, an apartment, or other vacation property to exchange for your own while on vacation, **become a member of a home-exchange organization**, which will send you its annual directories listing available exchanges and will include your own listing in at least one of them. Arrangements for the actual exchange are made by the two parties to it, not by the organization.

M
MONEY AND EXPENSES

ATMS

Chances are that you can **use your bank card at ATMs** to withdraw money from an account and get cash advances on a credit-card account if your card has been programmed with a personal identification number, or PIN. Before leaving home, **check on frequency limits** for withdrawals and cash advances.

On cash advances you are charged interest from the day you receive the money, whether from a teller or an ATM. Transaction fees for ATM withdrawals outside your home turf may be higher than for withdrawals at home.

TRAVELER'S CHECKS

Whether or not to buy traveler's checks depends on where you are headed; **take cash to rural areas and small towns, traveler's checks to cities.** The most widely recognized are American Express, Citicorp, Thomas Cook, and Visa, which are sold by major commercial banks for 1%–3% of the checks' face value—it pays to **shop around.** Both American Express and Thomas Cook issue checks that can be countersigned and used by you or your traveling companion. Record the numbers of the checks, cross them off as you spend them, and keep this information separate from your checks.

WIRING MONEY

You don't have to be a cardholder to send or receive funds through MoneyGram^{SM} from American Express. Just go to a MoneyGram agent, located in retail and convenience stores and in American Express Travel Offices. Pay up to $1,000 with cash or a credit card, anything over that in cash. The money can be picked up within 10 minutes in cash or check at the nearest MoneyGram agent. There's no limit, and the recipient need only present photo identification. The cost, which includes a free long-distance phone call, runs from 3% to 10%, depending on the amount sent, the destination, and how you pay.

You can also send money using Western Union. Money sent from the United States or Canada will be available for pickup at agent locations in 100 countries within 15 minutes. Once the money is in the system, it can be picked up at any one of 25,000 locations. Fees range from 4% to 10%, depending on the amount you send.

N
NATIONAL PARKS

If you are a frequent visitor, senior citizen, or a traveler with a disability, you can **save money on park entrance fees** by getting a discount pass. The Golden Eagle Pass can be a good deal if you plan to visit several parks during your travels. For $25, it entitles you and your companions to free admission to *all* parks for a year. It does not cover additional park fees such as those for camping or parking. Both the Golden Age Passport, for U.S. citizens or permanent residents 62 or older, and the Golden Access Passport, for travelers with disabilities, entitle holders to free entry to all national parks plus 50% off fees for the use of all park facilities and services except those run by private concessionaires. Both types of passports are free; you must show proof of disability or proof of age and U.S. citizenship or permanent residency (such as a U.S. passport, driver's license, or birth certificate). All three passes are available at all national park entrances.

P

PACKAGES AND TOURS

A package or tour to Santa Fe can make your vacation less expensive and more convenient. Firms that sell tours and packages purchase airline seats, hotel rooms, and rental cars in bulk and pass some of the savings on to you. In addition, the best operators have local representatives to help you out at your destination.

A GOOD DEAL?

The more your package or tour includes, the better you can predict the ultimate cost of your vacation. Make sure you know exactly what is included, and **beware of hidden costs.** Are taxes, tips, and service charges included? Transfers and baggage handling? Entertainment and excursions? These can add up.

Most packages and tours are rated deluxe, first-class superior, first class, tourist, and budget. The key difference is usually accommodations. If the package or tour you are considering is priced lower than in your wildest dreams, **be skeptical.** Also, **make sure your travel agent knows the hotels** and other services. Ask about location, room size, beds, and whether the facility has a pool, room service, or programs for children, if

you care about these. Has your agent been there or sent others you can contact?

BUYER BEWARE

Each year consumers are stranded or lose their money when operators go out of business—even very large ones with excellent reputations. If you can't afford a loss, take the time to **check out the operator**—find out how long the company has been in business, and ask several agents about its reputation. Next, **don't book unless the firm has a consumer-protection program.** Members of the United States Tour Operators Association and the National Tour Association are required to set aside funds exclusively to cover your payments and travel arrangements in case of default. Nonmember operators may instead carry insurance; look for the details in the operator's brochure—and the name of an underwriter with a solid reputation. Note: When it comes to tour operators, **don't trust escrow accounts.** Although there are laws governing those of charter-flight operators, no governmental body prevents tour operators from raiding the till. Next, **contact your local Better Business Bureau and the attorney general's office** in both your own state and the operator's; have any complaints been filed? Last, **pay with a major credit card.** Then you can cancel payment, provided that you can document your com-

plaint. Always **consider trip-cancellation insurance** (*see* Insurance, *above*).

BIG VS. SMALL➤ An operator that handles several hundred thousand travelers annually can use its purchasing power to give you a good price. Its high volume may also indicate financial stability. But some small companies provide more personalized service; because they tend to specialize, they may also be experts on an area.

USING AN AGENT

Travel agents are an excellent resource. In fact, large operators accept bookings only through travel agents. But it's good to **collect brochures from several agencies,** because some agents' suggestions may be skewed by promotional relationships with tour and package firms that reward them for volume sales. If you have a special interest, **find an agent with expertise in that area;** the American Society of Travel Agents can give you leads in the United States. (Don't rely solely on your agent, though; agents may be unaware of small-niche operators, and some special-interest travel companies only sell direct.)

SINGLE TRAVELERS

Prices are usually quoted per person, based on two sharing a room. If you are traveling solo, you may be required to pay the full double-occupancy rate. Some operators eliminate this surcharge if you agree to be matched up with a roommate of the same sex, even if one is not found by departure time.

PACKING FOR SANTA FE

Typical of the Southwest, temperatures can vary considerably from sunup to sundown. You should **pack for warm days and chilly nights.**

The areas of higher elevation are, of course, considerably cooler than are Carlsbad and other low-lying southern portions of the state. That means winter visitors should pack warm clothes—coats, parkas, and whatever else your body's thermostat and your ultimate destination dictate. Sweaters and jackets will also be needed for summer visitors because while days are warm, nights at the higher altitudes can be extremely chilly. And bring comfortable shoes; - you're likely to be doing a lot of walking.

New Mexico is one of the most informal and laid-back areas of the country, which for many is much a part of its appeal. Probably no more than three or four restaurants in the entire state enforce a dress code, even for dinner meals, though men are likely to feel more comfortable wearing a jacket in the major hotel dining rooms, and women in tennis shoes may receive a look of stern disapproval from the maître d'.

The Western look, popular throughout the country a few years back has, of course,

never lost its hold on the West. But Western dress has become less corny and more subtle and refined. Western-style clothes are no longer a costume; they're being mixed with tweed jackets, for example, for a more conservative, sophisticated image. Which is to say, you can dress Western with your boots and big belt buckles in even the best places in Santa Fe, Taos, Albuquerque, or Carlsbad, but if you come strolling through the lobby of the Eldorado Hotel looking like Hopalong Cassidy, you'll get some funny looks.

Depending on where - you're headed in New Mexico, you may find the sun strong, the air dry, and the wind hot and relentless. Don't neglect to **bring skin moisturizers** if dry skin's a problem, and **bring sunglasses** to protect your eyes from the glare of lakes or ski slopes. High altitude can be a problem (it may cause headaches and dizziness), so check with your doctor about medication to alleviate symptoms.

Bring an extra pair of eyeglasses or contact lenses in your carry-on luggage, and if you have a health problem, **pack enough medication** to last the trip. **Don't put prescription drugs or valuables in luggage to be checked,** for it could go astray.

LUGGAGE

Free airline baggage allowances depend on the airline, the route,

and the class of your ticket; ask in advance. In general, on domestic flights you are entitled to check two bags—neither exceeding 62 inches, or 158 centimeters (length + width + height), or weighing more than 70 pounds (32 kilograms). A third piece may be brought aboard; its total dimensions are generally limited to less than 45 inches (114 centimeters), so it will fit easily under the seat in front of you or in the overhead compartment. In the United States, the FAA gives airlines broad latitude to limit carry-on allowances and tailor them to different aircraft and operational conditions. Charges for excess, oversize, or overweight pieces vary.

SAFEGUARDING YOUR LUGGAGE➢ Before leaving home, **itemize your bags' contents** and their worth, and label them with your name, address, and phone number. (If you use your home address, cover it so potential thieves can't see it.) Inside your bag, **pack a copy of your itinerary.** At check-in, **make sure that your bag is correctly tagged** with the airport's three-letter destination code. If your bags arrive damaged or not at all, file a written report with the airline before leaving the airport.

PASSPORTS AND VISAS

CANADIANS

No passport is necessary to enter the United States.

SMART TRAVEL TIPS / THE GOLD GUIDE

U.K. CITIZENS

British citizens need a valid passport. If you are staying fewer than 90 days and traveling on a vacation, with a return or onward ticket, you will probably not need a visa. However, you will need to fill out the Visa Waiver Form, 1-94W, supplied by the airline.

While traveling, **keep one photocopy of the data page** separate from your wallet and leave another copy with someone at home. If you lose your passport, promptly call the nearest embassy or consulate, and the local police; having the data page can speed replacement.

R
RENTING A CAR

CUTTING COSTS

To get the best deal, **book through a travel agent and shop around.** When pricing cars, **ask where the rental lot is located.** Some off-airport locations offer lower rates—even though their lots are only minutes away from the terminal via complimentary shuttle. You may also want to **price local car-rental companies,** whose rates may be lower still, although service and maintenance standards may not be up to those of a national firm. Also **ask your travel agent about a company's customer-service record.** How has it responded to late plane arrivals and vehicle mishaps? Are there often lines at the rental counter, and, if you're traveling during

a holiday period, does a confirmed reservation guarantee you a car?

FOR U.K. CITIZENS

In the United States you must be 21 to rent a car; rates may be higher for those under 25. Extra costs cover child seats, compulsory for children under five (about $3 per day), and additional drivers (about $1.50 per day). To pick up your reserved car you will need the reservation voucher, a passport, a U.K. driver's license, and a travel policy covering each driver.

INSURANCE

When you drive a rented car, you are generally responsible for any damage or personal injury that you cause as well as damage to the vehicle. Before you rent, **see what coverage you already have** under the terms of your personal auto-insurance policy and credit cards. For about $14 a day, rental companies sell insurance, known as a collision damage waiver (CDW), that eliminates your liability for damage to the car; it's always optional and should never be automatically added to your bill.

SURCHARGES

Before picking up the car in one city and leaving it in another, **ask about drop-off charges or one-way service fees,** which can be substantial. Note, too, that some rental agencies charge extra if you return the car before the time specified

on your contract. To avoid a hefty refueling fee, **fill the tank just before you turn in the car.**

S

SENIOR-CITIZEN DISCOUNTS

To qualify for age-related discounts, **mention your senior-citizen status up front** when booking hotel reservations, not when checking out, and before you're seated in restaurants, not when paying your bill. Note that discounts may be limited to certain menus, days, or hours. When renting a car, **ask about promotional car-rental discounts**—they can net lower costs than your senior-citizen discount.

STUDENTS ON THE ROAD

To save money, **look into deals available through student-oriented travel agencies.** To qualify, you'll need to have a bona fide student I.D. card. Members of international student groups also are eligible. *See* Students *in* Important Contacts A to Z, *above.*

T
TELEPHONES

LONG-DISTANCE

The long-distance services of AT&T, MCI, and Sprint make calling home relatively convenient and let you avoid hotel surcharges; typically, you dial an 800 number in the United States.

W

The best time to go to New Mexico is a matter of personal preference. If you're interested in a particular sport, activity, or special event, go when that's available and don't worry too much about the weather. Most ceremonial dances at the Native American pueblos occur in the summer, early fall, and at Christmas and Easter. The majority of other major events are geared to the traditionally heavy tourist season of July and August: The Santa Fe Opera, Chamber Music Festival, and Indian and Spanish markets all take place during those two months. The Santa Fe Fiesta and New Mexico State Fair in Albuquerque are held in September, and the Albuquerque International Balloon Fiesta is in October.

The relatively cool climates of Santa Fe and Taos are a lure in summer, as is the skiing in Taos and Santa Fe in winter. Christmas is a wonderful time to be in New Mexico because of Native American ceremonials as well as the Spanish religious folk plays, special foods, and musical events. Hotel rates are generally highest during the peak summer season but fluctuate less than those in most major resort areas. If you plan to come in summer, be sure to **make reservations in advance for July and August.** You can avoid most of the tourist crowds by coming during spring or fall. Spring weather is unpredictable; sudden storms may erupt. October is one of the best months to visit: The air is crisp, colors are brilliant, and whole mountainsides become tumbling cascades of red and gold.

Climate

What follows are average daily maximum and minimum temperatures for Santa Fe and Albuquerque.

SANTA FE

Jan.	39F	4C	May	68F	20C	Sept.	73F	23C
	19	– 7		42	6		48	9
Feb.	42F	6C	June	78F	26C	Oct.	62F	17C
	23	– 5		51	11		37	3
Mar.	51F	11C	July	80F	27C	Nov.	50F	10C
	28	– 2		57	14		28	– 2
Apr.	59F	15C	Aug.	78F	26C	Dec.	39F	4C
	35	2		55	13		19	– 7

ALBUQUERQUE

Jan.	46F	8C	May	78F	26C	Sept.	84F	29C
	24	– 4		51	11		57	14
Feb.	53F	12C	June	89F	32C	Oct.	71F	22C
	28	– 2		60	16		44	7
Mar.	60F	16C	July	91F	33C	Nov.	57F	14C
	33	1		64	18		32	0
Apr.	69F	21C	Aug.	89F	32C	Dec.	48F	9C
	42	6		64	18		26	– 3

1 Destination: Santa Fe, Taos, Albuquerque

INTRODUCTION

T WAS WINTER, a good 25 years ago, when I first visited New Mexico. I was traveling with Gerta, the beautiful young German woman who was not yet my wife. We headed out from Tucson with the famous southwestern artist Ted DeGrazia and his wife, Marion, in DeGrazia's big Mercedes. DeGrazia wanted to sketch and paint Christmas ceremonial dances at the various pueblos. A fanatic about color, he was also looking for a red blanket of a certain shade. He'd been searching for months and he was sure he'd find it in New Mexico.

I don't recall where we stayed in Santa Fe, our first stop, but I remember being surprised at how shocked DeGrazia was when he learned that Gerta and I would be sharing the same room, even though we weren't married. I guess it just wasn't done in those days. I also recall that we shopped under the portals at the Palace of the Governors on the Santa Fe Plaza; I still have the inlaid turquoise and silver cuff links I bought there. I understand cuff links are coming back.

We went on to Taos, where we paid a perhaps-too-early-in-the-morning visit to the writer Frank Waters, a friend of De-Grazia's. I had a copy of Waters's *The Man Who Killed the Deer* that I was hoping to have autographed. Unannounced visits are quite common in the West, but ours couldn't have been more badly timed. Waters was just sitting down to breakfast and obviously having a tiff with his wife at the time (he has since remarried). Our arrival—"paying homage to the great writer" was his wife's ironic phrase, I think—set her off. A plate of scrambled eggs went flying across the kitchen, smashing into the wall. We could still hear the shouting as we got into the car. I never did get the book signed.

On Christmas Eve, we headed out to the services at Taos Pueblo. There was a huge crowd and no room to sit; we squeezed into the church balcony. A tall, powerfully built Indian standing next to me lit a cigarette. I told him he shouldn't smoke

in church. He told me we were in an "Indian place" and he'd smoke if he wanted to. I wasn't about to argue. After the priest said Mass, two Indian Deer dancers, bedecked in deerskins and antlers, came thumping down the center of the church aisle, rattles shaking, chanting; they were followed by others and then by a Buffalo dancer. DeGrazia sketched away.

At Nambe Pueblo, where we went next, we were surprised to discover the same priest celebrating Mass. In fact, this priest was at every pueblo we visited that night, eventually saying "midnight" Mass at 2 in the morning at Santa Clara. Somewhere along the way we got arrested. Driving down a long dirt road to one of the pueblos, we picked up a Native American who was going in the same direction. He was quite young and quite drunk, and it was the latter condition that found all four of us being led to the office of the tribal governor—who was apparently also a judge.

It was a serious offense, we were told, bringing alcohol into the pueblo. We hadn't, but because the intoxicated Native American was with us, it was assumed that we had contributed to his condition. For a while it looked as though we were going to spend Christmas Eve in jail, but then De-Grazia had a brainstorm. He opened his wallet and slowly laid out a string of credit cards, all gleaming plastic and bright colors. The governor-judge picked up each card and studied it carefully, running his finger over the embossed lettering. What message they transmitted, we don't know, but they did the trick. The cards were returned, and we were promptly released.

It was late and everyone was exhausted, but DeGrazia wanted to press on. An impressionist artist, he painted Native Americans with stylistic brilliance in a dazzling palette of colors. For the moment, however, he was making only quick pencil sketches. The more tired he was, he explained, the more blurred everything became, and only the most important details stood out. He worked best in that dreamlike state.

BEFORE VISITING THE PUEB-LOS, Gerta and I had noticed a blanket in the window of the local J. C. Penney. It was red, a terrible color red, a red that reminded us a bit of Campbell's tomato soup. We bought it, had it gift wrapped, and gave it to De-Grazia on Christmas morning. He seemed touched when he opened the box; it was just the color he was looking for, he said, trying to keep a straight face. How did we ever find it?

DeGrazia died in 1982. He had planned to move to Santa Fe and build a studio there in the foothills of the Sangre de Cristo Mountains, but that never came to pass. The city has expanded since that first visit and has changed, as have we all. Yet, like De-Grazia, I find New Mexico's spiritual pull at times overwhelming. And the impressions it leaves—especially after I go too long without sleep—are the most vivid of anywhere I've been.

Recently I was driving north from Carlsbad, alone, when I pulled up in front of the Inn of the Mountain Gods, centerpiece of the sprawling Mescalero Indian Reservation in the southern part of the state. Midway between Alamogordo and Roswell in Lincoln County, the reservation is home to more than 2,500 Mescalero Apaches, and the inn is Apache-owned and -run. The idea of vacationing for a few days on a Native American reservation appealed to me. I wanted to read, write, and relax away from it all. In the back of my mind were thoughts of hogans, tepees, and lazy curls of smoke rising from smoldering campfires.

These visions dissipated when a pleasant young man in jeans and a white shirt said, "Good morning, sir," as he unloaded my bags and then drove my car to an adjacent parking lot. Valet parking? I could have been in Beverly Hills.

But once inside, I knew I had come to the right place. The canyon-size lobby was dominated by a three-story-high copper-sheathed fireplace. Beyond, the glass-paneled walls looked out onto Mescalero Lake, and beyond the lake, the slender tips of ponderosa pine speared a bank of low-hanging clouds, all framed by a wall of jagged mountains. Native American paintings, artifacts, and wall hangings were displayed throughout the lobby. Even before I signed in I found myself pricing turquoise jewelry at a display case.

Three miles northeast is the town of Ruidoso, home of the Ruidoso Downs Racetrack. On Labor Day, the track's All-American Quarter Horse Futurity offers as much as $3 million in prize money; it's billed as the nation's richest purse. The town itself is small, one of those places where people still give directions by the number of bumps in the road. In addition to its shops and antiques stores, downtown Ruidoso has a number of saloons where the racetrack grooms, stable boys, and tipsters congregate. I stopped into one of these bars one night wearing a suit, and the bartender asked me if I was a doctor.

On the north, east, and west, Ruidoso is bordered by Lincoln National Forest. In 1950, after a devastating forest fire was brought under control in the Capitan Mountains, 30 miles northeast, firefighters found a badly burned bear cub clinging to a tree. Nursed back to health, the cub was later flown to the Washington, D.C., zoo. He was named Smokey, and became the symbol for the nation's campaign to prevent forest fires.

When I checked out of the hotel several days later, loaded down with Native American rugs, bracelets, pottery, and images of another way of life, I felt ready once again to face the rigors of city, traffic, and deadlines.

Extolling the glories of an area of which one is particularly fond invariably leaves one with a sense of misgiving. I can't help but wonder to what extent I'm contributing to changing the things that I value. With a statewide population of about 1.5 million, New Mexico isn't exactly being overrun. But I just heard that the Inn of the Mountain Gods was installing a hundred slot machines in its lobby. "I don't know why I paint Indians," DeGrazia once wrote to me. "Maybe I'm afraid that the Indians are going to vanish and I want to be around them to fill my eyes."

—*Ron Butler*

WHAT'S WHERE

Santa Fe and Vicinity

Perched on a 7,000-foot-high plateau at the base of the Sangre de Cristo Mountains in southern New Mexico, Santa Fe is one of the most popular cities in the United States, with an abundance of museums, art galleries, first-rate restaurants, and shops selling Southwestern furnishings and cowboy gear. Among the smallest state capitals in the country, the city has fine examples of traditional Southwestern-style homes made of adobe and stucco. Remnants of a 2,000-year-old Pueblo civilization surround the city, which is also filled with artifacts of Spanish rule, many of them on display in local museums. Other area highlights are excursions from Santa Fe to Pecos National Historic Park with ruins of Spanish missions and an ancient Native American pueblo; Las Vegas, a town that preserves the Old West; Los Alamos, the birthplace of the atomic bomb; and Chimayo, a small village famous for weaving, regional food, and the Santuario, which attracts thousands of worshipers each year.

Taos

About 70 miles north of Santa Fe, on a rolling mesa at the base of the Sangre de Cristo Mountains, Taos is a world-famous art and literary center that attracts artists and collectors to its copious museums and galleries. This enchanted town has romantic courtyards, stately elms and cottonwood trees, narrow streets, and a profusion of adobe buildings. Three miles northwest of the commercial center lies the Taos Pueblo, home of the Taos-Tiwa Indians, while 4 miles south of town is Ranchos de Taos, an adobe-housed farming and ranching community first settled centuries ago by the Spanish. Taos is also renowned for its fabulous ski slopes.

Albuquerque

With its own international airport, Albuquerque is the gateway to New Mexico. Like many other areas of the state, this large, sprawling city serves as a thriving center for artists, writers, poets, filmmakers, and musicians. Most of its citizens are descendants of Native American, Spanish, and Anglo settlers, and this blend of cultures is reflected in the city's architecture, cuisine, and artwork.

Carlsbad and Southern New Mexico

In southwestern New Mexico along the Pecos River, Carlsbad is a popular tourist destination with historic museums, 30 parks, 27 miles of beaches, and the nearby Living Desert State Park and Carlsbad Caverns National Park, the latter enclosing one of the largest and most spectacular cave systems in the world. Northwest of Carlsbad are the historic towns of Lincoln County (Ruiduso, San Patricio, and Lincoln, where Billy the Kid was jailed) and White Sands National Monument, an eerie wonderland of shifting sand dunes 60 feet high.

Pueblos of Rio Grande

The reservations of New Mexico are among the only places left in the United States where traditional Native American culture and skills are retained with a sense of dignity and pride. Descendants of the highly civilized Anasazi, the Pueblo peoples of northern New Mexico, continue to preserve their customs; each pueblo has its own personality, history, and specialties in art and design. Pueblos dating back centuries are located near Santa Fe, Taos, and Albuquerque; the best time to visit them is when they celebrate the harvest with special ceremonies, dances, and rituals.

PLEASURES & PASTIMES

Dining

A delicious and extraordinary mixture of Pueblo, Spanish Colonial, and Mexican and American frontier cooking, the regional cuisine is not only good, it's good for you. New Mexican restaurants are especially popular and are almost universally inexpensive. The traditional diet of New Mexico's Native American and Hispanic cultures is considered very healthy. Beans provide carbohydrates and protein; corn offers protein and calcium; and chiles, one of the most versatile seasonings known, contain an entire storehouse of vitamins and minerals—they're particularly rich with vitamin C.

Many New Mexico restaurants offer buffalo meat (stews, steaks, and burgers). Of course, there are a fair share of trendy and contemporary restaurants, particularly in the Santa Fe and Taos areas, as well as a respectable offering of gourmet grill rooms, French, Italian, Japanese, Greek, and other ethnic establishments.

The following list of names and terms may prove helpful for the newcomer to New Mexico who doesn't know what a great taste treat lies in store:

Aguacate. Spanish for avocado, the key ingredient of guacamole.

Albondigas. Meatballs, usually cooked with rice in a meat broth.

Burrito. A warm flour tortilla wrapped around meat, beans, or vegetables, and smothered in chile and cheese.

Chalupa. A corn tortilla deep fried in the shape of a bowl, filled with pinto beans (sometimes meat), and topped with cheese, guacamole, sour cream, lettuce, tomatoes, and salsa.

Chile relleno. A large green chile pepper, peeled, stuffed with cheese or a special mixture of spicy ingredients, dipped in batter, and fried.

Chiles. New Mexico's infamous hot peppers, which come in an endless variety of sizes and in various degrees of hotness, from the thumb-size jalapeño to the smaller and often hotter serrano. They can be canned or fresh, dried or cut up into salsa.

Chimichanga. The same as a burrito above, only deep-fried and topped with a dash of sour cream or salsa.

Chorizo. Well-spiced Spanish sausage, made with pork and red chile.

Enchilada. A rolled or flat corn tortilla, filled with meat, chicken, seafood, or cheese; covered with chile; and baked. The ultimate enchilada is made with blue Indian corn tortillas. New Mexicans order them flat, sometimes topped with a fried egg.

Flauta. A tortilla filled with cheese or meat and rolled into a flutelike shape (*flauta* means flute) and lightly fried. When eaten, they're usually dipped in salsa or chile.

Frijoles refritos. Refried beans, often seasoned with lard or cheese.

Guacamole. Mashed avocado, mixed with tomatoes, garlic, onions, lemon juice, and chile, used as a dip or a side dish.

Huevos rancheros. New Mexico's answer to eggs Benedict—eggs doused with chile and sometimes melted cheese, served on top of a corn tortilla. They're good accompanied by chorizos.

Posole. Resembling popcorn soup, this is a sublime marriage of lime hominy, pork, chile, garlic, and spices.

Quesadilla. A folded flour tortilla, filled with cheese and meat or vegetables, and warmed or lightly fried so the cheese melts.

Sopaipilla. Puffy deep-fried bread, served with honey.

Taco. A corn tortilla, fried and made into a shell that's then stuffed with spicy meat or chicken, and garnished with shredded lettuce, chopped tomatoes, onions, and grated cheese.

Tamale. Ground corn made into a dough and filled with finely ground pork and red chile, then steamed in a corn husk.

Tortilla. Thin pancake made of corn or wheat flour, used as bread, as an edible "spoon," and as a container for other foods. Locals place butter in the center of a hot tortilla, roll it up, and eat it as a scroll. It is also useful for scooping up the last bit in a bowl of chile.

Verde. Spanish for "green." Chile verde is a green chile sauce.

Shopping

ANTIQUES➤ The American West is still relatively young, but antiques shops and roadside museums dot the desert landscape. You'll find everything in New Mexico's antiques shops, from early Mexican typewriters to period saddles, ceramic pots, farm tools, pioneer aviation equipment, and yellowed newspaper clippings about Kit Carson and D. H. Lawrence.

ART➤ Santa Fe is the fine-arts capital of the Southwest, with more than 150 galleries. Albuquerque and Taos are not far behind. Native American art, Western art, fine art, junk art—it's all for sale in New Mexico, and in all mediums: sculptures, prints, posters, ceramics, etchings, drawings, photographs, and exquisite miniatures, by artists of both international and local renown.

CRAFTS➤ Hispanic handcrafted furniture and *santos* command high prices from collectors; santos are religious carvings and paintings in the form of *bultos* (three-dimensional carvings in the round) and *retablos* (holy images painted on wood or tin). Colorful handwoven Hispanic textiles, tinwork, ironwork, and straw appliqué are also much in demand. Native American textiles, rugs, kachina dolls, baskets, silver jewelry, turquoise, pottery, beadwork, ornamental shields, drums, and ceramics can be found almost everywhere in New Mexico, from Santa Fe Plaza to the Native American pueblos that range across the entire state. Prices range from thousands of dollars for a rare 1930s kachina doll to just a few cents for hand-wrapped bundles of sage, juniper, sweet grass, and lavender that are used by Native Americans in healing ceremonies, gatherings, and daily cleansing of the home. Ignited like incense, this herbal combination gives off a sacred smoke; passing it once around the room is enough to change and charge the air.

SPICES➤ You'll find stands beside the road selling *chile ristras,* strings of crimson chiles to hang in the kitchen or beside the front door, and you'll find shops everywhere selling chile powder and other spices. You'll catch the smell from the road; walk in the store, and your eyes begin to water and your mouth to salivate. For many, especially natives of the Southwest, *picante* is the purest, finest word in the Spanish language. It means hot—spicy hot. All around you, in boxes, bags, packets, jars, and cans, there's everything *picante*—salsas, chile pastes, powders, herbs, spices, peppers, barbecue sauce, and fiery potions in bottles.

Sports and the Outdoors

BICYCLING➤ Albuquerque is a biker's paradise, with miles and miles of bike lanes and trails crisscrossing and skirting the city. Not only is Albuquerque's Parks and Recreation Department aware of bikers' needs, but bike riding is heavily promoted as a means of cutting down on traffic congestion and pollution. Santa Fe and Taos, because of hilly terrain and narrow, frequently congested downtown streets, are less hospitable to cyclists. However, mountain biking is popular in both areas. With low gears and knobby tires, mountain bikes open back roads and trails to bike excursions of all kinds. Cycling events in New Mexico include the Santa Fe Century (50- or 100-mile recreational rides), the Sanbusco Hill Climb (an annual race to the Santa Fe Ski Area), and the Tour de Los Alamos (road race and criterium).

BIRD-WATCHING➤ Bird-watchers have wonderful opportunities to spot birds migrating from the jungles of South America to the tundra of the Arctic Circle. The Bosque del Apache National Wildlife Refuge, 90 miles south of Albuquerque, is the winter home of thousands of migrating birds, including one of only two wild flocks of the rare whooping crane.

CANOEING AND RIVER RAFTING➤ New Mexico's rivers offer a choice: A lazy glide along a serpentine waterway, past colorful mesas and soaring cliffs, or a heart-thumping ride through white-water rapids. The Taos Box, a 17-mile run through the churning rapids of the upper Rio Grande, is one of New Mexico's most exciting rafting experiences. Most of the hardcore river rafting is done in the Taos area. More leisurely trips can be had aboard the sightseeing craft that ply the Pecos, Rio Charma, and other meandering rivers.

FISHING➤ Fishing spots include the Rio Grande, which traverses New Mexico north to south; Abiquiu Lake, 40 miles northwest of Santa Fe; Heron Lake, 20 miles southwest of Chama via US 64 and NM 96; and Blue Water Lake in the northwest closer to Albuquerque, 28 miles west of Grants via NM 371. The San Juan's high-quality-water regulations make for some of the best trout fishing in the country. Six-thousand-acre Heron Lake offers rainbow trout, lake trout, and kokanee salmon. Trout fishermen will also find nirvana in the sparkling streams of the Sangre de Cristo range, bordering Santa Fe. The Pecos River and its tributaries offer excellent backcountry fishing. Fishing on Native American reservations is not subject to regulations but may require special permits.

GOLFING➤ The state has a respectable share of turf, with more than 60 courses offering recreation throughout the year. The dry climate here makes playing very comfortable. There are excellent public courses in Albuquerque, Angel Fire, Las Vegas, Los Alamos, Santa Fe, and Taos.

HIKING➤ Bring your walking shoes: Few states in the nation are as blessed with such a diverse network of trails. New Mexico's air is clean and crisp, and its ever-changing terrain is aesthetically rewarding as well. Carlsbad Caverns National Park in the southeast has more than 50 miles of scenic hiking trails.

HORSE RACING➤ Horse racing with parimutuel betting is very popular in New Mexico. Two of the more popular of the state's tracks are Downs at Santa Fe, 5 miles south of Santa Fe, and Downs at Albuquerque, a glass-enclosed facility in the center of the city at the New Mexico State Fairgrounds. Quarterhorse racing's Triple Crown events—Kansas Futurity, Rainbow Futurity, and All-American Futurity—take place in mid-June, mid-July, and Labor Day, respectively, at the Ruidoso Downs tracks in Lincoln County.

HOT-AIR BALLOONS➤ The Albuquerque International Balloon Fiesta in early October draws the largest number of spectators (an estimated 1.5 million people) of any sporting event in the state (see Festivals and Seasonal Events, below).

HUNTING➤ The New Mexico Game and Fish Department has instituted many innovative game-management and wildlife-restoration programs. As a result, hunters have a diverse selection of wildlife to pursue, including sizable herds of mule deer and elk. Waterfowl and upland game-bird hunting is also excellent. There are antelope in the wide, windswept eastern New Mexican plains, and bear in the mountainous backcountry. In addition, there are limited special hunts for Barbary and bighorn sheep, oryx, javelina, and Siberian and Persian ibex.

Four Native American reservations conduct hunts separate from the regular state hunts: the Jicarilla and Mescalero Apaches, the Navajos, and the Zunis all have extensive landholdings in the state and offer the opportunity to hunt certain species when the regular state season is closed.

RODEOS➤ Rodeos are a big draw from early spring through autumn. Besides big events in Santa Fe, Albuquerque, and Gallup, every county in the state has a rodeo competition during its county fair. Major Native American rodeos take place at Stone Lake on the Jicarilla Reservation, on the Mescalero Apache Reservation, at the Inter-Tribal Ceremonial in Gallup, and at the National Indian Rodeo Finals in Albuquerque.

SKIING➤ New Mexico offers many world-class downhill ski areas. Snowmaking equipment is used in most areas to ensure a long season, usually from Thanksgiving through Easter. The Santa Fe Ski Area averages 250 inches of dry-powder snow a year; it accommodates all levels of skiers on more than 40 trails. Within a 90-mile radius, Taos offers four ski resorts with excellent slopes for all levels of skiers, as well as snowmobile and cross-country ski trails. Taos Ski Valley resort is considered one of the best of its kind in the country.

For downhill skiing, Enchanted Forest near Red River has groomed trails in the state's best-known Nordic ski area. Head to the Sangre de Cristo Mountains for high-altitude terrain. There are also exciting cross-country trails north of Chama along the New Mexico–Colorado border, in the Tularosa Mountains in the Gila Wilderness, and to the south in the Sacramento Mountains adjacent to White Springs National Monument. The Sandia and Manzano mountains near Albuquerque are easily accessible for skiers.

Reservations

Two general classifications of Native Americans live in New Mexico: Pueblos, who established an agricultural civilization here many centuries ago, and the descendants of the nomadic tribes who came into the area much later—the Navajos, Mescalero Apaches, and Jicarilla Apaches. The Jicarilla Apaches live on a reservation of ¾ million acres in north-central New Mexico, the capital of which is Dulce. The terrain varies from mountains, mesas, and lakes to high grazing land, suited to cattle and horse ranching. The tribe has a well-defined tourist program promoting big-game hunting, fishing, and camping on a 20,000-acre game preserve. Nearly all the tribe members gather at Stone Lake on September 14 and 15 for the fall festival—two days of dancing, races, and a rodeo. For more information, contact the Tourism Department, Jicarilla Apache Tribe (Box 507, Dulce 87528, ☎ 505/759–3242).

A reservation of ½ million acres of timbered mountains and green valleys is home to the Mescalero Apaches in southeastern New Mexico. The tribe owns and operates the famous resort, Inn of the Mountain Gods, as well as Ski Apache, 16 miles from Ruidoso. For detailed information, *see* Chapter 5, Carlsbad and Southern New Mexico.

The Navajo Reservation, home to the largest Native American group in the United States, covers 16 million acres in New Mexico, Arizona, and Utah. More than any other tribe, the Navajos are still nomadic, following flocks from place to place and living in hogans (mud-and-pole houses). There are a few towns on the reservation, but for the most part it is a vast area of stark pinnacles, colorful rock formations, high desert, and mountains; the land encompasses several national and tribal parks, some of which include campgrounds. Navajos are master silversmiths and rug weavers, and their work is available at trading posts scattered throughout the reservation. The tribe encourages tourism; for more information, contact the Navajo Nation Tourism Office (Box 663, Window Rock, AZ 86515, ☎ 602/871–6659 or 602/871–7371, FAX 602/871–7381).

For detailed information about New Mexico's Pueblo peoples and their villages, *see* Chapter 6, Pueblos of the Rio Grande.

FODOR'S CHOICE

Historic Buildings

★ **KiMo Theater, Albuquerque.** At this 1927 movie palace on Central Avenue, restored to its original design—Pueblo Deco–style architecture painted in bright colors—a varied program is offered, including everything from traveling road shows to local song-and-dance acts.

★ **Palace of the Governors, Santa Fe.** The oldest public building in the United States, this Pueblo-style structure has served as the residence for 100 Spanish, Native American, Mexican, and American gov-

ernors; it is now the central headquarters of the Museum of New Mexico, a state system that includes four local museums.

★ **San Francisco de Asis Church, Ranchos de Taos.** First built in the 18th century as a spiritual and physical refuge from raiding Apaches, Utes, and Comanches and reconstructed in 1979, this church is a spectacular example of adobe Mission architecture that has inspired generations of painters and photographers, including Georgia O'Keeffe, Paul Strand, and Ansel Adams.

★ **San Miguel Mission, Santa Fe.** The oldest church still in use in the United States, this simple, earth-hued adobe structure built about 1625 has priceless statues and paintings on display, as well as the San José Bell, weighing nearly 800 pounds.

★ **Santuario de Chimayo, Chimayo.** Thousands flock each year to this small, frontier adobe church built on the site where believers say, a mysterious light came from the ground on Good Friday night in 1810; today the chapel sits above a sacred *pozito* (a small well), the mud from which is believed to have miraculous healing properties.

★ **Taos Pueblo, Taos.** For nearly 1,000 years, the Taos-Tiwa Native Americans have lived at or near this site, the largest existing multistory pueblo structure in the United States; within its mud-and-straw adobe walls—frequently several feet thick—it preserves a way of life barely changed by time's passage.

Lodging

★ **Inn of the Anasazi, Santa Fe.** In the heart of the historic Plaza district, this decidedly upscale hotel has individually designed rooms, each with a beamed ceiling, kiva fireplace, four-poster bed, and handcrafted desk, dresser, and tables. $$$$

★ **Hyatt Regency Albuquerque, Albuquerque.** In the heart of downtown, this gorgeous hotel has two soaring desert-colored towers climbing high above the city skyline. It's all totally modern and luxurious, from the private forest and a splashing fountain outside to the shopping promenade inside. $$$

★ **Inn of the Governors, Santa Fe.** Just two blocks from the Plaza, this is one of the nicest lodgings in town, with Mexican themed rooms filled with bright colors, hand-painted folk art, Southwestern fabrics, and handmade furnishings. $$$

★ **Inn of the Mountain Gods, Mescalero.** The Mescalero Apaches own and operate this spectacular year-round resort on the banks of Mescalero Lake, about 3 miles southwest of Ruidoso. $$$

★ **Casas de Suenos, Albuquerque.** Long a historic gathering spot for artists, the two-acre Casas de Suenos—Houses of Dreams—provides a magical setting of attractively decorated casitas amid lush English gardens and quiet patios; it's adjacent to Old Town on Rio Grande Boulevard SW. $$–$$$

★ **La Posada de Albuquerque, Albuquerque.** This historic, highly lauded hotel in downtown Albuquerque oozes Southwestern charm, with a tiled lobby fountain, massive vigas, encircling balcony, fixtures of etched glass and tin, and Native American war-dance murals behind the reception desk. $$–$$$

★ **Mabel Dodge Luhan House, Taos.** Once the home of an heiress and longtime Taos resident, this pleasant bed-and-breakfast is a National Historic Landmark frequently used for writing, art, cultural, and educational workshops. $$–$$$

★ **American Artists Gallery House, Taos.** At this unusual bed-and-breakfast, each guest room, furnished in charming southwestern style, has a gallery name; works by local, regional, and nationally known artists, including such Native American and southwestern favorites as R. C. Gorman, Amado Peña, and Veloy Virgil, are featured on the premises. $$

★ **Hotel La Fonda de Taos, Taos.** At this 1937 hotel, rooms have Turkish bedspreads and handmade wooden furniture, and showcased everywhere are framed newspaper and magazine stories from the old days—as well as photos, posters, Western paintings, Hopi shields, portraits, busts, Pueblo pottery, and Mexican paintings and artifacts. Eleven of D.H. Lawrence's erotic paintings are also on display. $$

★ **Inn of the Animal Tracks, Santa Fe.** At this enchanting 91-year-old restored adobe, with beamed ceilings, hardwood floors, handcrafted furniture, and fireplaces, each guest room is decorated with an animal theme:

Whimsical Rabbit, Gentle Deer, Soaring Eagle, Playful Otter, and Loyal Wolf. $$

Restaurants

★ **Anasazi, Santa Fe.** A half-block from the Plaza, the restaurant combines New Mexican and Native American flavors in exotic offerings; guests sit in a large dining room filled with beautiful, solid-wood tables and adobe banquettes upholstered with handwoven textiles from Chimayo. $$$

★ **Lambert's, Taos.** Set in the elegantly remodeled Victorian Randall House, this superb American restaurant is relaxed and intimate, with a stunning view of Taos Mountain. $$$

★ **Artichoke Cafe, Albuquerque.** In a turn-of-the-century brick building just east of downtown on Central Avenue, diners appreciate the excellent service and variety of cuisines—new American, Italian, French—at this outstanding café with dishes prepared using organically grown ingredients. $$

★ **Cafe Pasqual's, Santa Fe.** This tiny, cheerful eatery serves regional specialties and possibly the best breakfast in town, which is served all day. Forget the pancakes and order a *chorizo burrito,* made with Mexican sausages, scrambled eggs, home fries, and scallions. $$

★ **Encore Provence, Santa Fe.** Cuisine from the Provence region of southern France is the specialty at this unpretentious pale yellow wooden house with a stone front porch; in a dining room of 15 immaculately set tables, customers find impeccable service. $$

★ **Prairie Star, Albuquerque.** Facing east toward Albuquerque's majestic Sandia Peak, this rural restaurant serving New American, Southwestern, and classical cuisine is a favorite spot for sipping margaritas at sunset. $$

★ **Rancho de Chimayo, Chimayo.** This local favorite for northern New Mexico cuisine has cozy dining rooms within a century-old adobe hacienda tucked into the mountains. $$

Romantic Sites

★ **Any spot beside the road under a cottonwood tree during chile-harvesting season.** In August through September, enterprising farmers set up tumble dryer–like roasting machines under cottonwood trees to roast freshly picked chiles for sale to passing motorists.

★ **Millicent Rogers Museum, Taos.** At this Native American and Hispanic art museum, the courtyard with its Native American maiden statue by R. C. Gorman provides an enchanted atmosphere.

★ **Outdoor hot tubs at Ten Thousand Waves, Santa Fe.** Come to this Japanese-style health spa to unwind after a day's cavorting on the slopes or in the dusty desert.

★ **Santa Fe at Christmastime.** New Mexico's capital is at its most festive at the end of December, with incense and piñon smoke sweetening the air and the winter darkness illuminated by thousands *farolitos* (tiny lanterns).

★ **Taos Book Shop, Taos.** Many serious romances have begun in bookstores; this store, the oldest bookshop in New Mexico, provides a peaceful meeting spot in a lovely walled adobe building near Taos Plaza.

Scenic Drives

★ **The Enchanted Circle.** This 100-mile loop from Taos winds through canyon and alpine country, with a few colorful mining towns along the way.

★ **The High Road to Taos.** On the old road linking Santa Fe and Taos, the stunning drive—with a rugged alpine mountain backdrop—encompasses rolling hillsides studded with orchards and tiny picturesque villages noted for weavers and wood-carvers.

★ **Route 66.** America's most nostalgic highway takes in a colorful stretch that now constitutes Albuquerque's Central Avenue.

★ **Turquoise Trail.** This old route full of ghost towns between Albuquerque and Santa Fe ventures into backroad country, where the pace is slow, talk is all about weather and crops, and donkeys have right of way.

FESTIVALS AND SEASONAL EVENTS

DEC.➤ **Christmas Native American Dances,** various pueblos. The Spanish dance-drama *Los Matachines* is performed at Picuris and San Juan pueblos. There are also pine-torch processions at San Juan and Taos pueblos, the Kachina Dance at Taos, and Basket, Buffalo, Deer, Harvest, Rainbow, and Turtle dances at Acoma, Cochiti, San Ildefonso, San Juan, Santa Clara, and Taos pueblos. ☎ 505/ 852–4265.

DEC.➤ **Procession of the Virgin,** Taos Pueblo. After vespers on Christmas Eve, the procession of the Virgin Mary takes place, with dancers and bonfires. ☎ 505/758–9593.

DEC.➤ **Christmas Season,** Santa Fe. During the Christmas holidays the New Mexico capital is at its most festive, with incense and piñon smoke sweetening the air and the darkness of winter illuminated by thousands of *farolitos,* lunch sack–size paper bags weighted with sand and sheltering a candle. A custom believed to have derived from the Chinese lanterns the conquistadors brought with them, the glowing farolitos are everywhere, lining walkways, doorways, rooftops, walls, windowsills, and sometimes even gravesites with soft puddles of light. The songs of Christmas are sung around corner bonfires (*luminarias,* as the holiday bonfires are called in Santa Fe), and mugs of hot cider and melt-in-your-mouth Christmas cookies, *bizcochitos,* are offered to all who pass by. With glowing lights reflected on the snow, Santa Fe is never lovelier. Numerous religious pageants and processions take place. Early in the month are 10 days of **Las Posadas** at San Miguel Mission (401 Old Santa Fe Trail, ☎ 505/ 983–3974), during which the story of Mary and Joseph's journey to Bethlehem is reenacted. The **Feast Day of Our Lady of Guadalupe,** December 12, is grandly celebrated at Santuario de Guadalupe, and **Christmas at the Palace** resounds with hours of festive music emanating from the Palace of the Governors.

JAN.➤ **Native American New Year's Celebrations,** all pueblos. Comanche, Deer, and other traditional dances, including the Turtle dance (the men's traditional animal dance), are performed at the Taos Pueblo. ☎ 505/ 758–1028.

FEB.➤ **Winterfestival,** Santa Fe. This celebration of winter takes place in late February, both in town and on the slopes of the Santa Fe Ski Area. Events include snow-sculpture competitions, downhill racing, hot-air ballooning, music, and drama. ☎ 505/982–4429.

MAR.➤ **Fiery Foods Show,** Albuquerque. This annual one-weekend trade show specializes in everything you ever wanted to know about New Mexico's favorite spicy food. Chile is featured here in all its incarnations, from sizzling salsas and dips, to unusual beer and chocolate concoctions. Product demonstrations, panel discussions, and book signings all highlight the culinary qualities of this versatile state vegetable, making this free public event one of the hottest tickets in town. ☎ 505/ 873–2187.

APR.➤ **Albuquerque Founder's Day,** Albuquerque. This event commemorates the April 23, 1706, founding of Albuquerque by Governor Francisco Cuervo y Valdés, whose costumed persona presides over the event. The celebration takes place at the Old Town Plaza. ☎ 505/243–3696.

MAY➤ **Buzzard Days,** Carrizozo. Rattlesnake races and horseshoe competitions are held here during the second weekend in May. ☎ 505/648–2472.

JUNE➤ **New Mexico Arts and Crafts Fair,** Albuquerque. On the last weekend in June, the New Mexico State Fairgrounds hosts this crafts spectacular that brings together more than 200 artists and craftspeople to display their talents. Spanish, Native American, and other North American cultures are represented, and there's plenty of food and entertainment. ☎ 505/884–9043.

JULY➤ **Rodeo de Santa Fe,** Santa Fe. A taste of the Old West comes to Santa Fe in mid-July, with calf roping, bull riding, and a traditional rodeo parade. World-champion rodeo competitors come from all parts of the United States and Canada to this event, held since 1959. ☎ 505/471–4300.

JULY➤ **Spanish Market,** Santa Fe. Held on Santa Fe Plaza, this festive gathering features Spanish arts, crafts, and good things to eat—you can smell the burritos, tamales and chile from blocks around. Many exhibitors are from remote villages, where outstanding handicrafts are produced. Contact the Spanish Colonial Arts Society (Box 1611, Santa Fe 87501, ☎ 505/983–4038).

JULY–AUG.➤ **Shakespeare in Santa Fe,** Santa Fe. Theater fans reserve Fridays, Saturdays, and Sundays for free performances of great Shakespearean plays. An outdoor theater in the hills of eastside Santa Fe provides a beautiful backdrop for the immortal words of the Bard. ☎ 505/982–2910.

AUG.➤ **Bat Flight Breakfast,** Carlsbad. On the second Thursday of August, early risers gather at the entrance to Carlsbad Caverns to eat breakfast and watch tens of thousands of bats, who have been out for the night feeding on insects, fly back into the cave. ☎ 505/785–2232.

AUG.➤ **Indian Market,** Santa Fe. Native American arts, pottery, jewelry, blankets, and rugs are displayed and sold at the Indian Market on the Plaza in mid-August. Many of the town's 150 art galleries feature special shows of leading Native American artists. At least 800 artists and craftspeople are expected to attend the market. Contact Southwestern Association of Indian Affairs (SWAIA, Box 1964, Santa Fe 87501, ☎ 505/983–5220).

FALL

SEPT.➤ **Banjo and Fiddle Mini-Festival,** Santa Fe. This annual toe-tapping, banjo, fiddle, guitar, mandolin, old-time band, and bluegrass mountain-music festival takes place on Labor Day Weekend, attracting big-name folk musicians and thousands of loyal fans to the Santa Fe Rodeo Grounds. Contact the Banjo and Fiddle Contest (13213 Pinehurst NE, Albuquerque 87111, ☎ 505/298–3080).

SEPT.➤ **Las Fiestas de Santa Fe,** Santa Fe. The city's biggest celebration begins the first Friday after Labor Day and commemorates the reconquest of Santa Fe from the San Juan Indians by Don Diego de Vargas in 1692. Parades, dancing, pageantry, ethnic foods, arts and crafts, fireworks, and the burning of Zozobra (Old Man Gloom) are all part of the fun. Contact Las Fiestas de Santa Fe (Box 4516, Santa Fe 87505, ☎ 505/988–7575).

SEPT.➤ **New Mexico State Fair,** Albuquerque. One of the nation's liveliest state fairs takes place at the New Mexico State Fairgrounds, with arts, crafts, livestock shows, entertainment, a midway, a rodeo, and living early Spanish and Native American villages. ☎ 505/265–1791.

OCT.➤ **International Balloon Fiesta,** Albuquerque. More than 650 hot-air and gas balloons will participate in a mass ascension at sunrise during the first two weekends in October. This major event in the world of ballooning—you'll never see anything like it—takes place at Balloon Fiesta Park. ☎ 505/821–1000.

NOV.➤ **Weems Artfest,** Albuquerque. This annual arts and crafts festival features more than 200 artists from throughout the region and has been rated one of the top 75 arts and crafts events in the country. Held at the New Mexico State Fairgrounds, the artfest also includes an extensive children's artmart. ☎ 505/294–6494.

2   Santa Fe and Vicinity

WITH ITS CRISP, CLEAR AIR and bright, sunny weather, Santa Fe couldn't be more welcoming. Perched on a 7,000-foot-high plateau at the base of the Sangre de Cristo Mountains, the city is surrounded by the remnants of a 2,000-year-old Pueblo civilization, and filled with evidence of Spanish rule. Add rows of chic art galleries, smart restaurants, and shops selling Southwestern furnishings and cowboy gear, and you have a uniquely appealing destination that is growing increasingly popular every year.

La Villa Real de la Santa Fe de San Francisco de Asis (the Royal City of the Holy Faith of St. Francis of Assisi) was founded as early as 1607 by Don Pedro de Peralta, who planted his banner in the name of Spain: Although St. Augustine, Florida, is recognized by some as the oldest city in the United States, Santa Fe is actually older. Santa Fe's Paseo de Peralta—a paved loop that approximates the former boundaries of the original Spanish Colonial outpost—still protects the vital core of the city, if only symbolically. The nearly 400-year-old town plaza, now filled with Native American vendors, has been the site of bullfights, public floggings, gunfights, tribal wars, political rallies, and promenades, as well as public markets.

In 1680, the Native Americans of San Juan Pueblo sparked a revolt among all the northern pueblos, who subsequently drove the Spanish out, burning their churches and missions and turning the Palace of the Governors into a tribal dwelling. But the tide turned again 12 years later, when General Don Diego de Vargas returned with a new army from El Paso and recaptured Santa Fe. To commemorate Don Diego's triumph, Las Fiestas de Santa Fe has been held every year since 1712. The country's oldest community celebration traditionally takes place the weekend after Labor Day, with parades, mariachis, pageants, melodramas, arts-and-crafts shows, and nonstop private parties. Though the best-known, Las Fiestas de Santa Fe is but one of numerous opportunities for revelry throughout the year—everything from a Plaza parade to start the rodeo season in mid-July to traditional Pueblo dances at Christmastime.

The once-grand Camino Real (Royal Highway), as spectacular for its time as the transcontinental Pan American Highway is today, originally stretched from Mexico City to Santa Fe, bringing an army of conquistadores from the south to the northernmost reaches of their New World conquest. Now, however, visitors who drive along St. Francis Drive and Cerrillos Road into town from the south will find the two main arteries lined with motels, gas stations, fast-food restaurants, launderettes, and convenience stores.

The Old Santa Fe Trail from the northeast also brought newcomers—first traders to sell goods to the Spanish, then settlers from Missouri and beyond. The covered-wagon days of this famous route ended with the arrival of the railroad—the Atchison, Topeka and Santa Fe, a line made far more famous, perhaps, by the Andrews Sisters' hit recording than by its initial arrival in town in 1880. The Old Santa Fe Trail has survived the ravages of time and progress with far more grace than has El Camino Real, giving first-time visitors a more accurate impression of the town that lies ahead: The route is lined with splendid Southwest-style homes made of adobe and stucco. As one approaches town, the buildings become larger and closer together, but Santa Fe remains mercifully free of skyscrapers; a town ordinance keeps all buildings within a five-story limit.

Melded into the landscape with their earthen colors and rounded, flowing lines—and thus difficult to see from afar—the adobe pueblos of the area's original inhabitants were so styled as a means of protection from enemy tribes and, later, from Spanish explorers. Today the distinct Pueblo-style architecture that has come to characterize Santa Fe and its environs attracts rather than repels visitors—although the predominance of adobe, pure or ersatz, flat-roof Colonial style or climbing pueblo fashion, can be a bit overwhelming. As a result of the tendency to build in this style, the State Capitol, the Santa Fe Hilton, the Camera Shop of Santa Fe, and One Hour Martinizing all look pretty much alike.

Santa Fe is among the smallest state capitals in the country and is without a major airport. The city's population, an estimated 62,000, swells to nearly double that figure during the peak summer season and again in the winter, when skiers arrive, lured by the challenging slopes of the Santa Fe Ski Area and those of nearby Taos Ski Valley. Geared for tourists, Santa Fe can put a serious dent in your travel budget. Prices are highest in June, July, and August. September–October and the shoulder months, November and April, are lower. Rates are lowest (except for the major holidays) December–March. In general, hotel rates are on a par with top hotels and resorts in popular spots all over the globe, and prices charged for contemporary artwork in Santa Fe—which claims to be the third major art center in the country after New York and Los Angeles—can be astonishingly high.

EXPLORING

Humorist Will Rogers said on his first visit to Santa Fe, "Whoever designed this town did so while riding on a jackass, backwards and drunk." While the maze of narrow streets and alleyways may confound motorists, it's a delight for shoppers and pedestrians, who will find attractive shops and restaurants, a flowered courtyard, or yet another eye-catching gallery to explore at just about every turn.

Tour 1: Santa Fe Plaza

Numbers in the margin correspond to points of interest on the Santa Fe map.

★ ❶ A get-acquainted stroll of the city begins logically enough with the historic **Plaza** that forms its heart. Originally laid out around 1607 as the city's center for religious and military activities by New Mexico governor Don Pedro de Peralta, it witnessed the revolt of the Pueblos in 1680 and the Spanish recapture of Santa Fe in 1692. It once held a bullring, was the site of fiestas and fandangos, and was the actual end of the Santa Fe Trail, where freight wagons would unload after completing their arduous journeys. The American flag was raised over it in 1846, as was the standard of the Confederate army, some 20 years later, before Santa Fe was recaptured by Union forces. For a time it was a tree-shaded park, complete with a white picket fence, and later, in the Gay '90s, an expanse of lawn, where uniformed bands played from within the ornate gazebo at its center. Today, lined with shops, art galleries, and restaurants, it is as much the heart of the city as ever.

❷ The Pueblo-style **Palace of the Governors,** bordering the northern side of the Plaza on Palace Avenue, is the oldest public building in the United States. Built at the same time that the Plaza was laid out, it has been the key seat of government for four separate flags—Spain, Mexico, the Confederacy, and the U.S. territory that preceded New Mexico's state-

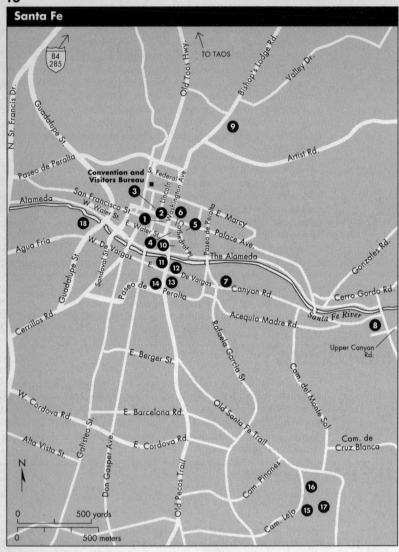

Barrio de Analco, **11**

Canyon Road, **7**

Cristo Rey Church, **8**

Fort Marcy, **9**

La Fonda, **4**

Loretto Chapel, **10**

Museum of Fine Arts, **3**

Museum of Indian Arts and Culture, **16**

Museum of the Institute of American Indian Arts, **6**

Museum of International Folk Art, **15**

The Oldest House, **12**

Palace of the Governors, **2**

Plaza, **1**

St. Francis Cathedral, **5**

San Miguel Mission, **13**

Santuario de Guadalupe, **18**

State Capitol building, **14**

Wheelright Museum of the American Indian, **17**

hood in 1912—serving as the residence for 100 Spanish, Native American, Mexican, and American governors.

Since 1913, the palace has been the central headquarters of the **Museum of New Mexico,** a state system that includes four museums in Santa Fe—the on-site **History Museum,** the adjacent **Museum of Fine Arts,** the **Museum of Indian Arts and Culture,** and the **Museum of International Folk Art**—and five state monuments scattered about New Mexico: the prehistoric ruins at **Jemez** and **Coronado,** the historic frontier forts **Sumner** and **Selden,** and the historic community of **Lincoln.** A three-day pass for $5.25 allows ☛ to all state museums. Individual ☛ to each monument costs $2. For information, call 505/827–6451.

Permanent exhibits at the **History Museum** in the Palace of the Governors chronicle 450 years of New Mexico history. In addition to displays of furniture, clothing, and housewares, a collection of rare mural-size works, painted on elk and bison hides, depicts key historical events. Themes of changing exhibits may include frontier firearms and the Civil War in New Mexico. In the same building, the Museum of New Mexico Press prints books, cards, and booklets on antique presses and offers bookbinding demonstrations, lectures, and slide shows. With advance permission, students and researchers have access to an extensive historical-research library and collections of rare maps and manuscripts, as well as photographs (more than 120,000 prints and negatives). *Palace Ave. (north side of the Plaza),* ☎ *505/827–6483.* ☛ *$4.20 single admission, 3-day pass $5.25, children under 17 free.* ☺ *Daily 10–5. Closed Mon. during Jan. and Feb.*

★ Under the shaded portals of the Palace of the Governors, **local Native American vendors** display and sell their wares as they've been doing for centuries. With few exceptions, the more than 500 vendors who are registered to sell under the portals are all members of New Mexico Pueblos or tribes. All merchandise on sale is required to meet Museum of New Mexico standards: Items are all handmade or hand-strung in Native American households; silver jewelry is either sterling (92.5% pure) or coin silver (90% pure); all metal jewelry bears the maker's mark, which is registered with the museum. Prices tend to reflect the high quality of the merchandise and the mastery of art forms that require years of apprenticeship and learning. Books, regional magazines, owners and salesclerks at reputable shops, and the vendors themselves are all good sources of information about Native American arts and crafts. No photographs should be taken unless permission is requested and granted.

❸ Across from the Palace of the Governors (turn right upon exiting and cross Lincoln Ave.), the **Museum of Fine Arts,** dating from 1917, was Santa Fe's first Pueblo Revival–style structure. More than any other building, it inspired the architectural trend in the region that continues to this day. Inside, the ceilings are made of split cedar *latillas* (branches set in a cross-hatched pattern) and hand-hewn vigas; many excellent examples of Spanish Colonial–style furniture are on display. The 8,000-piece permanent collection emphasizes the work of regional artists, including Georgia O'Keeffe and the Taos Masters (Ernest Blumenschein, Bert Geer Philips, Joseph Henry Sharp, and Eanger Irving Couse, among them), as well as that of Mexican (such as Diego Rivera), Southwestern, and Native American artists. Sculpture is displayed in three adjoining courtyards. *107 W. Palace Ave.,* ☎ *505/827–4468.* ☛ *$4.20 single admission, 3-day pass $5.25, children under 17 free, senior citizens free on Wed.* ☺ *Daily 10–5. Closed Mon. during Jan. and Feb.*

If you cross to the far corner of the Plaza, where Shelby and East San Francisco streets meet, you'll find yourself virtually in the lobby of Santa ④ Fe's landmark hotel, **La Fonda** (*see* Lodging, *below*). Built in 1864 and refurbished several times in recent years, the hotel is still known fondly as "The Inn at the End of the Trail" because of its history as a gathering place for cowboys, trappers, pioneers, soldiers, drummers, and frontier politicians. It's still a major social setting for many of the town's activities.

TIME OUT   Stop in at the lunch counter of **Woolworth's** on the Plaza (58 E. San Francisco St., ☎ 505/982–1062)—the only Woolworth's in New Mexico, opened in 1931—for some of its famous Frito pie. A small portion of this tasty concoction of Fritos, chile, and cheese costs $2.35 and a large portion is $4.

Tour 2: St. Francis Cathedral, Canyon Road

If the day's not too hot and you're in good physical condition, this tour can be done on foot. Be aware, however, that Canyon Road is a long stretch, all slightly uphill. In most cases, it's a good idea to drive.

★ ⑤ A block east of the Plaza is the magnificent **St. Francis Cathedral,** one of the rare departures from the city's steadfast pueblo design. Founded by Jean Baptiste Lamy, Santa Fe's first archbishop, it was built by French architects in 1869 in a French Romanesque style, with Italian stonemasons adding the finishing touches. The inspiration for Willa Cather's novel *Death Comes for the Archbishop,* the circuit-riding young Lamy, credited with resuscitating the Catholic faith in New Mexico, is buried in the crypt beneath the church's high altar. A small adobe chapel on the northeast side, the remnant of an earlier church built on the site, reveals the Spanish architectural influence so noticeably missing from the cathedral itself. Inside the chapel, *Nuestra Señora de la Paz* (Our Lady of Peace), is the oldest representation of the Madonna in the United States. This statue accompanied Don Diego de Vargas on his reconquest of Santa Fe in 1692, a feat attributed to the statue's spiritual intervention. Every Friday the faithful adorn *Nuestra Señora de la Paz,* now the patron saint of New Mexico, with a new dress. *231 Cathedral Pl.,* ☎ *505/982–5619.* ☉ *Daily. Mass celebrated daily at 6 and 7 AM and 5:15 PM; Sun. at 6, 8, and 10 AM, noon, and 7 PM.*

Across the street, in an expanded state-of-the-art facility in the reno-⑥ vated former Federal Post Office, is the **Museum of the Institute of American Indian Arts,** which has the largest collection of contemporary Native American art in the United States. Its paintings, photography, and traditional crafts showcase the work of the students and teachers, past and present, of the prestigious Institute of American Indian Arts, located across town on Cerrillos Road, where it was founded as a one-room studio classroom in the early 1930s. Established by Dorothy Dunn, a well-known teacher and promoter of the Native American cause, the school was taken over by the Bureau of Indian Affairs in 1962 and has since blossomed into the major learning center for Native American arts in the country. Famed artist Fritz Scholder taught here for years. (Straining against the bonds of rigid academia, he also taught informally at a compound on lower West Alameda.) Among his best-known disciples was T. C. Cannon, who was killed in Santa Fe in 1978 at the age of 38 when his pickup truck crashed into a shallow ravine. Today, Earl Biss, another Scholder protégé, paints dreamlike impressions of Native Americans on horseback moving relentlessly toward distant horizons, and he hasn't sold a dry painting in years. Long hair flying in the wind, he's frequently seen whipping around town in a white Cadillac convertible. Kevin Red Star, born on the Crow Reservation in Montana, as was Earl Biss, paints stylized warriors and chiefs in full regalia, using strong earth colors and bold interpretations. His work hangs in the Smithsonian and is sold in major galleries throughout the country. Allan Houser, a Chiricahua Apache (he Anglicized his original name, Alan Haozous, thinking it would broaden his appeal), became one of America's legendary sculptors before his death in 1994. Painter Harrison Begay, a former classmate of Houser's, is yet another illustrious alumnus of the institute. These artists are all represented in the permanent collection. *108 Cathedral Pl., ☎ 505/988–6281, or 505/988–6211 for events and parking information. ✒ $4 adults, $2 students and senior citizens, children under 16 free. ⊘ Weekdays 10– 5, weekends noon–5.*

★ **⑦** If you walk south to the end of Cathedral Place and turn left on Alameda for another block, crossing Paseo de Peralta, you'll come to **Canyon Road,** which once served as an Indian trail. During the early part of the century, woodcutters with their loaded burros used El Camino de Cañon as a route into town, where they sold bundles of chopped wood door to door. The road's 2-mile stretch from the center of town is now Santa Fe's most fashionable street, lined with many of the city's finest art galleries, shops, and restaurants—described affectionately by locals as "the art and soul of Santa Fe." If you're driving, remember that parking is at a premium on Canyon Road. A shopping complex at the lower end (225 Canyon Rd.) provides parking and rest rooms for customers only. The municipal parking lot at the juncture of Canyon Road and Camino del Monte Sol costs $1.50 per hour.

Upper Canyon Road is the site of some of the city's most elegant homes. At its terminus is the historic **Randall Davey Audubon Center,** once the home and studio of one of the most prolific early Santa Fe artists and, since 1975, the regional headquarters of the National Audubon Society. *Upper Canyon Rd., ☎ 505/983–4609. ✒ Free. ⊘ Daily 9–5 for self-guided tours.*

⑧ The **Cristo Rey Church,** at the corner of Upper Canyon Road and Cristo Rey, 1½ miles from the Plaza, was built in 1940 to commemorate the 400th anniversary of Coronado's exploration of the Southwest. Built the old-fashioned way, with parishioners mixing the more than 200,000 mud-and-straw adobe bricks themselves and hauling them into place, it's the largest adobe structure in the United States and is considered by many to be the finest example of Pueblo-style architecture anywhere. No less impressive is the church's magnificent 225-ton stone reredos (altar screen). *1120 Canyon Rd., ☎ 505/983–8528. ⊘ Daily 8–5.*

TIME OUT When you need a respite from shopping, drop into the **Backroom Coffeebar** (616 Canyon Rd., ☎ 505/988–5323) for a light snack and something to read.

⑨ If you don't want to spend the day along Canyon Road, another option when you're at St. Francis Cathedral is to head north. Within a few blocks of the Plaza, on a hill northeast of the city, lie the ruins of **Fort Marcy,** the first American military post in the Southwest (the entrance is just north of the junction of Bishops Lodge Road and Artist Road). Something of a white elephant that never justified its massive size (the walls are 9 feet high and 5 feet thick), the adobe fort—named after William L. Marcy, the secretary of war under President Polk— was eventually abandoned. Only a few mounds of earth mark its former existence, but the overview from the hilltop of the city and of nearby mountain ranges (and, on a clear day, of the Sandia Mountains bordering Albuquerque) is spectacular. On another nearby hilltop (on Paseo de Peralta between Otero Street and Hillside Avenue), the huge white **Cross of the Martyrs,** raised and dedicated during the fiesta, September 1920, commemorates the lives of the 23 Franciscan monks who were killed by Native Americans in the Pueblo Revolt of 1680.

Tour 3: Along the Old Santa Fe Trail

The first part of this tour can be done on foot, but you'll need a car to go beyond the State Capitol building. Most of the sights noted are along the route of the Old Santa Fe Trail, but the final two, the Wheelright Museum of the American Indian and Santuario de Guadalupe, are at opposite ends of town, both south of the Plaza, but not particularly accessible from the Old Santa Fe Trail.

★ ⑩ Behind the La Fonda Hotel and just to the left on the Old Santa Fe Trail is the **Loretto Chapel.** Started in 1873, the French-Romanesque chapel, modeled after the famous Parisian church Sainte-Chapelle, was built concurrently with the St. Francis Cathedral; the same French architects and Italian stonemasons worked on both projects. The chapel is known for the "Miraculous Staircase" that leads to the choir loft. Legend has it that the chapel was almost finished when it became obvious that there wasn't room enough to complete a staircase to the choir loft. In answer to the prayers of the cathedral's sisters, an old, bearded man arrived on a donkey, built a 20-foot staircase—using only a square, a saw, and a tub of water to season the wood—and then disappeared as quickly as he came. Many of the faithful believe it was St. Joseph himself. Considered an engineering marvel, the staircase contains two complete 360-degree turns, a double helix with no central or visible support; no nails were used in its construction and the wood is like none found in the region. The chapel is maintained by the Inn at Loretto (*see* Lodging, *below*), which adjoins it. *211 Old Santa Fe Trail,* ☎ *505/984–7971.* ☛ *$1 adults, children 6 and under free.* ☉ *Oct. 15–May 15, Mon.–Sat. 9–5, Sun. 10:30–5; May 16–Oct. 14, Mon.–Sat. 8–6, Sun. 10:30–5.*

⑪ Continuing south along the Old Santa Fe Trail, crossing the bridge over the Santa Fe River, one block farther, you'll come to **Barrio de Analco** (now called East De Vargas Street), believed to be one of the oldest continuously inhabited streets in the United States. Settled during the early 1600s by Mexican Indian mercenaries and Spanish colonists, it's also the oldest Spanish settlement in Santa Fe, with the exception of the Plaza area. Interpretive plaques highlight some of the more historic houses, including the Crespin, Alarid, Bandelier, and Boyle homes.

⑫ Here, too, on the right, you'll find the **Oldest House,** little more than a curiosity. Claimed to be the most ancient dwelling in America, built by Native Americans more than 800 years ago, it is constructed of "puddled" adobe, which predates the brick type. The building is now leased to a gift shop and museum, where T-shirts and souvenirs are sold. In the rear, a lifelike Native American dummy sits at a table with its head atilt beside a half-open coffin that supposedly contains the remains of a Spanish soldier. A few antique pots and pans, a lamp, and some tools complete the "museum" display. *215 E. De Vargas St.,* ☎ *505/983–8206. Donations accepted.* ☉ *Mon.–Sat. 10–5.*

⑬ Across the street, heading back toward the Old Santa Fe Trail, you'll see the **San Miguel Mission.** The oldest church still in use in the United

States, the earth-hued adobe structure was built about 1625 by the Tlax-calas (they originally came to New Mexico as servants of the Spanish troops and clergymen). Badly damaged in the 1680 Pueblo Revolt, the church was rebuilt in 1710. On display in the chapel is the San José Bell, weighing nearly 800 pounds, believed to have been cast in Spain in 1356 and brought to Santa Fe via Mexico several centuries later. This simple church, filled with priceless statues and paintings, is a must for any visitor to Santa Fe. Mass is held Sunday at 5 PM. *401 Old Santa Fe Trail,* ☎ *505/983–3974. Donations suggested.* ☉ *May–Sept., daily 9–4:30, Oct.–Apr., daily 10–4.*

TIME OUT Next door to the San Miguel Mission, **Upper Crust Pizza** (329 Old Santa Fe Trail, ☎ 505/982-0000) is a good place to sit and enjoy a slice out on the patio, watching the passing parade on Old Santa Fe Trail.

⑭ A block south of the San Miguel Mission, across the Old Santa Fe Trail, is the **State Capitol building,** built in 1966. Known as "the Roundhouse" (and sometimes "the Bullring"), it is modeled after a Southwestern Native American *zia*, representing the Circle of Life; four short walls—symbolizing the four winds, four directions, four seasons, and the four sacred obligations of Pueblo mythology—radiate from the central circular structure. Visitors may view the Governor's Gallery, as well as numerous historical and cultural displays, and enjoy 6 acres of landscaped gardens containing roses and sequoia, plum, and almond trees. *Old Santa Fe Trail at Paseo de Peralta,* ☎ *505/986–4589.* ☛ *Free. Guided tours offered.* ☉ *Weekdays 8–7.*

★ ⑮ About a mile farther south along the Old Santa Fe Trail, take the Camino Lejo turnoff. On the right, perched on a hillside overlooking the city, is the **Museum of International Folk Art,** the premier museum of its kind in the world. You'll need a car or taxi to get there; it's 2 miles from the Plaza and almost all uphill. Charming, handmade creations are everywhere you look—a Madonna painted on tin; papier-mâché pears and apples; a devil made from bread dough; rag dolls; clay pots; and much, much more. Founded by Florence Dibell Bartlett, a collector who built the museum and donated it and her collection of over 4,000 pieces of folk art to the state, the museum opened in 1953. In 1978, designer and architect Alexander Girard, who died in 1994 at the age of 86, turned over to the museum his lifelong collection of folk art—over 106,000 items. The Museum of International Folk Art was again enriched in 1989 with the opening of a new $1.1 million Hispanic Heritage Wing, designed to display Hispanic folk art from the Spanish Colonial period (in New Mexico, 1598–1821) to the present. The 5,000-piece exhibit includes religious folk art—particularly *bultos* (carved wooden statues of saints) and *retablos* (holy images painted on wood or tin). Along with the permanent collection, the museum frequently presents visiting exhibits, such as the recent "Swedish Folk Art: All Tradition is Change" and "Mud, Mirror, and Thread: Adornment in Rural India." A gift shop carries textiles, dolls, jewelry, ornaments, and other folk-art objects, as well as the excellent color-illustrated book *The Spirit of Folk Art,* to help explain it all. *706 Camino Lejo,* ☎ *505/ 827–6350.* ☛ *$4.20 single admission, 3-day pass $5.25, children under 17 free.* ☉ *Daily 10–5. Closed Mon. during Jan. and Feb.*

⑯ Next door, the **Museum of Indian Arts and Culture,** opened in 1987, focuses on the history and contemporary culture of New Mexico's Pueblo, Navajo, and Apache Native Americans. Along with its extensive collection of Southwestern Native American arts and crafts, the museum offers art demonstrations; Native American food concessions; and a Learning and Research Center, where visitors can weave on a Navajo loom or beat a Pueblo drum. Workshops and classes for children and adults are offered regularly. *710 Camino Lejo,* ☎ *505/827– 6344. For hours and prices, see Museum of International Folk Art, above.*

⑰ The privately owned **Wheelwright Museum of the American Indian,** housed in a building shaped like a traditional Navajo hogan behind the Museum of International Folk Art, first opened in 1937. Founded by Boston scholar Mary Cabot Wheelwright and Navajo medicine-man Hasteen Klah, it houses the works of all Native American cultures, exhibited on a single-subject rotating basis—silverwork, jewelry, pottery, basketry, paintings. On the lower level, the Case Trading Post, the museum shop, is modeled after those that dotted the Southwestern frontier over a hundred years ago. *704 Camino Lejo,* ☎ *505/982–4636. Donation suggested.* ⊘ *Mon.–Sat. 10–5, Sun. 1–5.*

⑱ Another of Santa Fe's historic gems lies at the other side of town. **Santuario de Guadalupe,** at the terminus of El Camino Real, 3½ blocks southwest of the Plaza, is the oldest shrine to Our Lady of Guadalupe, patron saint of Mexico, in the United States. It was built by Franciscan missionaries between 1776 and 1795 and has adobe walls nearly 3 feet thick. A museum administered by the nonprofit Guadalupe Historic Foundation, the Santuario contains several noteworthy paintings, including a priceless 16th-century work by Venetian painter Leonardo de Ponte Bassano, depicting Jesus driving the money changers from the temple, and a portrait of Our Lady of Guadalupe, one of the largest and finest oil paintings of the Spanish Southwest, by Mexico's renowned colonial painter José de Alzibar. Other highlights are an authentic 19th-century sacristy; a pictorial-history archives; a library devoted to Archbishop Lamy, furnished with many of his personal possessions; and gardens containing a number of plants from the Holy Land. Many local religious ceremonies, dramatic performances, art and educational events, and concerts are held at the Santuario. Adjacent is Agua Fria Street, filled with colorful shops and restaurants, all part of the Guadalupe Historic District. *100 Guadalupe St.,* ☎ *505/988–2027. Donation suggested.* ⊘ *Weekdays 9–4, Sat. 9–3.*

What to See and Do with Children

Santa Fe Children's Museum, next to the New Mexico Repertory Theater, less than a mile from the Plaza, offers stimulating hands-on exhibits in the arts and sciences. A solar greenhouse, waterworks, giant bubbles, oversize geometric forms, and a climbing area with a simulated 18-foot mountain-climbing wall all contribute to the museum's great popularity. Special performances—puppets, storytellers, and the like—and programs—including talks by scientists and artists—are offered on different days. A gift shop is open during museum hours. *1050 Old Pecos Trail,* ☎ *505/989–8359.* ☛ *$2.50 adults, $1.50 children old enough to walk.* ⊘ *Thurs.–Sat. 10–5, Sun. noon–5; also Wed., in June–Aug., 10–5.*

Wild Oats Market (1090 S. St. Francis Dr., 85701, ☎ 505/983–5333) offers free events for children 12 and under on the last Saturday of each month. Programs vary from arts and crafts and face painting to clowns and puppet shows.

Off the Beaten Track

The **Cumbres & Toltec Scenic Railroad** (in Chama, a 2-hour drive from Santa Fe via I–84) runs the 64 miles each way between Chama and

Antonito, Colorado, on the only surviving portion of track alongside the old 1,200-mile mountain route that the Denver and Rio Grande Railroad was forced to build when the Santa Fe beat it to Ratan Pass. A veritable rolling museum of antique narrow-gauge engines, equipment, and stock—including snow-fighting attachments that date from 1889 and are still working—the train provided the setting for key scenes in the film *Butch and Sundance: The Early Years.* It snakes back and forth over the Colorado border, whistle blowing and coal smoke belching; the climb up Cumbres Pass is so steep that a second engine is required to pull it up the grade. During the ride, the brakeman and conductor deliver a lively nonstop commentary about the history of the line and interesting sidelights about passing scenes. Dress warmly; the train is drafty. And take along sunglasses to protect your eyes from soot and cinders. *500 Terrace Ave., Chama,* ☎ *505/756–2151. Fares: one-way, returning by bus, $50 adults, $26 children 2–11. The train leaves at 10:30 daily, Memorial Day weekend–mid-Oct.*

A kind of Williamsburg of the Southwest, **El Rancho de las Golondrinas** (the Ranch of the Swallows), some 15 miles south of Santa Fe, is a reconstruction of a small New Mexican agricultural village. Originally a *paraje,* or stopping place, on El Camino Real, the village has restored buildings from the 17th and 18th centuries. Guided tours highlight Spanish Colonial lifestyles in New Mexico from 1660 to 1890; visitors view a molasses mill, threshing grounds, and wheelwright and blacksmith shops, as well as a mountain village and a *morada* (meeting place) of the order of Penitentes. Sheep, goats, and other farm animals wander about the sprawling 200-acre complex. During the Spring and Harvest Festivals, on the first weekends of June and October, respectively, the village comes alive with traditional music, Spanish folk dancing, and food and crafts demonstrations. There's a museum gift shop on the premises, but the nearest restaurant is 4 miles away. *Cienega, 15 mi south of Santa Fe on I–25,* ☎ *505/471–2261.* ☛ *$3.50 adults, $2 senior citizens, $1.50 children 5–12; during festivals, the rates are $5 for adults, $3 for senior citizens, and $2 for children 5–12.* ☉ *Apr.–Oct., daily 8–4.*

Founded as a Spanish Colonial outpost in 1614, when it was built largely from the rocks of Pueblo ruins, **Galisteo** is now a charming little village popular with artists and with equestrians who keep their animals boarded here (trail rides and rentals are available). There's a small church, open only on Sunday for services; a graveyard; and an old working brewery that welcomes visitors for tours and an occasional sampling. Twenty-three miles south of Santa Fe (take I–25 east to U.S. 285 south, then Route 41 south), Galisteo is mercifully free of fast-food and souvenir shops.

Ojo Caliente Mineral Springs (take I–25 to Espanola, then U.S. 285 to Ojo Caliente, ☎ 505/583–2233) was considered a sacred spot by the Native Americans who inhabited this area centuries ago. Today this famous turn-of-the-century resort, with its five bubbling hot springs, one hour north of Santa Fe, offers mineral baths, massages, facials, herbal wraps, a hotel-motel, gift shop, and a restaurant. This isn't Canyon Ranch; don't expect an up-to-date luxury spa. Come if you want to take a trip back in time when it was fashionable to "take the waters" (they contain healthful doses of some minerals not usually associated with beneficial effects, such as arsenic).

Ten Thousand Waves Japanese Health Spa (3½ mi outside town on Hyde Park Rd., ☎ 505/982–9304) is the perfect place to unwind after a day's cavorting on the slopes or in the dusty desert. Tucked into a pine-and-juniper-covered mountainside, this Japanese-style spa offers private and communal indoor and outdoor hot tubs, therapeutic massages, facials, herbal wraps, salt glows, and in-the-water *watsu* massage. Towels, kimonos, soaps, shampoos, sandals, and lockers are provided. Hot teas, juices, and pastries are available, too. Depending on the treatment, you'll part with anywhere from $12 to $115.

National Parks and Monuments

Chaco Culture National Historic Park, set in a canyon 17 miles long and 1 mile wide, with cliff faces rising 330 feet, protects the remains of 13 fully developed pueblos and about 400 smaller settlements. Pueblo Bonito, the largest prehistoric Southwest Indian dwelling ever excavated, contains 800 rooms covering more than 3 acres. This dwelling, the magnificent kivas, and other ancient structures, including a 1,200-mile network of paved roads and a solstice marker, all testify that the area was the highest point in the Anasazi culture, which peaked about AD 1150. Located at the park site is a visitor center, museum, and petroglyph displays. Overnight camping is permitted year-round.

To get here from Santa Fe, heading south–southwest via Route 44, in the direction of Bloomfield, drive to Cuba, New Mexico, and continue on to Anasazi. At Anasazi, head west (right) and drive on the dirt road all the way to Chaco Culture National Historic Park. The trip takes about 3½ to 4 hours. *Star Rte. 4, Box 6500, Bloomfield 87413,* ☎ *505/988–6716.* ☛ *$2 per individual or $4 per car.*

SHOPPING

Santa Fe has been a trading post for a long, long time. The great pueblos of the Hohokam and Anasazi civilizations 2,000 years ago were strategically located between the buffalo-hunting tribes of the Great Plains and the Native Americans of Mexico, who exchanged shells, metals, and parrots for sky-color turquoise, which was thought to have magical properties. After the arrival of the Spanish during the early 1600s and the subsequent development of the West, Santa Fe became the place in which to exchange silver, hides, and fur from Mexico for manufactured goods, whiskey, and greenbacks from the East. And following the building of the railroad in 1880, all manner of products came and went.

The legacy remains, but today downtown Santa Fe caters almost exclusively to tourists. J.C. Penney was demolished to make way for art galleries. Big Joe's Lumberyard became the Eldorado Hotel. The major commodity in today's Santa Fe is something known as Santa Fe style, as distinctive as the city's architecture. The clean lines, strong colors, and Native American patterns that characterize the style have a great deal of charm. True, because of its popularity, it's become a bit of a cliché; a locally produced poster, titled "Another Victim of Santa Fe Style," shows a Santa Fean lying faceup on a Native American rug, surrounded by howling-coyote carvings, a kiva fireplace, a beamed ceiling, a sun-bleached cattle skull, a string of red chile peppers, and other trendy ornaments. Detractors have named the movement "Santa Fake." But the style remains highly infectious just the same—visitors can't seem to get enough of it and can't wait to take it home.

Santa Fe may strike newcomers as one massive shopping mall, with stores and shopping nooks sprouting up in the least likely places. Nevertheless, a few shopping areas stand out. Canyon Road is the most famous and most expensive. The downtown district offers a mix of shops, galleries, restaurants, and crafts nooks within a five-block radius of

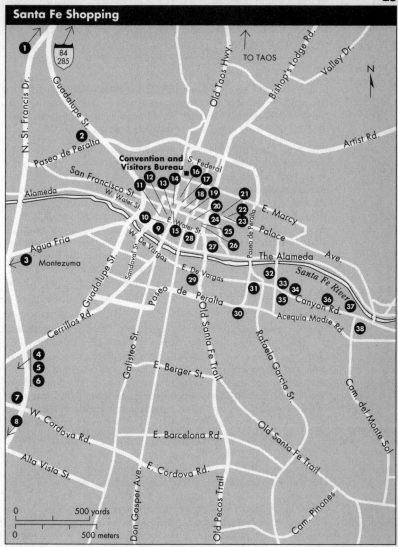

Santa Fe Shopping

Altermann & Morris Gallery, **34**

Arrowsmith's, **29**

Artesanos, **9**

Bellas Artes, **37**

Canyon Road Fine Art, **36**

Cline Fine Art, **35**

Collected Works Book Shop, **12**

Coopers Western Warehouse, **2, 5**

Deborah Hudgins Fine Art, **25**

Dewey Galleries, **26**

Horwitch Lewellen Gallery, **16**

Fenn Galleries, **30**

Footsteps Across New Mexico, **27**

Foreign Traders, **10**

Frank Patania, **17**

Gary Mauro Gallery, **31**

Glenn Green Galleries, **20**

Handsel Gallery, **38**

Jane Smith, **15**

Joshua Baer & Co., **21**

Kachina House and Gallery, **32**

Montecristi Custom Hat Works, **13**

Montez Gallery, **22**

Morning Star Gallery, **33**

New Mexico Outlet Center, **8**

New Millennium Fine Art, **11**

Packard's Indian Trading Co., **24**

Prairie Edge, **28**

The Rainbow Man, **23**

Santa Fe Boot Company, **7**

Santa Fe Factory Stores, **6**

Santa Fe Western Mercantile, **4**

Spanish Pueblo Doors, **3**

Trade Roots Collection, **14**

Trader Jack's Flea Market, **1**

Wadle Galleries, **18**

William R. Talbot Fine Art, **19**

the Plaza. At the southwest perimeter of town, the Guadalupe neighborhood is great for strolling and for relaxing at a sidewalk café as a break from shopping.

Art Galleries

Santa Fe's brilliant light, limpid skies, and timeless landscape of mountains and mesas have long hypnotized artists. "The world is wide here," said Georgia O'Keeffe, in her usual get-right-to-the-point manner. "It's very hard to feel that it's wide in the East."

Well before the arrival of such artists as Ernest Blumenschein and John Sloan to the state during the early 20th century, an earlier form of art was popular in northern New Mexico. Bultos and retablos, both commonly known as santos, or saints, remain a unique, little-heralded art form as indigenous to the Southwest as is an oil painting by Ted DeGrazia. These devotional images were part of everyday life in Mexico and the American Southwest in the years following the conquistadores and the founding of Christianity in the New World. Today they have captured the attention of serious art collectors and leading museums. Although the santos now being made seem destined more for the tourist trade than for regional churches, no attempt has been made to mass-produce them, and no two are exactly alike. As a result, they still retain their charm.

Santa Fe is also the epicenter of contemporary Native American art, the breakaway and sometimes satirical styles of Fritz Scholder, R. C. Gorman, Earl Biss, Kevin Red Star, Robert Redbird, Amado Maurilio Peña, and others who are strongly identified with the Santa Fe movement. Before the introduction of blurred images and shocking colors, Native American art was traditionally flat and static, with Bambi-like deer with big, sad eyes, and lifeless corn dancers in pueblo rituals. Today, top Native American painters, such as Gorman and Cherokee artist Bert Seabourn, are as celebrated in the galleries of Berlin and Tokyo as they are on Canyon Road.

Santa Fe has 150 art galleries (and no one knows how many painters). The following selection represents a good cross section; the Santa Fe Convention and Visitors Bureau (*see* Santa Fe Essentials, *below*) has a fuller listing, and *The Wingspread Collectors Guide to Santa Fe and Taos* (*see* More Portraits *in* Chapter 7) is a good bet for those who are seriously interested in buying art in Santa Fe.

Altermann & Morris Gallery (225 Canyon Rd., ☎ 505/983–1590) features works of the Cowboy Artists of America, original Remingtons and Bierstadts, the Wyeths, and the Hurds. It occupies the former Janus Gallery.
Bellas Artes (653 Canyon Rd., ☎ 505/983–2745), a landmark crafts gallery and sculpture garden, next to the popular Compound Restaurant, carries a wide selection of contemporary arts and crafts, pre-Columbian works, ceramics, and textiles.
Canyon Road Fine Art (621 Canyon Rd., ☎ 505/988–9511, FAX 505/988–2108) specializes in works by early Santa Fe and Taos artists, as well as by selected contemporary impressionist painters.
Cline Fine Art (526 Canyon Rd., ☎ 505/982–5328), in a 200-year-old landmark adobe, specializes in early to mid-20th-century American art, with an emphasis on pre–World War II New Mexico. Selected contemporary artists are also represented.
Deborah Hudgins Fine Art (80 E. San Francisco St., ☎ 505/988–9298) was formed with the merger of two previous galleries, El Taller Santa Fe and the Plaza Gallery. A full range of original paintings, drawings,

and graphics is available here. Among the artists represented is Amado Peña, a master painter of Mexican and Yaqui ancestry, noted for his bold color schemes and strong graphic use of lines.

Dewey Galleries (74 E. San Francisco St., ☎ 505/982–8632 or 800/327–7721) is housed in the historic Spiegelberg Building on the south side of the Plaza. In a spacious showroom under the original 20-foot-high pressed tin ceilings, is a huge collection of historic Navajo textiles and jewelry, plus paintings and sculpture by contemporary and past artists.

Horwitch Lewellen Gallery (129 W. Palace Ave., ☎ 505/988–8997) sells paintings, sculptures, and graphics by internationally known artists as well as by up-and-coming painters from the Southwest. The Horwitch firm also has a gallery in Scottsdale.

Fenn Galleries (1075 Paseo de Peralta, ☎ 505/982–4631) specializes in works of the celebrated Taos Society of Artists and their successors, in addition to those of early Santa Fe painters, including such luminaries as Maxfield Parrish, Maynard Dixon, and Georgia O'Keeffe. One of the best-known galleries in the Southwest, its list of clients includes former president Gerald Ford, Cher, and Cybill Shepherd. Its garden has a Vietnamese potbellied pig in residence.

Gary Mauro Gallery (233C Canyon Rd., ☎ 505/988–3048) focuses on this native Santa Fe artist's many interpretations of the female form. Though best-known for his bas-relief nudes, which are drawn and painted on muslin, then contoured to create a quiltlike form, Mauro also casts figures in bronze or aluminum. This one-artist showcase features all of the above, plus Mauro's drawings, paintings, and more.

Glenn Green Galleries (50 E. San Francisco St., ☎ 505/988–4168) displays paintings and photographs by internationally known artists. Founded in 1975, the spectacular two-story gallery exclusively represents the work of Native American sculptor Allan Houser, as well as other noted Native American and Anglo artists.

Handsel Gallery (306 Camino del Monte Sol, ☎ 505/988–4030) moved from its downtown site to its present location just off Canyon Road. Owner Michael Matassa features work by artist Susan Contreras, sculptor Elizabeth Rose, and glass designers Martha Wolf and Louise Falls.

Joshua Baer & Co. (116½ E. Palace Ave., ☎ 505/988–8944), a half block from the Plaza, focuses on 19th-century Navajo wall hangings, serapes, and blankets, as well as pre-Columbian Mimbres pottery.

Morning Star Gallery (513 Canyon Rd., ☎ 505/982–8187) is the largest gallery in the world specializing in antique Native American art and artifacts. Located in a landmark Spanish hacienda and shaded by a huge cottonwood tree, it's a virtual museum of antique basketry, pre-1940 Navajo silver jewelry, Eskimo ivories, Northwest Coast Native American carvings, classic Navajo weavings, and art of the Plains Buffalo culture. (Gallery director Joe Rivera operated trading posts on the Rosebud Sioux Reservation for 12 years.)

New Millennium Fine Art (217 W. Water St., ☎ 505/983–2002), founded by Stephen Fox in 1980, is a huge street-level showroom filled with contemporary Native American paintings and antique pawn jewelry, signed posters and prints, and an excellent collection of photographs of Southwestern and Native American subjects by Yousuf Karsh, Myron Wood, Tracey Pierre, and Edward Curtis. One of Santa Fe's best-known dealers, Fox has also turned to jewelry crafting of late and offers his own fine line of Native American pawn-style jewelry.

Wadle Galleries (128 W. Palace Ave., ☎ 505/983–9219) carries works of national and regional painters, bronze and stone sculpture, Pueblo pottery, jewelry, and American folk art. This spacious gallery, with plenty of chairs and seating space, is a good place for unwinding and soaking up the arty Southwestern ambience.

William R. Talbot Fine Art (129 W. San Francisco St., ☎ 505/982–1559) features antique maps of the Americas and natural-history paintings.

Factory Outlets

New Mexico's first factory outlets opened recently. **New Mexico Outlet Center** (601 W. Frontage Rd., 31 mi south of Santa Fe via the Budagher exit, ☎ 505/867–6329) houses 38 stores in its $12 million facility, including Van Heusen, Liz Claiborne, Levi's, and Bass Shoes. **Santa Fe Factory Stores** (8380 Cerrillos Rd., ☎ 505/474–4000) a $110-million, 42-store shopping center includes Jockey, Donna Karan, Dansk, Brooks Bros., and Royal Doulton.

Flea Markets

Trader Jack's Flea Market (7 mi north of Santa Fe on U.S. 84/285, ☎ 505/455–7874), also known as the Santa Fe Flea Market, has been dubbed the best flea market in America by its habitual legion of bargain hunters. It's open dawn to dusk every Friday, Saturday, and Sunday except during December, January, and February—and sometimes even then if the weather's right. You can buy everything here from a half-wolf puppy or African carvings to vintage cowboy boots, fossils, or a wall clock made out of an old hubcap. Sprawled over 12 acres on land belonging to the Tesuque Pueblo, the flea market is located right next to the Santa Fe Opera. ("There goes the neighborhood," says Trader Jack, when the opera season starts.)

Specialty Stores

Books

Collected Works Book Shop (208B W. San Francisco St., ☎ 505/988–4226), an independent bookstore, is a popular stop for art and travel books as well as a wide selection of literary paperbacks. Its downtown location makes it the perfect place to pick up a good book and stroll to the nearby plaza for a pleasurable afternoon of reading. And if you're in town awhile, and the book you want isn't in stock, the friendly staff is always willing to special order even the most obscure titles for you. At **Footsteps Across New Mexico** (211 Old Santa Fe Trail, ☎ 505/982–9297), the emphasis is on the "Land of Enchantment." The shop easily contains the most comprehensive selection of books and guidebooks on Santa Fe and New Mexico, from regional cookbooks to area histories. The firm recently opened a second branch in Albuquerque's Old Town.

Clothing

Function dictates form in cowboy fashions. A wide-brimmed hat is essential in sun country; not only does it protect the wearer from heat, but it's effective in warding off gnats, flies, and other insects. Cowboy hats made by Resistol, Stetson, Bailey, and other leading firms range in price from $50 to $500, but hats made of exotic materials, such as fur, can go for thousands. Small wonder that when it rains in Santa Fe or Albuquerque, a man is more apt to be concerned with protecting his hat than with letting it protect him.

While tenderfeet may guess that cowboy boots are worn to protect against rattlesnakes, they serve other practical purposes as well. Pointed toes slide easily in and out of the stirrups, and high heels—worn for the same reason by Mongolian tribesmen—help keep feet in the stirrups. Tall tops protect ankles and legs on rides through brush and cactus country and can save the wearer a nasty shin bruise from a skittish horse.

Some Western accessories, now mostly worn to be stylish, were once also functional. A colorful bandanna protected an Old West cowboy from sunburn and windburn and served as a mask in windstorms; when riding drag behind a herd; or, on occasions far rarer than Hollywood would have us believe, when robbing trains. A cowboy's sleeveless vest offered maneuverability during roping and riding chores and provided pocket space that his skintight pants—snug to prevent wrinkles in the saddle area—didn't. Of all the accessories today, however, belt buckles are probably the most important to Western dressers, and it's not unusual for them to spend thousands of dollars for gold ones.

Coopers Western Warehouse (De Vargas Center, ☎ 505/982–3388, and Villa Linda Mall, ☎ 505/471–8775) sells all the top names and top lines—hats, boots, belts, buckles, and complete outfits for the well-dressed cowboy and cowgirl.

Jane Smith (122 W. San Francisco St., ☎ 505/988–4775) features extraordinary—and pricey—handmade Western wear for women and men. The store's contemporary incarnations of days past include everything from beaded doeskin gloves to handmade cowboy boots to Plains Indian–style beaded tunics. The ubiquitous broomstick skirt and concho belt can also be found here in a wide range of colors and styles.

Montecristi Custom Hat Works (118 Galisteo St., ☎ 505/983–9598) is where the smart set goes for custom-made straw hats that fit so perfectly they're all but guaranteed to stay on, even when driving in an open convertible. Felt toppers with bejeweled and unusual hatbands are also available. The smooth-talking sales force will make you feel like a movie star—like those whose autographed photos hang on the wall.

Santa Fe Boot Company (950 W. Cordova Rd., ☎ 505/983–8415) stocks boots by all major manufacturers, as well as more exotic styles designed by owner Marian Trujillo. The store also sells hats and Western outerwear.

Santa Fe Western Mercantile (6820 Cerrillos Rd., ☎ 505/471–3655) offers a seemingly inexhaustible supply of hats, boots, jeans, English and Western saddles, buckles, belts, and feed and health-care products for horses and livestock.

Home Furnishings

Artesanos (222 Galisteo St., ☎ 505/983–5563 or 505/983–1743), a Mexican marketplace only a block from the Santa Fe Plaza, has a warehouse-size showroom and an open courtyard filled with arts and crafts from south of the border—everything from leather chairs to papiermâché *calaveras* (skeletons used in Day of the Dead celebrations), tinware, Colonial furniture, Talavera tiles, lighting fixtures, and more. The prices are reasonable, too.

Foreign Traders (202 Galisteo St., ☎ 505/983–6441), a Santa Fe landmark—founded as the Old Mexico Shop in 1927 and still run by the same family—offers high-quality handicrafts, antiques, and accessories from Mexico and other parts of the world. A section of outstanding collectible pieces includes mesquite *escritorios* (writing tables), antique wooden tortilla presses, and burro pack saddles.

Montez Gallery (Sena Plaza Courtyard, 125 E. Palace Ave., ☎ 505/982–1828) offers "masterpieces" of New Mexican art, including retablos, bultos, tinwork, furniture, painting, pottery, weaving, and jewelry, all by Hispanic artists.

Spanish Pueblo Doors (1091 Siler Rd., ☎ 505/473–0464), established in 1952, is the buyer's gateway to a wide selection of handcrafted wood doors and gates in Spanish Colonial and custom designs.

Native American Arts and Crafts

Arrowsmith's (402 Old Santa Fe Trail, ☎ 505/989–7663), neighboring the popular Pink Adobe restaurant, offers an eclectic collection of artifacts and early crafts from cowboy-and-Indian days. Prices range from a few dollars for arrowheads and Native American fetishes to $24,000 for a saddle embellished with 200 pounds of silver. The buffalo head on the wall isn't for sale.

Frank Patania (119 E. Palace Ave., ☎ 505/983–2155), just off the Plaza, carries on the name of the Tucson-based family long known for excellence in sterling silver and top-of-the-line Native American jewelry and crafts. This shop offers New Guinea and Oceanic art and artifacts as well.

Kachina House and Gallery (236 Delgado St., ☎ 505/982–8415) features an incomparable collection of authentic Hopi kachina dolls, along with a vast selection of Navajo pottery, sculpture, and jewelry.

Packard's Indian Trading Co. (61 Old Santa Fe Trail, on the east side of the Plaza, ☎ 505/983–9241), is the oldest authentic Native American arts and crafts store on the Santa Fe Plaza. This veritable museum is filled with old pottery, leather garments, saddles, kachina dolls, and silver and turquoise jewelry.

Prairie Edge (102 E. Water St., El Centro, ☎ 505/984–1336) offers classic Lakota art, artifacts, and jewelry, created by contemporary Sioux artists and craftspeople in the style and tradition of the past. Hides, beaded and quilled clothing, shields, weapons, buffalo skulls, and sterling and bead jewelry are all sold here.

The Rainbow Man (107 E. Palace Ave., ☎ 505/982–8706), established in 1945, does business in the rebuilt remains of a building that was damaged during the legendary 1680 Pueblo Revolt. Today, the shop offers an eclectic mix of jewelry, vintage Native American blankets, historic photographs, and railroad memorabilia. The shop's collection of miniature kachina dolls, some standing only 1 inch tall, is a main attraction.

Trade Roots Collection (38 Burro Alley, ☎ 505/982–8168) is the place to go if you're heavily into Native American ritual objects—outstanding fetishes, fetish jewelry, and Hopi rattles. This handsome showroom, one block west of the Plaza, also has an extensive collection of handwoven rugs, pillows, fabrics, and accessories.

SPORTS AND THE OUTDOORS

Participant Sports

Bicycling

The streets of Santa Fe are narrow and winding, but the roads and byways are generally level, and the scenery is spectacular. While the city is an ideal size for biking, unfortunately no special bike lanes are available. A suggested route map for bikers can be picked up at the information desk of the Convention and Visitors Bureau (201 W. Marcy St., ☎ 505/984–6760). Because of the high density of out-of-state tourist traffic and erratic drivers, bikers are cautioned to stay alert.

Rentals are available at the **Palace Bike Rentals** (409 E. Palace Ave., ☎ 505/984-2151) and **Rob and Charlie's** (1632 St. Michael's St., ☎ 505/471–9119).

Golf

Cochiti Lake Golf Course (5200 Cochiti Hwy., Cochiti Lake, ☎ 505/465–2239) was designed by Robert Trent Jones, Jr., and is set against a stunning backdrop of steep canyons and red-rock mesas. A 45-minute drive southwest of the city, it's rated among the top 25 public golf courses in the country.

Quail Run (3101 Old Pecos Trail, ☎ 505/986–2255), opened in 1987, is a beautiful, well-balanced course set amid piñon and juniper. The club is private, so you'll have to find a member to take you.

Santa Fe Country Club (Airport Rd., ☎ 505/471–0601), a close-to-town, tree-shaded, semiprivate course, was designed more than 50 years ago. There's a pro shop, club and electric-cart rentals, and private lessons by appointment.

Valle Grande (288 Prairie Star Rd. [I–25/Route 44 West], ☎ 505/867–9464), about 45 minutes south of Santa Fe, offers 18 holes of golf, a driving range, a putting area, a fully stocked pro shop, the Prairie Star restaurant, and a bar and grill.

Horseback Riding

New Mexico's rugged mountain country has been the scene of many Hollywood Westerns, including, in recent years, *Wyatt Earp*. Whether you want to ride the range that Kevin Kline and Gregory Peck rode or just go out and feel tall in the saddle, try the following. Rentals average about $20 an hour.

Pool Wells Station (40 mi north of Santa Fe on Route 68, ☎ 505/852–2013) is a former stagecoach stop where you can make reservations for trail rides, hayrides, barbecues, mock hangings, gunfights, and barn dancing.

Vientos Encantados (Round Barn Stables, Ojo Caliente, one hour north of Santa Fe on U.S. 84/285, no ☎) offers trail rides and pack trips near the hot mineral springs of northern New Mexico (*see* Off the Beaten Track, *above*). After a long ride, a hot soak may be in order!

River Rafting

The mention of no other sport conjures up as much excitement as does white-water rafting, and justly so. White-water rafting provides the kind of walloping action-packed thrill that belongs to the rocky, bone-thumping country that gave birth to it. Of course, if you prefer something less invigorating than heart-stopping, hair-raising Class V rapids, there are always more leisurely sightseeing possibilities on a river trip along the Rio Chama or one of the more gentle rivers of northern New Mexico, gliding past colorful mesas, ancient ruins, and fields ripening in the sun. The river trips are run only in the summertime.

Los Rios River Runners (desk in La Fonda Hotel, ☎ 505/983–6565 or 800/338–6877) provides a variety of white-water adventures, including the famous Taos Box, a 17-mile run on the rolling rapids of the upper Rio Grande.

Native American Tours (142 Lincoln Ave., Suite 103, Box 22658, ☎ 505/986–0804 or 800/578–3256, FAX 505/986–0812) offers rafting trips on the Rio Grande and the Rio Chama. Half-day, full-day, and overnight trips are available, all with Native American guides, gourmet meals, and storytelling.

New Wave Rafting Company (103 E. Water St., Suite D, ☎ 505/984–1444) features full-, half-day, and overnight river trips, with daily departures from Santa Fe.

Santa Fe Rafting Company and Outfitters (Box 28525–3525, ☎ 505/988–4914 or 800/467–7238) customizes rafting tours. Tell them what you want—they'll do it.

Southwest Wilderness Adventures (information and reservations through Galisteo News and Ticket Center, ☎ 505/983–7262 or 800/869–7238) handles local and international river tours, from the Rio Chama to China.

For a complete list of outfitters who guide trips on the Rio Grande and the Rio Chama, write the **Bureau of Land Management, Taos Resource Area Office** (224 Cruz Alta Rd., Taos 87571, ☎ 505/758–8851).

Running

With the city's 7,000-foot altitude, newcomers to Santa Fe may feel as if they're running in the Chilean Andes. Once they adjust, however, they'll find it a great place to slip into their running shoes. The city obliges its runners with a jogging track that runs along the Santa Fe River, parallel to Alameda, and one on Washington Avenue near Fort Marcy. There's lots of local organized activity as well, in which visitors may participate. **The Santa Fe Runaround,** a 10-kilometer race held in early June, begins and ends at the Plaza. The **Women's Five-Kilometer Run** is held in early August, and joggers turn out in droves on Labor Day for the most popular run of all, the annual **Old Santa Fe Trail Run.** More a weekly social event than a minimarathon is the **Fun Run** that starts out every Wednesday evening from the Plaza.

Skiing

The ski season in Santa Fe runs from Thanksgiving through Easter and averages 250 inches of dry-powder snow a year. The **Santa Fe Ski Area,** with blue skies above, blue-silver snow below, and green pines dotting the horizon like exclamation marks, has a 1,650-foot vertical rise and more than 40 trails (20% beginner, 40% intermediate, 40% advanced). The resort's six ski lifts include an Easy Street beginner's chair lift and a swift, breath-halting 5,000-foot triple chair to the summit. New Mexico's first quad chair lift, the Santa Fe Super Chief, makes the ride up almost as much fun as the downhill run. Chipmunk is a free run for small fry who measure less than 46 inches in their ski boots, provided they're in the company of a paying adult. Open bowls at the peak and more sheltered runs through the trees make for pleasant skiing even when the high winds blow. A ski-area restaurant, the **Evergreen** (High Park Rd., ☎ 505/984–8190), serves warming soups and chowders, as well as other hearty dishes.

For ski-area information, call the Santa Fe Ski Area (☎ 505/982–4429 or 505/983–9155) or Santa Fe Central Reservations (☎ 505/983–8200 or 800/776–7669 outside New Mexico). Snow-condition information is available by calling 505/984–0606. For cross-country skiing conditions, contact the **Santa Fe National Forest Office,** ☎ 505/988–6940.

Tennis

Santa Fe has 27 public tennis courts, including four asphalt courts at **Alto Park** (1035½ Alto St.), four concrete courts at **Herb Martinez/La Resolana Park** (Camino Carlos Rey), three asphalt courts at **Ortiz Park** (Camino de las Crucitas), and two asphalt courts at **Fort Marcy Complex** (Prince and Kearney Aves.). They are all available on a first-come, first-served basis. For the location of additional public facilities, call the **City Parks Division** (☎ 505/473–7236). Among the major private tennis facilities, including indoor, outdoor, and lighted courts, are **Club at El Gancho** (Old Las Vegas Hwy., ☎ 505/988–5000), **Sangre De Cristo Racquet Club** (1755 Camino Corrales, ☎ 505/983–7978), **Santa Fe Country Club** (Airport Rd., ☎ 505/471–3378), and **Shellaberger Tennis Center** (St. Michaels Dr., on the campus of the College of Santa Fe, ☎ 505/473–6144). Check for limited membership privileges.

Windsurfing

Strong summer breezes and a proximity to numerous lakes have made northern New Mexico a popular destination for windsurfers. **Abiquiu Lake** (40 mi northwest of Santa Fe, via U.S. 84/285; Drawer D, Abiquiu,

87510, ☎ 505/685–4371), **Cochiti Lake** (off U.S. 85 between Los
Alamos and Santa Fe; Cochiti Lake, Pena Blanca, 87041, ☎ 505/242–
8302), **Conchas Lake** (three hours east of Santa Fe, via I–25 to Las Vegas
and Route 104 to Conchas Lake; Box 976, Conchas Dam, 88416, ☎
505/868–2270), and **Storrie Lake** (an hour east, via I–25 to Las Vegas;
Box 3157, Las Vegas, 87701, ☎ 505/425–9231), all with warm water
and good winds, have developed a legion of devoted regulars. Most
of the windsurfing lakes have no on-site rental facilities, so you'll have
to bring your own equipment, which can be rented or purchased from
sporting-goods and water-sports stores in Santa Fe. **Water Sports** (1301
Escalante St., ☎ 505/982–8085) has a good selection.

Northern New Mexico is in a constant thunderstorm pattern during
the summer, so early morning sessions are recommended for beginning
windsurfers or anyone who can't get off the lakes in a hurry.

Spectator Sports

Horse Racing
Horse racing at the Santa Fe Downs, a beautiful 1-mile track in the
foothills of the towering Sangre de Cristo Mountains (on I–25, just 6
minutes southwest of town), attracts nearly a quarter-million spectators each year. The racing season begins mid-June and runs through
Labor Day. Races are held each Wednesday, Friday, Saturday, and
Sunday and on holidays, with the first race starting at 1:30 or, on Wednesday and Friday, at 3. The $100,000 Santa Fe Futurity for two-year-
olds is New Mexico's richest Thoroughbred purse. There's pari-mutuel
betting, of course, a Jockey Club, a Turf Club, ultramodern grandstands,
and plenty of parking, something rare in Santa Fe. For more information,
contact **Santa Fe Racing, Inc.** (☎ 505/471–3311).

DINING

A delicious mixture of Pueblo, Spanish, Mexican, and American-fron-
tier cooking, Santa Fe cuisine is like none other. Recipes that came from
Spain via Mexico were adapted generations ago for local ingredients—
chiles, corn, pork, beans, honey, apples, piñon nuts, jicama, and leaves
of the prickly pear cactus—and have remained much the same ever since.
New Mexican dishes, such as *carne adovada* (red chile–marinated
pork), burritos, chile rellenos, *flautas* (rolled corn tortillas filled with
shredded beef or chicken), and *chalupas* (bowl-shape corn tortillas filled
with beans, chicken, or beef), are particularly distinctive in flavor.
Pinto beans, *posole* (hominy stew), and Spanish rice are often served
on the side.

In northern New Mexico, babies cut their teeth on fresh flour tortillas.
And how quickly they develop a taste for sopaipillas, deep-fried, puff-
pastry pillows, drizzled with honey. But it is the chile, whether red or
green, that is the heart and soul of northern New Mexican cuisine. Visitors from other parts of the country are always a bit surprised to learn
that *ristras,* those strings of bright red chile peppers that seem to hang
everywhere, are sold more for eating here than for decoration. More
varieties of chiles—upwards of 90—are grown in New Mexico than
anywhere else in the world.

But if you can't stand the heat, you don't have to get out of the Santa
Fe kitchen. The city has 200 restaurants to suit all tastes and budgets,
from a riot of fast-food outlets on the outskirts of town, particularly
along Cerrillos Road, to elegant downtown restaurants near the Plaza,

Santa Fe Dining

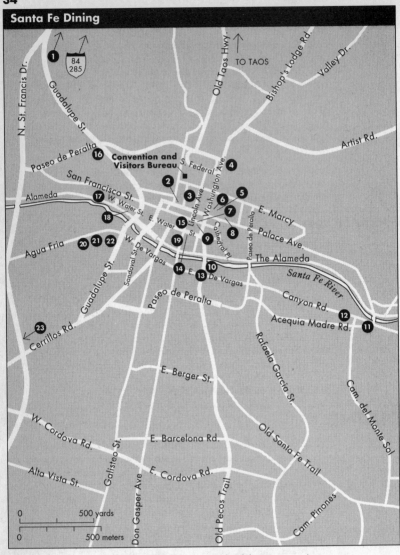

Anasazi, **6**

Bistro 315, **10**

Cafe Escalera, **3**

Cafe Pasqual's, **19**

The Compound, **11**

Corn Dance Cafe, **18**

Coyote Cafe, **15**

El Nido, **1**

Encore Provence, **20**

Geronimo, **12**

Guadalupe Cafe, **22**

India Palace, **14**

La Casa Sena, **8**

La Tertulia, **21**

Old Mexico Grill, **23**

Ore House on the
Plaza, **7**

The Palace, **2**

Pink Adobe, **13**

Plaza Cafe, **9**

Santacafe, **4**

The Shed, **5**

Vanessie, **17**

Whistling Moon
Cafe, **16**

where you can hobnob with film stars and publishers. There are also health-food and vegetarian restaurants and a wide selection of ethnic eating places.

What to Wear

You can dress in most restaurants as casually as you like. Restaurants in the major business hotels tend to be a bit more formal, of course, but as the evening wears down, so do the restrictions.

CATEGORY	COST*
$$$	over $20
$$	$10–$20
$	under $10

per person, excluding drinks, service, and sales tax (6.25%)

$$$ **Anasazi.** The dim, dramatic Southwestern interior of Anasazi echoes
★ that of the hotel it sits in. A mere half-block from the Plaza, the restaurant has quickly become one of the city's finest, thanks to the imaginative creations of Chef Peter Zimmer, who combines New Mexican and Native American flavors into such exotic offerings as Navajo flat bread with fire-roasted sweet peppers, sage-and-juniper-seared river trout, and cinnamon-chile grilled beef tenderloin with chipotle potatoes. Guests are seated in a large dining room filled with beautiful hand-hewn appointments including solid wood tables and *bancos* (adobe banquettes) upholstered with handwoven textiles from the famous northern New Mexico weaving village of Chimayo; groups of up to 12 can request to dine in the private wine cellar. No matter where you sit, service is always prompt and friendly. ✕ *113 Washington Ave.,* ☎ *505/ 988–3030. Reservations advised. AE, D, DC, MC, V.*

$$$ **The Compound.** With its crisp white linen tablecloths, heavy crystal, gleaming silver, elaborate floral arrangements, white-glove service—and the only rigidly enforced dress code in Santa Fe—this restaurant is the most formal, and the most expensive, in town. The main dining room, draped with colorful fabrics, overlooks an Italian garden where a playful fountain splashes; the other, with Navajo-rug hangings, overlooks a Spanish patio. Described as American Continental, the menu includes breast of chicken in champagne, fresh foie gras, roast loin of lamb, baked salmon, Russian caviar, and raspberries from New Zealand. ✕ *653 Canyon Rd.,* ☎ *505/982–4353. Reservations required. Jacket and tie required. AE. Closed Sun. and Mon. No lunch.*

$$$ **Coyote Cafe.** Flashy colors, modern art, oversize folk-art figures, and
★ howling-coyote silhouettes fill this former Greyhound bus depot, now one of the trendiest spots in town. The imaginative menu changes every other week and might include the signature steak—a 26-ounce ribeye called The Cowboy, served with barbecued black beans and red chile-dusted onion rings. Other crowd-pleasers include lobster enchiladas, squash blossom and corn cake appetizers, and ravioli filled with wild-boar-and-goat-cheese sausage. The wine list offers more than 500 selections. For less expensive but equally exotic fare, the Rooftop Cantina serves such dishes as sea bass tacos and barbecued duck quesadillas during the summer months. A shop adjoining the café sells a wide variety of Southwestern foodstuffs plus Coyote Cafe chef-and-owner Mark Miller's best-selling cookbooks. ✕ *132 W. Water St.,* ☎ *505/983– 1615. Reservations required. AE, D, DC, MC, V.*

$$$ **La Casa Sena.** This elegant restaurant occupies a 19th-century Territorial-style adobe house in the courtyard of lovely Sena Plaza, one of the most charming spots in Santa Fe, especially when the hollyhocks are in bloom. The house was once part of a large hacienda owned by the prominent Sena family, but was transformed into a restaurant a

few years back when local art dealer and developer Gerald Peters bought the entire plaza. The menu includes a delicious mix of New Mexican and Continental fare, including one of the best—and most expensive—red chile enchiladas in town, the popular *truchas en terracotta* (fresh trout baked in clay), and a strange but wonderful avocado cheesecake with a piñon nut crust. An incredible selection of more than 700 wines also earned this restaurant the *Wine Spectator*'s award of excellence. For a musical meal (evenings only), sit in the restaurant's adjacent Cantina, where staff members serve up Broadway show tunes along with your food. ✕ *125 E. Palace Ave.,* ☎ *505/988–9232. Reservations required. AE, D, DC, MC, V.*

$$–$$$ **Cafe Escalera.** Ride the only escalator in Santa Fe to this second-floor
★   hot spot serving fine Mediterranean-influenced fare. The spacious restaurant and bar have a minimalist look, with billowy ceiling canopies that match the white tablecloths. The menu changes daily, but may include spaghettini with English peas, pancetta, sage, and pecorino Romano cheese, or a fried oyster sandwich with arugula, smoked bacon, and aïoli. Entrées are accompanied by fresh seasonal vegetables and great bread. For an appetizer, you can't go wrong with the potatoes—a heaping mound of matchstick potatoes with homemade ketchup, or roasted potatoes served with aïoli—or the soup of the day. ✕ *130 Lincoln Ave.,* ☎ *505/989–8188. Reservations required. MC, V. Closed Sun.*

$$ **Bistro 315.** This tiny, 27-seat bistro feels like something you might find on a trendy thoroughfare in Paris rather than on the Old Santa Fe Trail. Chef Matt Yohalem creates classically prepared bistro fare that features organic vegetables and heirloom beans, locally raised beef and lamb, free-range chicken, and fresh seafood. The ever-changing menu is highlighted by such seasonal specials as potato-crusted salmon with *beurre rouge* sauce, and might include herb-roasted chicken on a bed of creamy polenta, spinach and endive salad with mushroom sherry vinaigrette, and other delicious seafood dishes. French and California wines, tangy lemon pound cake, real New York cheesecake, and variations on classic bread pudding round out an intimate dining experience within the bistro's sunny interiors. In good weather, diners can sit on the patio and be happy they're not in pretentious Paris, but in pretty Santa Fe instead. ✕ *315 Old Santa Fe Trail,* ☎ *505/986–9190. Reservations required. AE, MC, V.*

$$ **Cafe Pasqual's.** On a busy corner a block southwest of the Plaza, this
★   tiny, cheerful eatery offers regional specialties and possibly the best breakfast in town, which is served all day for the benefit of local sleepyheads. Forget the pancakes and order a chorizo burrito (Mexican sausages, scrambled eggs, home fries, and scallions wrapped in a flour tortilla and doused with red or green chile), or the succulent corned beef hash and a steamy *caffe latte* (coffee with hot milk). For dinner, there's fresh trout with green chile and toasted piñon nuts, and for dessert, a sinful caramel sundae with homemade piñon-nut ice cream. High ceilings and huge colorful murals lend a spacious feel to the small restaurant, and piñatas, ristras, and ceramic pottery add a festive tone, highlighted by the friendly service. Expect a line at breakfast and lunch. ✕ *121 Don Gaspar Ave.,* ☎ *505/983–9340. Reservations required for dinner. AE, MC, V.*

$$ **Corn Dance Cafe.** Proprietress Loretta Barrett Oden, a member of the Oklahoma Potawatomi Indian Tribe, spent three years sitting in the kitchens of Native American cooks—from the Mississippi Chippewa tribes to the Houma peoples of the Southeast coast—gathering recipes that honor the ancient culinary traditions of the first Americans. People who come to New Mexico in search of authentic Native American food will be pleasantly surprised by the bounty presented here. The menu spotlights fresh, healthy foods that are indigenous to the United States before the European conquest; items like corn, beans, squash, buffalo, rabbit, and venison are prepared simply to allow their natural flavors to come bursting through. House favorites include butternut squash soup, wild turkey with cornbread-sage dressing, wood-grilled buffalo burgers, and "Kick Ass" buffalo chile in an edible jalapeño bread bowl. Tempt your taste buds with the Houma barbecued shrimp in a rich and spicy sauce of butter, garlic, and dark beer. Try the "Little Big Pie"—air-baked flat bread topped with a number of savory combinations such as barbecued buffalo, fresh seasonal vegetables, or chicken with grilled mushrooms and corn chile. The atmosphere is pleasant in this squat, unassuming adobe on the western edge of downtown, and the service is warm and accommodating. In summer, you can sit out on the backyard patio, where Native American cooking demonstrations and storytelling complement your unique dining experience. ✗ *409 W. Water St., 505/986–1662. AE, D, DC, MC, V. Closed Tues. mid-Oct.–Apr.*

$$ El Nido. For more than 50 years, Santa Feans have made the 10-mile drive to the tiny village of Tesuque to visit this former dance hall and trading post, now known for its cozy ambience and a solid menu of choice aged beef, fresh seafood, and such New Mexican specialties as green chile chicken enchiladas or chunky green chile stew. Among the highlights are oysters Rockefeller, prime rib, and an excellent broiled salmon. Only a five-minute drive from the Santa Fe Opera, El Nido is a favorite of opera fans, who may find themselves dining next to their favorite divas. ✗ *Rte. 285 10 mi north of Santa Fe to Tesuque exit, then about ¼ mi more to restaurant,* ☎ *505/988–4340. Reservations required. MC, V. Closed Mon.*

$$ Encore Provence. Santa Fe's only truly southern French restaurant—
★ it features cuisine from the Provence region of France—is in an unpretentious little pale yellow wooden house with a stone front porch. Its interior, however, glows with elegance and warmth; 15 tables are immaculately set with linens, flowers, and crystal, and the service is equally impeccable. Every night chef-owner Patrick Benrezkellah offers a selection of some seven fish dishes and three meat dishes—from steamy, tantalizing bouillabaisse to a seven-hour leg of lamb. The wine list is half-French, half-Californian, and the desserts—particularly the crème brûlée—are decadently delicious. ✗ *548 Agua Fria St.,* ☎ *505/ 983–7470. Reservations required. AE, MC, V. ☽ Mon.–Sat. No lunch.*

$$ Geronimo. This is one of many restaurants in recent years to occupy
★ the historic Borrego House, whose structure dates to 1753, but given it's popularity, it appears it will be around for some time to come. Italian chef Gina Ziluca mixes her Italian influences with southwestern spices to create some of the most innovative menus in town. The menu changes daily, but you're likely to choose from such items as smoked quail on sweet potato gravy, cinnamon chicken breast with green chile cheese sauce, and grilled fillet of salmon with an interesting spicy sauce. Meals are complemented by home-baked breads, crisp arugula salads, fine wines, and desserts whose intriguing ingredients are also selected daily. And the special Sunday brunch always features something exciting and new. The white dining rooms with beamed ceilings and wood floors are pristine and romantic; corner fireplaces and cushioned bancos compliment the intimate seating arrangements. In the warmer months, customers dine under the front portal, which looks out upon the galleries and sights of Canyon Road. But no matter where you sit, the service is as excellent as the view. ✗ *724 Canyon Rd.,* ☎ *505/982–1500. Reservations required. AE, MC, V. No lunch Sat.–Mon.*

$$ India Palace. The thought of an East Indian restaurant in Santa Fe probably never occurred to most locals until one suddenly appeared in the spot where the favorite Little Chief Grill once stood. Now, many locals wouldn't think of living without the exotic and spicy dishes of chef Bal Dev Singh, who cooked in New York, Dallas, and Los Angeles before settling in Santa Fe. The serene, deep pink interior sets the scene for such authentic East Indian favorites as tender tandoori chicken, lamb, and fish; superb curried vegetables, meats, and seafood; saffron rice dishes; and an assortment of soft, warm Indian breads. Meals are cooked as hot or mild as you wish, and vegetarians have much to choose from. Don't be daunted by the restaurant's location in the far corner of a downtown parking lot; this is some of the best ethnic food to be found in Santa Fe. ✗ 227 Don Gaspar Ave. (at the rear of the El Centro shopping compound through the Water St. parking lot), ☎ 505/986–5859. Reservations required. AE, D, MC, V.

$$ La Tertulia. A splendid Spanish Colonial art collection surrounds diners feasting on fine New Mexican cuisine in this converted 19th-century convent. Among the culinary highlights are tender carne adovada (pork marinated in red chile), chalupas (bowl-shape corn tortillas stuffed with beans, guacamole, sour cream, and chicken or beef), and Spanish paella (a chunky mix of chicken, seafood, saffron, and rice). Try the traditional New Mexican flan (egg custard) for dessert, and don't miss the extraordinary house sangria. The service is gracious and the dim adobe interiors create a cozy dining experience. ✗ 416 Agua Fria St., ☎ 505/988–2769. Reservations required. AE, MC, V. Closed Mon.

$$ Old Mexico Grill. For a taste of Old Mexico in New Mexico, this colorful restaurant is a town favorite. Regional Mexican dishes featuring fish and fowl are grilled to perfection, then spiced up with any of 20 varieties of Mexican chile. The arracheras, the traditional name for fajitas, are a heaping serving of beef, chicken, or fish grilled with peppers and onions and served with corn or flour tortillas and all the traditional toppings. Equally enticing are the tacos al carbon (shredded pork cooked in a supreme mole sauce and folded into corn tortillas) or shrimp sautéed in tequila cream sauce. Start the meal with a fresh ceviche appetizer and a cool lime margarita, and finish with bread pudding smothered in a piñon nut caramel sauce. The dining room is open and airy, with beautiful Mexican tile decor throughout. The restaurant's Cerrillos Road shopping center location makes parking a snap. ✗ 2434 Cerrillos Rd., College Plaza S, ☎ 505/473–0338. D, MC, V. Closed weekend lunch.

$$ Ore House on the Plaza. This restaurant is known more for its perfect location—with a dining balcony overlooking the Plaza—than its food. Salmon, swordfish, lobster, oysters, ceviche, and steaks are all solidly prepared, though rather ordinary. The specialty margaritas, however, are anything but ordinary: They come in 80 customized flavors, ranging from cool watermelon to zippy jalapeño. ✗ 50 Lincoln Ave., upstairs on the southwest corner of the Plaza, ☎ 505/983–8687. Reservations required. AE, MC, V.

$$ The Palace Restaurant. This lively saloon-style restaurant—with up-
★   holstered banquettes and chairs, crystal chandeliers, and rich red wallpaper—was indeed an infamous saloon, gambling hall, and house of ill repute in the mid-1800s. Then in 1959, a renovation turned it into one of Santa Fe's most popular restaurants, which today specializes in superb Continental and northern Italian cuisine. Owned by the charming Pertusini brothers of Lake Como, Italy, the restaurant serves up a large selection of seafood, steak, veal, and pasta entrées; try the sautéed sweetbreads and cannelloni stuffed with pheasant, eggplant, and zucchini. The Caesar salad, homemade pastries, and extensive wine se-

lection are memorable. Ditto for the fine service. ✕ *142 W. Palace Ave.,* ☎ *505/982–9891. Reservations required. AE, D, MC, V. Closed Sun. lunch.*

$$ **Pink Adobe.** Rosalea Murphey has been the owner of this Santa Fe gold mine—one of the best-known restaurants in town—for 50 years. (She's the author on the covers of the acclaimed *The Pink Adobe* and *In the Pink* cookbooks, which can be purchased at the restaurant.) She still lends a hand in the kitchen, and her grandson is one of the managers. The historic adobe has several cozy dining rooms with fireplaces and an array of art by well-known artists, including stunning works by Rosalea, herself. Continental, New Orleans Creole, and local New Mexican favorites are served daily. Steak Dunnigan, smothered in green chile and mushrooms, and savory Shrimp Louisianne—fat and crispy deep-fried shrimp—are perennial specials; so is the famous apple pie drenched in brandy sauce. A limited menu is served in the adjacent Dragon Room bar, one of the most popular local hangouts in town. No smoking is allowed. ✕ *406 Old Santa Fe Trail,* ☎ *505/983–7712. Reservations required. AE, D, DC, MC, V.*

$$ **Santacafe.** The thick adobe walls of this romantic restaurant, two blocks north of the Plaza in the historic Padre Gallegos House, are decorated with floral bouquets. The menu is inspired by an eclectic array of international cuisines. Chef Marion Gillcrist creates such specialties as crispy Asian duck breasts with cranberry *hoisin* sauce, noodle pillow, and sesame bok choy; grilled venison loin with kumquat-pistachio chutney, herb potatoes and Asian-scented vegetables; marinated rack of lamb with jalapeño mint jelly; and a wide variety of homemade breads and desserts. High-quality ingredients, artful presentation, and pleasant service combine to make this one of Santa Fe's finest restaurants and a favorite spot for Sunday brunch. ✕ *231 Washington Ave.,* ☎ *505/984–1788. Reservations required. MC, V.*

$$ **Vanessie.** You'd better be hungry: This longtime local favorite serves up huge portions of beef, chicken, fish, and rack of lamb, along with massive baked potatoes; salads are enormous. Onion-lovers will be awestruck by the size of the onion-loaf appetizer. High beamed ceilings and massive oak tables with high-back chairs create a cozy lodge-like ambience. After dinner, the popular piano bar is a perfect place to sit, listen to wistful tunes, and digest your food. ✕ *434 W. San Francisco St.,* ☎ *505/982–9966. No reservations. AE, DC, MC, V.*

$ **Guadalupe Cafe.** This informal café, open from breakfast to dinner, is
★ a local haven for efficient service and quality American and New Mexican fare. Try any of a half-dozen enchiladas and tacos smothered in red or green chile. The sizeable sopaipillas (fluffy fried bread) served with honey, make a good dessert, or splurge on the restaurant's classic Adobe Pie—coffee ice cream on a chocolate cookie crust. Breakfast is a popular attraction here, undoubtedly due to the fresh raspberry pancakes, the rich eggs Florentine, and the imaginative breakfast burrito—sautéed spinach and mushrooms rolled in a flour tortilla and buried in red or green chile. If you don't show up early, be prepared to wait. ✕ *313 Guadalupe St.,* ☎ *505/982–9762. No reservations. MC, V. Closed Mon.*

$ **Plaza Cafe.** This large busy-beehive restaurant has been a fixture on the Santa Fe Plaza since 1918 and run with homespun care by the Razatos family since 1947. From all appearances, the decor hasn't changed much since then: red leather banquettes, black Formica tables, tile floors, vintage Santa Fe photos, and a coffered tin ceiling. A 1940s-style service counter runs along a wall. Standard American fare, such as hamburgers and tuna sandwiches, is served, along with an interesting mix of New Mexican and Greek specialties, including spanakopita (spinach pie) and baklava. A bowl of green chile and beans will leave your tongue burning—that's the way the locals like it. You can cool it off, however, with a number of old-fashioned ice cream treats from the soda fountain or a towering slice of coconut, banana, or chocolate cream pie. There's a good wine and beer selection. The service is friendly. ✗ *54 Lincoln Ave., ☎ 505/982–1664. No reservations. MC, V.*

$ **The Shed.** Judging by the long lines, this downtown spot serving clas-
★   sic New Mexican cuisine and fabulous homemade desserts is a favorite of Santa Feans. Housed in a rambling, historic adobe hacienda dating from 1692, the restaurant is decorated throughout with festive folk art. Specialties include red-chile enchiladas, green chile stew (green chile with potatoes and pork), *posole* (hominy stew), and charbroiled "Shedburgers." For dessert, the mocha cake is a must. The place exudes charm, and the neighborly service will make you feel like you never left home. ✗ *113½ E. Palace Ave., ☎ 505/982–9030. No reservations. No credit cards. No weekday dinner. Closed Sun.*

$ **Whistling Moon Cafe.** This new eatery has become a local fast-food fa-
★   vorite for quality traditional Middle Eastern and other Mediterranean fare. Simple, inexpensive, and scented with unusual spices, the menu entrées encompass nicoise salad, pasta primavera, Greek salad, Tunisian eggs, Moroccan lamb sausage, and Turkish coffee. The Middle Eastern Sampler (hummus with pita, tahini, fresh eggplant salad, coriander-accented grape leaves, and five varieties of olives) offers a little of everything, while the flavorful falafel, kefta lamb burger, and rosemary chicken sandwich come in generous portions. The coriander-cumin fries are irresistible as are such homemade desserts as Greek honey cheesecake and pistachio-and-apricot baklava. Although the small ochre dining room with red Moroccan weavings is a touch noisy, and the lack of parking out front can be frustrating, the food and low prices more than make up for it. ✗ *402 N. Guadalupe, ☎ 505/983–3093. Reservations required for parties of 6 or more. No credit cards.*

LODGING

Santa Fe is a hot tourist destination that attracts lots of upscale travelers. As a result, prices have been escalating steadily in recent years and are likely to continue to climb as long as a steady stream of fat cats continues to show up and pay them. Low-season hotel rates, which fluctuate considerably from place to place, are generally in effect from the beginning of November until the end of April (excluding the Thanksgiving and Christmas holidays), and then they soar. But the savings are far from spectacular, even at no-frills hotels.

CATEGORY	COST*
$$$$	over $150
$$$	$100–$150
$$	$65–$100
$	under $65

All prices are for a standard double room, excluding tax (5.8% in New Mexico).

Hotels

$$$$ **Eldorado Hotel.** This is the city's largest hotel—a bit too modern for some—located in the heart of downtown, not far from the Plaza. Its rooms are stylishly furnished with carved Southwestern-style desks and chairs, nature prints, and large upholstered club chairs, all in warm, desert colors. Many rooms have terraces or kiva-style fireplaces. Baths

Santa Fe Lodging

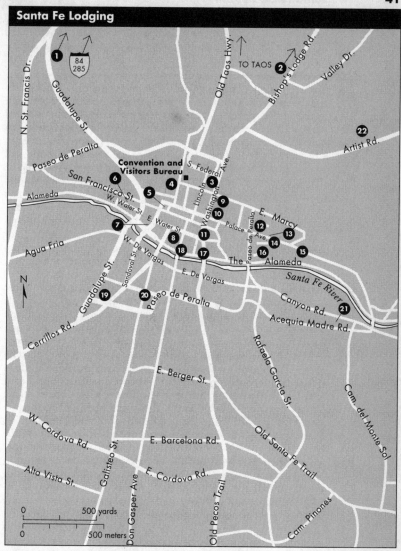

Alexander's Inn, **15**
The Bishop's Lodge, **2**
Dunshee's, **21**
Eldorado Hotel, **5**
The Grant Corner Inn, **4**
Hilton of Santa Fe, **7**
Hotel Plaza Real, **9**
Hotel St. Francis, **8**

Hotel Santa Fe, **19**
Houses of the Moon, **22**
Inn at Loretto–Best Western, **17**
Inn of the Anasazi, **10**
Inn of the Animal Tracks, **12**
Inn of the Governors, **18**

Inn on the Alameda, **16**
La Fonda, **11**
La Posada de Santa Fe, **13**
Preston House, **14**
Pueblo Bonito B&B Inn, **20**
Rancho Encantado, **1**
Territorial Inn, **3**
Water Street Inn, **6**

are spacious and completely tiled. ⌕ *309 W. San Francisco St., 87501,* ☎ *505/988–4455 or 800/955–4455,* FAX *505/988–4455, ext. 143. 214 rooms and minisuites, 5 suites. Restaurant, bar, pool, shops. AE, D, DC, MC, V.*

$$$$ **Inn on the Alameda.** Nestled between the Santa Fe Plaza shopping dis-
★ trict and gallery-filled Canyon Road is one of the city's most prestigious small hotels. This inn on the Santa Fe River (Alameda means "place
by the river"), with its adobe architecture and enclosed courtyards and
portals, combines a relaxed New Mexico country atmosphere with the
luxury and amenities of a world-class hotel. The Southwest color
scheme in the bedrooms carries over into the accessories, beds, wall
hangings, and wood-framed mirrors. Handmade armoires, oversize
chairs, headboards, and ceramic lamps and tiles all exemplify local
artistry. While the inn has no dining room, its complimentary gourmet
breakfast is a wonder: homemade muffins, bagels, creamy pastries, cinnamon rolls, fruit, juice, teas, and special Kona coffee, all served by a
friendly staff. ⌕ *303 E. Alameda, 87501,* ☎ *505/984–2121 or
800/289–2122,* FAX *505/986–8325. 66 rooms and suites. Bar, refrigerators, 2 hot tubs, spa, exercise room, library, laundry service. AE,
D, DC, MC, V.*

$$$$ **Inn of the Anasazi.** One of Santa Fe's showplaces in the heart of the
★ historic Plaza district, this hotel was clearly designed with the upscale
traveler in mind. Each individually designed room has beamed ceilings;
a kiva-style fireplace; a handcrafted desk, dresser, and tables; and a four-
poster bed. Services include a personal attendant who acts as a concierge,
twice-daily maid service, and room delivery of exercise bikes upon request. The restaurant is headed by renowned chef Peter Zimmer whose
cuisine celebrates the foods of Native Americans and the North American cowboy. Guests can browse in the library, which focuses on the
lore and legends of New Mexico and the Southwest. ⌕ *113 Washington
Ave., 87501,* ☎ *505/988–3030 or 800/688–8100,* FAX *505/988–3277.
59 rooms and suites. Minibars, in-room safes, in-room VCRs. AE, D,
DC, MC, V.*

$$$$ **Inn at Loretto–Best Western.** Built in the traditional Pueblo style, this
hotel has been designed with historical accuracy in mind, with such
touches as light fixtures custom-made of tinwork or pottery, and ancient designs on the walls. Rooms are decorated in light colors and have
beds with handmade oak headboards and nightstands inlaid with re-
cessed tile work. The inn, built on the site of the Sisters of Loretto
Academy, is adjacent to the famous Loretto Chapel (*see* Tour 3 in Exploring Santa Fe, *above*). ⌕ *211 Old Santa Fe Trail, 87501,* ☎ *505/988–
5531 or 800/528–1234 outside NM,* FAX *505/984–7988. 137 rooms.
Restaurant, lounge, pool, beauty salon, shops. AE, D, DC, MC, V.*

$$$$ **La Posada de Santa Fe.** This Spanish Colonial inn, only two blocks
from the Plaza, is situated on 6 acres of beautifully landscaped gardens and expansive green lawns shaded by giant elms and cottonwoods.
Some of the charming rooms have fireplaces, beamed ceilings, and Native American rugs. In the center of this hotel complex is the excellent
Victorian-style Staab House. ⌕ *330 E. Palace Ave., 87501,* ☎ *505/986–
0000 or 800/727–5276 outside NM,* FAX *505/982–6850. 119 rooms
and suites. Restaurant, pool, health club. AE, D, DC, MC, V.*

$$$ **Hilton of Santa Fe.** This downtown establishment has a comfortable
and spacious lobby with a beamed ceiling, a huge wrought-iron chan-
delier, and colorful Native American wall hangings. The large guest
rooms, done in muted Southwestern tones of golden brown, feature
locally crafted table lamps, fine modern furniture, and hanging or pot-
ted plants. The hotel is built around the Casa de Ortiz, a historic home

whose now-enclosed patio houses the hotel's delightful Chamisa Court-yard restaurant, open for breakfast and lunch. The intimate Piñon Grill serves entrées grilled over western hardwoods; try the marinated rack of lamb with apple blackberry chutney or the free range chicken breast with smoked tomato *coulis* (liquid puree) The cozy El Canon is a casual breakfast and lunch spot featuring a constantly changing selection of fine wines and specialty beers. ☒ *100 Sandoval St., 87501,* ☎ *505/988–2811 or 800/336–3676,* FAX *505/986–6439. 155 rooms. 2 restaurants, bar, pool. AE, D, DC, MC, V.*

$$$ Hotel Plaza Real. One of the city's newer hotels (it opened four years ago, just one block from the downtown plaza), this place was built in traditional Territorial style, unique to the region, with massive wood beams and old Native American designs throughout. The large rooms are decorated with Southwest handcrafted furniture. Most have wood-burning fireplaces, and patios or balconies; several are accessed from an interior brick courtyard. Continental breakfast is complimentary. ☒ *125 Washington Ave., 87501,* ☎ *505/988-4900 or 800/279–7325,* FAX *505/988–4900. 56 rooms and suites. Lounge, concierge, parking (fee). AE, D, DC, MC, V.*

$$$ Hotel St. Francis. Listed in the National Register of Historic Places, this
★ three-story building, constructed in 1920, has walkways lined with turn-of-the-century lampposts. In addition to a prime location—one block southwest of the Plaza—the hotel offers small and simple rooms with high ceilings, casement windows, brass-and-iron beds, marble and cherry wood antiques, and original artwork. A carved wooden angel floats on the wall above each bed. Bathrooms feature the original hexagonal tile and porcelain pedestal sinks. Afternoon tea, with scones and finger sandwiches, is served daily in the huge lobby, which rises 50 feet from a floor of blood-red tiles. The On Water restaurant offers innovative meat and fish specialties, and the hotel bar is one of the only places in town that serves food until 1 AM. ☒ *210 Don Gaspar Ave., 87501,* ☎ *505/983–5700 or 800/529–5700 outside NM,* FAX *505/989–7690. 81 rooms. Restaurant, bar. AE, D, DC, MC, V.*

$$$ Inn of the Governors. This hotel, just two blocks from the Plaza, is one
★ of the nicest in town. A small, intimate lobby makes the traveler feel quickly at home. Standard rooms have a Mexican theme, with bright colors, hand-painted folk art, Southwestern fabrics, and handmade furnishings; deluxe rooms are balconied Southwestern-style minisuites with fireplaces. The dining room specializes in native New Mexican dishes and lighter fare. ☒ *234 Don Gaspar Ave. (at W. Alameda), 87501,* ☎ *505/982–4333 or 800/234–4534 outside NM,* FAX *505/989–9149. 100 rooms. Restaurant, piano bar, pool, free parking. AE, D, DC, MC, V.*

$$$ La Fonda. When Santa Fe was established in 1610, official records
★ show that the town already had an adobe *fonda,* or inn, to accommodate travelers. Two centuries later, the original hotel was still welcoming guests—traders, trappers, mountain men, soldiers, and politicians. The present structure was built on the site of the original inn in 1864 and has been refurbished countless times since. The only lodging directly on the Plaza, it is perhaps also the only hotel in the world that can boast having had both Kit Carson and John F. Kennedy as guests. A spacious tiled lobby is decorated with Spanish Colonial antiques, early Mexican pieces, and classic Native American art. Each room is unique, with hand-decorated wooden furniture, wrought-iron light fixtures, beamed ceilings, oak door paneling, and motifs painted by local artists; many accommodations have turn-of-the-century pieces, and all the suites have fireplaces. ☒ *100 E. San Francisco St., 87501,* ☎ *505/982–5511 or 800/523–5002 outside NM,* FAX *505/988–2952. 132 rooms, 21 suites. Restaurant, bar, lounge, pool, 2 hot tubs. AE, D, DC, MC, V.*

\$\$ **Hotel Santa Fe.** Controlling interest in this Pueblo-style three-story hotel is owned by the Picuris Pueblo, smallest of the eight northern New Mexico Native American tribes. Rooms and suites are decorated in traditional Southwestern style, with locally handmade furniture and Pueblo paintings (*Picuris* means "those who paint"), many by well-known artist Gerald Nailor. All suites have microwave ovens, and smaller rooms have access to a common kitchen. The lobby is decorated with Native American art, including a large hand-loomed rug and the tower bell from the pueblo's 200-year-old mission. The lobby bar serves a Continental breakfast. The hotel gift shop, the only such tribal-owned store in Santa Fe, has prices lower than most nearby retail stores. Most staff members are from the Picuris Pueblo and travel the 60 miles to and from work each day by van. ☎ *1501 Paseo de Peralta, 87501, ☎ 505/ 982–1200 or 800/825–9876 outside NM, ℻ 505/984–2211. 40 rooms, 91 suites. Bar, deli, pool, hot tub. AE, D, DC, MC, V.*

Bed-and-Breakfasts

\$\$\$ **Houses of the Moon.** Santa Fe Style gives way to Japan Style in the moon-
★   lit mountains above Santa Fe, where the local Ten Thousand Waves Japanese Health Spa provides the same kind of high quality lodging experiences that it has been giving its hot-tub and massage customers for years. Visitors choose from three small houses—"Full Moon," "Rising Moon," and "Blue Moon"—which are set on a hillside, and reached by a path through the piñons, just south of the spa. All of the accommodations have brick floors, marble fireplaces, and adobe-color walls, plus Japanese art, fine woodwork, and other Asian touches. Each house sleeps up to four—two on a queen-size futon and two on a queen-size sofa bed—and have outdoor decks that overlook the city lights and other pristine mountain views. Although no food service is offered, "Full Moon" comes with a full kitchen and may also connect to "Rising Moon" for parties that need more space. This is a popular overnight spot for skiers, who head just a few miles up the road to hit the slopes. And for those who enjoy the outdoor hot tubs, variety of massage, and other luxuries that Ten Thousand Waves has to offer, lodgers get 10% off for all services at the spa. ☎ *3.5 miles from downtown Santa Fe on the road to the Santa Fe Ski Basin, Box 10200, 87504, ☎ 505/ 982–9304, ℻ 505/989–5077. 3 cottages. MC, V.*

\$\$ **Alexander's Inn.** This 1903 Victorian house exudes all the charm of an old country inn, with American country-style wooden furnishings, flower arrangements, and lots of open space. A colorful flowered walkway runs alongside the building. In a lovely east-side residential area, only a few blocks from the Plaza and the Canyon Road shops and galleries, Alexander's Inn serves a generous Continental breakfast, including homemade bread and muffins. ☎ *529 E. Palace Ave., 87501, ☎ 505/986–1431. 6 rooms, 4 with private bath, 2 with shared bath, and 2 cottages. MC, V.*

\$\$ **Dunshee's.** This pretty B&B, set in a quiet neighborhood just a mile from the Plaza, is so romantic that its patio has been used for weddings. Guests have two options. One is a spacious suite in the restored adobe home of artist Susan Dunshee, the proprietor. The suite has its own private entrance and includes a cozy living room, a bedroom with a double bed, and a Mexican tile bath. The rooms have kiva-style fireplaces and viga ceilings and are furnished with antiques, quilts, and folk art, and you get a full gourmet breakfast in the bargain. The other, more expensive, choice is an adobe casita with two bedrooms, a living room, a Mexican tile bath, a patio, and a kitchen complete with iron, dishwasher, and a refrigerator amply stocked for a do-it-yourself breakfast. It, too, features vigas, a kiva-style fireplace, decorative linens, and folk art. All in all, a good buy for upscale Santa Fe. ⊡ *986 Acequia Madre, 87501,* ☎ *505/982–0988. Suite and 2-bedroom casita. MC, V.*

$$ **Grant Corner Inn.** This delightful Colonial-style lodging, located downtown, but surrounded by a patio and garden, combines antique Spanish and American country furnishings with potted greens and knickknacks. Room accents include tile stoves, old-fashioned fixtures, quilts, and Native American blankets. The ample breakfast includes home-baked breads and pastries, jellies, and such unique local treats as blue-corn waffles. ⊡ *122 Grant Ave., 87501,* ☎ *505/983–6678. 7 rooms with bath, 2 with shared bath, 1 minisuite, and 2 rooms with bath in a nearby hacienda. MC, V.*

$$ **Inn of the Animal Tracks.** Three blocks east of the Plaza is this enchanting
★ 91-year-old restored adobe, with beamed ceilings, hardwood floors, handcrafted furniture, and fireplaces. Each guest room is decorated with an animal theme: Whimsical Rabbit, Gentle Deer, Soaring Eagle, Playful Otter, and Loyal Wolf. Be prepared for cuteness: The Whimsical Rabbit room, for instance, is filled with stuffed and terra-cotta rabbits, rabbit books, rabbit drawings and paintings; bunny-rabbit slippers are tucked under the bed. A full breakfast and high tea are served; high tea is also available by reservation for nonguests. ⊡ *707 Paseo de Peralta, 87504,* ☎ *505/988–1546. 5 rooms with bath. AE, D, MC, V.*

$$ **Preston House.** This 1886 Queen Anne house, the only one of its kind in the city, is tucked away in a quiet garden setting not far from the Plaza. Its pleasant rooms highlight period furnishings, Edwardian fireplaces, and stained-glass windows. Fruit bowls and fresh-cut flowers add to the appeal. ⊡ *106 Faithway St., 87501,* ☎ *505/982–3465. 15 rooms. AE, MC, V.*

$$ **Pueblo Bonito B&B Inn.** Minutes from the Plaza is this century-old adobe compound—one of the few bed-and-breakfast inns in Santa Fe that retain the pure Southwest Pueblo design throughout. The handmade and hand-painted furnishings are all in the traditional Old Santa Fe style; works by local Native American and Western artists hang on the walls, and pottery made by New Mexican craftspeople grace the shelves, bookracks, and mantels. All the rooms have fireplaces. A filling breakfast is served in the main dining room (there's also room service), which has French doors that open onto a patio. ⊡ *138 W. Manhattan Ave., 87501,* ☎ *505/984–8001. 11 rooms with bath, 7 suites. Laundry. MC, V.*

$$ **Territorial Inn.** Creature comforts are a high priority in this elegant 100-year-old brick structure, nestled amid restaurants and shops; it's one of Santa Fe's leading bed-and-breakfasts, only one block from the Plaza. The decor is Victorian throughout; among the well-maintained rooms, No. 9 has a canopied bed and a fireplace. A hot tub is also available, with robes provided. In addition to Continental breakfast, the inn offers afternoon treats and brandy in the evening. ⊡ *215 Washington Ave., 87501,* ☎ *505/989–7737,* ⅮⅩ *505/986–1411. 11 rooms, 8 with bath, 3 with shared bath. MC, V.*

$$ **Water Street Inn.** This intimate, restored adobe house blends regional Southwestern furnishings with period antiques. All the rooms have fireplaces and private baths. ⊡ *427 W. Water St., 87501,* ☎ *505/984–1193. 8 rooms with bath. MC, V.*

Resorts

$$$$ **The Bishop's Lodge.** This resort sits 3 miles north of downtown Santa Fe, in the rolling foothills of the Sangre de Cristo Mountains. Geared

toward families, particularly during the summer, the property offers a variety of outdoor activities, including horseback riding, hiking, skeet shooting, tennis, swimming in an outdoor heated pool, and lawn games. Guests can use the 18-hole golf course at the Santa Fe Country Club, about 20 minutes away. Guest rooms and public spaces in the one- and three-story lodges have old Southwestern furnishings, such as shipping chests, tables, and desks dating from 1917–1920, when the hotel was built, along with tinwork from Mexico and original Native American and Western art. An additional lodge with 14 rooms was just completed. The dining room offers a bountiful luncheon buffet; Sunday's meal draws large crowds of nonguests from town. Jackets are required for dinner. ⌂ *Bishop's Lodge Rd., 87504, ☎ 505/983–6377, FAX 505/989–8739. 70 rooms, 18 suites. Restaurant, bar, pool, hot tub, 4 tennis courts, horseback riding, airport shuttle, shuttle to Santa Fe. AE, MC, V.*

$$$$ **Rancho Encantado.** This elegantly casual resort offers horseback riding, indoor and outdoor swimming, hiking, jogging, and seasonal skiing in the rolling, piñon-covered hills above the sprawling Rio Grande Valley. The guest rooms have Southwestern-style furniture, handmade and hand-painted by local craftspeople, in addition to fine Spanish and Western antiques from the 1850s and earlier. Some rooms have fireplaces and/or private patios; some are carpeted, while others have tile floors. The acclaimed dining room specializes in rack of lamb and fresh fish. ⌂ *Located on U.S. 285 near Tesuque, 8 mi north of Santa Fe (State Rd. 592), 87574, ☎ 505/982–3537 or 800/722–9339 (reservations), FAX 505/983–8269. 22 rooms, 36 villas. Restaurant, 2 pools, hot tub, 2 tennis courts. AE, DC, MC, V.*

Camping

With its wide, open spaces, good roads, and knock-'em-dead scenery, northern New Mexico draws camping enthusiasts and RV road warriors like teenagers to a rock concert. The Santa Fe National Forest is right in the city's backyard and includes the Dome Wilderness (5,200 acres in the volcanically formed Jemez Mountains) and the Pecos Wilderness (223,333 acres of high mountains, forests, and meadows at the southern end of the Rocky Mountain chain). Administrators of the Santa Fe National Forest have spent $600,000 to open a 14-site campground, 12 shaded picnic units, and a 45-vehicle parking area, and to improve trout habitats along a six-mile stretch of the Jemez River, and they spent an additional $450,000 to open a 22-unit campground and a separate 90-vehicle parking area along the Rio Chama. Public sites remain open from May through October. For specifics, call the **Santa Fe National Forest Office** (1220 S. St. Francis Dr., Box 1689, 87504, ☎ 505/988–6940). Some private campground operators provide literature at the **La Bajada Welcome Center** (La Bajada Hill, 13 mi southwest of Santa Fe on I–25, ☎ 505/471–5242). The following are a few of the main campground and recreational vehicle facilities:

Los Campos Recreational Vehicle Park. The only full-service RV park within the city limits, Los Campos even has a swimming pool. Tucked behind a car dealership on one side, it offers open vistas on the other: poplars and Russian olive trees, a dry riverbed, and mountains rising in the background. ⌂ *3574 Cerrillos Rd., 87501, ☎ 505/473–1949. 94 hookups plus assorted tent sites (back-ins and pull-throughs $22.75). Showers, bathrooms, LP gas, pool, picnic tables.*

Rancheros de Santa Fe Camping Park. Located on I–25N (at Exit 290 on the Las Vegas Hwy., 10½ mi from the Santa Fe Plaza), this beautiful camping park is set on a hill in the midst of a piñon forest. ⌂ *Old*

Las Vegas Hwy., 87505, ☎ 505/983–3482. RV and tent sites ($14.50 plus $2 per person for more than 2 people, children $1.50, children under 3 free), hookups ($17.50), pull-throughs ($19.50). Bathrooms, hot showers, LP gas available, grocery, ice, pool, laundry.

Santa Fe KOA. Set in the southwestern foothills of the Sangre de Cristo Mountains, this large campground is well treed with piñon, cedar, and juniper. ⊠ *Old Las Vegas Hwy. (Rte. 3), Box 95-A, 87501, ☎ 505/466–1419. RV sites ($15.50), full hookups ($19.95), tent sites ($14.95, plus $2 per person for more than 2 people), cabins ($25.95). Bathrooms, showers, grocery, recreation room (billiards, Ping-Pong, video games), laundry.*

Tesuque Pueblo RV Campground. This campground, operated by the Tesuque Pueblo, 10 miles north of Santa Fe (St. Francis exit off I–25), is on an open hill with a few cedar trees dotting the landscape; off to the west is the Tesuque River. ⊠ *Tesuque 87501, ☎ 505/455–2661. RV sites ($16), tent sites ($13 plus $2 per person for more than 2 people), 63 full hookups ($16). Toilets, showers, drinking water, security gate, laundry.*

THE ARTS AND NIGHTLIFE

Check the entertainment listings in Santa Fe's daily newspaper, the *New Mexican,* or the complimentary *Inside Santa Fe,* available at most hotels and shops, for special performances and events.

The Arts

Music

Artistically and visually the city's crowning glory, the famed **Santa Fe Opera** is housed in a strikingly modern structure, a spectacular, 1,173-seat, indoor-outdoor amphitheater carved into the natural curves of a hillside, 7 miles north of the city. It overlooks a vast panorama of mountains, mesas, and sky. Blend in some of the most acclaimed singers, directors, conductors, musicians, designers, and composers from Europe and the United States, and you begin to understand the excitement that explodes each July and August amid the tall pines of the Sangre de Cristo Mountains. Founded in 1957 by John Crosby, who remains its general director, the company offers a blend of seasoned classics, neglected masterpieces, and innovative premieres. For schedules and further information, call 505/986–5900, FAX 505/986–5999, or write the Santa Fe Opera, Box 2408, 87504.

Under the direction of maestro Stewart Robertson, the **Santa Fe Symphony** (☎ 505/983–3530, Box 9692, 87504) performs seven concerts each season (September through May) to sold-out audiences at Sweeney Center. Also from September through May, regular orchestral and chamber concerts are given by the professional **Santa Fe Pro Musica** (☎ 505/988–4640, Box 2091, 87504). Its Mozart Festival in February and its annual holiday presentation of Handel's *Messiah* have become local traditions. In addition, **Santa Fe Summerscene** (☎ 505/438–8834) offers a series of free concerts (rhythm and blues, light opera, jazz, Cajun, salsa, folk, and bluegrass), dance performances (modern, folk), lectures, and storytelling sessions staged on the Santa Fe Plaza each Tuesday and Thursday from mid-June through August at noon and 7 PM.

Theater

On Friday, Saturday, and Sunday nights during July and August, **Shakespeare in Santa Fe** (☎ 505/982–2910) presents free performances of the Bard's finest at the courtyard of the John Meem Library at St. John's College (Camino de Cruz Blanca, the next left past the cutoff for the International Folk Art Museum on the Old Santa Fe Trail). The music begins at 6, the show at 7. Picnic baskets are welcome, in the tradition of the Old Vic, but, please, no ripe tomatoes. There's also a concession stand. Seating is limited to 350, so it's best to get tickets in advance.

Staging at least four productions each October through May, the beautiful **Greer Garson Theater** (☎ 505/473–6511 or 505/473–6439, College of Santa Fe, St. Michael's Dr., 87501) is the scene of some of northern New Mexico's most spirited comedies, dramas, and musicals. (The actress after whom it is named is a principal contributor to the college's performing-arts program and a part-time resident of Santa Fe.)

Live theatrical performances are also available throughout the year at the **Santa Fe Actors' Theater** (☎ 505/982–8309), dedicated to fostering the growth of the performing arts in Santa Fe and staging the works of playwrights ranging from Euripides to Sam Shepard; the **Santa Fe Community Theater** (☎ 505/988–4262), with its adventurous mix of avant-garde, established drama, and musical comedy; and the **Santa Fe Performing Arts Company** (☎ 505/473–2240), offering a five-week intensive training program for students 8–19, culminating with a major production at the end of the summer session.

Nightlife

The lounges, hotels, and night spots of Santa Fe offer a wide variety of entertainment options, from lively dancing at a frontier saloon to quiet cocktails beside the flickering embers of a piñon fire. You can throw both your wallet and your hip out of joint at any of the following: **Badlands** (213 W. Alameda, ☎ 505/820–2985) offers a mix of live and DJ rock, disco, and alternative dance music. **Edge** (135 W. Palace Ave., ☎ 505/986–1700) offers mostly DJ-powered music but veers to live sounds on Monday and Tuesday. **El Farol** (808 Canyon Rd., ☎ 505/983–9912) is where the locals like to hang out and listen to live music nightly. **Rodeo Nites** (2911 Cerrillos Rd., ☎ 505/473–4138) attracts a country-Western crowd. **The Bull Ring** (414 Old Santa Fe Trail, ☎ 505/983–3328) presents a live rock band on weekends. Rock and roll is also the mainstay at **Shooters** (1196 Harrison Rd., ☎ 505/438–7777), which offers dance instructions on Wednesday night.

EXCURSION 1: PECOS NATIONAL HISTORIC PARK AND LAS VEGAS

A visit to the ancient New Mexican past and to a contemporary town that lives in the past are highlighted in this pleasant excursion to the region south of Santa Fe.

Exploring

Pecos National Historic Park

Pecos National Historic Park is the site of what was perhaps the greatest Native American pueblo. Located in a fertile valley and strategically situated between the buffalo hunters of the Great Plains and the farmers of the Rio Grande Valley, Pecos was an early trading center. It was the largest and easternmost pueblo reached by the Spanish conquistadores, who built two missions here in their zeal to convert the Indians to Catholicism, and it became a major landmark on the Santa Fe Trail.

The ruins of the missions and of the excavated and partially stabilized pueblo may be visited on a self-guided tour, which can be completed in about one hour. Containing more than 1,100 rooms and once the multidwelling home of as many as 2,500 Native Americans, the pueblo was four stories high in places. It was abandoned in 1838, and its 17 surviving occupants moved to the Jemez Pueblo. Today's visitors will find an exhibit and information center at the monument entranceway, where an introductory film is screened. *Pecos National Historic Park, Drawer 418, Pecos 87552, ☎ 505/757–6414.* ☛ *$4 per car, $2 per bus passenger.*

Las Vegas

The antithesis of its Nevada namesake, Las Vegas was once an oasis for stagecoach passengers on the Santa Fe Trail who were seeking refuge from Native Americans and outlaws. And it was once, in the late-19th century, one of the state's major centers of commerce. Now the seat of San Miguel County, Las Vegas lies where the Sangre de Cristo Mountains merge with the high plains of New Mexico. At an altitude of 6,470 feet, its climate is delightful—summer days averaging in the low to mid-80s, winter days rarely below freezing. If you like to go traipsing through the past, back to a time when men were slow on words but fast on the draw, you'll enjoy a day in this town.

Sheriff Pat Garrett, who killed Billy the Kid, lived in the building that now houses the **Las Vegas Chamber of Commerce** (727 Grand Ave.). Teddy Roosevelt held a Rough Riders reunion in the Castaneda Hotel—once a crown jewel in the Fred Harvey chain—which has clearly seen better days. And, fresh from his triumph at San Juan Hill, he announced his candidacy for the vice-presidency in the lobby of the Las Vegas Harvey House. **Theodore Roosevelt's Rough Riders Memorial and City Museum** houses Native American artifacts, documents pertaining to the city's history, and memorabilia from the Spanish-American War. *Chamber of Commerce Bldg., 727 Grand Ave., ☎ 505/425–8726.* ☛ *Free. ☉ Mon.–Sat. 9–4.*

Las Vegas's 15,000 inhabitants unabashedly live in the past. Today's Las Vegas is built around old churches, old salons, old hotels, old houses, and old shops (many selling memorabilia and antiques of the period). Las Vegas has nine historic districts and some interesting lodgings, including the elegant, historic 1882 Plaza Hotel on the Old Town Plaza (☎ 505/425–3591) and the Inn on the Santa Fe Trail, 2 miles away (☎ 505/425–6791).

TIME OUT In Old Town, on the Plaza, **Byron T's Lounge** (Plaza Hotel, 230 Old Town Plaza, ☎ 505/425–3591) serves up American favorites (steaks, chops, and chicken), as well as Southwestern cuisine, including steaming bowls of chili and hearty soups. Half a block away, **El Realto** (141 Bridge St., ☎ 505/454–0037) offers seafood and Mexican specialties in a historic 1890s building furnished with Victorian and early West antiques.

Pecos National Historic Park and Las Vegas Essentials

Arriving and Departing

Pecos National Historic Park is about 25 miles southeast of Santa Fe via I–25. Continuing another 35 miles on I–25 in the same direction brings you to Las Vegas.

Important Addresses and Numbers

The **visitor center** of Pecos National Historic Park (Drawer 418, Pecos 87552, ☎ 505/757–6414), at the monument entranceway, offers information about the area, including a free brochure, a 10-minute film, and a small exhibit.

Las Vegas Chamber of Commerce (727 Grand Ave., Box 148, Las Vegas 87701, ☎ 505/425–8631) provides brochures and other printed matter about the town and its colorful history.

EXCURSION 2: AROUND LOS ALAMOS

With the Jemez Mountains on one side and the Sangre de Cristo range on the other, Los Alamos's mesa-top location provides spectacular scenery and clean mountain air that's pleasantly cool in summer and ideal for outdoor pursuits in winter. There are plenty of fine accommodations, good food, convenient shopping, and several excellent museums. Hundreds of archaeological sites dot the Los Alamos area. Many of the best are located in Bandelier National Park—where cave and cliff dwellings, ancient ceremonial kivas, and other stone structures stretch out for more than a mile as the sheer walls of the Frijoles Canyon rise to a tree-fringed rim—and in Jemez State Monument. Nearby Valle Grande and Soda Dam provide insight into the geology of the region.

Los Alamos, birthplace of the atomic bomb, spreads over fingerlike mesas at an altitude of 7,300 feet. While research continues at the Los Alamos National Laboratory (in areas such as lasers, nuclear energy, superconductivity, and medicine), the community now emphasizes its link to the prehistoric past, promoting the more than 7,000 archaeological sites in the area (*see* Bandelier National Monument, *below*).

Exploring

The community of Los Alamos was founded in absolute secrecy in 1943 as a center of defense research. The disclosure of its existence two years later made international headlines. A visitor today might suspect the place was kept secret because it's so ugly, with its army barracks and middle-income tract houses.

Bradbury Science Museum is the Los Alamos National Laboratory's public showcase. It allows visitors to experiment with lasers, use advanced computers, and witness research in solar, geothermal, fission, and fusion energy. You can get a glimpse of World War II's historic Project Y, as well as some of today's advanced science and technology, at the Los Alamos National Laboratory. *Los Alamos National Laboratory, 15th St. and Central Ave.* ☎ *505/667–4444.* ☛ *Free.* ☉ *Tues.–Fri. 9–5, Sat.–Mon. 1–5.*

Housed in a national historic landmark, **Fuller Lodge Art Center** features works of northern New Mexican artists and traveling exhibits of both national and regional importance. The massive log structure, built in 1928, served as the dining and recreation hall for students of the Los Alamos Ranch School before World War II. *Fuller Lodge, 2132 Central Ave.,* ☎ *505/662–9331.* ☛ *Free.* ☉ *Mon.–Sat. 10–4, Sun. 1–4.*

Also located on the grounds of the former ranch school, **Los Alamos Historical Museum** displays artifacts of early Native American life, as well as photographs and documents of the community's history, before and after World War II. *Fuller Lodge, 2132 Central Ave.,* ☎ *505/ 662–4493.* ☛ *Free.* ☉ *Mon.–Sat. 10–4, Sun. 1–4.*

From Los Alamos, take Route 502 (Trinity Dr.) west and then Route 501 (West Jemez Rd.) south until you reach Route 4 at a "T" intersection. Turn left (east) and drive 6 miles to the entrance of **Bandelier National Monument.**

Seven centuries before the Declaration of Independence was signed, egalitarian, compact cities existed in the desert Southwest. Remnants of one of the most impressive of them, the **Anasazi Ruins,** can be seen at Frijoles Canyon in Bandelier National Monument. At the canyon's base, beside a gurgling stream, are the ruins of a three-story-high pueblo, crumbling walls representing an irregular circle of small stone rooms. Visitors using primitive wooden ladders, rungs lashed into place with leather strips, can squeeze through the doorway and get a feel for what it was like to live within the cell-like, 4' × 4' rooms. As the population expanded, additions were made to the original buildings. Natural caves in the soft volcanic tuff nearby were enlarged, and houses were built out from the cliffs.

For hundreds of years, the Anasazi people, early relatives of today's Rio Grande Pueblo Native Americans, thrived on wild game and crops of corn and beans. Suddenly, for reasons that are still undetermined, the settlements were abandoned. Climatic changes? A great drought? Crop depletion? No one knows for sure what caused the hasty retreat.

Visitors may ponder these and other mysteries while following a paved, self-guided trail through the site. Bandelier National Monument, named after author and ethnologist Adolph Bandelier (his novel, *The Delight Makers,* is set in Frijoles Canyon), contains 37,737 acres of wilderness, waterfalls, and wildlife, traversed by 60 miles of trails. A small museum in the visitor center focuses on Native American culture and artifacts from AD 1200 to modern Pueblo times. Some information about the area's wildlife is also displayed. *Bandelier National Monument, Los Alamos 87544,* ☎ *505/672–3861.* ☛ *$3 per individual; $5 per car.*

Take a left when you leave the national monument onto Route 4 west and follow the winding, scenic road up through the mountain forest to Jemez Springs; the drive should take about 45 minutes. Between Bandelier and Jemez, you'll pass magnificent **Valle Grande,** the world's largest volcanic caldera, only a fraction of which can be seen from the road. Once a bubbling inferno of lava, it's now a lush green high-mountain valley with herds of grazing cattle. The entire 50-mile Jemez range, formed by cataclysmic upheavals, is now filled with gentle streams, hiking trails, and campgrounds.

Jemez State Monument, on Route 4, 1 mile north of Jemez Springs, contains another impressive Native American ruin. Approximately 600 years ago, ancestors of the people of Jemez Pueblo built several villages in and around the narrow mountain valley. One of the villages was Guisewa, or "Place of the Boiling Waters," a name that refers to the numerous hot mineral springs in the area. The Spanish colonists discovered it in 1598 and built a mission that was abandoned in 1630. Jemez is a year-round vacation destination, with hiking, cross-country skiing, and camping in nearby U.S. Forest Service areas. ☎ *505/829–3530.* ☛ *$2.10 adults, children under 15 free.* ☉ *May–Sept. 15, daily 9–6; Sept. 16–Apr., daily 8:30–4:30.*

A mile north of Jemez State Monument, just off Route 4, is a geological wonder known as **Soda Dam.** The so-called dam was created over thousands of years, formed by travertine deposits from mineral precipitation as waters cooled the earth's surface. The site's strange, mushroom-shape exterior and the natural caves that have formed in and around it create the mystical aura that made it a sacred place to the ancient Native Americans. Numerous artifacts, prayer sticks, and rabbit clubs have been found here, as well as the mummy of a Native American baby wrapped in a blanket. In the warm summer months, the Jemez River at Soda Dam is a popular swimming spot.

Dining

$$ Ashley's. This handsome restaurant and lounge located in the Los Alamos Inn serves American and Southwest regional specialties for breakfast, lunch, and dinner; the Sunday brunch is a local favorite. The large dining room, decorated in modern Southwestern style, is filled with booths and rows of tables. ✕ *2201 Trinity Dr.,* ☎ *505/662–7211. Reservations advised for dinner. AE, D, DC, MC, V.*

$–$$ Hill Diner. This large, friendly restaurant used to be called the Good Eats Café; it still boasts the finest gourmet burgers in town ($5.99), along with chicken-fried steaks, chicken-fried chicken, homemade soups, and heaps of fresh vegetables. Hill Diner is a good buy, with generous portions and relatively painless prices. A steak and shrimp dinner tops the menu at $10.99. ✕ *1315 Trinity Dr.,* ☎ *505/662–9745. AE, D, DC, MC, V. Closed Sun.*

Lodging

$$ Hilltop House Hotel. Minutes from the Los Alamos National Laboratory, the three-story Hilltop House is geared toward traveling scientists and businesspeople as well as vacationers. Deluxe rooms have kitchenettes, and mini- and executive suites offer full kitchen facilities. All accommodations are furnished with modern Southwestern-style beds, desks, chairs, and tables. Guests get a complimentary cooked-to-order breakfast on weekdays, and the hotel's Trinity Sights restaurant offers good American and Southwestern cuisine in an elegant, white-tablecloth and flickering candlelight setting. ☎ *Trinity Dr. at Central Ave., Box 250, Los Alamos 87544,* ☎ *505/662–2441,* FAX *505/662–5913. 88 rooms. Restaurant, lounge, indoor pool, coin laundry, car rental. AE, DC, MC, V.*

$–$$ Los Alamos Inn. Rooms in this sprawling ground-level hotel feature modern Southwestern decor and provide sweeping canyon views. Its dining room, Ashley's (*see* Dining, *above*), does a Sunday brunch that's popular with locals as well as vacationing visitors. ☎ *2201 Trinity Dr., Los Alamos 87544,* ☎ *and fax 505/662–7211. 114 rooms. Restaurant, bar, pool. AE, DC, MC, V.*

$–$$ Orange Street Inn. Situated in a rather unremarkable 1948 wood-frame house in a quiet residential neighborhood, this B&B offers the usual amenities. Rooms are furnished in Southwest and contemporary styles; the public area has cable TV and a VCR; guests may use the kitchen facilities and the laundry. Breakfast is an ample Continental-plus. In the summer you get afternoon wine and hors d'oeuvres, and pay-as-you-go soft drinks and snacks are always available. ☎ *3496 Orange St., Los Alamos 87544,* ☎ *and fax 505/662–2651. 7 rooms, 3 with bath. D, MC, V.*

Los Alamos Essentials

Arriving and Departing

Los Alamos is 45 minutes north of Santa Fe, west of U.S. 84–285, on Route 502. **Gray Line of Santa Fe** (☎ 505/983–9491) runs a four-hour tour of Los Alamos and the nearby Bandelier Cliff Dwellings.

Los Alamos County Chamber of Commerce (Fuller Lodge, 2132 Central Ave., Box 460 VG, Los Alamos 87544, ☎ 505/662–8105) offers a free *Visitor Guide,* brochures, and other promotional material upon request.

EXCURSION 3: THE HIGH ROAD TO TAOS

If time isn't important, your drive from Santa Fe to Taos can be far more scenic and memorable if you detour a bit, skip the main highway (Route 68), and take the high road, a trip that takes you back in time. The drive through the rolling hillsides studded with orchards and tiny picturesque villages noted for weavers and wood-carvers, all set against the rugged alpine mountain backdrop, is stunning. A note of caution, however. As pretty as the high-road country is in winter, when the fields turn deep, soft white and the villages, fences, and naked trees are silhouetted like bold pen-and-ink drawings against the sky, the roads can be icy and treacherous. Check on weather conditions before attempting the drive, or stay with the more conventional Santa Fe–Taos route.

Out of Santa Fe past Tesuque on U.S. 84/285, turn northeast at Pojoaque on Route 503 (about 12 miles north of Santa Fe). You'll come first to Nambe Pueblo and the lovely Nambe Falls picnic area. Continue on through the village of Cundiyo to **Chimayo,** sometimes called "the Lourdes of the Southwest." Nestled into the rugged hillsides where gnarled piñons seem to grow from bare bedrock, Chimayo is a town famous for its weaving, regional food, and the **Santuario de Chimayo** (once you reach the village, you can't miss it; signs everywhere point the way). The Santuario is a small, frontier adobe church built on the site where, believers say, a mysterious light came from the ground on Good Friday night in 1810. Some men from the village investigated the phenomenon, trying to find its source. Pushing away the earth, they found a large wooden crucifix. Today the chapel sits above a sacred *pozito* (a small well), the mud from which is believed to have miraculous healing properties, as the dozens of abandoned crutches and braces left at the altar—along with many notes, letters, and photos left behind in thanksgiving and prayer—dramatically testify. The Santuario draws a steady stream of worshipers all year long, but during Holy Week as many as 50,000 people visit. The shrine is a National Historic Landmark, but unlike similar holy places, it remains free of hysteria, and the commercialism is limited to a small adobe shop nearby that sells brochures, books, and religious articles. ☎ *505/351-4889.* ☛ *Free.* ☉ *Daily 9–5:30.*

TIME OUT Off to the left of the Santuario is **Leona's de Chimayo** (☎ 505/351-4660), a fast-food–style burrito and chile stand with a few tables in front and a constant crowd of people waiting to be served. Leona Tiede's tiny establishment has become so successful that she recently opened a tortilla factory in Chimayo's Manzana Center that does a thriving mail-order business all over the country. Her specialty is flavored tortillas—everything from butterscotch to jalapeño.

Chimayo is also known for its colorful weaving. At the junction of Route 520 and Route 76, **Ortega's Weaving Shop** offers high-quality Rio Grande work by a family whose Spanish ancestors brought the craft to New Mexico in the 1600s. Adjacent to the weaving shop is the **Ga-**

leria Ortega, featuring traditional New Mexican Hispanic and contemporary Native American arts and crafts. The mailing address for both shops is Box 325, Chimayo 87522, ☏ 505/351–4215.

About 4 miles east–northeast of Chimayo, just off Route 76 (look for the clearly marked signs), is the town of **Cordova.** Hardly more than a mountain village with a small central plaza, Cordova is the center of the regional wood-carving industry. Craftspeople whose ancestors carved santos and other religious and ornamental figures for church altars and private chapels still fashion them here from local wood. There's not much to see in the village, which consists of a schoolhouse, post office, and a few stores, except for the **St. Anthony of Padua Chapel,** which is filled with beautiful handcrafted statues and retablos.

Cordova supports no fewer than 35 full-time and part-time carvers. Most of them are descendants of Jose Dolores Lopez, who in the 1920s created the unpainted "Cordova Style" of carving that the village is famous for. Most of the *santeros* (makers of religious images) in Cordova have signs outside their homes indicating that the statues are for sale. The pieces are expensive, ranging from several hundred dollars for small ones to several thousand for larger figures. Collectors snap them up at any price.

Continuing north on Route 76, about 1½ miles from Cordova, you'll come to **Truchas,** where Robert Redford shot the movie *The Milagro Beanfield War* (based on a novel written by Taos author John Nichols). This breathtakingly beautiful village is perched on the rim of a deep canyon with the towering Truchas Peaks, mountains high enough to be almost perpetually capped with snow, dominating the horizon. The tallest of the Truchas Peaks is 13,102 feet, the second-highest mountain in New Mexico. Truchas (Spanish for "trout") has a colorful array of shops and galleries, the best-known of which is **Cordova's Weaving Shop** (Box 425, Truchas 87579, ☏ 505/689–2437). Proprietor Harry Cordova, whose son played a part in the Redford movie, is quick to point out that his shop's back door was also in the film as the front door of the town's newspaper office.

Next is the village of Trampas, founded in 1751. Turn right on winding Route 75, then left on Route 518 to Talpa and on to Rancho de Taos, site of the famous San Francisco de Asis church. Turn right on Route 68 to Taos.

Dining

$$ **Rancho de Chimayo.** Where aficionados of northern New Mexican cook-
★   ing go to find the best of it. Set in a century-old adobe hacienda tucked into the mountains, with whitewashed walls and hand-stripped vigas, cozy dining rooms, and lush, terraced patios, the Rancho de Chimayo is still owned and operated by the family who originally occupied the house. They use locally grown products and recipes that are generations old. (On sale at the cash register and in bookstores everywhere is the *Rancho de Chimayo Cookbook.*) There's a roaring fireplace in the winter and summer dining alfresco. ✕ *Rte. 520,* ☏ *505/351–0444. Reservations required. AE, MC, V.*

Lodging

$$–$$$ **Casa Escondida.** This intimate Spanish Colonial–style home, set on 6 fertile acres 30 miles north of Santa Fe, offers sweeping views of the Sangre de Cristo Mountains. Owner Irenka Taurek speaks several languages; with Chopin on the CD player and the scent of fresh-baked strudel wafting through the rooms, the inn provides a quick fix for the many international travelers who visit. In the main house, French doors open onto a roof deck and patio. A large hot tub is hidden in a grove behind wild berry bushes. All rooms are decorated with Native American and other regional arts and crafts, as well as handpicked antiques. The Sun Room, large and bright with a private patio, has viga ceilings and a brick floor. Upstairs, the Kiva Room boasts a queen-size bed, a kiva-style fireplace, and an oversize tub. The separate one-bedroom Casita Escondida also has a kiva-style fireplace and viga ceilings, along with tile floors and a lovely sitting area. ⌕ *Box 142 (off Rte. 76 at Road Marker 0100), Chimayo 85722,* ☎ *505/351–4805. 5 rooms with bath, 1-bedroom house with full kitchen and microwave. MC, V.*

$$ Hacienda de Chimayo. Across the street from the Rancho de Chimayo restaurant (*see above*) and owned by the same people is the Hacienda de Chimayo, more of a country inn than a bed-and-breakfast (though a Continental breakfast is served). Its rooms are all decorated with turn-of-the-century antiques, and each has a private bath and a fireplace. The lovely mountain setting and the charming furnishings make this a delightful accommodation. ⌕ *Rte. 520, Chimayo, 87522,* ☎ *505/351–2222,* ᖴᴀX *505/351–4038. 6 rooms, 1 suite. AE, MC, V.*

$$ La Posada de Chimayo. This small country inn features two guest houses (one built in 1891) of typical northern New Mexico adobe, with brick floors, viga ceilings, and traditional kiva fireplaces. The cozy rooms have Mexican rugs, handwoven bedspreads, comfortable regional furniture, and some good books. Owner Sue Farrington, an expert on Mexico and Mexican cooking, offers a full gourmet breakfast in a variety of south-of-the-border flavors. ⌕ *279 Rio Arriba (Box 463), Chimayo 87522,* ☎ *and fax 505/351–4605. 2 rooms with bath, 2 suites. MC, V.*

SANTA FE ESSENTIALS

Arriving and Departing

By Bus
Greyhound/Trailways (858 St. Michaels Dr., ☎ 800/231-2222) offers comprehensive daily service to and from Santa Fe.

By Car
Although located in a secluded mountain setting, Santa Fe is easily accessible; it's a day's drive from several metropolitan areas from points north and south via I–25 or U.S. 84/285.

By Plane
See Air Travel in Important Contacts A to Z.

By Train
Amtrak's (☎ 800/872–7245) *Southwest Chief* serves Santa Fe via the village of Lamy, 17 miles from town, daily on routes from Chicago and Los Angeles. A connecting Amtrak shuttle-bus service (☎ 505/982-8829; reserve a day in advance) is available to and from town. The one-way fare is $14.

Getting Around

Downtown Santa Fe is easily maneuvered on foot, with the majority of its museums, galleries, shops, and restaurants located within a comfortable radius of the famous Santa Fe Plaza. But you'll need transportation for the city's outer reaches, including such attractions as the

International Folk Art Museum and the Museum of Indian Arts and Culture. Even a tour of the art galleries along Canyon Road can be a hilly 2-mile stretch. Fortunately, the city has inaugurated its first major bus system, **Santa Fe Trails.** So far, the line's 11 smart tan buses cover six major routes: Agua Fria, Cerrillos, West Alameda, Southside, Eastside, and Galisteo. For information, telephone 505/984–6730. Tell the operator where you are and where you want to go, and advice will be forthcoming. Fares are 50¢ adults; 25¢ students under 18 (with school ID), senior citizens, and people with disabilities. Buses run approximately every 30 minutes weekdays, every hour weekends. Service continues until 10 PM weekdays and until 8 PM Saturday. There is no bus service on Sunday.

By Car
Following is a list of car-rental services in Santa Fe: **Adopt-A-Car** (3570 Cerrillos Rd., ☎ 505/473–3189), **Enterprise** (1911 Fifth St., ☎ 505/473–3600), **Avis** (Garrett's Desert Inn, 311 Old Santa Fe Trail, ☎ 505/982–4361), **Budget** (1946 Cerrillos Rd., ☎ 505/984–8028), **Hertz** (100 Sandoval St., in the Hilton of Santa Fe lobby, ☎ 505/982–1844), **Snappy** (3012 Cielo Ct., ☎ 505/473–2277), and **Sears** (1946 Cerrillos Rd., ☎ 505/984–8038).

By Limo
If you're feeling flush or the occasion warrants it, you can call the **Limotion** (☎ 505/471–1265). Fares are $65 per hour, with a two-hour minimum.

By Taxi
Public transportation in town is monopolized by **Capital City Cab Company** (☎ 505/438–0000), the only taxi service in Santa Fe. The taxis aren't metered; you pay a flat fee determined by the distance you're going. There are no official cab stands in town; you must phone to arrange a ride—and if you're lucky, a cab will show up. Rates for various points within the city range from $4 to $7. You can pick up a 40% taxi discount coupon at the Santa Fe Public Library (*see* Visitor Information, *below*).

Guided Tours

General-Interest
Aboot About/Santa Fe Walks (309 W. Francisco St., 87504, ☎ 505/988–4455, ext. 108) is a 2½-hour walking tour through the "City Different" led by a long-time resident historian. It leaves the Eldorado Hotel daily at 9:30 and 1:30. The fee is $10.

Afoot in Santa Fe Walking Tours (211 Old Santa Fe Trail, 87501, ☎ 505/983–3701) offers a 2½-hour get-acquainted, close-up look at the city with the help of resident guides. It leaves from the Inn at Loretto daily at 9:30 and 1:30. The fee is $10.

Discover Santa Fe (508 W. Cordova, 87501, ☎ 505/982–4979) provides specially tailored tours and vacation itineraries for individuals and families, as well as for tour and business groups, including airport transfers, hotel arrangements, and guides.

Gray Line Tours of Santa Fe (1330 Hickox St., 87501, ☎ 505/983–9491) features a variety of daily tours leaving from and returning to the Santa Fe Bus Depot (hotel and motel pickups by advance arrangement). Taos, Bandelier Cliff Dwellings, Los Alamos, and the Santa Clara Pueblo are among the company's destinations. In winter, the availability of tours is subject to road and weather conditions.

Recursos (826 Camino de Monte Rey, 87505, ☎ 505/982–9301) runs historical, cultural, and nature tours.

Santa Fe Detours (La Fonda Hotel lobby, 100 E. San Francisco St., 87501, ☎ 505/983–6565 or 800/338–6877) includes tours by bus, river, and rail; city walks; trail rides; and ski packages.

Learning Experiences

Santa Fe School of Cooking (116 W. San Francisco St., ☎ 505/983–4511) offers both night and day classes that allow visitors to capture the flavor of regional New Mexican fare. Classes range from a two-hour basic demonstration exploring the rich flavors and history of northern New Mexican and Southwestern cuisine to more elaborate undertakings, with particular emphasis on exploring the wonders of special chile sauces. The results, good or bad, may be eaten. There are 11 classes, usually in the morning, which include recipes and lunch; fees range from $25 to $43. The school, located on the upper level of Plaza Mercado, only a block from the main Plaza, is headed by Susan Curtis, who suggests that reservations be made in advance.

Travel Photography Workshop is a week-long photography blitz headed by Lisl Dennis, a noted photographer whose work appears regularly in *Outdoor Photographer* and other major publications and who has authored a number of books on photographic techniques. A tuition of $1,250 includes workshop sessions; photo field trips to Chimayo, Rancho de Taos, and Taos; critiques; lodging; and some meals. Lisl Dennis and her husband, author Landt Dennis, also offer a number of international photography workshop tours. For inquiries, contact Travel Photography Workshop in Santa Fe (Box 2847, 87504, ☎ 505/982–4979, FAX 505/983–9489).

Special-Interest

Art Tours of Santa Fe (310 E. Marcy St., 87501, ☎ 505/988–3527 or 800/888–7679) specializes in five- to seven-day excursions to historic sites, museums, galleries, artists' studios, private homes, and collections; tours are accompanied by authorities on art, archaeology, and New Mexican history.

Atwell Fine Art (5741 Cerrillos Rd., 87505, ☎ 800/235–8412) arranges half- and full-day custom art and cultural tours for individuals and groups to area artists' studios, private collections, local foundries, historical sights, and more.

Ghost Tours of Santa Fe (142 Lincoln Ave., Suite 103, 87501, ☎ 505/984–2080) takes its often-apprehensive group of evening travelers on an eerie, 90-minute journey through the alleyways, hidden graveyards, and haunted buildings of downtown Santa Fe, where, it is believed, witches once roamed and the ghosts of brokenhearted women and gamblers still linger. Tours are by appointment only for groups of 10 or more, at $10 per person.

House and garden tours have always been popular in Santa Fe and are scheduled periodically, depending on the mood and disposition of property owners and guides. The **Santa Fe Architect Society** (☎ 505/983–7421) opens a different home each year to visitors, usually in August, a week after the Sunday of Indian Market Weekend. **Behind Adobe Walls and Garden Tours** (☎ 505/983–6565 or 800/338–6877) generally schedules tours during the last two Tuesdays of July and the first two Tuesdays of August. Contact the Santa Fe Convention and Visitors Bureau (*see* Important Addresses and Numbers, *below*) for late-breaking house-tour announcements.

Native American Tours (142 Lincoln Ave., Suite 103, Box 22658, 87502, ☎ 505/986–0804 or 800/578–3256, FAX 505/986–0812) is a newly formed group, completely operated by Native Americans, covering such sights and attractions as the ruins of Bandelier, pueblos, petroglyphs, Indian arts and crafts, storytelling sessions, Chaco Canyon, and Canyon de Chelly. Founder Elaina Ortiz of the San Juan Pueblo is the daughter of an archaeologist. Both standard and customized tours are available.

Rain Parrish (535 Cordova Rd., 87501, ☎ 505/984–8236), former curator of the Wheelwright Museum of the American Indian, is a Navajo art consultant and guide who customizes tours of Native American pueblos, art studios, and archaeological sites. Rates for two people are $125 for four hours; longer tours are available.

Rojo Tours (228 Old Santa Fe Trail, 87501, ☎ 505/983–8333) designs a variety of specialized trips—to view wildflowers, pueblo ruins and cliff dwellings, galleries and studios, Native American arts and crafts, and private homes—as well as adventure tours, such as ballooning, whitewater rafting, hiking, and horseback riding, all with hotel and motel pickups.

Southwest Adventure Group (142 Lincoln Ave., Suite 103, 85701, ☎ 505/984–2080 or 800/723–9815), along with adventure tours, also has a number of special-interest offerings, such as guided photo walks, studio tours of artists' galleries and workshops, craft tours, and cooking-tasting tours.

Opening and Closing Times

Store and commercial hours may vary from place to place and season to season (remaining open longer in summer than in winter), but the following is a general guide: banks, weekdays 9–3; museums, daily 10–5; stores, Monday–Saturday 10–6; post office, weekdays 8–5.

Important Addresses and Numbers

Emergencies
Fire, ambulance, police (☎ 911).

Medical Emergency Room. St. Vincent Hospital (455 St. Michaels Dr., ☎ 505/983–3361; 24-hour hospital hot line, ☎ 505/820–5242).

Medical Clinics. Lovelace Urgent Care (901 W. Alameda, ☎ 505/986–3656; 440 St. Michaels Dr., ☎ 505/986–3556).

Dental Clinics. Medical Dental Center (465 St. Michaels Dr., Suite 205, ☎ 505/983–8089) will see walk-in patients on an emergency basis.

Late-Night Pharmacies
Lee Pharmacies (**Medical Center Pharmacy,** 465 St. Michaels Dr., ☎ 505/983–4359, and **Fraser Pharmacy,** 501 Old Santa Fe Trail, ☎ 505/982–5524) and **Medicap Pharmacy** (2801 Rodeo Rd., ☎ 505/471–6177) all offer 24-hour emergency service. Pharmacies at **Lovelace Urgent Care** (*see above*) are open until 8 PM.

Visitor Information
The **Santa Fe Convention and Visitors Bureau** (201 W. Marcy St., Box 909, 87504, ☎ 505/984–6760 or 800/777–2489, FAX 505/984–6679) has Santa Fe visitor guides, brochures, maps, and calendar listings. The **Santa Fe Chamber of Commerce** (510 N. Guadalupe St., Suite L, De Vargas Center N, 87504, ☎ 505/983–7317) is geared more toward the traveling businessperson and individuals relocating to Santa Fe, pro-

viding assistance and general information. The **New Mexico Department of Tourism** (Lamy Bldg., 491 Old Santa Fe Trail, 87503, ☎ 505/827–7400 or 800/545–2070, ℻ 505/827–7402) offers a wealth of booklets and printed material on all areas of New Mexico. The **Santa Fe TeleGuide** (☎ 505/820–2020), a computerized library, carries ski and tourist information for Santa Fe. Except for the long-distance toll, the 24-hour service is free to anyone with a modem-equipped computer.

Another good source of information is the **Santa Fe Public Library,** whose main branch (145 Washington Ave., ☎ 505/984–6780) is just off the Plaza in a historic building that has served at various times as city hall and police and fire stations (the large windows in front are where the fire engines used to rush out). Here you'll find bus route maps, discount taxi coupons, and a wealth of local literature.

Weather Information, Time, and Temperature
☎ 505/473–2211.

3 Taos

MYSTERIOUS, SPIRITUAL, AND AGELESS, Taos is an enchanted town of soft lines and delineations that once viewed will remain etched in the mind forever. Romantic courtyards, stately elms and cottonwood trees, narrow streets, and the profusion of adobe all add to its timeless appeal.

Just as layers of history can be read on the rock walls of the 650-foot-deep Rio Grande Gorge, carved into the otherwise table-flat landscape just west of Taos, so, too, are layers of history revealed in the town itself. The tawny one- and two-story adobe buildings that line the two-centuries-old Plaza reveal the influence of Native American and Spanish settlers. Overhanging balconies supported by slender beams were added later by American pioneers who came west after the Mexican War of 1846. Some of the roads extending from the Plaza are still unpaved today; when it rains, they're not unlike the rutted streets of yesteryear. Taos is actually three towns in one.

The first is the community itself, which many compare to Santa Fe before all the glitz and glamour arrived. The second, 3 miles northwest of the commercial center, is the Taos Pueblo, the home of the Taos-Tiwa Indians, whose apartment-house–style pueblo dwelling is one of the oldest continually inhabited communities in the country. The third Taos, 4 miles south of town, is Ranchos de Taos, an adobe-housed farming and ranching community settled by the Spanish centuries ago. A bit scruffy these days, Ranchos de Taos is best known for the San Francisco de Asis Church, with its massive buttressed adobe walls and graceful towers. Generations of painters and photographers—including Georgia O'Keeffe, Paul Strand, and Ansel Adams—have been inspired by its beauty. Its graveyard, or *campo santo,* is one of the most photographed in the country, with a beauty surpassed only by the church's wealth of religious artifacts and paintings. The church is the focal point of St. Francis Plaza and its shops and antiques galleries.

These three distinct faces of Taos merge at the place where the sky meets the mountains, in a magnificent 7,000-foot-high plateau. With a combined population of under 5,000, Taos, the Taos Pueblo, and Ranchos de Taos offer a unique blend of history and culture. Add to this a remarkable literary and artistic heritage, names like D. H. Lawrence, Mabel Dodge Luhan, Frank Waters, Lady Dorothy Brett, and a score of other well-known artists and writers, and the town's appeal is evident.

Life at the Taos Pueblo predates Marco Polo's 13th-century travels in China and the arrival of the Spanish in America in 1540. The northernmost of the 19 Pueblo Native American settlements scattered throughout the Rio Grande Valley, Taos Pueblo is now the home of some 200 of the more than 2,000 members of the reservation (most of whom live in fully modern homes elsewhere on the Pueblo's 95,000 acres). It retains much of its rich cultural heritage, as exemplified by the soft, flowing lines of the dramatic architecture and in the seasonal dances performed on the open plaza. The Taos Pueblo has no electricity, no telephones (except at the visitor center), and no plumbing; water is carried by bucket from the crystal-clear stream that rushes through the Pueblo's center. A sign reading "Please, No Wading" warns thoughtless tourists away from this sacred river, the pueblo's only source of drinking water. Unlike many Native American tribes that were forced to relocate to government-designated reservations, the Taos Pueblo Native Americans have resided at the base of the 12,282-foot-high Taos Mountain for centuries, remaining a link between pre-Columbian inhabitants who originally lived in the Taos Valley and their descendants who reside there now.

In many ways Taos is still very much a frontier town. In the dry summer months, dust covers everything, giving the place a comfortably worn, weathered look.

EXPLORING

Taos is a year-round destination. Its fabulous ski slopes beckon in the wintertime, and summer brings a flood of tourists, both longtime regulars and newcomers who have heard or read about the enchanting little town in northern New Mexico and want to see it for themselves. Situated on a rolling mesa at the base of the rugged Sangre de Cristo Mountains, where lofty Wheeler Peak, the state's highest mountain, rises 13,161 feet, Taos has more than enough attractions to stand on its own and is worth more than a day trip out of Santa Fe. The town, with its intrinsically rustic charm, is a world-famous art and literary center, drawing both artists and collectors to the many museums and galleries surrounding the historical Plaza. Another of its primary appeals is that it is a tricultural community, with strong Native American, Spanish, and Anglo influences. A visit to the Taos Pueblo north of town is a good introduction to the centuries-old culture of the Pueblo Native Americans. Restored haciendas and the famous San Francisco de Asis Church to the south of the Plaza reflect Taos's strong Spanish heritage. There are also numerous sights of interest outside Taos proper, including the Enchanted Circle, the Rio Grande Gorge, and the haunts of well-known Taos personalities, such as D. H. Lawrence and Georgia O'Keeffe.

Tour 1: The Plaza Tour

Numbers in the margin correspond to points of interest on the Taos map.

★ ❶ The **Taos Plaza** bears only a hint of the grace, dignity, and stateliness of the Plaza in Santa Fe, although its history is drawn with the same pen. The first Europeans to appear in the Taos Valley were led by Captain Alvarado, who was exploring the area for the 1540 Coronado Expedition. Don Juan de Onate, the official colonizer of the province of Nuevo México, arrived in Taos in July 1598. An established mission, trading arrangements with the Taos Pueblos, and abundant water and timber attracted early Spanish settlers. Because of the many fires that plagued the city, none of the buildings on the Plaza predates the 19th century. At the center of the Plaza, the U.S. flag flies night and day, as authorized by a special act of Congress in recognition of Kit Carson's heroic stand, when he and his men stood guard over the flag to protect it from Confederate sympathizers during the Civil War. Next to a covered gazebo, donated by heiress and longtime Taos resident Mabel Dodge Luhan, is the Tiovivo, an antique carousel that delights children when it's put into operation during summer fiestas (only three days per year, in late July during the Fiestas de Santiago y Santa Ana; tickets are 50¢ per ride).

A walking tour of historic Taos begins logically enough on the Plaza, with its many smart shops and galleries. On the south side of the Plaza, don't miss the extraordinary **La Fonda de Taos Hotel,** with all its eccentric charm. For an ☛ fee of $3, you can enter the manager's office and view the erotic paintings done by D. H. Lawrence. The paintings were banned in London, as were many of the author's books. Hardly

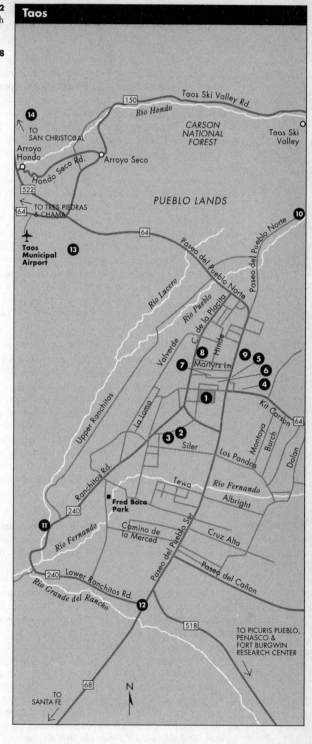

scandalous by today's standards, the paintings are certainly worth a visit for anyone with more than a passing interest in Lawrence and his work.

Next, take a detour off the southeast corner of the Plaza to Ledoux Street, where a number of historic adobe buildings can be explored.

★ ❷ Two blocks from the Plaza is the **Blumenschein Home,** a fully restored, original adobe masterpiece. Ernest L. Blumenschein was the cofounder of the Taos Society of Artists, an art colony that flourished from 1912 to 1927. His paintings and those of his talented wife, Mary Green Blumenschein, and their daughter, Helen, are on display inside, along with works of other Taos artists. Blending the sophistication of European charm with the beauty of classic adobe, the house is furnished with handmade Taos furniture, as well as with European antiques and artifacts gathered by the artist and his family from all over the world. The house creates a colorful picture of the life of the early Taos Society of Artists. *222 Ledoux St., ☎ 505/758–0505.* ☞ *$4 adults, $2.50 children 6–15, children under 6 free, $3 senior citizens.* ☉ *Daily 9–5. Note: The Blumenschein Home is part of the Kit Carson Historic Museums of Taos, a private nonprofit organization that also includes the Kit Carson Home and the Martinez Hacienda (see below). Combined tickets for 2 of the sites is $6 adults, $4 children 6–15, children under 6 free, $5 senior citizens; for all 3, $8 adults, $5 children 6–15, children under 6 free, $6 senior citizens. Special family rates are also available.*

❸ Farther along Ledoux Street is the **Harwood Foundation Library and Museum,** the former home of Burt C. Harwood, a member of the original Taos art colony. On display are more than 100 paintings by early and modern Taos artists, plus rare santos (saints) carvings done by early Spanish wood-carvers—almost all from the private collection of Taos art patron Mabel Dodge Luhan. This is where the Museum of Taos Art exhibits and researches the art, artists, and history of Taos County. It's also the site of the Taos Public Library, which houses an excellent collection of volumes on the Southwest, Western and Native American art, and volumes by and about D. H. Lawrence. *238 Ledoux St., ☎ 505/758–3063 (library), 505/758–9826 (museum).* ☞ *$2. Library open Tues.–Thurs. 10–8, Fri. and Sat. 10–5, closed Sun. and Mon.; museum open weekdays 10–5, Sat. 10–4.*

TIME OUT   If you're ready for a break, stop off at **Marciano's Ristorante** (112 Placitas St., ☎ 505/751–0805) for a light repast in a courtyard. If you just want to rest your feet, head for the peaceful garden behind the Harwood Museum.

If you head east from the Plaza across the intersection of Paseo del Pueblo Norte and Paseo del Pueblo Sur, you'll find more fine shops, some of
❹ the best in town. Here, too, is the **Kit Carson Home and Museum,** once home of the famous mountain man and scout who left an indelible mark on the history of Taos. Carson purchased the 12-room adobe home in 1843 as a wedding gift for his young bride, Josefa Jaramillo, the beautiful daughter of a powerful and politically influential Mexican family. Josefa was 14 when Carson, dashing in dun-colored buckskins with long fringes and colorful beadwork, began courting her; he was 32 and already twice married to Native American maidens. The couple lived in the house for more than 25 years. Three of the rooms are furnished as they were when the Carson family lived here, offering a glimpse of Taos's rich and colorful history. The rest of the museum is devoted to gun and mountain-man exhibits, as well as to Native American, Span-

ish, and early Taos antiques, artifacts, and manuscripts. In the patio outside, the Carson House Shop has four rooms filled with gifts and collectibles, Native American art, folk art, jewelry, kachinas, and hand-crafted furniture. *Kit Carson Rd.,* ☎ *505/758–4741.* ☛ *$4 adults, $2.50 children, $3 senior citizens; family and combination tickets are available (see Blumenschein Home, above).* ☉ *Early Oct.–mid-June, daily 9–5; mid-June–Sept., daily 8–6.*

Back at the intersection of Paseo del Pueblo Norte and Paseo del Pueblo Sur, turn right and walk to the **Taos Inn,** a historical landmark and the site of the original town well, now a fountain in the hotel lobby.

5 Next door to the Taos Inn is the **Stables Art Center,** the visual arts gallery of the Taos Art Association. The association purchased the handsome adobe building, formerly a private home, in 1952. It was in the stables in back of the house that the association first began exhibiting the work of members and of invited nonmember artists from all over northern New Mexico—thus the gallery's name. The main building was once the home of Arthur Manby, a recluse who gained considerable notoriety by securing himself behind barred doors and snarling guard dogs for most of his 30 years in Taos. The Stables presents changing exhibits almost monthly; all the artwork is for sale. *133 Paseo del Pueblo Norte, Taos 87571,* ☎ *505/758–2036.* ☛ *Free.* ☉ *Mon.–Sat. 10–5, Sun. noon–5.*

Leaving the Stables, cross Paseo del Pueblo Norte and you'll be on Bent Street, one of the town's major shopping venues, lined with at-

6 tractive galleries and boutiques. The **John Dunn House** (124A Bent St., no ☎) was the onetime homestead of a notorious Taos gambler and entrepreneur, who founded the town's first transportation company. It contains a number of interesting shops, including G. Robinson Old Prints and Maps and Moby Dickens, a popular and eclectic bookstore and prime gathering spot for the local literati (*see* Shopping, *below*).

7 Also on this small street is the **Governor Bent Museum.** In 1846, when New Mexico became a United States territory during the Mexican War, Charles Bent, an early trader, trapper, and mountain man, was appointed governor. A year later he was killed in his house by an angry mob protesting New Mexico's annexation by the United States. The well-kept adobe building where Bent lived is filled with his family's pos-sessions, furniture, and Western Americana. Governor Bent was married to Maria Ignacia, older sister of Kit Carson's wife, Josefa Jaramillo. *117A Bent St.,* ☎ *505/758–2376.* ☛ *$1 adults, 50¢ chil-dren.* ☉ *Daily 10–5.*

8 Two blocks north of Bent Street on the corner of Armory Street and Placitas Road is the Taos Volunteer Fire Department, home of the **Fire-house Collection.** More than 100 paintings by Taos artists, including some of the town's most famous—Joseph Sharp, Ernest Blumenschein, Bert Phillips, and others—are on display. The paintings are exhibited in the Fire Department's meeting hall, adjoining the station house, where five fire engines are maintained at the ready. An antique fire engine is housed here as well. *323 Placitas Rd., Box 4591, Taos 87571,* ☎ *505/ 758–3386.* ☛ *Free.* ☉ *Weekdays 9–4.*

If you head east from the Firehouse back to Paseo del Pueblo Norte, and turn left, you'll come to the wooded, 20-acre **Kit Carson Park,** two blocks farther. Kit Carson's grave is located here, marked with a *cerquita,* a spiked wrought-iron rectangular fence, traditionally used to outline and protect grave sites. Mabel Dodge Luhan, the art patron and longtime guiding light of the Taos social scene, is also buried in the same small graveyard.

❾ A short walk north is the **Fechin Institute,** housed in a traditional Southwestern adobe house with a Russian-style interior. Filled with extraordinary hand-carved doors, windows, and gates, the home was built between 1927 and 1933 by artist Nicolai Fechin, a Russian émigré who arrived in Taos one year earlier. Fechin designed the extraordinary house, with its exotic hand-carved architectural motifs and Russian furnishings, to showcase his daringly colorful portraits and landscapes. Listed in the National Register of Historic Places, the Fechin Institute hosts annual exhibits and special workshops devoted to the artist's unique approach to learning, teaching, and creativity. *227 Paseo del Pueblo Norte,* ☎ *505/758–1710.* ☛ *$3.* ⊘ *Memorial Day weekend–Oct., Wed.–Sun. 1–5:30, or by appointment.*

Tour 2: The Taos Pueblo

★ ❿ Three miles north of town, driving on Paseo del Pueblo Norte, you'll come to Taos's number-one tourist attraction, the **Taos Pueblo,** selected in 1993 as a World Heritage Site (the United Nations' world-scale equivalent of a National Historic Landmark). For nearly 1,000 years, the Taos-Tiwa Native Americans have lived at or near the present pueblo site. The northernmost of New Mexico's 19 Native American pueblos, it is the largest existing multistory pueblo structure in the United States. Continuously inhabited for centuries, it holds within its mud-and-straw adobe walls—frequently several feet thick—a way of life little changed by the passage of time. Two separate buildings rise in earthy magnificence, containing many individual homes built side by side and in layers, with common walls but no connecting doorways. (Because there were neither doors nor windows, access to the dwellings was gained only from the top, via ladders that were retrieved after entering.) Small buildings and corrals are scattered about. The two main buildings, Hlauuma (north house) and Hlaukwima (south house), separated by a creek, are believed to be of a similar age, most likely constructed between AD 1000 and 1450.

The pueblo today appears much as it did when the first Spanish explorers arrived in New Mexico in 1540: Seeing the golden shades of its smooth adobe walls, the conquistadores thought they had discovered one of the fabled Seven Cities of Gold. The outside surfaces are continuously maintained by replastering with thin layers of mud, and the interior walls are frequently coated with thin washes of white earth to keep them clean and bright. The roofs of each of the five stories are supported by large timbers—vigas—hauled down from the mountain forests. Rotted vigas are replaced as needed. Smaller pieces of wood—pine or aspen *latillas*—are placed side by side between the vigas; the entire roof is then packed with dirt.

Tribal ritual allows no electricity or running water within the pueblo, where approximately 200 Taos Native Americans live full-time. Some 2,000 others live in conventional homes on the pueblo's land, which extends over 95,000 acres, television antennas poking out from above the roofs. Inside the pueblo, the traditional Native American way of life has endured even after 400 years of Spanish and Anglo presence. The crystal-clear waters of the Rio Pueblo de Taos, originating high above in the mountains at the sacred Blue Lake, still serve as the primary source of drinking water and irrigation. Bread is still baked in outdoor domed ovens, a system unchanged for centuries. Artisans of the Taos Pueblo produce handcrafted wares by using techniques that have been passed down through the generations; the mica-flecked pottery and silver jewelry made in the pueblo are sold at many of the individually owned curio shops within the compound. Great hunters, the Taos Native Americans are also renowned for their work with animal skins, creating excellent moccasins, boots, and drums.

The pueblo dwellers are about 90% Catholic, but they practice their religion alongside ancient Native American religious rites that remain an important part of life in the Taos Pueblo. This combination derives from a concession often made by the Spanish missionaries, who were anxious to convert the "pagan savages." A costumed Native American Deer dancer in full regalia often comes thumping down the church aisle during or immediately after the celebration of the Catholic mass. The striking adobe Church of San Geronimo (St. Jerome, the patron saint of the Taos Pueblo) on the pueblo grounds was completed in 1850 to replace a church that was destroyed by the U.S. Army in 1847 during the Mexican War. With its graceful flowing lines, arched portal, and twin bell towers, the church is a popular subject of photographers and artists (but, please, no photographs inside).

Although many religious activities are restricted to tribal members, the public is invited to witness certain ceremonial dances. These include the following: January 1, Turtle Dance; January 6, Buffalo or Deer Dance; May 3, Feast of Santa Cruz–Foot Race and Corn Dance; June 13, Feast of San Antonio–Corn Dance; June 24, Feast of San Juan–Corn Dance; July (2nd weekend), Taos Pueblo Powwow; July 25 and 26, Feast of Santa Ana and Santiago–Corn Dance; September 29–30, Feast of San Geronimo–Sunset Dance; Christmas Eve, Procession; Christmas Day, Deer Dance or *Matachines*. Although there is no charge for general ☛ to the Taos Pueblo, certain rules must be observed. These include respecting the "restricted area" signs that protect the privacy of pueblo residents and sites of native religious practices; not entering private homes or opening any doors not clearly labeled as curio shops; not photographing tribal members without asking permission; not entering the cemetery grounds; and not wading in the Rio Pueblo de Taos, the community's sole source of drinking water. *Taos Pueblo, Box 1846, Taos 87571, ☎ 505/758–9593. Tourist fees: $5 per vehicle (for parking), $10 for tour buses (plus $1 per passenger, 50¢ for students); $5 for a still-camera permit, $10 for a movie-camera permit, $10 for a video camera permit, artist's sketching fee $15, and artist's painting fee $35. ☻ Apr.–Nov., daily 8–5:30; Dec.–Mar., daily 8:30–4:30. Closed during funerals or religious ceremonies and often for a one-month "quiet time" in late winter or early spring; check before planning a visit at this time.*

TIME OUT When you're ready for a quick snack, look for the "Fry Bread" signs on individual dwellings. You can enter the kitchen and enjoy fresh fry bread—bread dough that is flattened and deep-fried until it's puffy and golden brown and then topped with honey or powdered sugar—and a cup of coffee while watching the Native American women cook.

Tour 3: The Spanish Colonial Heritage

In Taos, one quickly steps into the town's rich Spanish past with a visit to the outstanding Martinez Hacienda Museum and the cherished, oft-photographed and -painted Ranchos de Taos.

★ ⓫ Two miles south of Taos Plaza, on Ranchitos Road (Route 240), is **La Hacienda de Don Antonio Severino Martinez,** one of the only fully restored Spanish Colonial adobe haciendas open to the public in New Mexico. The fortlike building, on the banks of the Rio Pueblo, served as the Martinez family's home and a community refuge against Comanche and Apache raids. With massive adobe walls and no exterior windows, the hacienda has 21 rooms surrounding two courtyards. Magnificently restored period rooms illustrate the lifestyle of the Spanish Colonial era, when the only supplies to Taos came by oxcart on the Camino Real over the "Journey of Death." Built in progressive additions between 1804 and 1827 by Severino Martinez, the house gives testimony to the pure, rich Spanish heritage that survived the rugged colonial conditions and remains to this day. Padre Antonio José Martinez, Severino's son, became a famous leader of his people and founder of *El Crepúsculo* (The Dawn), possibly the first newspaper published west of the Mississippi.

Along with the room exhibits, the fortresslike house is also used for changing exhibits on Spanish culture and history and photography shows. In addition, there's a working blacksmith's shop, and other living-history demonstrations. On the last weekend in September, the hacienda hosts the annual Old Taos Trade Fair, which reenacts the fall trading fairs of the 1820s, when Plains Native Americans and trappers came to trade with Spanish and Pueblo Native Americans in Taos. The two-day event includes traditional crafts demonstrations, native foods, entertainment, traditional-style caravans, and music. *Ranchitos Rd. (Rte. 240),* ☎ *505/758–1000.* ☛ *$4 adults, $2.50 children and senior citizens; family and combination tickets are available (see Blumenschein Home, above).* ☉ *Daily 9–5.*

★ ⓲ Four miles east of the Martinez Hacienda on Ranchitos Road (Route 240) is **Ranchos de Taos** (on Route 68), an adobe-house Spanish Colonial ranching and farming community. An early home of Taos Native Americans, it was settled by Spaniards in 1716. The centerpiece of Ranchos de Taos is the monumental adobe masterpiece, the **San Francisco de Asis Church,** first built in the 18th century as a spiritual and physical refuge from raiding Apaches, Utes, and Comanches. In a state of deterioration, the church was rebuilt by community volunteers in 1979, using traditional adobe bricks. It's a spectacular example of adobe Mission architecture, and the shapes and shadows of the walls and supporting bulwarks have inspired generations of painters and photographers, including Georgia O'Keeffe, Paul Strand, and Ansel Adams. If you've got a camera handy and want to try it yourself, late afternoon offers the best exposure of the heavily buttressed rear of the church, while morning is best for the front. Bells in the church's twin belfries call faithful Taoseños to services on Sunday and holidays, when worshipers fill the church to overflowing.

In the parish hall nearby, a 15-minute video presentation every half hour explains the history and restoration of the church, and the famous mystery painting *Shadow of the Cross* may be seen throughout the day. In the evening, the shadow of a cross, which isn't there in daylight, appears over Christ's shoulder. Scientific studies made on the canvas and the paint pigments cannot explain the phenomenon. *Ranchos de Taos,* ☎ *505/758–2754.* ☛ *$1.* ☉ *Mon.–Sat. 9–4, Sun. and holy days during church services: Sun. Mass 7 (in Spanish), 9, and 11:30 AM.*

Many of the old adobe homes around Ranchos Plaza now house shops, restaurants, and galleries. The **Hacienda de San Francisco Galeria** (4 St. Francis Plaza, ☎ 505/758–0477), with its collection of fine Spanish Colonial antiques and sculptured bronzes by such masters as Mexico's Francisco Zúñiga.

Tour 4: Artistic and Literary Taos

★ ⑬ If you have time to visit only one museum in Taos, make it the **Millicent Rogers Museum,** 4 miles northwest of the Plaza, just off Route 522 (turn left at the blinking light and follow the signs to the museum). Founded in 1953, it contains more than 5,000 pieces of Native American and Hispanic art, the core of Standard Oil heiress Millicent Rogers's private lifetime collection. The granddaughter of Henry Huttleston Rogers, one of John D. Rockefeller's partners in the Standard Oil Company and founder of Anaconda Copper and U.S. Steel, she visited New Mexico in 1947 and, like many others, fell in love with the country and its people. A woman of keen intellect and artistic talent, she became intently interested in the area's culture and art. She gathered baskets, blankets, rugs, jewelry, kachina dolls, santos, carvings, and paintings—a collection that remains unsurpassed to this day. A recent acquisition of major importance is the pottery and ceramics of Maria Martinez and members of the famous San Ildefonso family of potters. The museum's Hispanic collection, including recently acquired rare pieces of religious and secular artifacts, is equally impressive. Missing, of course, is the presence of Millicent Rogers herself, a striking beauty with a flair for fashion and a love of costumes. A debutante in the heyday of the Jazz Age, she was tall, with a perfectly proportioned figure, a born "clotheshorse" with long, painted nails, wide-set eyes, and alabaster skin. Married three times, she numbered among her suitors Clark Gable, Serge Obolensky, Ian Fleming, and James Forrestal. Many of her costumes and jewelry designs are included in the museum's holdings. The Millicent Rogers Museum offers permanent and changing exhibits, guided tours on request, and a gift shop, as well as educational activities, such as field trips, lectures, films, workshops, and demonstrations. *Box A, Taos 87571,* ☎ *505/758–2462,* FAX *505/758–2462.* ☛ *$4 adults, $3 senior citizens and students, $2 children 6–16, $8 family groups.* ☉ *Daily 9–5, closed holidays and Mon., Nov.–Mar.*

★ ⑭ Leaving the Millicent Rogers Museum, follow Route 522 north for 10 miles, and you'll reach the **D. H. Lawrence Ranch** and the **D. H. Lawrence Shrine.** The noted British author lived in Taos only briefly, about 22 months over a three-year period between 1922 and 1925. He and his wife, Frieda, arrived in Taos at the behest of Mabel Dodge Luhan, who collected famous writers and artists the way some people collect butterflies. Luhan provided them with a place to live, Kiowa Ranch, on 160 acres in the mountains north of Taos. Rustic and remote, it's now known as the D. H. Lawrence Ranch, although Lawrence never actually owned it. Nearby is the smaller cabin where Dorothy Brett, the tag-along companion of the Lawrences, stayed while traveling with the couple. The houses, now owned by the University of New Mexico, are not open to the public. The D. H. Lawrence Shrine, nearby at the end of a step walk on wooded Lobo Mountain, can be visited, however. A small white shedlike structure, it is simple and unimposing. The writer fell ill while visiting France and died in a sanatorium there in 1930. Five years later, his wife, subsequently married in Italy to Angelo Ravagli, had Lawrence's body disinterred, cremated, and brought back to Taos. Frieda Lawrence is buried, as was her wish, in front of the shrine. *Rte. 522, San Cristobal 87564,* ☎ *505/776–2245.* ☛ *Free. The D. H. Lawrence Shrine is open daily.*

Tour 5: The Enchanted Circle

Numbers in the margin correspond to points of interest on the Enchanted Circle map.

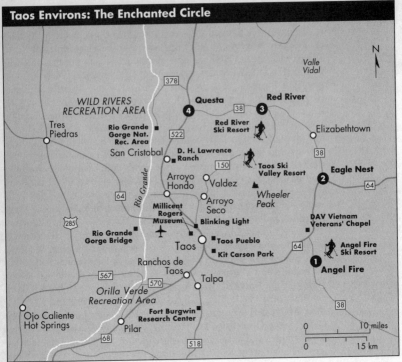

Taos Environs: The Enchanted Circle

No visit to northern New Mexico is complete without experiencing the 84-mile day trip through the Enchanted Circle, a breathtaking panorama of deep canyons, passes, alpine valleys, and towering mountains of the verdant Carson National Forest. It's a journey that in many ways will take you into another century. This tour can easily be combined with Tour 4, *above*. Both the D. H. Lawrence Ranch and the Millicent Rogers Museum are on the loop.

Traveling east from Taos along U.S. 64, you'll soon be winding your way through Taos Canyon, climbing toward 9,000-foot-high Palo Flechado Pass (Pass of the Arrow). On the opposite side of the pass are stunning vistas—Moreno Valley, and the towns of Angel Fire and

❶ Eagle Nest. Now known primarily as a ski resort, **Angel Fire** was for hundreds of years little more than a long, empty valley, the fall meeting grounds of the Ute Indians. The name derives from the glow that covers the mountain in the late autumn and early winter. Here you'll find the stunning Vietnam Veterans Memorial, a 50-foot-high gull wing-shape monument built in 1971 by D. Victor Westphall, whose son David was killed in that war. The memorial's textured surface captures the constantly changing sunlight of the New Mexican mountains, vividly changing their colors throughout the daylight hours as the sun moves across the sky. It's on the north side of U.S. 64, 8½ miles southwest of Eagle Nest.

❷ At **Eagle Nest,** a tiny village surrounded by thousands of acres of national forest, you'll get on to U.S. 38 and head over Bobcat Pass (just

❸ under 10,000 ft elevation) to **Red River,** another major ski resort, with 33 trails and a bustling little downtown community filled with shops and sportswear boutiques. Red River came into being as a miners' boom town during the last century, taking its name from the river whose mineral content gave it a rich, rosy color. When the gold petered out, Red River died, only to be rediscovered in the 1920s by migrants who were escaping the dust bowl. Situated at 8,750 feet above sea level at the base of Wheeler Peak (New Mexico's tallest mountain), Red River is the highest, if not the loftiest, town in the state. Much of the Old West flavor remains in Red River, with Main Street shoot-outs, a genuine melodrama, and plenty of square dancing and two-stepping. In fact, because of its many country dances and festivals, Red River is affectionately called "The New Mexico Home of the Texas Two-Step."

❹ From Red River, the Enchanted Circle heads west to **Questa** ("hill" in Spanish), a town settled in the 1840s with considerable difficulty because of Native American raids. In 1870, it was officially established—as were many Western towns—with the opening of its first post office; to date, Questa has had only six postmasters. Don't miss St. Anthony's Church, built of adobe with 5-foot-thick walls and viga ceilings. The Red River Trout Hatchery (*see* Off the Beaten Track, *below*) is also worth a visit. Known as the "Heart of the Sangre de Cristo Mountains," Questa is a small, quiet village, nestled between Taos and the Red River amid some of the most beautiful mountain country in New Mexico. Turning left at downtown Questa's main intersection, you're on your way back to Taos on Route 522, passing through the picturesque communities of San Cristobal and Arroyo Hondo. It's on this last stretch that you can stop and visit the D. H. Lawrence Ranch or the Millicent Rogers Museum, both off Route 522.

TIME OUT In Red River, stop by the **Sundance** (High St., ☎ 505/754–2971) for Mexican food or **Texas Red's Steakhouse** (Main St., ☎ 505/754–2964) for steaks, chops, burgers, or chicken. If you want to stay overnight, try the **Red River Lodge** (Box 818, Red River 87558, ☎ 505/754–6280), which has 26 moderately priced rooms, hot tubs in the winter, and picnic tables in the summer.

What to See and Do with Children

Anyone who has children and goes to Taos without them is bound to regret it. Almost everywhere they turn, parents will find something they wish their children were there to see. The **Taos Pueblo** (*see* Tour 2, *above*) offers insights into a way of life that has remained virtually unchanged over the centuries. The **Kit Carson Home and Museum** and **Kit Carson Park** (*see* Tour 1, *above*), where Carson's grave is located, are bound to be spellbinders. In Kit Carson Park there's a playground for youngsters, picnic tables and grills, an ice-skating rink in winter, and bicycle and walking paths. **Fred Baca Park,** 2 miles west, also has tennis courts, a playground, a baseball field, and basketball hoops. The **Red River Trout Hatchery** in Questa (*see* Off the Beaten Track, *below*) will fascinate the younger set. And if your child is one that has to be bribed, bound, and chained before being dragged screaming and kicking into an art gallery, you may find the **Firehouse Collection** (*see* Tour 1, *above*) a painless introduction. After all, there are all those beautiful fire engines to ogle.

Off the Beaten Track

Fort Burgwin Research Center, 10 miles southeast of Taos on Route 518, is a restored fort that once housed the First Dragoons of the United States Cavalry (1852–60). Their function was to protect the citizens of Taos and the travelers coming from and going to Santa Fe, the territorial capital, from renegade Native Americans. Operated by the

Southern Methodist University of Dallas, Texas, the center now conducts extension courses for its university students, particularly in theater, music, and the arts. Summer concerts, plays, and lectures are presented to the public free of charge. *Box 300, Ranchos de Taos 87557,* ☎ *505/758–8322.* ☉ *Daily 9–5.*

Of **Ghost Ranch/Abiquiu,** Georgia O'Keeffe wrote, "When I first saw the Abiquiu house it was a ruin with an adobe wall around the garden broken in a couple of places by fallen trees. As I climbed and walked about in the ruin I found a patio with a very pretty well house and a bucket to draw up water. It was a good-sized patio with a long wall with a door on one side. That wall with a door in it was something I had to have. It took me 10 years to get it—three more years to fix the house up so I could live in it—and after that the wall with the door was painted many times." After a long history of regular visits to New Mexico and the Southwest, the artist moved permanently to Abiquiu, New Mexico, in 1949. The rocky desert vistas between Ghost Ranch, where O'Keeffe purchased her first home in New Mexico, and Abiquiu, 20 miles to the south, where she had her second home, are all that remain open to public scrutiny; both homes are in private hands.

Before her death in 1986 at the age of 98, O'Keeffe added special provisions in her will to ensure that the houses would never be turned into public monuments, in order to protect the land she loved so much from an onslaught of tourists. Thus a pilgrimage to O'Keeffe country, a good 60 miles east of Taos (Route 68 south of Espanola, U.S. 84 to Abiquiu; look for a dirt road off 84 marked with a cattle-skull highway sign), is purely what the visitor makes of it. Ghost Ranch was originally called *El Rancho de los Brujos,* the Ranch of the Witches. A Spanish rancher was murdered in the sprawling adobe homestead, and the villagers believed that the voices of the female spirits who roamed there could be heard howling through the nearby canyons. Anglos shortened the name to Ghost Ranch. Possessed or not, the area remains hauntingly beautiful.

In Questa, about 20 miles north of Taos (at the end of Route 515), the **Red River Trout Hatchery** offers a fascinating look at how the king of freshwater fish is hatched, reared, stocked, and controlled. There's a visitor center with displays and exhibits, a show pond, and a machine that dispenses fish food, so you can feed the trout yourself. Self-guided tours last anywhere from 20 to 90 minutes, depending on how enraptured visitors become. Guided tours are available for groups upon request. Parking space and a picnic area are on the grounds. *Box 410, Questa 87556,* ☎ *505/586–0222.* ☉ *Daily 8–5.*

Rio Grande Gorge Bridge (west of Taos on U.S. 64) is the second highest expansion bridge in the country. Viewing the dramatic gorge, with the Rio Grande River 650 feet below, is a breathtaking experience. Hold on to your camera and eyeglasses when looking down, and watch out for low-flying planes. The Taos Municipal Airport is close by, and daredevil private pilots have been known to challenge one another to fly *under* the bridge.

Camposantos means "holy fields," as the Spanish-speaking New Mexicans call their parish and community graveyards. More than 400 such graveyards can be found in New Mexico, usually next to a church or off on a country road. Numerous crosses, some made of wood, others of iron or even welded pipes, dot the lonely grave sites. Anonymous graves are marked with the same devotional images. Paper flowers, hand-carved angels, wrought-iron rectangular fences (*cerquitas*) used for defining and protecting grave sites, and candles whose flames have long since burned away commemorate the dead while recalling the living who so lovingly tend and care for them.

SHOPPING

When it comes to shopping, Taos is basically an extension of Santa Fe, with many of the same shops and galleries (as well as some restaurants) represented in both cities. If Taos has any edge over the capital in this regard, it's in the craftsmanship of its Spanish carvers and carpenters, whose techniques have been handed down from father to son for nearly 300 years. Complementing such skills is the work of talented young artists, who have been drawn to the town's legendary reputation as an art center and as a place of spiritual fulfillment. This energy can be seen everywhere in Taos, in the decor of buildings, in the presentation of food in restaurants and dining rooms, in the attitude and enthusiasm of the people, and in the wares that fill the galleries and showcases.

Shopping Districts

The main concentration of shops in Taos is directly on or just off the historic central Plaza. That area includes the John Dunn Boardwalk and Bent Street, running parallel to the Plaza on the north, and Kit Carson Road, extending east off the northeast corner. With plenty of municipal parking just beyond Bent Street, these shopping districts, concentrated as they are, are easy to maneuver on foot. Except for its broad open space in the center, there isn't a spare niche anywhere along the Plaza that isn't a shop or restaurant of some kind or another, from Charley's North and West, two large gift shops on the northwest corner, to the Clothes Horse on the southeast corner. It's pockets of unrelieved commercialism such as these, as appealing as they may be to some, that have critics complaining that Taos is going the way of tourist centers everywhere and is quickly losing its distinctive charm. Cheap souvenir stores and fast-food outlets are popping up everywhere, and the downtown traffic bottleneck is at times beyond comprehension.

Bent Street, happily, seems less overdone. Named in honor of New Mexico's first governor, Bent Street was long home to mountain men, traders, and artists of the Old West. The street now houses some of the finest galleries and shops in town. Kit Carson Road, named in honor of the legendary scout, also hosts top art galleries, as well as El Rincón, the oldest trading post in Taos. In addition, the Ranchos de Taos area, 4 miles south of the Plaza, contains a number of fine shops, including some of the town's priciest.

Galleries

Bert Geer Phillips and Ernest Blumenschein, traveling from Denver on a planned painting trip into Mexico in 1898, stopped in Taos to have a broken wagon wheel repaired—a chance occurrence that led to the development of Taos as a major art center. Enthralled with the dramatic Taos landscape, earth-hued adobe buildings, thin, piercing light, and clean mountain air, they decided to stay. Word of their discovery soon spread to fellow artists. In 1912, the Taos Society of Artists was formed. At its nucleus were Blumenschein, Phillips, Joseph Henry Sharp, and Eanger Irving Coue Couse, all graduates of the celebrated Parisian art school Académie Julian. Members of the society painted in Taos but shipped their work to art markets on the East Coast and in Europe.

Most of the early Taos artists spent their winters in New York or Chicago teaching, painting, or illustrating to earn enough money to free them for their summers in New Mexico, where they worked under difficult conditions at best, often without running water or electricity. Most were fascinated with Native Americans, their customs, modes of dress, and ceremonies, feeling—rather romantically—a spiritual kinship with them. The society was disbanded in the late 1920s, but Taos continued to attract artists. Several galleries opened, and in 1952 local painters joined to form the Taos Artists' Association, forerunner to today's highly active Taos Art Association. At present, more than 80 galleries and shops display original art, sculpture, and crafts.

For a unique opportunity to have one-on-one contact with nationally known artists who are residing in Taos, the Taos Inn (☎ 505/758–2233) sponsors a free meet-the-artist series in spring (mid-May–mid-June) and again in fall (mid-Oct.–mid-Dec.) every Tuesday and Thursday evening at 8.

Clay and Fiber Gallery (126 W. Plaza Dr., ☎ 505/758–8093), on the southwest corner of the Plaza, emphasizes ceramics and such cloth work as hand-painted silks and traditional and contemporary weavings.

El Taller Taos Gallery (119A Kit Carson Rd., ☎ 505/758–4887) is the exclusive Taos representative of original works by Amado Peña. It also handles sculpture, jewelry, weavings, glass, and clay.

Mission Gallery (138 E. Kit Carson Rd., ☎ 505/758–2861), now in its 33rd year, features early Taos artists, early modernists, and important contemporary artists. The gallery is located in the former home of early Taos painter Joseph H. Sharp.

Navajo Gallery (210 Ledoux St., ☎ 505/758–3250) offers the varied works of Navajo artist R. C. Gorman, widely considered the best Native American artist and probably the best known of all the modern Southwestern artists. Dubbed "the Picasso of Indian Art" by the *New York Times,* Gorman opened the Navajo Gallery in 1968, becoming the first Native American artist to operate his own gallery. A branch of the Navajo Gallery was opened in Albuquerque's historic Old Town district in 1989.

R. B. Ravens (St. Francis Plaza, Ranchos de Taos, ☎ 505/758–7322) presents paintings by the founding artists of Taos, weavings, ceramics, and sketches by famous Native American painter Elbridge Ayer Burbank. It also features Navajo textiles—both blankets and rugs—pottery, regalia, and pawn jewelry.

The Shriver Gallery (401 Paseo del Pueblo Norte, ☎ 505/758–4994) handles traditional bronze sculpture and paintings, including oils, watercolors, and pastels, as well as drawings and etchings.

The Taos Gallery (403 Paseo del Pueblo Norte, ☎ 505/758–2475) features Western and Southwestern impressionism and an exclusive collection of bronzes.

Taos Traditions Gallery (221 Paseo del Pueblo Norte, ☎ 505/758–0016), next to the Fechin Institute, mainly showcases the works of contemporary artists, including oils, pastels, and watercolors.

Western Heritage Art (110 S. Plaza, ☎ 505/758–4376), established in 1985, handles paintings, alabaster and bronze sculpture, Navajo rugs, and Native American artifacts and pottery. Bill Rabbit and Robert Redbird are among the artists represented here.

Specialty Stores

Books

The Brodsky Bookshop (218 Paseo del Pueblo Norte, ☎ 505/758–9468) has a fine selection of contemporary books and Southwestern classics. If you don't see what you want, Brodsky's will order it on the spot.

Fernandez de Taos Book Store (109 N. Plaza, ☎ 505/758–4391), located right on the Plaza, has books, art magazines, and major out-of-town newspapers, such as the *New York Times* and the *Washington Post.*

G. Robinson Old Prints and Maps (124D Bent St., ☎ 505/758–2278), located in the John Dunn House, has a wide selection of original antique maps and prints (16th- to 19th-century), Edward Curtis Native American photographs, and rare books.

Moby Dickens (No. 6, John Dunn House, 124A Bent St., ☎ 505/758–3050) is roomy and well lit, with lots of windows that let in the bright Taos sun. A bookstore for all ages, it has a good selection of contemporary best-sellers, as well as an outstanding selection of books on the Southwest.

Taos Book Shop (122D Kit Carson Rd., ☎ 505/758–3733), a half block east of the Taos Plaza in a lovely walled adobe building, is the oldest bookshop in New Mexico. It was founded in 1947 by Genevieve Janssen and Claire Morrill, whose recollections of their years in Taos, *A Taos Mosaic* (University of New Mexico Press), remains by far the best local history of the Taos area. Frequent book signings and receptions for authors are held in the shop, which specializes in out-of-print and Southwestern selections.

Ten Directions Books (228C Paseo del Pueblo Norte, ☎ 505/758–2725) buys and sells new and used books. It welcomes book searches, locating out-of-print and hard-to-find volumes.

Clothing

Mariposa Boutique (John Dunn House, 120F Bent St., ☎ 505/758–9028) sells original contemporary Southwestern clothing and accessories by leading Taos designers. Handcrafted jewelry is also featured.

Martha of Taos (121 Paseo del Pueblo Norte, ☎ 505/758–3102), next to the Taos Inn, specializes in Southwestern-style dresses, pleated Navajo "broomstick" skirts, Navajo blouses, and velvet Navajo dresses with silver.

Overland Sheepskin Company (Rte. 522, ☎ 505/758–8822) has a huge selection of high-quality sheepskin coats, hats, mittens, and slippers, many using Taos beadwork, Navajo rug insets, and buffalo hides for exotic new styles. There are branches in Santa Fe, San Francisco, and the Napa Valley area of California.

Home Furnishings

Casa Cristal Pottery (on Rte. 522 in El Prado, ☎ 505/758–1530), 2½ miles north of the Taos Plaza, has it all: stoneware, serapes, clay pots, Native American ironwood carvings, ceramic sunbursts, straw and tin ornaments, *ristras* (strings of chile peppers), fountains, sweaters, ponchos, clay fireplaces, Mexican blankets, clay churches, birdbaths, baskets, tile, piñatas, and blue glassware from Guadalajara. Also featured are antique reproductions of park benches, street lamps, mailboxes, bakers' racks, and other wrought-iron products. Casa Cristal also has an outlet in Colorado Springs, Colorado.

Dwellings Revisited (107 Bent St., ☎ 505/758–3377) offers time-worn, authentic primitive pine furniture and other antique treasures from New Mexico.

Hacienda de San Francisco (4 St. Francis Plaza, Ranchos de Taos, ☎ 505/758–0477) has an exceptional collection of Spanish Colonial antiques.

High Mesa Furniture (S. Rte. 68, Ranchos de Taos, ☎ 505/758–4253) sells handcrafted ranch-style log furniture. You can visit their workshop, across the highway from the Taos Drum factory.

Lo Fino (201 Paseo del Pueblo Sur, ☎ 505/758–0298), in a contemporary adobe, provides one of the largest selections of handcrafted furniture in New Mexico, with the works of 10 top Southwestern furniture and lighting designers featured in one large showroom. Hand-carved beds, tables, chairs, cupboards, chests, lamps, and doors are all on display, along with Native American alabaster sculptures, basketry, and pottery.

Taos Blue (101A Bent St., ☎ 505/758–3561) specializes in Taos-style interior furnishings and just about everything else you might need to beautify your space. Behind the blue door on the corner of Bent Street and Paseo del Pueblo Norte is an extensive collection of one-of-a-kind accessories. On display are Pawnee/Sioux magical masks, decorated with feathers, horsehair, and scarves; "storyteller figures" from the Taos Pueblo; ceramic dogs baying at the moon; and Native American shields and rattles, sculptures, leather hassocks, and painted buckskin pillows.

Native American Arts and Crafts

Broken Arrow (222 N. Plaza, ☎ 505/758–4304) specializes in collector-quality Native American arts and crafts, including sand paintings, rugs, prints, jewelry, pottery, artifacts, and Hopi kachina dolls.

Buffalo Dancer (103A E. Plaza, ☎ 505/758–8718) buys, sells, and trades Southwestern Native American arts and crafts, including pottery, concho belts, kachina dolls, hides, and silver-coin jewelry.

Don Fernando Curio and Gift Shop (104 W. Plaza, ☎ 505/758–3791) is the oldest Native American arts shop on the Taos Plaza. It opened in 1938, hoping to catch some business from the newly opened La Fonda Hotel across the Plaza. Guests from La Fonda still wander in to pick out a turquoise bracelet, a kachina mud man, a woven straw basket, or some colorful beads.

El Rincón (114 E. Kit Carson Rd., ☎ 505/758–9188), housed in a traditional adobe from the turn of the century, was and still is a trading post, the oldest in Taos. Native American items of all kinds are bought and sold here: drums, feathered headdresses, Navajo rugs, beads, bowls, baskets, shields, beaded moccasins, jewelry, arrows, and spearheads. A free museum of Native American and early Spanish American artifacts is located off the main room of the shop. One of its most prized acquisitions is a pair of Kit Carson's buckskin pants. In back of the shop is the El Rincón Bed and Breakfast, reminiscent of the era when Native Americans often traveled for days on horseback to visit the reservation trading post and were invited to spend the night.

R. B. Ravens (St. Francis Plaza, Ranchos de Taos, ☎ 505/758–7322) offers the best in Navajo blankets and rugs, historical pots, regalia, pawn jewelry, and fine paintings, many from the founding artists' group of Taos painters.

Southwest Moccasin & Drum (803 Paseo del Pueblo Norte, ☎ 505/758–9332 or 800/447–3630) has one of the country's largest selections: 716 native moccasin styles and 72 sizes of drums, many painted by local artists.

Taos Drums (Santa Fe Hwy., Rte. 68, ☎ 505/758–3796 or 800/424–3786) is the factory outlet for the Taos Drum Factory (5 miles south of the Taos Plaza on Route 68; look for the large tepee). For sale are authentic handmade Pueblo log drums, leather lamp shades, and wrought-iron and Southwest furniture.

SPORTS AND THE OUTDOORS

Whether you're going to be pumping iron or jogging along Paseo del Pueblo Norte, the altitude in Taos (over 7,000 feet) takes a toll. Even your car will be gasping, getting too much gas and not enough air. Your body works almost the same way at high altitudes, with decreased oxygen content and decreased humidity. You may experience symptoms of nausea, insomnia, shortness of breath, diarrhea, sleeplessness, and tension. Eat lightly during the first few days and try to avoid alcohol, which aggravates "high-altitude syndrome." Keep physical exertion to a minimum. And, voilà! After a few days you should be your old self again and ready to hit the road running.

Participant Sports

Bicycling

"Gearing Up" Bicycle Shop (129 Paseo del Pueblo Sur, ☎ 505/751-0365), a full-service bike shop that also has information on tours and guides, and **Taos Mountain Outfitters** (114 S. Plaza, ☎ 505/758-9292), an outdoor sporting-equipment store, both have bicycles to rent. **Bikemeister Tours** (El Prado, ☎ 505/758-1194) offers back-road bike tours for families. The Taos-area roads are steep and hilly, and none have marked bicycle lanes. Be cautious; drivers, many from out of state, may be as unfamiliar with a passing bicycle as they are with a passing deer. Serious bikers may want to participate in the annual autumn **Enchanted Circle Wheeler Peak Bicycle Rally** and the **Aspen-cade,** both held in late September: Hundreds of cyclists challenge the 100-mile route through Red River, Taos, Angel Fire, Eagle Nest, and Questa, past a brilliant blaze of fall color.

Golf

If golf's your game, take your clubs to Angel Fire's 18-hole PGA mountain course, one of the highest in the nation. Contact the **Angel Fire Pro Shop** (Drawer B, Angel Fire 87710, ☎ 505/377-3055 or 800/633-7463) for tee times and greens fees. The **Taos Country Club** (south of Taos at Rte. 240, ☎ 505/758-7300), an 18-hole championship course with separate practice facility, opened in August 1992. Greens fees for 18 holes are $20 on weekdays, $22 on weekends.

Health Clubs

The **Taos Spa and Court Club** (111 Doña Ana Dr., ☎ 505/758-1980) has indoor and outdoor pools, a sauna, a Jacuzzi, tennis and racquetball courts, and aerobics classes. All are open to nonmembers for a $10.68 fee. Hotel health facilities are generally reserved only for the use of guests.

Jogging

The Taos mountain roads are challenging to a jogger, to say the least. You might try the running track that rings the football field at Taos High School (134 Cervantes St., ☎ 505/758-5230). It isn't open to the public, but no one seems to object if nonstudents, within reasonable numbers, jog there. The paths through Kit Carson Park are also suitable.

River Rafting

White-water rafting through the Taos Box section of the Rio Grande Wild and Scenic River is a growing sport in the region. **Native Sons Adventures** (☎ 505/758-9342 or 800/753-7559) and **Native Sons Tours** (☎ 505/986-0804 or 800/578-3256) run full- and half-day rafting trips. Contact the **Bureau of Land Management** (☎ 505/758-8851) for a list of other registered river guides or for information on running the river on your own.

Skiing

RESORTS

In winter, within a 90-mile radius, Taos offers five ski resorts with beginning, intermediate, and advanced slopes, as well as snowmobile and cross-country skiing trails. These resorts include the **Angel Fire Resort** (Drawer B, Angel Fire 87710, ☎ 505/377–6401 or 800/633–7463 outside NM), open from December 15 through the first week in April; the **Red River Ski Area** (Box 900, Red River 87558, ☎ 505/754–2382), open from Thanksgiving to Easter; the **Sipapu Lodge and Ski Area** (Rte. Box 29, Vadito 87579, ☎ 505/587–2240), open from mid-December to the end of March; and the **Taos Ski Valley** (Box 90, Taos Ski Valley 87525, ☎ 505/776–2291, reservations 800/776–1111 or 505/776–2233, FAX 505/776–8596), open from November 22 through the first week in April.

CROSS-COUNTRY

At the **Enchanted Forest Cross-Country Ski Area** (Box 521, Red River 87558, ☎ 505/754–2374), the season runs from the end of November to Easter. The **Carson National Forest Service** (Box 558, Taos 87571, ☎ 505/758–6200) can provide a good self-guide map of cross-country trails throughout the park.

Swimming

The **Don Fernando Municipal Swimming Pool** (124 Civic Plaza Dr., ☎ 505/758–9171) is open for recreational swimming from 1 to 5 daily. The charge is $2 for adults, $1 for children.

Tennis

Kit Carson Park and Fred Baca Park both have free public tennis courts, available on a first-come, first-served basis. For information, call the Taos Department of Parks and Recreation (☎ 505/758–4160). The **Quail Ridge Inn and Tennis Ranch** (Taos Ski Valley Rd., ☎ 505/776–2211) has eight Laykold tennis courts (two indoors), which are free to guests. Nonguests can play on the two indoor courts for $30 an hour.

Spectator Sports

Spectator sports include the annual **Rodeo de Taos,** held at the Taos County Fairgrounds in mid-June, and the **Taos Mountain Balloon Rally,** held in a field south of downtown during the last week in October in conjunction with the "Taste of Taos" food and wine tasting.

DINING

For a city with a population of fewer than 5,000, Taos has an extraordinary number of fine restaurants. As in Santa Fe, many of the restaurants rely heavily on northern New Mexico–style cooking, offering flavorful dishes that are rooted deep in the Spanish culture, with recipes that, for the most part, have been handed down for generations. (*See* Pleasures and Pastimes *in* Chapter 1 for an explanation of New Mexican food terms.) The clientele at all these establishments is a cross section of locals and seasonal tourists, skiers in the winter and art and nature lovers in the summer.

What to Wear

Taos caters to tourists who have come to the town to relax. You can dress in most restaurants as casually as you like.

CATEGORY	COST*
$$$	over $15
$$	$10–$15
$	under $10

*per person, excluding drinks, service, and sales tax (6.8% in the town
of Taos, 6.3% in the county)*

$$$ **Apple Tree.** In a historic adobe Territorial house on Bent Street, only
★   a block from the Plaza, this cozy and casual restaurant is a popular
luncheon and early dinner spot for locals as well as visitors. A series
of intimate dining rooms divided by open archways have pastel walls
and wooden tables flanked with straw chairs. Kiva (beehive) fireplaces
burn brightly in winter, and there's patio dining in summer; the large
tree in the courtyard gives the restaurant its name, but beware of
falling apples when eating outdoors in the fall. Among the excellent
dinner entrées are mango chicken enchilada, shrimp quesadillas, filet
mignon with a madeira mushroom sauce, and fresh fish dishes. Two
hot homemade soups are prepared daily, as are vegetarian dishes, and
the weekend brunch, served from 11:30 to 3, is a Taos tradition. Lunch
is also served on weekdays from 11:30 to 3. ✗ *123 Bent St.,* ☎ *505/
758–1900. Reservations advised. AE, D, DC, MC, V.*

$$$ **Brett House.** Four miles north of Taos is the former home and literary
★   salon of Lady Dorothy Brett, friend and frequent traveling compan-
ion of Frieda and D. H. Lawrence. Opened in 1983 as a restaurant,
the Brett House is now one of the finest in Taos. Chef-owners Steve
and Cindie White offer a wide selection of international cuisine with
an emphasis on Continental and American classics, including beef
Wellington with a béarnaise sauce; rack of lamb Provençal with mint
sauce; roasted breast of duck with cherry wine sauce; steaks; seafood;
and nightly specials. Service is impeccable and the views of the Sangre
de Cristo Mountains are superb. Set in a traditional old Taos adobe,
painted white, are four small rooms with half fireplaces, wood floors,
and viga ceilings. Several articles about Lady Brett are framed on the
wall, along with photos taken when she still lived in the house, and a
large pastel portrait by R. C. Gorman, completed just before she died
in 1977. One of the dining rooms is called the R. C. Gorman Room,
and a table there is reserved for the artist. His graceful portraits of Indian maidens line the wall, and two bronze sculptures outside can be
seen from the window tables. ✗ *No. 7 on Rte. 150 (Ski Valley Rd.),*
☎ *505/776–8545. Reservations advised. MC, V.*

$$$ **Casa Cordova.** The domain of Johnny Montano, who meets and greets,
this L-shape adobe building with a wooden portal, in a woodsy set-
ting at Arroyo Seco, is the place where chefs go when their own restau-
rants are closed. A separate lounge and large dining area with two
fireplaces form a cozy place for a meal. Menu highlights include es-
cargots à la bourguignonne and homemade pâté among the appetiz-
ers, and fresh trout, steak au poivre, quail, and sweetbreads among the
entrées. ✗ *Rte. 150 (Ski Valley Rd.) at Arroyo Seco,* ☎ *505/776–2500.
Reservations advised. AE, MC, V. Closed Sun.*

$$$ **Casa de Valdez.** A large A-frame building with wood-paneled walls
and beamed ceilings, Casa de Valdez has a rustic, mountain-lodge feel-
ing. The tables and chairs are handmade, as are the colorful drapes on
the windows. Owner-chef Peter Valdez specializes in hickory-smoked
barbecues, charcoal-grilled steaks, and regional New Mexican cuisine. ✗ *1401 Paseo del Pueblo Sur, 2½ mi south of the Taos Plaza,* ☎
505/758–8777. Reservations advised. AE, D, MC, V. Closed Wed.

$$$ **Doc Martin's.** The Taos Inn's restaurant, long a popular gathering
★   place for locals, is known for traditional and contemporary Southwestern

80

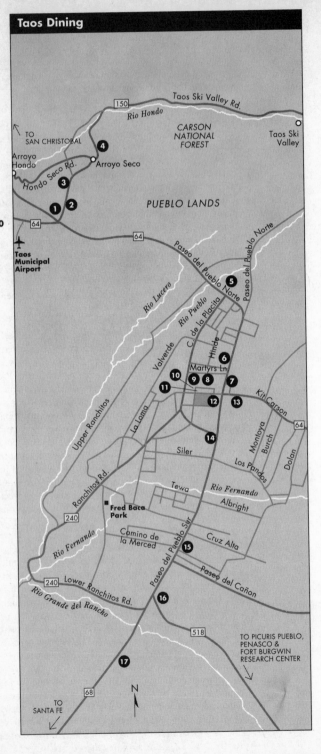

Taos Dining

cuisine, fresh seafood, distinctive game specialties, and an award-winning wine list. Doc Martin's takes its name from the building's original owner, a local physician who performed operations and delivered babies in the rooms that now make up the dining areas. The decor is the epitome of Southwestern: viga and latilla ceilings (beams and small strips of wood arranged to create a herringbone effect), *nichos* (wall niches) containing pottery and carved wooden santos, fireplaces, balconies with intricately carved railings draped with Native American saddle blankets, and handcrafted wooden tables and chairs. Breakfast and lunch menus are predominantly New Mexican; try the shrimp burrito smothered in vegetarian green chile for lunch. Dinner favorites here include the piñon nut–breaded chicken breasts and the grilled lamb satay with spicy cashew sauce. ✗ *Taos Inn, 125 Paseo del Pueblo Norte,* ☎ *505/758–1977. Reservations advised. MC, V.*

\$\$\$ **Don Fernando's.** The dining room at the Holiday Inn, 1 mile south of the Taos Plaza, is modern in concept, with Taos flourishes—kiva-style fireplaces, Indian art, and handcrafted tables and lamps. Out of its busy kitchen comes a wide selection of authentic Southwestern dishes, including enchiladas Puerto Vallarta (stuffed with crab and baby shrimp), shrimp Veracruz (marinated and grilled), and *carne asada* (broiled steak fillet). The adjoining lounge, Fernando's Hideaway (*see* Nightlife, *below*), features live entertainment, with intimate seating around a large adobe fireplace. ✗ *1005 Paseo del Pueblo Sur,* ☎ *505/758–4444. AE, D, DC, MC, V.*

\$\$\$ ★ **El Patio de Taos.** A Taos favorite for over 40 years, El Patio is set in a traditional adobe touted as the oldest structure in Taos. The building was the Taos Pueblo trading post during the 17th century, and later served as administrative offices for the Spanish government. The main dining room has a skylight, flagstone floors, and a stone fountain covered by a small green sea of potted plants. A second, smaller dining room, which seats 20, has viga ceilings and hand-painted walls featuring traditional Spanish floral patterns. The restaurant offers classic Mexican and New Mexican cuisine, featuring authentic chile rellenos and blue-corn enchiladas. Portions are large, and the Caesar salad is probably the best in town. ✗ *121 Teresina La., northwest corner of Taos Plaza,* ☎ *505/758–2121. Reservations advised. D, DC, MC, V.*

\$\$\$ ★ **Lambert's of Taos.** Considered by many locals to be the best restaurant in town, Lambert's was opened in 1989 by the former head chef of the Taos Inn. The historic Randall House, two and a half blocks south of the Plaza, is the culinary province of chef-proprietors Zeke and Tina Lambert. The remodeled Victorian houses a series of elegantly simple, white dining rooms; the atmosphere is laid-back and intimate. If you arrive before dark, try to sit at a table with a stunning view of Taos Mountain. The contemporary American menu changes according to what's fresh at the market. Trusty specialties include pepper-crusted lamb and crab cakes, accompanied by your choice of an array of fine California vintages. For dessert, try the chocolate mousse with raspberry sauce. ✗ *309 Paseo del Pueblo Sur,* ☎ *505/758–1009. Reservations advised. AE, DC, MC, V.*

\$\$\$ **The Stakeout Grill and Bar.** Tucked into the foothills of the Sangre de Cristo Mountains, 9 miles south of Taos Plaza, at a place called Outlaw Hill, this old adobe homestead offers views that stretch up to a hundred miles and sunsets that dazzle. Clearly marked by a huge cowboy hat next to the turnoff from the highway, the restaurant has rustic decor, with wood-paneled walls, viga ceilings, hardwood floors, wooden tables and chairs, and muted-glass wall lamps. Changing exhibits of locally produced Western artworks—which are for sale—are displayed throughout, but the main attraction is the food: New York strip steaks, filet mignon, roast prime rib, shrimp scampi, swordfish steak, duck, chicken, and daily pasta specials. ✕ *Stakeout Dr. (off Rte. 68),* ☎ *505/758–2042. Reservations advised. AE, D, DC, MC, V.*

$$$ **Villa Fontana.** This two-story adobe houses two intimate, candlelit din-
★   ing rooms, with gleaming hardwood floors, well-appointed tables, and starched linens. Master chef Carlo Gislimberti and his wife, Siobhan, prepare authentic northern Italian cuisine, including the house specialty of locally picked wild mushrooms and a variety of seasonal game, such as venison and pheasant. ✕ *Rte. 522, 5 mi north of Taos Plaza,* ☎ *505/758–5800. Reservations advised. AE, D, DC, MC, V.*

$$ **Bent Street Deli.** You might think you're in New York City when you
★   try the hearty Reuben sandwich here, though the friendly service and simple, unpretentious setting will reassure you of your New Mexican surroundings. This small deli offers an extensive selection of great soups, sandwiches, salads, and desserts as well as gourmet coffees, beer, and wine. Besides the Reuben, the Taos—fresh turkey, bacon, green chile, and guacamole rolled in a flour tortilla—is an excellent and filling sandwich. But don't get too full; there's cheesecake and other sweet treats in the glass counter at the front. The dinner menu is equally extensive, and diners can choose from a menu featuring fresh salmon with a Szechuan glaze, a primavera Sumatra with Indonesian peanut sauce, or the ever-popular *camarones* (shrimp) in pesto sauce. There are also fresh seafood specials nightly. Breakfast lasts until 11. ✕ *120 Bent St.,* ☎ *505/758–5787. MC, V. Closed Sun.*

$$ **Chile Connection.** Six minutes north of the Taos Plaza on Ski Valley Road, Chile Connection is housed in a sprawling ranch-style adobe building with a large patio offering spectacular mountain views. The patio is open for dining in summer and on mild sunny winter days; otherwise, meals are served in four separate dining rooms, each with a kiva-style fireplace, handcrafted tables and chairs, Western art, and decorations from south of the border. Specialties of the house include blue-corn tortillas, homemade salsa, buffalo burgers and steaks, and fajitas. Although chile is supposed to be the restaurant's forte, some locals claim that it's less than fabulous. The award-winning margaritas, however, just might make up for it. ✕ *Ski Valley Rd. (Rte. 150)* ☎ *505/776–8787. Reservations advised. D, DC, MC, V.*

$$ **Ogelvie's Bar and Grill.** Occupying the second floor of an old two-story adobe building on the east side of the Taos Plaza, Ogelvie's is the perfect spot for people-watching from on high, especially from the outdoor patio in summer. Inside, the restaurant's two adjoining dining rooms and full-service lounge are decorated with a strange mix of paintings, vintage black-and-white photos, antiques, and assorted knickknacks. People wait in line to sample such entrées as prime Angus beef, shrimp scampi, grilled Rocky Mountain trout, and meat or cheese enchiladas. A special light-and-healthy menu is available. ✕ *103 E. Plaza,* ☎ *505/ 758–8866. No reservations. AE, DC, MC, V.*

$–$$ **Michael's Kitchen, Coffee Shop, and Bakery.** It seems almost required
★   by law that all Western communities have one top spot for breakfast; in Taos, this is it. Housed in a traditional old adobe, four blocks north of the Plaza, Michael's has been turning out huevos rancheros, fat pancakes and waffles, and traditional bacon and eggs to get the day going for over 15 years. The restaurant's unique decor reflects its past as a curio shop—an antique washing machine, a wood-burning stove, vintage picture frames and mirrors, a turn-of-the-century coat rack, 10-gallon hats, Native American pottery, and a pitcher and commode. The ceilings are beamed, the floors are polished hardwood, and the tables and chairs are all handcrafted. Chef-owner Michael Ninneman also serves lunch and dinner, but it's breakfast that brings the faithful back

for more. ✕ *314 Paseo de Pueblo Norte,* ☎ *505/758–4178. AE, D, MC, V.* ☾ *7 AM–8:30 PM.*

$ Roberto's. Housed in a 150-year-old adobe, across from the Kit Carson Museum, this New Mexican restaurant affords an ambience of rustic elegance and grace. Owners Bobby and Patsy Garcia reveal a deep-rooted love for their native heritage, using prized recipes handed down through the Garcia family for generations to create authentic native dishes from scratch. Three intimate dining rooms are decorated in Southwestern style throughout, with art and cherished family antiques, including handcrafted lamps and furniture. The chile rellenos are particularly good. ✕ *122B E. Kit Carson Rd.,* ☎ *505/758–2434. Reservations advised. AE, D, MC, V. Closed Tues.*

$ Tapas de Taos Cafe. This offbeat eatery, in a 300-year-old adobe, has a decor that echoes the themes of the Mexican *Dia de los Muertos,* or Day of the Dead. But if you don't find imitation black skulls appetizing, there's sure to be something on the tasty tapas (appetizers) menu that is. The beauty of tapas is that you can order one dish as an appetizer, or make a meal out of two or three. Try pairing up the fried calamari with the shrimp and vermicelli pancake. If you find you're still hungry after that, order one of the larger Mexican dishes on the menu. In the warmer months, two pleasant patios offer a lovely alternative to the rather grim interior. ✕ *136 Bent St.,* ☎ *505/758–9670. D, MC, V.*

$ Wild and Natural Cafe. "We Think Before You Eat" is the slogan of this healthy and hip Taos café. Chef-owner Carol Wildman serves an array of good-for-you foods that, unlike the fare in some natural eateries, tastes good, too. Whole grains and local organic ingredients are used whenever possible, and all entrées are low-fat and made without eggs, refined sugar, saturated fats, or cholesterol. The Veggie Plate is a heaping helping of steamed veggies, beans, and brown rice served with a special sauce of the day—such as ginger curry—and a cup of miso soup. Other popular items include the Vegerito, a whole wheat tortilla stuffed with fresh steamed vegetables and doused with green chile; the Bubba Burger, marinated tempeh burger with green chile and avocado on a whole wheat roll with eggless mayonnaise; and Wild and Natural Enchiladas, blue corn tortillas layered with tofu filling and smothered in red or green chile. Healthy drink items include fresh organic carrot juice, herbal teas, and fruit smoothies, while dessert choices like Brown Rice Krispie Bars and organic carrot cake are good alternatives to their less-healthy counterparts. Local beer, organic wine, and gourmet coffee drinks—made with soy milk, upon request—are available. ✕ *812B Paseo del Pueblo Norte,* ☎ *505/ 751–0480. No reservations. D, MC, V.*

LODGING

Taos is a tourist town, and it has a broad range of accommodations. There are hotels and motels to suit every need and budget, from big-name chains with all the extra amenities to smaller roadside establishments offering basic accommodations. There's no drastic variation in hotel rates from season to season, but you'll find more rooms available in the spring and late fall.

Most of the art and social events take place May through October; lodging rates are about 20% higher during the peak summer period (July and August) and reservations are highly recommended during this time.

With the development of the Taos Ski Valley and several other nearby ski resorts in the mid-1950s, Taos, long a virtual ghost town in winter, blossomed into one of the premier ski destinations in the country. Depending on snow conditions, the season generally runs from about the third week in November through the first week in April. Skiers now have many deluxe resorts to choose from for comfortable and convenient accommodations.

In order to accommodate the large influx of visitors into their small town, many Taos residents decided to open up their homes. Bed-and-breakfast Taos style means traditional adobe houses and haciendas, some 200 years old, and special Southwestern-flavor breakfasts—blue-corn pancakes and huevos rancheros. Innkeepers often act as concierges, directing guests to specialty shops, arranging river rafting or hot-air balloon excursions, or suggesting the perfect place for dining. For information, contact **Bed and Breakfast of New Mexico** (Box 2805, Santa Fe 87504, ☎ 505/982–3332) or the **Taos Bed and Breakfast Association** (Box 2772, Taos 87571, ☎ 800/876–7857).

CATEGORY	COST*
$$$	over $95
$$	$50–$95
$	under $50

All prices are for a standard double room, excluding 3.5% city room tax or 3% county room tax; 6.75% city sales tax or 6.25% county sales tax; and service charges.

Hotels/Motels

$$$ **Sagebrush Inn.** With its graceful portals, enchanting patios, and charming adobe architecture, the two- and three-story Sagebrush Inn is one of the prettiest hotels in town. It's also one of the noisiest, so ask for a room well away from the live lounge entertainment. Built in adobe Pueblo-Mission style in 1929, the inn is furnished with authentic Navajo rugs, rare pottery, Southwestern and Spanish antiques, fine carved pieces, and paintings from many of the old Southwestern masters. Georgia O'Keeffe once lived and painted in one of the third-story rooms. The two large dining rooms (specializing in prime rib and New Mexican cuisine) are decorated in the Southwestern mode, as are rooms and suites, which feature wall niches containing antique religious figures, Native American wall hangings, and Native American–design rugs and bed coverings. Many have kiva-style fireplaces; some have balconies looking out onto the magnificent Sangre de Cristo Mountains. The Sagebrush Village offers alternative family lodging, condominium style. ☒ *1508 Paseo del Pueblo Sur, 3 mi south of the Plaza, Box 557, Taos 87571, ☎ 505/758–2254 or 800/228–2828,* ℻ *505/758–5077. 80 rooms. 2 restaurants, lounge, pool, 2 hot tubs, 2 tennis courts. AE, D, DC, MC, V.*

$$–$$$ **Taos Inn.** This sprawling hotel, only steps from the Taos Plaza, is a prized
★   local landmark, exemplifying Southwestern rustic charm with its adobe walls, wood-burning fireplaces, hand-stripped viga ceilings, hand-loomed rugs, and wrought-iron fixtures. It's listed in the National Register of Historic Places; parts of the structure date from the 1600s. The guest rooms, all individually furnished in warm Southwestern style, are filled with antiques; handmade Native American bedspreads; custom-made Taos-style furniture built by local artists; and fireplaces created by Carmen Velarde, the local Michelangelo of fireplace design. In summer there's dining alfresco on the patio. Paintings on the walls of the dining rooms, as well as in the dramatic two-story lobby, are by Na-

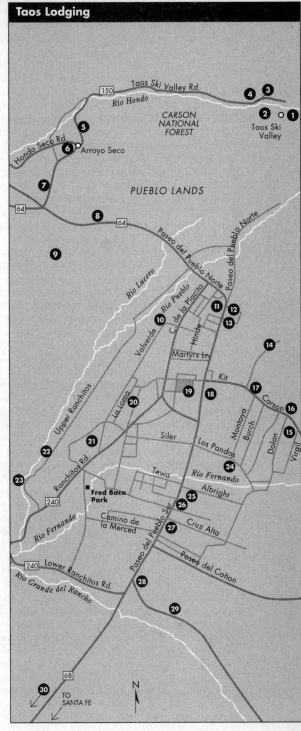

Abominable Snow-Mansion Skiers' Hostel and Summer Center, **6**

Adobe & Pines, **30**

American Artists Gallery House, **25**

Amizette Inn & Restaurant, **3**

Austing Haus, **4**

Blue Door, **29**

Brooks Street Inn, **13**

Casa de las Chimeneas, **24**

Casa de Milagros, **16**

Casa Europa, **23**

Don Fernando de Taos Holiday Inn, **27**

El Monte Lodge, **17**

El Pueblo Lodge, **11**

Hacienda del Sol, **8**

Harrison's Bed and Breakfast, **9**

Hotel Edelweiss, **2**

Hotel La Fonda de Taos, **19**

Kachina Lodge de Taos–Best Western, **12**

Koshari Inn, **15**

La Posada de Taos, **20**

Mabel Dodge Luhan House, **14**

Orinda, **10**

Quail Ridge Inn Resort, **7**

Rancho Ramada Inn de Taos, **26**

Ruby Slipper, **21**

Sagebrush Inn, **28**

Salsa del Salto, **5**

Taos Country Inn at Rancho Rio Pueblo, **22**

Taos Inn, **18**

Thunderbird Lodge and Chalets, **1**

Taos Lodging

tive American and Southwestern artists. The comfortable, inviting lobby is built around an old town well, from which a fountain now bubbles forth; nearby is a sunken fireplace, rimmed with *bancos* (cushioned adobe seating areas). Most of the town's shops and restaurants are within walking distance of the hotel, which is adjacent to the Stables Art Center and the Taos Community Auditorium. ☎ *125 Paseo del Pueblo Norte, Taos 87571,* ☎ *505/758–2233 or 800/TAOS–INN,* FAX *505/758–5776. 39 rooms. Restaurant, bar, lounge, library. DC, MC, V.*

$$ Don Fernando de Taos Holiday Inn. This is one of the newer hotels in Taos, but it has a venerable past. The original Don Fernando, built in the 1920s by a German entrepreneur, was considered one of the most charming hotels in the Southwest. At the time, Taos was populated by a colorful assortment of Native Americans, trappers, miners, and desperadoes. Hotel guests were met at the train depot in Lamy by guides from the Fred Harvey Company and then endured an arduous 12-hour journey by Model-T Ford to the hotel, 1 mile south of the Taos Plaza. The old Don burned to the ground in 1933, and the new one rose in its place in 1989. It's built in a distinct Pueblo-style design, with rooms grouped around central courtyards and connected by meandering walkways. Accommodations are tastefully appointed with hand-carved New Mexican furnishings, accented with specially designed fabrics in rich Southwestern colors. Many of the rooms have kiva-style fireplaces. Suites named after D. H. Lawrence, Lady Brett, and others of the charmed literary circle miss a bet by not including a memento or two—not even a photograph—of their celebrated namesakes. Because of its amenities, including the lounge, this is probably the best choice for single travelers. ☎ *1005 Paseo del Pueblo Sur, Drawer V, Taos 87571,* ☎ *505/758–4444 or 800/759–2736,* FAX *505/758–0055. 126 rooms. Restaurant, bar, lounge, pool, hot tub, tennis court. AE, D, DC, MC, V.*

$$ El Monte Lodge. Nestled among cottonwoods in a quiet residential area four blocks east of the Taos Plaza is the El Monte Lodge, in business for over 50 years. It consists of several one-story white-painted adobe buildings, similar to guest-house cottages in the privacy of their arrangement among the trees. Local color is afforded by beamed viga ceilings, corner fireplaces, bright Native American rugs, and tinwork mirrors and frames. All rooms have refrigerators; some have kiva-style fireplaces and kitchenettes. A laundry on the premises is available for the guests' use, as are picnic tables outside. Owners George and Pat Schumacher know all the ins and outs of Taos life and are happy to help guests plan their vacation schedules. ☎ *317 Kit Carson Rd., Box 22, Taos 87571,* ☎ *505/758–3171 or 800/828–8262,* FAX *505/758– 1536. 7 rooms, 4 2-bedroom suites. Picnic area, refrigerators, coin laundry. AE, D, DC, MC, V.*

$$ El Pueblo Lodge. This low-to-the-ground Pueblo-style adobe, only blocks north of the Taos Plaza, is as practical as it is charming. In-room refrigerators, kitchenettes, and the use of a complimentary guest laundry room make it an ideal home away from home for traveling families. There's even cable TV. The lodge is located on the Ski Valley side of Taos, pointing skiers in the right direction. Room appointments include pale desert colors and traditional Southwestern furnishings—handmade furniture, lamps, and mirrors and Native American and Western art throughout. Many of the rooms have fireplaces. Free Continental breakfast is served in the lobby. ☎ *412 Paseo del Pueblo Norte, Box 92, Taos 87571,* ☎ *505/758–8700 or 800/433–9612,* FAX *505/758– 7321. 58 rooms. Pool, hot tub. AE, D, MC, V.*

$$ Hotel La Fonda de Taos. Tourists on the trail of D. H. Lawrence should make this their first stop. The novelist often took to the easel as a form of relaxation, and for $3 you can enter the manager's office and view Lawrence's erotic paintings. Saki Karavas, the hotel's owner, bought the 11 paintings from Lawrence's widow. They had been banned in London (as were many of Lawrence's books); by today's standards, however, they seem about as offensive as the White Rock fairy. James Karavas, father of the present owner, built the hotel in 1937, and early on it catered to European and American celebrities (Tyrone Power honeymooned here). Karavas's son, the present owner, is, at 73, every bit as gregarious and as sentimental. Although the hotel has been spruced up considerably of late, with new Turkish bedspreads in the rooms, new paint on the handmade wooden furniture, and more lighting in the lobby, it has seen better days. Showcased everywhere are framed newspaper and magazine stories from the old days—as well as photos, posters, Western paintings, Hopi Native American shields, portraits, busts, Pueblo pottery, and Mexican paintings and artifacts. Near the reception desk, two "suits of lights" have been mounted: bullfighters' costumes, in full pose, frequently mistaken by older guests for bellhops. *Taos Plaza, Box 1447, Taos 87571, ☎ 505/758–2211 or 800/833–2211, FAX 505/758–8508. 24 rooms with bath. Lounge. AE, MC, V.*

$$ **Kachina Lodge de Taos–Best Western.** ★ Just down the road from the historic Taos Pueblo and only minutes from the Taos Plaza is this large, comfortable lodge, built in a two-story Pueblo-style adobe. A kachina theme runs throughout the hotel, with rare and historic kachina dolls, carved from the root of cottonwood trees, decorating many of the hotel's public areas and others—newer, and somewhat more commercial—offered for sale in the hotel shops and lobby area. Chairs and couches, upholstered in fabrics inspired by Southwest Native American designs and colors, rim the large lobby fireplace. Hopi and Pueblo art hangs on the walls. In the hotel's Kiva Coffee Shop (there's also a Hopi Dining Room and Zuni Cocktail Lounge), a huge hand-carved totem pole behind the counter dominates the room. The guest rooms continue the Southwestern Native American theme, with handmade, hand-painted furnishings, colorful fabric bedspreads, and decorative lamps. Every night from Memorial Day through Labor Day, a troupe from the nearby Taos Pueblo performs ritual dances outside by firelight. During the day, the hotel's 7 acres of wooded landscape invite picnics and quiet walks. *413 Paseo del Pueblo Norte, Box NN, Taos 87571, ☎ 505/758–2275 or 800/522–4462, FAX 505/758–9207. 118 rooms. Restaurant, bar, coffee shop, pool, hot tub, shops. AE, D, DC, MC, V.*

$$ **Koshari Inn.** ★ Nestled under centuries-old silver aspens in the foothills of Taos Canyon is the Koshari Inn—a former motel that has been painstakingly converted into a traditional Southwestern inn, in the Taos mold. Recently refurbished units have handmade wooden chairs, desks, and end tables painted in the pale colors so popular in northern New Mexico. Framed posters by favorite regional artists, including Georgia O'Keeffe and R. C. Gorman, hang on the walls, and the Native American motif is everywhere. Beyond the inn, which is part adobe, part cement block, is the Rio Fernando, more a trickling stream than a mighty river. The inn offers its guests free use of 10-speed all-terrain bicycles for touring the countryside or for trips into town, 2 miles to the west. There's also a small swimming pool on the property for guests' use. Rooms are spacious, and each has a motel-style private entrance. Continental breakfast is served in the lobby during peak seasons. Pets are welcome. *910 E. Kit Carson Rd., Box 6612, Taos 87571, ☎ 505/758–7199, FAX 505/751–0370. 12 units. Pool, mountain bikes. MC, V.*

$$ **Rancho Ramada Inn de Taos.** The two-story adobe-style Ramada Inn, 1 mile south of the Taos Plaza, recently underwent a transformation of sorts, putting more of a Taos stamp on the familiar Ramada mold.

The remodeled dining room now features desert colors, Western art, and Native American pottery; the lobby has a fireplace. Even the guest-room furnishings have been modified to reflect a Southwestern flavor. The hotel's Fireside Cantina specializes in spicy Southwestern cuisine as well as American favorites, and you can enjoy hors d'oeuvres here while sitting by a cozy fireplace. There is also live music here during peak summer months. ☎ *615 Paseo del Pueblo Sur, Box 6257, Taos 87571,* ☎ *505/758–2900 or 800/272–6232,* FAX *505/758–1662. 124 rooms. Dining room, lounge, pool, meeting rooms. AE, D, DC, MC, V.*

Resorts and Ski Lodges

$$–$$$$ **Quail Ridge Inn Resort.** The 20th century comes to sleepy Taos with this all-things-to-all-people family resort and conference center. One- and two-story modern would-be adobe bungalows offer a variety of room choices—plain rooms, studios with kitchen, one- and two-bedroom suites, and rooms with balconies or patios, all decorated in Southwestern contemporary, with viga ceilings and kiva-style fireplaces. Four miles north of Taos Plaza, the Quail Ridge offers a touch of modern elegance set against the magnificent natural backdrop of northern New Mexico. What it lacks in rustic charm it makes up for in a host of recreational amenities, from organized trail rides to hot-tub soaks. ☎ *Ski Valley Rd. (Rte. 150), Box 707, Taos 87571,* ☎ *505/ 776–2211 or 800/624–4448,* FAX *505/776–2949. 110 rooms and suites. Restaurant, lounge, pool, hot tub, 8 tennis courts, exercise room, racquetball, squash, volleyball. Complete ski, tennis, rafting, mountain-bike, and fly-fishing packages are available for groups or individuals. D, DC, MC, V.*

$$$ **Hotel Edelweiss.** This quiet, elegant resort hotel, directly on the ski slopes, offers a touch of European alpine flavor, complete with floral arrangements on the dining tables and fresh-baked breads and rolls at the hotel's La Croissanterie restaurant. The large lobby is dominated by a gigantic fireplace, where après-ski coffee and pastries are served; it's the place to meet and socialize. Owners and chefs Timothy and Ann-Marie Wooldridge make their own hearty soups, sandwiches, and desserts. Rooms are more practical than posh, offering just the basics. In summer, the hotel converts to a bed-and-breakfast inn. ☎ *Box 83,Taos Ski Valley 87525,* ☎ *505/776–2301 or 800/458–8754,* FAX *505/ 776–2533. 24 rooms. Hot tub, massage, sauna. AE, MC, V. Closed mid-Apr.–Memorial Day.*

$$$ **Thunderbird Lodge and Chalets.** Only 150 yards from the main lifts, on the sunny side of the valley, this large, two-story wood-frame inn is the ultimate ski-lodge resort, owned and managed by live-in residents Elizabeth and Tom Brownell. Its dining room is one of the most popular in the valley, with all breads, soups, salads, entrées, pastries, and ice cream made on the premises. A large conference room also serves as a games room, with TV, board games, and a library. Guest rooms are small and functional, typical of ski-resort accommodations. Supervised children's activities include early dinners, movies, and games. ☎ *Box 87, Taos Ski Valley 87525,* ☎ *505/776–2280 or 800/776–2279,* FAX *505/776–2238. 32 rooms. Restaurant, bar, hot tub, massage, sauna. MC, V.*

$$ **Amizette Inn & Restaurant.** A small, wood-frame mountain inn on the banks of the Rio Hondo, 1½ miles from the ski lifts, the Amizette offers all the amenities (as well as the decor) of a traditional alpine chalet—hot tub, redwood sauna, sun deck, trout stream and hiking trails, and comfortable rooms with queen-size beds, private baths, and color TV. The decor, as you might expect, is alpine. ☎ *Taos Ski Valley Rd.,*

Box 756, Taos Ski Valley 87525, ☎ 505/776–2451 or 800/446–TAOS. 12 rooms. Hot tub, sauna. AE, D, MC, V.

$$ **Austing Haus.** Billed as the largest and tallest timber-frame building in
★ the United States, the Austing Haus is made of over 70,000 board feet
of heavy timbers, with more than 3,000 interlocking joints—held to-
gether by wooden pegs. The beams are exposed inside and out, pro-
viding structural stability and a pleasantly aesthetic design. All the
furniture is handmade as well: Owner Paul Austing, an award-winning
chef, is as handy with a mallet and saw as he is with his sauces and
soufflés. The full front exterior of the building is paneled glass, offer-
ing stunning views of the valley from inside and a glimpse of the cozy
interior from outside. The hotel's aptly named Glass Dining Room has
large picture windows, stained-glass paneling, a fireplace, and a Na-
tive American loom with a partially completed blanket mounted on
the wall. House specialties are veal Oscar and steak au poivre. Guest
rooms are sparse and functional, not unlike those of ski lodges all over
the world. The ski lifts are just 1½ miles away. In summer, the hotel
converts to a bed-and-breakfast inn. ☎ *Taos Ski Valley Rd. (Rte. 150),
Box 8, Taos Ski Valley 87525, ☎ 505/776–2649, 505/776–2629, or
800/748–2932, FAX 505/776–8751. 36 rooms with bath. Restaurant,
hot tub. DC, MC, V.*

$ **Abominable Snow-Mansion Skiers' Hostel and Summer Center.** This
large old adobe building, midway between Taos and the Ski Valley (15
minutes either way), is designed for the budget-minded who don't
mind bedding down in bunks, dormitory style. You can't miss the gar-
ish lettering out front, painted directly on the adobe facade. Inside, the
front part of the two-story building is a large general room where ev-
erything happens; there are video games, a piano, a fireplace, chairs,
couches, and books. Meals are served here buffet style during the ski
season. No food is offered during the summer, but kitchen facilities are
available to guests. In back and upstairs are six dormitory rooms with
bunk beds, mostly five beds to a room; each room has its own bath.
During the summer, three of the rooms are offered as private accom-
modations. There are two cabin units out back and an area set aside
for tent camping (conventional and tepee). It's all clean, comfortable,
and fun, and a great way to meet people. ☎ *Taos Ski Valley Rd. (Rte.
150), in Arroyo Seco, Box 3271, Taos 87571, ☎ 505/776–8298, FAX
505/776–8746. 96 beds. No liquor permitted during the summer
months. MC, V.*

Bed-and-Breakfasts

$$$ **Adobe & Pines.** With its 80-foot-long portal, stretching the entire ex-
panse of the main entranceway, this 150-year-old adobe home on four
acres of pines, fruit trees, and pastures couldn't be more impressive.
The bed-and-breakfast, set against the Taos Mountains, was opened
in 1991 after extensive renovations. Owners Chuck and Charuil Fulk-
erson traveled the world before settling on, and in, Taos. Four guest
rooms in the main house have queen-size beds with fluffy goose-down
comforters and pillows, Mexican-tile baths, and fireplaces. A separate
cottage has a canopy bed, whirlpool bath, two fireplaces, cable TV,
and a kitchen. The public area—a living room where hors d'oeuvres
are served in the afternoon—and a glass-enclosed sunroom and dining area where breakfast is unveiled, are spaciously Western. ☎ *U.S.
68, Box 837, Ranchos de Taos 87557, ☎ 505/751–0947 or 800/723–
8267, FAX 505/758–8423. 4 rooms with bath, 1 cottage with bath. No
smoking. Sauna. MC, V.*

$$$ **Casa de las Chimeneas.** Just 2½ blocks from the Plaza, secluded be-
★   hind thick adobe walls, the "House of Chimneys," with its formal gar-
dens and cool, stately entranceway, could serve as the approach to a
castle. The interior of this Spanish-style hacienda, originally built in
1912 and renovated a decade ago, is equally grand. The living room
features regional art, tile hearths, French doors, and traditional viga
ceilings. Each guest room has its own private entrance and fireplace
and each is individually furnished with hand-carved, hand-painted
traditional New Mexican chests, tables, chairs, and headboards. Rooms
also have tile bar areas with minifridges stocked with complimentary
juices, sodas, and mineral waters; there are also Hobbes-Russell tea
kettles with tea and coffee setups. A special two-room suite includes
a large sitting room with a sofa bed. All rooms overlook the inn's for-
mal gardens and fountains. Large common areas contain cozy nooks
for reading or relaxing. The Taos Plaza is just a short walk away, two
blocks southeast of the inn. Innkeeper Susan Vernon and her artist hus-
band, Ron Rencher, share the stage with two resident cats. Full com-
plimentary breakfasts—served in the guest rooms, on the terrace, or
in the dining room—feature huevos rancheros, blue-corn pancakes with
fresh berries and maple syrup, and the like. Nobody goes away hun-
gry. Hors d'oeuvres are served in the late afternoon. ☎ *405 Cordoba
Rd., Box 5303, Taos 87571,* ☎ *505/758–4777,* FAX *505/758–3976. 3
rooms with bath, 1 suite. No smoking. Outdoor hot tub. MC, V.*

$$$ **Casa Europa.** There's a marvelously ornate 200-year-old bed in the French
★   Room at the Casa Europa that must take an army of maids to keep
polished. But gleaming and polished it is, and you'll feel a little like
Louis XIV as you drift off to sleep, with sounds of crickets and field
frogs wafting in through the partially open French windows above the
courtyard of this two-century-old adobe farmhouse. The inn is run with
care and precision by German-born Rudi Zwicker (former owner of
the popular Greenbriar Restaurant in Boulder, Colorado) and his wife,
Marcia. It was restored in 1983 with its adobe bricks and wood vigas
intact. The rooms, whose whitewashed walls are splashed with sunlight, are furnished with an eclectic collection of European antiques
and treasured Southwest pieces—including the oldest door in Taos, discovered years ago in the basement of the Guadalupe Church. Breakfasts are elaborate. ☎ *840 Upper Ranchitos Rd., Los Cardovas Rte.,
HC, Box 3F, Taos 87571,* ☎ *505/758–9798. 6 double rooms with bath.
Hot tub, sauna. MC, V.*

$$$ **Salsa del Salto.** Seven miles from the Taos Plaza, on the way to the
★   Taos Ski Valley, is this large Western ranch–style home including a two-
story common room with a massive stone fireplace, heated outdoor
pool, hot tub, and tennis court. Located at the edge of the Sangre de
Cristo Mountains, overlooking the Taos mesa, it was designed for own-
ers Mary Hockett and Dadou Mayer by well-known architect Antoine
Predock. Each of the guest rooms is furnished with handcrafted, hand-
painted New Mexican furniture. All have king-size beds with goose-
down comforters and tile bathrooms, and all have spectacular views.
The Master–Honeymoon Suite has a fireplace with copper detailing.
Full gourmet breakfasts are served each morning. During the summer,
the gentle clack of croquet balls can be heard on the front lawn; ev-
eryone dresses in white to play. In the winter, Mayer, a renowned
French chef, doubles as a ski instructor at Taos Ski Valley. ☎ *Rte. 150,
Box 1468, El Prado 87529,* ☎ *and fax 505/776–2422. 8 rooms with
bath. Pool, hot tub, tennis court. MC, V.*

$$$ **Taos Country Inn at Rancho Rio Pueblo.** The aroma of strong coffee and
good things to eat floats through the rooms and hallways of this sprawl-
ing hacienda, parts of it built nearly two centuries ago by settlers named

Rivera. Yolanda Deveaux, the current owner, comes from an old Taos family; her father, Dr. Reynoldo Deveaux, "delivered half the people in Taos," she says. The inn stands amid 22 acres of pastureland, gardens, and orchards, graced with olive trees, cottonwoods, and willows, a brook here, a sturdy wooden fence there. The guest rooms, with white plaster fireplaces and sitting areas, are spacious and sunny; they all have king- or queen-size beds, leather sofas, and local artifacts and artwork. The public rooms are filled with handcrafted furniture and, owing to their large windows, with plenty of light. Breakfast entrées include cream-cheese-and-salmon omelets and such regional specialties as butter crunch eggs and eggs rancheros. ☎ *Box 2331, Upper Ranchitos and Karavas Rds., Taos 87571,* ☎ *505/758–4900 or 800/866–6548,* FAX *505/758–0331. 9 suites. VCR on request, massage. MC, V.*

$$–$$$ **American Artists Gallery House.** The 7-foot-tall flat black iron sculpture in front isn't Kokopelli (whose fluty tunes can be heard in every gift shop between San Diego and Santa Fe) but the *God of Bed and Breakfasts,* a special creation of artist Pozzi Franzetti. (And it may be the only piece among the 500 or so works at the inn that doesn't have a price tag on it.) Works by local, regional, and nationally known artists, including such Native American and Southwestern favorites as R. C. Gorman, Amado Peña, and Veloy Virgil, are featured at this bed-and-breakfast art gallery. Each of the guest rooms has a gallery name, and each is individually furnished in charming Southwestern style. For example, the Garden Gallery room is set in a courtyard with brick and fieldstone areas abundant with flowers, while the Gallery Lilac room is in a separate guest house with high wood ceilings, a kiva-style fireplace, and a kitchen. There's a "honeymoon cottage" in a separate casita. Guests may also enjoy the main living room with its large fireplace, as well as a brick portico and side gardens. Taos Plaza is only minutes away, and owners LeAn and Charles Clamurro are on hand to offer travel advice and information about the city. Full breakfasts include such specialties as French toast stuffed with nuts and soft cheese, along with fresh fruit, coffee, and bagels. ☎ *132 Frontier Rd., Box 584, Taos 87571,* ☎ *505/758–4446 or 800/532–2041,* FAX *505/758–0497. 7 rooms with bath, 2 minisuites with kitchens. Hot tub. MC, V.*

$$–$$$ **Casa de Milagros.** A single-story, turn-of-the-century adobe house, a half-mile east of the Taos Plaza, Casa de Milagros (House of Miracles) offers the texture and flavor of the Taos of long ago, with all the conveniences of today, from hot tub to cable TV. The inn, actually two buildings connected by a portal (where the hot tub is located), is furnished in an eclectic style. Southwestern decor predominates—viga ceilings, Mexican tile bathrooms, custom cabinets, and lots of pottery, tapestry, and weavings. Native American art, particularly the works of Taos Pueblo artist Jonathan Warm Day, hangs on the walls, along with the works of other local artists. Much of it is for sale, and some is commissionable—a portrait, a landscape, if you like. When available from local Native Americans, breakfast includes breads baked in traditional Pueblo *hornos* (ovens), as it has been baked for centuries. There are also fresh fruit, muffins, bread pudding, and homemade granola. ☎ *321 Kit Carson Rd., Box 2983, Taos 87571,* ☎ *505/758–8001 or 800/243–9334,* FAX *505/758–0127. 6 rooms with bath, 1 2-bedroom suite. No smoking. MC, V.*

$$–$$$ **La Posada de Taos.** Within walking distance of the Taos Plaza is this provincial adobe with beamed ceilings, a portal, kiva-style fireplaces, and the intimacy of a private hacienda. Four of its five guest rooms are in the main house; the fifth is a separate cottage with a sky-lit double loft bed, a sitting room, and a fireplace—all cozy and pretty enough to be dubbed *La Casa de la Luna de Miel* (The Honeymoon House).

Wood-burning stoves or adobe fireplaces can be found in the guest rooms, which have either mountain or flowered courtyard views. Innkeepers Bill Swan and Nancy Brooks-Swan offer a full, hearty breakfast, from traditional ham and country eggs to a spicy burrito. ☎ *309 Juanita La., Box 1118, Taos 87571, ☎ 505/758–8164 or 800/645–4803,* FAX *505/751–3294. 5 rooms with bath, 1 cottage. No credit cards.*

$$–$$$ **Mabel Dodge Luhan House.** The home of the heiress and longtime Taos resident, now a bed-and-breakfast inn and conference center, was recently declared a National Historic Landmark. Luhan bought the 200-year-old three-room adobe structure, along with the 12 acres surrounding it, in 1915. Then, with the determination of the pharaohs building the pyramids, she enlarged and expanded it, with the intention, some say, of duplicating her palatial villa in Italy. The three rooms grew to 17; the house rose from one story to three. What it resembled, though, was not an Italian villa but a pueblo—and indeed it was built for and with her fourth husband, Tony Luhan, a full-blooded Taos Pueblo Indian. (Originally the only way to enter was pueblo fashion—by ladder. The ladders are still there, but today's guests can use the front door.) Past guests, from pre-bed-and-breakfast days, included D. H. and Frieda Lawrence, Georgia O'Keeffe, Willa Cather, Mary Austin, John Collier, and John Marin. Mabel Dodge Luhan herself died here in 1962 at the age of 83. Today's owners, George Otero and Susan Chambers-Cooke, bought the house 15 years ago from actor Dennis Hopper. There are 10 guest rooms in the main house, 10 more in a separate guest house. The inn is frequently used for literary workshops and artistic, cultural, and educational meetings and workshops. A full Southwest-style buffet breakfast is served. Don't go if you're looking for crisp linen, designer soaps, and a lot of pampering; the buildings are rumpled and frayed, the stairs creak. Ah, but if you want to soak up some of the magic that made Taos what it is today, this is the place. Meal service is available, and public tennis courts are nearby. ☎ *Box 3400, 240 Morada La., Taos 87571, ☎ 505/758–9456 or 800/846–2235,* FAX *505/751–0431. 18 rooms, 16 with bath; 2 suites. Meeting rooms. MC, V.*

$$–$$$ **Ruby Slipper.** This 1930s farmhouse is one of the few adobe structures in Taos with a gabled roof. The inn includes five guest rooms in the main house and two more in an adjoining building, also styled in adobe. All the rooms have private entrances and include kiva-style fireplaces, Mexican tile baths, and locally crafted furniture—simple and practical, handmade and hand-painted in the brighter colors of the Santa Fe school. Owners Diane Fichtelbert and Beth Goldman envision Taos as a mythical land and have used characters from *The Wizard of Oz* as themes for all their guest rooms. As innkeepers they are environmentally conscious (only natural foods are served) and spiritually aware (God's-Eye symbols are used for do-not-disturb signs, and the Neem Karoli Baba Ashram Hindu Temple is just down the road). The inn reaches out to the gay community and welcomes honeymooners. There's a full breakfast during ski season; the rest of the year, a gourmet basket is delivered to each room. The owners blend their own fine Ruby Slipper coffee. ☎ *416 La Lomita Rd., Box 2069, Taos 87571, ☎ 505/758–0613. 7 rooms with bath. No smoking. Hot tub. AE, D, MC, V.*

$$ **Blue Door.** In the foothills between Taos and Ranchos de Taos, the Blue Door is a 100-year-old adobe farmhouse situated amid orchids, flower gardens, lawns, and patios. Nearby is the famous San Francisco de Asis Church, surrounded by colorful shops. Each of the bedrooms is decorated in country style, with viga ceilings, wood floors, hand-carved beds, and Native American–drum end tables. Owner Bruce Allen makes and markets traditional Taos drums, crafted from carved tree trunks and covered with tautly stretched leather. (His **Taos Drums** factory outlet is on Route 68 on the outskirts of town.) His wife, Pat, runs the inn and also raises Arabian horses. Breakfast at the Blue Door is a particular treat—green-chile quiche, juice, fresh fruit, muffins, blueberry pancakes, bacon, waffles, coffee, and homemade jams from the orchard. ⌦ *La Morada Rd., Box 1168, Taos 87571,* ☎ *505/758–8360. 2 rooms with bath. MC, V.*

$$ **Brooks Street Inn.** A large, rambling adobe house with a circular drive and an adjoining guest house comprise the Brooks Street Inn, at one time an artist's residence. Although constructed in 1956, the house was built in the traditional manner with adobe bricks made on the property, beamed ceilings, polished wood floors, and a large stone fireplace. An elaborately carved corbel arch (the handiwork of Japanese carpenter Yaichikido) spans the entranceway, and alongside is a shaded, walled garden. The guest rooms show great attention to detail—the perfect basket; fresh-cut flowers; plump, fluffy pillows. In the large living room, paintings by local artists share wall space with family photographs. The full breakfast features blue corn pancakes with pineapple sauce, stuffed french toast with apricot glaze, and other home-baked delights, all complemented by coffee, espresso, and cappuccino, fresh from the expresso machine. When the weather is warm, breakfast is served at umbrella tables on the patio; in the winter, it's served by the fireplace. ⌦ *119 Brooks St., Box 4954, Taos 87571,* ☎ *800/758–1489. 6 rooms with bath. No smoking. AE, MC, V.*

$$ **Hacienda del Sol.** This is a house with a history. Bordering the Taos
★ Pueblo, it was acquired in the 1920s by art patron Mabel Dodge Luhan. She and her fourth husband, Tony Luhan, lived here while building their main house, Las Palomas de Taos. After moving, they kept Hacienda del Sol as a private retreat and as a guest house for visiting notables; author Frank Waters wrote *People of the Valley* while staying here. Overlooking 95,000 acres of pueblo land and shaded by huge cottonwood, ponderosa pine, blue spruce, and willow trees, the site offers a majestic, uninterrupted view of the Taos mountains, one particularly enjoyed by today's guests while soaking in the secluded outdoor hot tub. Most of the rooms feature kiva-style fireplaces, Spanish antiques, Southwestern-style handcrafted furniture, and original artwork, much of it for sale. (The inn has a complete gift shop, just off the reception area.) The Los Amantes Room has a large bedroom with seating area adjoining a room with a double-size black Jacuzzi on a mahogany platform amid a jungle of potted plants. There's a skylight for stargazing while you soak, and the attached bathroom, with its jet-black sink, tub, shower, and toilet—all with gleaming gold fixtures—is a celebration of decadence. A full gourmet breakfast is served. ⌦ *109 Mabel Dodge La., Box 177, Taos 87571,* ☎ *505/758–0287,* FAX *505/751–0319. 7 rooms with bath, 2 with shared bath, 1 suite. Outdoor hot tub. MC, V.*

$$ **Orinda.** Surrounded by open meadows and tall trees, Orinda, built in 1947, is a dramatic adobe estate with spectacular views and country privacy, and it's within walking distance of the Taos Plaza. Even getting there is fun: It's off bustling Placitas Road, down a drive flanked by pastures with grazing horses and groves of cottonwoods and elms. The spacious one- and two-bedroom suites have separate entrances, kiva-style fireplaces, traditional viga ceilings, and Mexican tile baths. The thick adobe walls ensure peace and quiet. Wisconsinites George and Cary Pratt, the owners since 1992, have remodeled and enlarged the original adobe structure. The main house has a library with a fireplace and a picture window looking onto the Taos Mountains. A hearty breakfast is served in the two-story sun atrium amid a gallery of art works, all for sale. ⌦ *461 Valverde, Box 4451, Taos 87571,* ☎

505/758–8581 or 800/847–1837. 2 rooms with bath, 1 suite. No smoking. D, MC, V.

$ **Harrison's Bed and Breakfast.** In a rural setting 2½ miles north of the Taos Plaza, this large adobe home is convenient for trips to the Taos Ski Area. It is the domain of Bob and Jean Harrison, who have lived in Taos for 26 years. The house overlooks a wooded area and the town from the foot of the west mesa and is beautifully set off by trees and bushes. The guest rooms are furnished with handmade and hand-painted desks, tables, and headboards crafted in northern New Mexico, less ornate than their Santa Fe–style counterparts. Breakfast—tailored to guests' preference—is served in the rooms or, weather permitting, on the flower-bedecked patio. ▨ *1134 Millicent Rogers Rd., Box 242, Taos 87571, ☎ 505/758–2630. 4 double rooms with bath, 2 double rooms with shared bath. No credit cards.*

Camping

Thousands of miles of unspoiled wilderness await campers in and around the Taos area. The **Orilla Verde Recreation Area** (Bureau of Land Management, Cruz Alta Rd., Taos 87571, ☎ 505/758–8851), located 10 miles south of Taos along the banks of the Rio Grande, offers opportunities for camping, hiking, fishing, and picnicking. It's open year-round; camping fees are $7 per night, $3 per vehicle for day use. The **Carson National Forest** (208 Cruz Alta Rd., Box 558, Taos 87571, ☎ 505/758–6200) has more than 30 campgrounds (and 400 miles of cool mountain trout streams), including those of the Wheeler Peak Recreational Area, the highest point in New Mexico at 13,161 feet. Most campgrounds are free; some charge a $5–$8 camping fee.

A number of commercial campgrounds can be found as well, among them the **Taos RV Park** (Rte. 68, 1799 Paseo del Pueblo Sur, Box 729F, Ranchos de Taos 87557, ☎ 505/758–1667 or 800/323–6009), next to the Taos Motel just off the intersection of Route 518. The park has 29 spaces: 22 full hookups with cable TV capacity, and 7 tent sites with water and electricity. Hot showers are available. The trailer sites are $17 per night for two; the tent sites are $12 for two. Located in the Sangre de Cristo Mountains, 5 miles from the Rio Grande Gorge, the area is grassy, with a few small trees. ☉ Year-round.

Taos Valley RV Park (120 Estes Rd., Box 200, Ranchos de Taos 87557, ☎ 505/758–4469), a former Campgrounds of America (KOA) franchise, has complete campground facilities, with 60-foot pull-throughs and full hookups. Facilities for tenters are also available. In the Rio Grande Valley, 2½ miles south of the Taos Plaza, the campground is at an elevation of 7,000 feet and has been in operation for over 20 years. It has 92 sites, with prices ranging from $12.25 to $17.75, depending on size and requirements. Local TV signals come in sharp and clear. ☉ March–November 1.

Questa Lodge (Questa, Box 155, Questa 87556, ☎ 505/586–0300) has 24 units on the banks of the Red River, two blocks from Route 522. Fees are $6 for the tent sites, $15 for full hookups. ☉ May–mid-October.

The Roadrunner Campground (Red River, Box 588, Red River 87558, ☎ 505/754–2286 or 800/243–2286) has 155 units located at the end of Red River–Route 578 in a spectacular wooded mountain setting, with the Red River running right through the campground. Fees are $20 ($22 for a river site), which includes water and electrical hookup, cable TV, and sewer. ☉ Year-round.

THE ARTS AND NIGHTLIFE

Taos Magazine (Whitney Publishing, Box 1236, Santa Fe 87504, ☎ 505/989–7603), published eight times a year, covers events, fashion, arts, and the general cultural beat in town.

The Arts

The **Taos Community Auditorium** (133 Paseo del Pueblo Norte, ☎ 505/758–4677) offers performances of modern dance groups and the local theater group, concerts, movies, and even the sounds of Andean folk music. For a weekly entertainment listing, check the "Tempo" section of the *Taos News*. Contact the **Taos Art Association** (☎ 505/758–2052), which owns and operates the Taos Community Auditorium, for ticket information. The **Taos Spring Arts Celebration** (May) and the **Taos Arts Festival** (Sept. 18–Oct. 4) are the major arts gatherings in Taos. Both events highlight the visual, performing, and literary arts of the community and allow visitors to rub elbows with the many artists who call Taos home. For information, call Taos Arts Celebration (☎ 505/758–3873) and the Taos County Chamber of Commerce (☎ 505/758–3873 or 800/732–8267). The **Wool Festival** (late Sept. or early Oct.), held in Kit Carson Park, features everything from sheep to shawl, with demonstrations of shearing, spinning, and weaving, handmade woolen items for sale, and tastings of favorite lamb dishes.

Music

From mid-June through early August, the Taos School of Music and the International Institute of Music fill the evenings with the sounds of chamber and symphonic orchestras at the **Taos Chamber Music Festival.** This is the oldest summer music program in America and possibly the largest enclave of professional musicians in the Southwest. It has been furthering the artistic growth of young string and piano students for over 30 years. Concerts are presented every Saturday evening from mid-June through August at the Taos School of Music, Taos Community Auditorium (☎ 505/776–2388). The tickets are $12. Concerts and recitals are also presented at the **Hotel Saint Bernard** (☎ 505/776–2251) in the Taos Ski Valley. Admission is free. **Music from Angel Fire** is a series of classical and jazz concerts presented at the Community Auditorium from mid-August to early September. The series is now in its 12th season. Tickets cost around $12 per concert. For information, call 505/758–4667.

Nightlife

Bars and Lounges
Fernando's Hideaway (Holiday Inn, Paseo del Pueblo Norte, ☎ 505/758–4444) presents live entertainment nightly, alternating rock, jazz, vocals, and country music. Saturday is reserved for karaoke. Lavish complimentary Happy Hour buffets are offered on weekday evenings. The **Taos Park Inn International** (Paseo del Pueblo Sur, ☎ 505/758–8610) features dancing and live entertainment on weekends, usually of the rock or country variety. The **Adobe Bar** (Taos Inn, 125 Paseo del Pueblo Norte, ☎ 505/758–2233), Taos's local meet-and-greet spot, offers talented local live acts, from a flute choir to individual guitarists and small jazz, folk, and country bands.

Cabaret
The **Kachina Lodge Cabaret** (413 Paseo del Pueblo Norte, ☎ 505/758–2275) brings in headline acts, such as Arlo Guthrie and the Kingston Trio, on a regular basis and is open for dancing.

Country-and-Western Clubs

The **Sagebrush Inn** (Paseo del Pueblo Sur, ☎ 505/758–2254) offers live entertainment—mostly of the country-Western variety—nightly in its spacious lobby lounge. There's no cover charge, and if you show up on a Thursday, you can learn to two-step.

Jazz Clubs

Each January, **Thunderbird Lodge** (3 Thunderbird Rd., ☎ 505/776–2280) in the Taos Ski Valley presents Jazz Legends, an annual series of concerts that bring world-famous jazz musicians to the intimate setting of the Thunderbird Bar. The concerts are popular and seating is limited, so early reservations are recommended.

TAOS ESSENTIALS

Arriving and Departing

By Bus

Texas, New Mexico, Oklahoma Coaches (a subsidiary of Greyhound/Trailways) runs buses once a day from Albuquerque to the Taos Bus Station (corner of Paseo del Pueblo Sur and Paseo del Cañon, ☎ 505/758–1144).

By Car

The main route from Santa Fe to Taos is Route 68. From points north, take Route 522; from points east or west, take Route 64. Roads can be treacherously icy during the winter months; call New Mexico Road Conditions (☎ 800/432–4269) before heading out. The altitude in Taos will affect your car's performance, causing it to "gasp" because it's getting too much gas and not enough air.

By Plane

The closest major airport is in Albuquerque, 2½ hours south of Taos. The **Taos Municipal Airport** (U.S. 64, ☎ 505/758–4995), 12 miles west of the city, services only private planes and air charters. For air-charter information, call 505/758–4995.

BETWEEN THE AIRPORT AND DOWNTOWN

Pride of Taos (☎ 505/758–8340) runs daily shuttle service to the Albuquerque Airport ($35 one-way, $65 round-trip) and between Taos and Santa Fe ($25 one-way, $50 round-trip). Advance reservations are strongly recommended.

Faust's Transportation (in nearby El Prado, ☎ 505/758–3410 or 505/758–7359) offers radio-dispatched taxis between the Taos Airport and town ($12), and between the Albuquerque airport and Taos ($35 one-way, $65 round-trip).

By Train

Amtrak (☎ 800/872–7245) provides service into Lamy Station (County Rd. 41, Lamy 87500) half an hour outside Santa Fe, the closest train station to Taos. **Faust's Transportation** (in nearby El Prado, ☎ 505/758–3410 or 505/758–7359) offers radio-dispatched taxis to the train station.

Getting Around

Taos, like Santa Fe, radiates around its famous central Plaza and is easily maneuvered on foot. And, like Santa Fe, it has a La Fonda Hotel directly on the Plaza, although the two hotels have no official affiliation. Since the Plaza is the city's prime location, many of the top

No matter where you go, travel is easier when you know the code.^{sm}

dial 1 8 0 0 CALL ATT®

Dial 1 800 CALL ATT and you'll always get through from any phone with any card* and you'll always get AT&T's best deal.** It's the one number to remember when calling away from home.

*Other long distance company calling cards excluded.
**Additional discounts available.

AT&T
Your True Choice

All the best trips start with **Fodor's**.

restaurants, stores, boutiques, and galleries are either on it or within its immediate vicinity. The main street through town is Paseo del Pueblo Norte, which turns into Paseo del Pueblo Sur. All the major hotels have ample parking space, and parking areas can be easily found just beyond the Plaza (though space may be tight during the peak summer months). To reach many of the sights of interest outside town, transportation will be necessary.

By Car
CAR RENTAL
Hertz Rent-A-Car (☎ 505/751–1292) is located on Paseo del Pueblo Sur; **Payless Rent-A-Car** (☎ 505/758–9501) is at the Taos Municipal Airport; and **Jeep Trailways Rentals** (☎ 505/754–6443, open May 15–Oct. 15) is located at Alpine Lodge, Red River.

By Taxi
Taxi service is sparse. However, **Faust's Transportation** (☎ 505/758–3410 or 505/758–7359), in nearby El Prado, has a fleet of radio-dispatched cabs.

Guided Tours

Orientation
Pride of Taos Tours (Box 1192, Taos 87571, ☎ 505/758–8340) provides 70-minute narrated trolleylike bus tours of Taos highlights, including the San Francisco de Asis Mission Church that Georgia O'Keeffe painted, the Martinez Hacienda that portrays Spanish Colonial life during the 17th and 18th centuries, and Kit Carson's House and Museum near the Plaza. The cost is $15 for adults, and children under 11 go free. A longer "deluxe" tour covering the Millicent Rogers Museum, San Francisco de Asis Church, and other outlying attractions costs $30 (there is a minimum of five passengers, children under 11 go free). The departure points for tours, shuttles, and pickups is next to the Chamber of Commerce office on Paseo del Pueblo Sur and the Taos Plaza.

Special-Interest
Native Sons Adventures (715 Paseo del Pueblo Sur, Taos 87571, ☎ 505/758–9342 or 800/753–7559) organizes biking, backpacking, rafting, snowmobiling, and horseback and wagon expeditions. **Roadrunner Tours** (Box 274, Angel Fire 87710, ☎ 505/377–6416) is run by Nancy and Bill Burch, who offer car, Jeep, ski, and horseback rentals, as well as snowmobile tours and sleigh rides. **Taos Fitness Adventures** (216-M Paseo del Pueblo Norte, Suite 173, Taos 87571 ☎ 505/776–1017) provides week-long hiking and fitness programs during the summer and fall, limited to eight persons housed in a luxury mountain lodge. Hikes range from easy to advanced, covering up to 15 miles a day. **Taos Indian Horse Ranch** (Taos Pueblo 87571, ☎ 505/758–3212 or 800/659–3210) features two-hour trail rides, as well as old-fashioned horse-drawn sleigh rides through the Taos Pueblo backcountry, winter weather permitting, complete with brass bells, a Native American storyteller, toasted marshmallows, and green chile roasts. Escorted horseback tours and hayrides are run through Native American lands during the remainder of the year. (By reservation only. No liquor permitted.) The Ranch closes for 42–48 days each year to observe the Taos Pueblo Sweats Ceremony. Call the Taos Pueblo Governor's Office (☎ 505/758–9593) for exact dates.

Opening and Closing Times
Banks, weekdays 9–5; museums, daily 9–5; stores, daily 9 or 10–5 or 6; post office, weekdays 9–5.

Important Addresses and Numbers

Emergencies
Fire, medical, or police (☎ 911). **Taos police** (☎ 505/758–2216), **state police** (☎ 505/758–8878).

Ambulance (☎ 505/758–1911).

Hospital emergency room: Holy Cross Hospital (630 Paseo del Pueblo Sur, ☎ 505/758–8883).

Pharmacies
Taos Pharmacy (S. Santa Fe Rd., ☎ 505/758–3342); **Furr's Pharmacy** (1100 Paseo del Pueblo Sur, ☎ 505/758–9891); **Springer's Drug** (825 4th St., Springer, ☎ 505/483–2356).

Visitor Information
Brochures, maps, a calendar of events, and general information are available from the **Taos County Chamber of Commerce** (1139 Paseo del Pueblo Sur, Post Office Drawer 1, Taos 87571, ☎ 505/758–3873 or 800/732–8267). Its visitor-information center, two blocks south of the Plaza on Paseo del Pueblo Sur, is open 9–6 daily during the summer months, 9–5 daily during the rest of the year.

4 Albuquerque

A LARGE CITY—its population is nearing the half-million mark—Albuquerque spreads out in all directions, with no apparent ground rules. No cohesive pattern, either architecturally or geographically, seems to hold it together; the city seems as free and free-spirited as all those hot-air balloons that take part in the Albuquerque International Balloon Fiesta every October. Even residents seem confused by the street system that, like the city itself, goes this way and that. Each main street and boulevard has a direction designation after it, NE, SW, or what have you, so people can find out where they are.

Once the code is broken, however, it's a marvelous city. Like all of New Mexico, it blends its cultures well; its citizens are descendants of the Native Americans who first inhabited the land and defended it bravely, of the Spanish who came on horseback to conquer and settle, and of the Anglos who were trappers and hunters and traders and pioneers in a new and often inhospitable land. From the beginning, Albuquerque was a trade and transportation center. It was an important station on the Old Chihuahua Trail, an extension of the Santa Fe Trail winding down into Mexico.

Albuquerque's incredible sprawl can be explained in a number of ways. The city was founded in 1706 on the banks of the Rio Grande near a bend in the river, an ideal location for crop irrigation, transportation, and protection. The settlement prospered, thanks to its strategic trade-route location and its proximity to several Native American pueblos that offered mutual support and commerce. The settlers built a chapel and then a church, San Felipe de Neri Catholic Church (named after a 16th-century Florentine saint). Their homes were built close together around a central plaza for protection, as were those in other early Spanish settlements in the hostile new land. Entrance to the fortresslike community could be gained only at the four corners, making it easier to defend.

That original four-block downtown area is now known as Old Town, the city's tourist hub, with all its galleries and trendy restaurants. Had the city simply continued to grow, progressively expanding from its central hub, that would have made sense. But something happened. First the Rio Grande gradually changed its course, moving farther and farther west. That caused a shift in the population. Then, in 1880, the railroad came to Albuquerque, its tracks skirting Old Town by a good 2 miles. The result was another population shift. Old Town wasn't exactly abandoned, but "New Town" began to sprout up along the train depot, and it grew until it eventually enveloped Old Town. Finally, there was Route 66. Designated in 1926, called the "Mother Road" by John Steinbeck, it sparked much of Albuquerque's early economic development. During the '30s and '40s it surged through town with as much impact as the railroad and the river combined, and the burgeoning city swelled around the asphalt pavement—motels, gas stations, diners, and truck stops, a sea of neon that celebrated America's new independent mobility.

Today Albuquerque is a thriving arts center, as are many other areas of New Mexico. From the moment visitors step off a plane at Albuquerque International Airport, they're surrounded by art. Throughout the terminal building, special display areas are devoted to the works of New Mexican artists—a collection assembled by the Albuquerque Arts Board as part of the city's 1% For Art Program, in which 1% of Albuquerque's

municipal budget is devoted to public art projects. In addition, the city
has numerous privately owned museums and galleries and is a growing center for artists, writers, poets, filmmakers, and musicians.

EXPLORING

Historic and colorful Route 66 is Albuquerque's Central Avenue, uni-
fying, as nothing else, the diverse areas of the city—Old Town cradled
at the bend of the Rio Grande, the University of New Mexico to the
east, and Nob Hill (a lively strip of restaurants, boutiques, galleries,
and shops farther east along Central Avenue). The railroad tracks and
Central Avenue/Route 66 divide the city into quadrants, or quarters—
SW, NW, SE, NE.

Because Albuquerque covers such a large geographical area, its terrain
is rather diverse. Along the river in the north and south valleys, ele-
vations hover at around 4,800 feet. To the northeast, land rises over
mesas to the foothills of the Sandia Mountains at an elevation of 6,500
feet; the Sandia Crest is a grand spot from which to view the city spread
below and get a feel for its layout. West of the Rio Grande, where much
of Albuquerque's growth is taking place, the mesa rises more abruptly
than it does in the east—with a difference in elevation of 1,700 feet in
the lowlands and highlands of the city. There are corresponding changes
in temperature, as much as 10°F at any time; it's even been known to
snow or rain in one part of town while remaining dry and sunny in
another.

Tour 1: Old Town

*Numbers in the margin correspond to points of interest on the Albu-
querque Old Town and Albuquerque maps.*

An exploration of Albuquerque begins where the city began, in Old
Town. It was here on the Plaza in 1706 that Don Francisco Cuervo y
Valdes, a New Mexico provincial governor, decided to seal his mark
in history by founding a town. No slouch when it came to political
maneuvering, he named the new town, or *villa*, after the Duke of Alburquerque, viceroy of New Spain, hoping that the flattery would
cause the duke to overlook the fact that the newly formed community
had only 15 families instead of the required 30 needed for a charter.
The Duke of Alburquerque acquiesced, of course, but somewhere
down the line the first "r" in his name was dropped. Don Francisco
couldn't have made a better choice for the town's location. The new
settlement was on the banks of the Rio Grande where the river made
a wide curve, providing good irrigation for crops, and where several
Native American pueblos already existed, meaning mutual aid, protection, and trade. The nearby mountains and forest offered ample
wood—cottonwoods, willows, and olive trees. The weather was ideal.

★ ❶ Today, Albuquerque's **Old Town Plaza** remains the heart of the city's
heritage. While the modern city of nearly 500,000 residents grew up
all around it, the four-square-block area of Old Town clings fiercely
to the past, at least in spirit. The tree-shaded Plaza of today is much
the Plaza of the past, except that a graceful white gazebo and lacy
wrought-iron benches have been added. The **San Felipe de Neri Catholic
Church** (2005 North Plaza NW, ☎ 505/243–4628), enlarged and expanded several times over the years, still stands facing the Plaza, its
massive adobe walls and other original sections intact. Most of the old
adobe homes surrounding the church and the Plaza have been converted
into shops, galleries, and restaurants, and many of the hidden *placitas,*

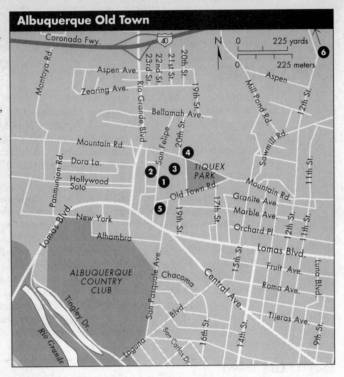

or little plazas, offer more of the same. The best time to visit Old Town is early in the morning before the stores have opened and the daily rush of activity begins. In the defused light of morning, you can almost hear the strum of a Spanish guitar and the click of heels, possibly a dancer, a conquistador, or a woman opening her shop.

Old Town, which is one block north of Central Avenue (the city's main street) at Rio Grande Boulevard, is a beehive of activity, with nearly 200 shops, restaurants, cafés, and delis. The scent of bubbling vats of green chile, enchiladas, and burritos hangs in the air. Gunfights are staged on Romero Street on Sunday afternoon, and during times of fiesta Old Town is alive with mariachi bands and dancing señoritas. You can pick up schedules of events and maps, which contain a list of public rest rooms, at the **Old Town Visitors Center** across the street from the San Felipe de Neri Catholic Church. *305 Romero St. NW,* ☎ *505/243–3215.* ☉ *Mon.–Sat. 10–5, Sun. 11–5.*

Adjacent to Old Town, just off the northeast corner on Mountain Road, are two of the city's major museums. The solar-heated **Albuquerque Museum** enshrines relics of the city's birth and development and is home to the largest collection of Spanish Colonial artifacts in the nation. The centerpiece of the exhibit is two life-size models of Spanish conquistadores in chain mail and armor, one on horseback, representing the arrival of Francisco Vásquez de Coronado and his soldiers on their quest for gold in 1540, the turning point of New Mexico's history. Among the museum's attractions are early maps (some from the 15th century showing California as an island and the Rio Grande spilling into the Pacific), treasure chests once filled with pearls and gold coins, colonial and contemporary paintings, and religious artifacts. A multimedia audiovisual presentation chronicles the development of the city since

1875. *2000 Mountain Rd. NW,* ☎ *505/243–7255 or 505/242–4600.*
☛ *Free.* ⊙ *Tues.–Sun. 9–5.*

★ ❹ The **New Mexico Museum of Natural History,** across the street from
the Albuquerque Museum, is the city's newest showpiece. The striking glass and sand-color building with slanted roofs opened in 1986.
Its spectacular world of wonders, rumored to have been mounted, in
part, with the help of Disney experts, includes an active volcano (its
river of bubbling hot lava flows beneath museum visitors under a see-
through glass floor), a frigid Ice Age cave, dinosaurs, and an Evolator
(short for Evolution Elevator), a six-minute high-tech ride through 35
million years of New Mexico's geological history via a mountain of
video wizardry. An on-board video host on the large elevator escorts
25 passengers per ride, during which the floors and video-screen walls
move, simulating a ride through the dimensions. The Dynamax Theater makes viewers feel equally involved. An 85-foot-long replica of
the Rio Grande flows from its source in Colorado, all the way down
through Texas. A full-size replica of a 100-million-year-old Quetzal-
coatlus, with a wingspan of 38 feet, hovers over the museum's central
atrium, while visitors arriving via the front walkway outside share space
with a life-size sculpture of a Pentaceratops, a 21-foot-long horned dinosaur, and an Albertosaur, a 30-foot-long carnivorous dinosaur. The
museum has a Fossil Hot Line (call the main number) to assist ama-
teurs in identifying paleontological finds. *1801 Mountain Rd. NW,* ☎
505/841–8837. ☛ *$4 adults, $3 senior citizens and students, $1 chil-
dren 3–11, toddlers free. Combination tickets for museum and Dynamax Theater: $7 adults, $5 senior citizens and students, $3 children
3–11.* ⊙ *Daily 9–5.*

❺ For some more specialized natural history, go back down to Old Town,
at the corner of San Felipe and Old Town Road: In the **American International Rattlesnake Museum,** the largest exhibit of rattlesnakes and
rattlesnake memorabilia ever mounted can be viewed. Included are rare
and unusual specimens, such as an albino rattlesnake. There are also
rattlesnake artifacts, videos, and a Southwestern gift shop. *202 San Felipe NW,* ☎ *505/242–6569.* ☛ *$2 adults, $1 children under 16.* ⊙ *10–
9 in summer, 10–7 in winter.*

★ ❻ A short drive north of Old Town brings you to the **Indian Pueblo Cultural Center.** Its unique multilevel semicircular design was inspired by
that of Pueblo Bonito, the famous prehistoric ruin in Chaco Canyon
in the northwestern section of New Mexico. The cultural center is owned
and operated by the 19 Pueblo tribes of New Mexico, each of which
has an upper-level alcove devoted to its particular arts and crafts.
Lower-level exhibits trace the history of the Pueblo Native Americans
from prehistoric times to the present. Original paintings and sculpture
of the highest quality, jewelry, leather crafts, rugs, souvenir items,
drums, beaded necklaces, painted bowls, and fetishes on display are
for sale. It's the largest collection of Native American arts and crafts
in the Southwest and the richest resource for the study of America's
first inhabitants of the region. Native American ceremonial dances are
performed during the summer and on special holidays. *2401 12th St.
NW,* ☎ *505/843–7270 or 800/766–4405.* ☛ *$3 adults, $2 senior citizens, $1 students and children 6–18, children under 6 free.* ⊙ *Daily
9–5:30; restaurant open 7:30–3:30. Closed major holidays.*

TIME OUT The Indian Pueblo Cultural Center has a restaurant, open for lunch, that
serves Native American food exclusively, including blue-corn enchiladas, posole, Native American bread pudding, and, of course, fry

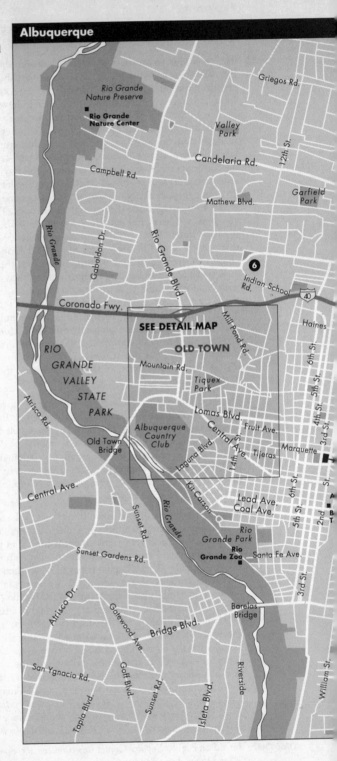

Albuquerque

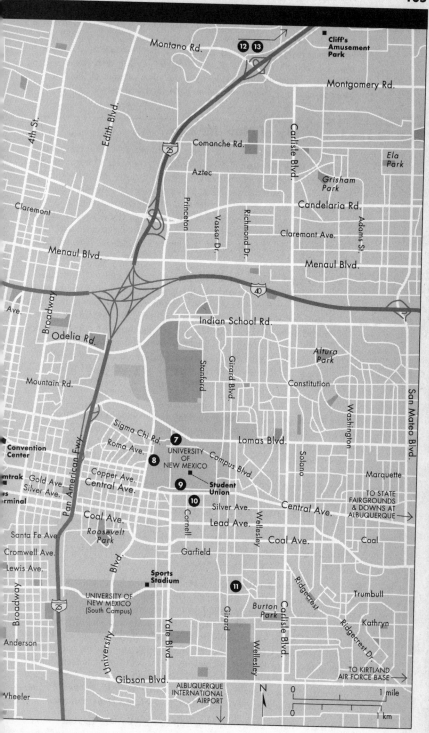

Montano Rd.

⑫ ⑬

Cliff's
Amusement
Park

Montgomery Rd.

4th St.

Edith Blvd.

I-25

Comanche Rd.

Aztec

Princeton

Carlisle Blvd.

Ela
Park

Claremont

Grisham
Park

Candelaria Rd.

Vassar Dr.

Richmond Dr.

Claremont Ave.

Adams St.

Menaul Blvd.

Menaul Blvd.

Broadway

I-40

Odelia Rd.

Indian School Rd.

Altura
Park

Mountain Rd.

Stanford

Girard Blvd.

Constitution

Washington

San Mateo Blvd.

Convention
Center

Sigma Chi Rd.

Roma Ave.

⑦

UNIVERSITY
OF
NEW MEXICO

⑧

Campus Blvd.

Lomas Blvd.

Solano

Marquette

Amtrak
Gold Ave.
Silver Ave.

Copper Ave.

Central Ave.

⑨

⑩

Student
Union

Silver Ave.

Lead Ave.

Wellesley

Central Ave.

TO STATE
FAIRGROUNDS
& DOWNS AT
ALBUQUERQUE →

bus
terminal

Santa Fe Ave.

Cromwell Ave.

Lewis Ave.

Coal Ave.

Roosevelt
Park

Blvd.

Cornell

Garfield

Coal Ave.

Coal

Pan American Fwy.

Broadway

I-25

Anderson

Wheeler

Sports
Stadium

UNIVERSITY OF
NEW MEXICO
(South Campus)

University

Yale Blvd.

Gibson Blvd.

⑪

Girard

Burton
Park

Wellesley

Carlisle Blvd.

Ridgecrest

Ridgecrest Dr.

Trumbull

Kathryn

TO KIRTLAND
AIR FORCE BASE →

ALBUQUERQUE
INTERNATIONAL
AIRPORT

N

0   1 mile
0   1 km

bread—that addictive popoverlike creation topped with honey, beans, chile, or powdered sugar or gobbled up plain. In Old Town, **Zane Graze Cafe & News** (308 San Felipe NW, ☎ 505/243–4377) is delightful for lunch or refreshments. A good alternative is the **Owl Cafe** (800 Eubank Blvd. NE, directly north of I–40, ☎ 505/291–4900), a nostalgic 1950s-style diner with a soda fountain, jukebox, pictures of Marilyn Monroe, and milk shakes and green chile cheeseburgers.

Tour 2: The University of New Mexico

Just east of I–25 on Central Avenue is Albuquerque's 106-year-old **University of New Mexico** (☎ 505/277–0111), the state's largest university, internationally recognized for its programs in anthropology, biology, Latin American studies, and medicine. It's also noted for its Pueblo Revival–style architecture and superb landscaping. A central oasis within its 700 acres contains knolls, a duck pond, fountains, waterfalls, and benches. Throughout the campus are large-scale sculptures by internationally known artists and murals by famous New Mexican painters.

The university is a mainstay of Albuquerque's cultural and educational life, and its many outstanding galleries and museums, open to the public free of charge, shouldn't be missed. Included among them

★ ➐ is the **Jonson Gallery,** containing the works of the late modernistic painter Raymond Jonson (1891–1982), as well as those of contemporary artists. This intimate gallery is Jonson's former home and studio. A special retrospective exhibit of his work is presented each summer. *1909 Las Lomas NE (University of New Mexico campus),* ☎ *505/277–4967.* ☛ *Free.* ☺ *Tues. 9–4 and 5–8, Wed.–Fri. 9–4; closed Sat.–Mon. and all major holidays.*

➑ The **Maxwell Museum of Anthropology,** in the university's Anthropology Building, one block north of Grand Avenue on University Boulevard, has two permanent galleries. In one, the "Ancestors" exhibit chronicles 4 million years of human emergence. In the other, "Peoples of the Southwest" explores the lifeways, art, and cultures of 11,500 years of human occupation in the Southwest. The museum shop offers a wide selection of traditional and contemporary Southwestern Native American jewelry, rugs, pottery, basketry, beadwork, and folk art from around the world. It also has a children's section with inexpensive books and handmade tribal artifacts. *Maxwell Museum of Anthropology (University of New Mexico campus),* ☎ *505/277–4405.* ☛ *Free.* ☺ *Weekdays 9–4, Sat. 10–4, Sun. noon–4.*

➒ The **University Art Museum,** located in the Fine Arts Center just northwest of the entrance on Stanford Drive and Central Avenue, features permanent and changing displays of contemporary and historical art. Its fine-art collection is the largest in the state and includes the work of such Old Masters as Rembrandt and such newer ones as Picasso and (of course) Georgia O'Keeffe. The museum also has one of the largest holdings of prints and photographs in the country, including contemporary leaders and early pioneers in the field. *Fine Arts Center (University of New Mexico campus),* ☎ *505/277–4001.* ☛ *Free.* ☺ *Tues. 9–4 and 5–8, Wed.–Fri. 9–4, Sun. 1–4; closed Mon. and Sat.*

At the corner of Central Avenue and Cornell Drive is the sales and exhibit gallery of the **Tamarind Institute,** an internationally renowned school and workshop for lithographers, where fine-art prints pulled from stones and metal plates are created. A Tamarind Master Printer certification is to an artist what a degree from Juilliard is to a musician. Tamarind maintains a gallery where prints and lithographs done by professionals, as well as those recently produced by students, are on display. Special guided tours are conducted on the first Friday of each month at 1 PM. *108 Cornell Dr. SE, ☎ 505/277–3901. ☛ Free. ⊘ Weekdays 9–5 and by appointment.*

⑪ Two blocks south of the university on Girard Boulevard SE, you'll find the **Ernie Pyle Memorial Library,** the memorabilia-filled home of the beloved Pulitzer Prize–winning war correspondent, now the smallest branch of the Albuquerque Public Library. Pyle bought the house in 1940 after several visits to New Mexico with his wife, Jerry. On display are photos, handwritten articles by Pyle, and news clippings of his career and of his death by a sniper's bullet on April 18, 1945, on the tiny Pacific island of Ie Shima; he's buried in the National Cemetery of the Pacific in Punchbowl Crater, near Honolulu. "There are really two wars," wrote John Steinbeck. "One is the war of maps, logistics, campaigns, ballistics, divisions. . . . Then there is the war of the homesick, the weary, the wounded and dying, the common man . . . that is Ernie Pyle's war." *900 Girard Blvd. SE, ☎ 505/256–2065. ☛ Free. ⊘ Tues. and Thurs. 12:30–9, Wed., Fri., and Sat. 9–5:30. Closed Sun. and Mon.*

TIME OUT The university's **Student Union Building** (☎ 505/277-2331) on Central Avenue, just north of the visitors' parking area, is a good spot to grab a burger or just rest your feet for a while. Here you'll also find changing exhibits and students' showings in three exhibit spaces—the Centennial (on the main level), Union (north end, lower level), and ASA (south end, lower level) galleries.

Tour 3: Sandia

For a view of Albuquerque on high—and of half of New Mexico for that matter—head for **Sandia Crest,** the 10,678-foot summit of the Sandia Mountains. The road to the Crest, the Sandia Crest National Scenic Byway (east on I–40 to NM 14, north to NM 536), is well paved and carefully maintained year-round. Of course, there's more than one

★ ⑫ way to get to the top. The **Sandia Peak Aerial Tramway,** the world's longest single-span tramway, takes visitors from a point outside Albuquerque's city limits on an awesome 2.7-mile climb to the top of Sandia Peak, where at sunset the desert skies produce a kaleidoscope of changing colors. From its lower terminal the tram car glides across a terrain of jagged boulders and clawing peaks, causing deer or perhaps a family of Rocky Mountain bighorn sheep to scamper away from the strange sight. The tram cars were custom-made in Switzerland with plenty of window space. From the sky-top observation deck at the summit, you can see Santa Fe to the northeast and Los Alamos to the northwest. And isn't that Tucson over there? Heading back, you can go the way you came or take the double-chair skiers' chair lift 7,500 feet down the other side. To reach the tramway's base, take I–25 north to the Tramway Road exit, then east on Tramway Road, or take Tramway Boulevard north from I–40 and Central Avenue for 8½ miles to the stop sign, then head right on Tramway Road. *Sandia Peak Tramway, 10 Tramway Loop NE, ☎ 505/298–8518. ⊘ Memorial Day–Labor Day, daily 9 AM–10 PM; Labor Day–Memorial Day, Sun.–Thurs. 9–9 (opens later on Wed.), Fri.–Sat. 9 AM–10 PM. Weekends only during the 2nd and 4th wks of April. Tickets for the 90-min round-trip are $12.50 adults, $9.50 senior citizens and children 5–12.*

TIME OUT   There's a pricey restaurant atop the tramway called, appropriately, **High Finance** (Sandia Peak, ☎ 505/243–9742). Needless to say, the view is outstanding. An alternative is the **Firehouse Restaurant** (☎ 505/856–3473), at the base of the tram. If you choose to drive to Sandia Crest, try **Sandia Crest House Gift Shop and Restaurant** (Sandia Crest, ☎ 505/243–0605), which provides snacks and refreshments and more spectacular views.

⑬   A few miles farther north, the **Sandia Pueblo** is one of the most industrious of the Rio Grande Pueblos. *See* Pueblos Near Albuquerque *in* Chapter 6.

What to See and Do with Children

Cliff's Amusement Park, on Osuna Road at San Mateo Boulevard, includes 24 thrill rides, live entertainment, games, an arcade room, and private picnic areas. *4800 Osuna Rd. NE,* ☎ *505/881–9373.* ☛ *For unlimited rides: $10.95.* ☛ *Without rides: $3.50.* ⊙ *Apr. 3–Oct. 14. Call ahead for hours.*

The Hands-on Corner at the **Indian Pueblo Cultural Center** (*see* Tour 1, *above*) allows youngsters to touch Native American pottery, jewelry, dried corn, weaving, and tools. Children can draw their own petroglyphs or design pots. Colorful Native American dances in the museum's courtyard will impress the entire family.

Go about 30 miles north of Albuquerque on NM 14, which runs between Albuquerque and Santa Fe, where you can visit the **Old Coal Mine Museum** in the quasi ghost town of **Madrid,** now populated with writers, artists, potters, and poets, and home to a sprinkling of unusual shops and galleries. Children love exploring the old coal mine tunnel, with its vein of coal; climbing aboard a 1906 steam train; and nosing through a variety of antique buildings full of marvelous old relics, including 1920s movie projectors, early hospital and dental equipment, antique cars, and even a 1928 International dump truck. Tickets for the museum are available at the Mine Shaft Tavern out front. If you're there on a weekend between Memorial Day and Labor Day, catch the museum's old-fashioned melodrama, staged in a former roundhouse machine shop that's been converted into the **Engine House Theater.** It's probably the only theater anywhere with a full-size steam train that comes chugging onto the stage; the rear of the theater opens onto the tracks. In this production, when the pretty heroine gets tied onto the tracks, she's really got something to worry about. *Old Coal Mine Museum, Madrid,* ☎ *505/473–0743.* ☛ *$3 adults, $1 children under 12. Melodrama tickets: $8 adults, $6.50 senior citizens, $4 children under 12.* ⊙ *Daily 9:30–dusk, weather permitting.*

New Mexico Museum of Natural History (*see* Tour 1, *above*) is particularly appealing to children, since a number of interesting programs and exhibits have been designed just for them. A big favorite is the Evolator, which takes visitors through 35 million years, back to a seacoast where dinosaurs roamed. The naturalist center lets children touch snakes and frogs, see objects through microscopes, and make animal tracks in a sand box. The museum also arranges camp-ins in which groups of children can sleep overnight—if they dare close their eyes—with dinosaurs, giant flying reptiles, and an active volcano.

What child doesn't love the zoo? Albuquerque's **Rio Grande Zoological Park** is home to more than 1,300 animals from around the world, from pink flamingos to chest-thumping gorillas. Don't miss Moon-shadow, the snow leopard, one of the rarest of its kind. Sprawled over 60 acres, the zoo is especially well known for its spacious naturalistic exhibits and lush landscaping, including a half-dozen waterfalls. *903 10th St. SW,* ☎ *505/843–7413.* ☛ *$4.25 adults (ages 16–64), $2.25 senior citizens and children 3–15.* ☉ *Daily 9–5.*

While in the Sandia Mountains, you'll find lots to do with the children. A quick stop at the **Sandia Ranger Station** (☎ 505/281–3304), off NM 14 South, will provide you with pamphlets, maps, and a fire-prevention program with a *Smokey the Bear* movie and occasional tours to the nearby fire station; call to reserve a time. You might also take a couple of hours to see **Sierra Goat Farms,** 15 miles south of NM 14. Here you and your little ones will meet Carmen Sanchez, the Goat Lady, who owns the farm and delights in teaching children. Ms. Sanchez shows children how to milk the animals and care for them. The farm has plenty of outdoor grills and picnic tables, and a variety of goat cheeses, cheesecakes, and chocolates are for sale. *Sierra Goat Farms, Hwy. NM 40, Tijeras,* ☎ *505/281–5061.* ☛ *Free.* ☉ *Tues.–Sun. 10–6.*

There are plenty of interesting attractions for small-fry travelers in Albuquerque, but perhaps none more so than the **Tinkertown Museum** in Sandia Park on the way to Sandia Crest. Run by Ross and Carla Ward, the museum houses a world of miniature carved-wood characters. It contains the results of more than 30 years of carving and collecting by its owners, including an animated miniature Western village. The latest addition is a circus exhibit with wooden merry-go-round horses from the 1940s and original circus emblems. Tiny vendors sell cotton candy, pink lemonade, and popcorn; other figures include trapeze artists, a bear act, a fire eater, a tiger trainer, and an animated fat lady. Visitors entering the roadside attraction, passing through the building's colorful glass-bottle facade, are greeted by ragtime piano music. There's a life-size general store, where deliveries arrive by horse-drawn wagon. Put a quarter in a slot and Boot Hill Cemetery comes to life, as lightning crackles and the devil and an angel do battle over a poor lost soul. Tinkertown and most of its delightful creations represent a lifetime of carving for Ross Ward, whose dream was hatched in the late 1950s. Today, more than 900 figures populate the tiny village. *Tinkertown Museum, NM 536, Sandia Park,* ☎ *505/281–5233.* ☛ *$2.50 adults, $2 senior citizens, $1 children 4–16, children under 4 free.* ☉ *Apr. 1–Oct., daily 9–6.*

Off the Beaten Track

The **National Atomic Museum** is devoted to an exploration of atomic energy and the role New Mexico played in nuclear technology. Exhibits include replicas of Little Boy and Fat Man, the atomic bombs dropped on Japan. In the Missile Park section you can examine a B-52 bomber and an F-105D fighter bomber, touch the rocket that was used to boost Alan Shepard into space, and see an array of historic flying machines with names like *Hound Dog, Bomarc, Mace,* and *Snark.* David Wolper's film *Ten Seconds That Shook the World* can also be seen here; call ahead for movie times. *Kirtland Air Force Base, Wyoming Gate,* ☎ *505/845–6670.* ☛ *Free.* ☉ *Daily 9–5.*

A scenic drive initiated nearly a quarter-century ago and still popular, the **Turquoise Trail** departs from freeway travel and ventures into back-road country, where the pace is slow, talk is all about weather and crops, donkeys have the right of way, and Albuquerque seems like another planet. It's the old route between Albuquerque and Santa Fe, now full of ghost towns that are being restored, thanks to writers, artists, and travelers who pass through.

Heading east on I–40, the NM 14 North exit takes you to the back road of Sandia Crest (NM 536), snaking up through a portion of Cibola National Forest and on to the 10,678-foot crest. Stop to enjoy the view. Back on NM 14, again heading north, you'll hit **Golden,** site of the first gold rush (1825) west of the Mississippi. Golden has a rock shop and a mercantile store, and its rustic adobe church and graveyard send photographers into a state of euphoria. La Casita, a shop at the north end of the village, serves as a kind of unofficial Chamber of Commerce, in case you've got any questions.

Twelve miles past Golden, you'll come to **Madrid.** Long abandoned, Madrid has been rebuilding, but slowly. Weathered old houses have been repaired and a shop opens here, and another one there, mostly converted company stores or old homes. Some of the shops are definitely worth a visit—**Sundance Originals** (☎ 505/471–8393), for Southwestern fashions, blankets, coats, and such; **Madrid Earthenware Pottery** (☎ 505/471–3450); **Manos Imports** (☎ 505/471–7904), for handmade Mexican furniture; the **Tapestry Gallery** (☎ 505/471–0194), for hand-loomed knits and rugs; and **Maya Jones Imports** (☎ 505/473–3641), for Guatemalan imports. You'll probably also want to visit the **Old Coal Mine Museum** and its **Engine House Theater,** remnants of a once-flourishing coal mining business. During melodramas staged here on summer weekends, you can cheer the hero and hiss the villain (*see* What to See and Do with Children, *above*).

A few miles farther north on NM 14, **Cerrillos** comes into view, yet another echo of bygone days. A boomtown in the 1880s, its mines brimmed with gold, silver, and turquoise; it had eight newspapers, four hotels, and 21 taverns flourishing. Then the mines went dry, and the town went bust. More recently, Cerrillos has been the location site for a number of television and Hollywood Westerns (*Young Guns, Lonesome Dove*). The town has a number of interesting shops along its tree-shaded streets, including **What Not Shop** (☎ 505/471–2744), which carries a little bit of just about everything. **Casa Grande** (☎ 505/438–3008), a sprawling 21-room adobe, offers early mining exhibits, a gift shop, a petting zoo, and a scenic overlook.

When you're ready to return to Albuquerque, you can turn around and drive back the way you came, or head west when you reach NM 22 and drive to the **Santo Domingo Reservation and Trading Post** (*see* Pueblos Near Albuquerque *in* Chapter 6), then drive south to town.

Parks and Monuments

Aztec Ruins National Monument

So named because early 19th-century settlers believed they had stumbled upon the Halls of Montezuma, Aztec contains 500 rooms laid out in an E-shape plan around a plaza. In 1934, archaeologists restored the 12th-century Great Kiva here to mint condition, complete with a timbered roof packed with mud. The site even offers mood music; stereophonic Navajo chants can be summoned by the mere push of a button. There's a visitor center and a museum (ancient pottery, clothes, tools, and artifacts). A complete tour of the site takes about 90 minutes. *Aztec Ruins National Monument, Box 640, Aztec 87410,* ☎ *505/334–6174. I–25 north from Albuquerque to Bernalillo, NM 44 north another 140 mi to Aztec. Total driving time is 3½–4 hours one-way.* ☛ *$2 per person.* ☉ *Daily 8–5; closed Dec. 25 and Jan. 1.*

Coronado State Monument

Coronado State Monument is named in honor of the first Spanish expedition into the Southwest (1540–42). This prehistoric Kuaua pueblo, on a bluff overlooking the Rio Grande, is believed to have been the headquarters of Francisco Vásquez de Coronado's army of 1,200, who came seeking the legendary Seven Cities of Gold. The pueblo's restored kiva contains copies of magnificent frescoes done in black, yellow, red, blue, green, and white, depicting fertility rites, rain dances, and hunting rituals; the original frescoes are preserved in a small, nearby museum next to the visitor center. The area is lovely. The Sandia Mountains rise abruptly from 5,280 to 10,678 feet a mere 6 miles away. The small community of Bernalillo, settled by Spanish colonists before Albuquerque was founded in 1706, is nearby. In the autumn, the views are especially breathtaking, with the trees turning russet and gold. Coronado State Monument is part of Coronado State Park, which has campsites and picnic grounds. *Coronado State Park, Box 95, Bernalillo 87004, ☎ 505/867–5351. 1 mi northeast of Bernalillo on NM 44, off I–25. From Albuquerque's Old Town, travel 20 mi north on I–25 and take either the first turnoff (Bernalillo) or the second directly to the monument on NM 44. ☛ $2 adults, children 17 and under free. ☉ 8–5 in winter, 9–6 in summer, except holidays.*

Fort Selden State Monument

Established in 1865 to protect settlers of the Mesilla Valley and pioneers who were traveling through, this fort was typical of frontier posts in the Southwest, consisting of flat-roofed adobe brick buildings arranged around a drill field. In the early 1880s, Captain Arthur MacArthur was appointed post commander. With him was his young son Douglas, who spent several years on the post. He grew up to become World War II hero General Douglas MacArthur. A permanent exhibit called "Fort Selden: An Adobe Post on the Rio Grande" depicts the roles of officers, enlisted men, and women on the American frontier during the Indian Wars. Food and gas are available locally, and there are camping facilities at the adjacent Leasburg State Park. *Fort Selden State Monument, 13 mi north of Las Cruces at the Radium Springs exit, off I–25, ☎ 505/526–8911. I–25 south from Albuquerque to Exit 19, about 225 mi. ☛ $2.10 adults, children under 16 free. ☉ May 1– Sept. 15, daily 9:30–5:30, Sept. 16–Apr. 30, daily 8:30–5:30. Closed all state holidays except July 4, Memorial Day, and Labor Day.*

Fort Sumner State Monument

Established in 1862, Fort Sumner is located in De Baca County, 2 miles east of the town of Fort Sumner and 4 miles south of U.S. 60 on Billy the Kid Road along the east bank of the Pecos River. Artifacts and photographs on display—the Soldiers, the Native Americans, and Billy—relate to Fort Sumner and the Bosque Redondo Reservation, where 9,000 Navajos and Mescalero Apaches were interred from 1863 to 1868. Forced to make the infamous "Long Walk," on which many died, they were brought to the site by Colonel Kit Carson from their original homeland in Canyon de Chelly, Arizona. The land was far from hospitable. Natural disasters destroyed crops, wood was scarce, and even the water from the Pecos proved unhealthy. Those who survived the harsh treatment and wretched living conditions (3,000 didn't) were allowed to return to Arizona in 1868. When the garrison left, the post was sold at auction and eventually converted into a large ranch. It's the same ranch where, in 1881, Sheriff Pat Garrett gunned down Billy the Kid, who's buried in a cemetery just off nearby NM 212. Adjacent is the Billy the Kid museum. *Fort Sumner State Monument, 2 mi east and 2 mi south of the town of Fort Sumner on NM 212, ☎ 505/355–2573.*

I–40 east from Albuquerque to Santa Rosa, then NM 84 south for 45 mi and look for signs. Total distance from Albuquerque: about 180 mi. ☛ *$1.05 adults, children under 17 free.* ☉ *May–mid-Sept., daily 9:30–5:30; mid-Sept.–Apr., daily 8:30–5:30. Closed all state holidays except July 4, Memorial Day, and Labor Day.*

Petroglyph National Monument

★ Located 8 miles west of Albuquerque in the West Mesa area, at the site of five extinct volcanoes, the Petroglyph National Monument contains more than 17,000 ancient Native American rock drawings (petroglyphs) inscribed on the 17-mile-long West Mesa escarpment. Native American hunting parties camped at the base of the lava flows for thousands of years, chipping and scribbling away. Archaeologists believe the petroglyphs were carved on the lava formations between AD 1100 and 1600. Four walking trails at this former state park allow views of many of the drawings. *Petroglyph National Monument, 6900 Unser Blvd. NW, Albuquerque 87120,* ☎ *505/897–8814.* ☛ *$1 weekdays, $2 weekends.* ☉ *Daily 9–5, except major holidays.*

Rio Grande Nature Center State Park

★ On the east bank of the Rio Grande in a cottonwood forest known as the "bosque," the Rio Grande Nature Center State Park is home to all manner of birds and migratory fowl that can be viewed year-round. Its unique visitor center is constructed half above and half below ground; viewing windows provide a look at what's going on at both levels as birds, frogs, ducks, and turtles do their thing. *2901 Candelaria Rd. NW, Albuquerque 87107,* ☎ *505/344–7240.* ☛ *Adults $1, children 50¢; under 6 free.* ☉ *Daily 10–5, closed major holidays.*

SHOPPING

Shopping anywhere in northern New Mexico brings on a feeling of déjà vu: After a while, one shop looks like the next. Still the prowl, shopping bag in hand, is well worth the effort. The tourist trail in New Mexico is paved with Native American arts and crafts (handsome turquoise and silver jewelry, baskets, blankets, pottery, etc.), Spanish Colonial handmade furniture, leather goods, textiles, colorful items from south of the border, trendy Taos and Santa Fe designs in interior furnishings, and antique mementos of the early West—everything from Billy the Kid's gun belt (of dubious authenticity) to Kit Carson's hat (well, maybe). Tourist demand has forced prices up, but if you diligently stalk the fairs and powwows, the back-street shops, flea markets, and secondhand stores, you'll surely come away with a treasure or two.

When it comes to art, buy what you like and let the experts hiss and howl. But unless you're really knowledgeable, beware of those high-priced, once-in-a-lifetime purchases. You'll also find some funky, good-natured souvenir art and merchandise that's always worth a few dollars, if only as a keepsake of happy days spent visiting dusty pueblos or flea markets in the sun.

As with most large, sprawling Western cities, Albuquerque's main shopping areas are malls and shopping centers scattered throughout the community. Hours are generally 10–9 weekdays, Saturday 10–6, and Sunday noon–6.

Shopping Malls

Among the major shopping centers are **Coronado Center** (Louisiana Blvd. NE and Menaul Blvd. NE, ☎ 505/881–2700), New Mexico's largest shopping center, with over 160 stores including May D&F, The Gap, and Victoria's Secret; **Fashion Square** (1100 San Mateo Blvd., ☎ 505/ 265–6931), anchored by Kistler Collister department store, but mostly filled with boutiques selling jewelry, shoes, home furnishings, children's clothes, and beauty products; **First Plaza Galeria** (20 First Plaza, ☎ 505/242–3446), with a variety of small shops and restaurants; and **Winrock Center** (Louisiana Blvd. exit off I–40, ☎ 505/883–6132), with 120 stores, including Dillard's and Montgomery Ward, and 17 restaurants, from fast-food to upscale fare.

Nob Hill Shops

Nob Hill is the city's newest and trendiest shopping district. Stretching for seven blocks along Central Avenue from Girard Boulevard to Washington Street, the area began in 1947 as the city's first car-oriented shopping center. A 1985 government grant gave the historic area a face-lift, and today, instead of cars, neon-lit boutiques, restaurants, galleries, and performing arts spaces encourage foot traffic day and night. Among the highlights are **Wear It!** (107 Amherst Dr. NE, ☎ 505/266–7764), for contemporary clothing and accessories; **Beeps** (3500 Central Ave. SE, in the Nob Hill Business Center, ☎ 505/262– 1900), a card and novelty store that is a city favorite; and **P.T. Crow Trading Co.** (114 Amherst Dr. SE, ☎ 505/256–1763 or 800/657– 0944), for one of the best selections of vintage and custom-made cowboy boots in the state.

Specialty Stores

Antiques
The **Antique Specialty Mall** (4516 Central Ave. SE, ☎ 505/268–8080, and 330 Washington St. SE, ☎ 505/256–9653) is Albuquerque's most prestigious center for collectibles and fine antiques, with special emphasis on memorabilia from the early 1880s to the 1950s. When the set designers for the hit television miniseries *Lonesome Dove* needed special props to establish authenticity, they came here. At the mall's two locations, collectors will find Art Deco and Art Nouveau items, Depression-era glass, pottery, Native American arts and crafts, quilts and linens, vintage clothes, cherry wood furniture, antique jewelry, and Western memorabilia.

Books
Salt of the Earth Books (3025 Central Ave. NE, ☎ 505/265–6355) is a popular university-area bookstore specializing in Southwestern fiction and nonfiction, politics, and Chicano, Native American, and Latin American studies. The diverse selection includes new and hard-to-find titles. The store features frequent book-signings, readings, and community forums, which are always entertaining events.
Page One (11018 Montgomery Blvd. NE, ☎ 505/294–2026), voted the best bookstore in Albuquerque by *Albuquerque Monthly Magazine,* is certainly one of the biggest, claiming the largest selection of titles in New Mexico. It also handles computer software, technical and professional books, maps, globes, racing forms, and 150 out-of-state and foreign newspapers.

Native American Arts and Crafts
Adobe Gallery (413 Romero St. NW, ☎ 505/243–8485) specializes in historic and contemporary art of the Southwestern Native Americans: Pueblo pottery; Hopi kachinas; Navajo rugs, blankets, and paintings. Founded in 1978, the shop is housed in a historic *terrones adobe* (bricks were cut from the ground rather than formed from mud and

dried) homestead that dates from 1878; it is owned and managed by Alexander E. Anthony, Jr. The shop also has an extensive stock of books about Southwestern Native Americans.

Andrews Pueblo Pottery (Suite 8, 303 Romero NW, ☎ 505/243–0414) handles Pueblo pottery, fetishes, kachina dolls, and baskets for the beginning and seasoned collector.

Nizhoni Moses, Ltd. (326 San Felipe St. NE, ☎ 505/842–1808) features a vast selection of Pueblo pottery, including the black earthenware pottery of Maria Martinez of San Ildefonso, as well as potters from Acoma, Santa Clara, Isleta, and Zia. Rare Zuni and Navajo jewelry are showcased, as are select Navajo weavings from 1900 to the present.

Penfield Gallery of Indian Arts (2043 S. Plaza Ave. NW, ☎ 505/242–9696) is owned by Julia Reidy, who specializes in Pueblo pottery, storytellers, Hopi jewelry, kachina dolls, Zuni fetishes, and sand paintings.

Skip Maisel Wholesale Indian Jewelry and Crafts (510 Central Ave. SW, ☎ 505/242–6526) sells quality Indian arts and crafts at truly wholesale prices. The warehouse-like store is rather plain, but it's packed with Zuni, Navajo, and Santo Domingo jewelry; pottery from Santa Clara and Acoma; textiles, paintings, sculpture, and more.

Tanner Chaney Gallery (410 Romero St. NW, ☎ 505/247–2242 or 800/444–2242) is housed in a beautiful old pre–Civil War adobe hacienda in Old Town. On display in several showrooms is an extensive collection of jewelry, sculpture, contemporary and historic pottery, and weaving by Native Americans. Huge hand-carved wooden doors lead from the showrooms to a flagstone patio, shaded by old *latillas* (strips of wood laid in a herringbone pattern); bougainvilleas and hibiscus tumble this way and that; and the famous Angel of Old Town fountain bubbles forth. It's one of the prettiest courtyards in town. The main showroom, the Great Gallery, is filled with Navajo rugs (some dating from the early 1800s), pottery, baskets, and an extensive selection of books on the Southwest. The shop also has a branch at the Hyatt Regency.

Wright's Collection of Indian Arts (6600 Indian School Rd., ☎ 505/883–6122), one block north of the Marriott in Park Square, was founded as a trading post in 1907. Considerably more upscale these days, Wright's offers authentic Native American arts and crafts, from the traditional to the contemporary. Shoppers may also visit the unique museum on the premises, with its impressive display of Southwestern art and pottery.

Art Galleries

Amapola Gallery (2045 S. Plaza St. NW, ☎ 505/242–4311), just west of the Plaza near Rio Grande Boulevard, has a lovely cobbled courtyard and an indoor space, both of which are overflowing with pottery, paintings, textiles, carvings, baskets, jewelry, and more. It's worth a visit just to see the handsome displays. Amapola is one of the largest co-op galleries in New Mexico.

Cafe (516 Central Ave. SW, ☎ 505/242–8244), which claims to be Albuquerque's largest gallery, exhibits non-traditional works—contemporary painting, collage, photography, sculpture, and printmaking—by New Mexico artists. Some of the big names include Carlos Quinto Kemm, Beverly Magennis, and Valerie Arber. The gallery also hosts frequent "live art" performances.

DSG (3011 Monte Vista Blvd. NE, ☎ 505/266–7751) is owned by John Cacciatore, who handles contemporary paintings and tapestries by regional artists, including Larry Bell, Nancy Kozikowski, Angus Macpherson, and Joan Boyden.

Mariposa Gallery (113 Romero St. NW, ☏ 505/842–9097) is a six-room Old Town space handling contemporary American crafts, including jewelry, sculptural art glass, mixed media, clay works, and fiber arts. The changing gallery exhibits spotlight some of the area's best upcoming artists. And the *Día de los Muertos* (Day of the Dead) display shouldn't be missed.

Navajo Gallery (323 Romero St. NW, ☏ 505/843–7666) is the Albuquerque branch of famed Navajo artist R. C. Gorman's trend-setting Taos space. The first Native American painter to open his own fine-arts gallery, Gorman now has outlets in Hawaii, New York, and Tokyo that represent his work exclusively.

Weems Gallery (2801-M Eubank Blvd. NE, ☏ 505/293–6133) represents over 150 artists, with emphasis on originality and quality. Featured are paintings, pottery, sculpture, jewelry, weaving, stained glass, and original-design clothes. Gift items and a framing service are also available.

SPORTS AND THE OUTDOORS

Participant Sports

The **Albuquerque Parks and Recreation Department** (400 Marquette Ave. NW, Box 1293, Albuquerque 87103, ☏ 505/768–3490) maintains a widely diversified network of parks and recreational programs, encompassing over 20,000 acres of open space, four golf courses, 200 parks, six paved tracks for biking and jogging, as well as numerous recreational facilities, such as swimming pools, tennis courts, ball fields, playgrounds, and even a shooting range.

Ballooning

Known for the Albuquerque International Balloon Fiesta (*see* Spectator Sports, *below*), Albuquerque also offers myriad opportunities for those who want to take to the skies themselves. If you'd like to give it a try, contact any of the following:

Ad Venture Balloons (31232 San Mateo NE, ☏ 505/298–8887).
AERCO Balloon Port (523 Rankin Rd., ☏ 505/344–5844).
Balloon Fiesta (8309 Washington Pl. NE, ☏ 505/821–1000).
Braden's Balloons (3212 Stanford Ave. NE, ☏ 505/281–2714).
Duke City Balloonport (12100 Anaheim Ave. NE, ☏ 505/299–5481).
Rainbow Ryders (430 Montclaire Dr. SE, ☏ 505/268–3401).
World Balloon Corporation (4800 Eubank Blvd. NE, ☏ 505/293–6800).

Bicycling

Albuquerque is big on biking, both as a recreational sport and as a means of cutting down on automobile traffic and its resulting emissions. In 1973, the city established a network of bikeways, recommending existing streets and roadways as bike routes, lanes, and trails. Since then, many new ones have been added, and the program continues to expand. On designated bike routes, bicycles share lanes of traffic with automobiles, with no separation between car and bicycle; the bicyclist has the same right to use the street as does the motorist and must obey the same traffic laws and signals. Bike lanes, on the other hand, are designated exclusively for bike riders. Designated Recreational Trails are shared with pedestrians and provide the safest off-road area for both (*see* Jogging, *below,* for a list of these routes). An elaborately detailed **Metropolitan Albuquerque Bicycle Map** can be obtained free of charge by calling 505/768–3550. The foldout map also includes rules and regulations concerning biking in the city, as well as safety tips. For information about mountain biking in the adjacent national forest, call the **Sandia Ranger Station** (☎ 505/281–3304).

Golf

The Albuquerque Parks and Recreation Department maintains four public golf courses. Greens fees range from $7.35 for nine holes to $11.55 for 18 holes, with special discount rates for early bird and sundown play. (The courses are open from sunup to sundown.) Each has a clubhouse and pro shop, where clubs and equipment can be rented. Weekday play is on a first-come basis, but reservations are advised for weekend use. The city's **Golf Management Office** (6401 Osuna Rd. NE, ☎ 505/888–8115) can provide more information.

Arroyo del Oso (7001 Osuna Rd. NE, ☎ 505/888–8115) has an 18- and a 9-hole regulation course and practice facilities. Selected as one of the top 50 27-hole public golf courses in the country by *Golf Digest,* **Puerto del Sol** offers a driving range, a full-service restaurant, and an up-to-the-hour information line for tee-off status (☎ 505/889–3699).

At **Ladera** (3401 Ladera Dr. NW, ☎ 505/836–4449), 10 miles west of downtown, there are an 18-hole regulation course, practice facilities, a 9-hole executive course, a large driving range, a restaurant, and a full-service pro shop.

Los Altos (9717 Cooper Ave. NE, ☎ 505/298–1897) includes an 18-hole regulation course, a short 9-hole course, and practice facilities. One of the Southwest's most popular facilities, Los Altos has a driving range, grass tees, a restaurant (serving mainly New Mexican food), instructors for individuals or groups, and a large selection of rental equipment.

Located near the Albuquerque airport, **Puerto del Sol** (1800 Girard Blvd. SE, ☎ 505/265–5636) has a 9-hole regulation course, a lighted driving range, and a full-service pro shop. There are no reservations for tee times.

The University of New Mexico also maintains two public golf courses. One, **UNM North** (2201 Tucker Rd. NE, between Stanford Ave. and University Blvd., ☎ 505/277–4146), is a first-class 9-hole course on campus; the other, **UNM South** (off Rio Bravo on University Blvd., ☎ 505/277–4546), is an 18-hole championship course, including an excellent beginners' 3-hole regulation course. Both are open daily (except Christmas) and have full-service pro shops, instruction, and snack bars offering New Mexican favorites.

Health Clubs

Most of the large hotel health clubs are reserved for guests' use only. However, keeping fit in Albuquerque is easy, with numerous health clubs, gyms, and fitness centers from which to choose in virtually every neighborhood.

Albuquerque Rock Gym (3300 Princeton Dr. NE, ☎ 505/881–3073) has a complete indoor climbing facility, with a pro shop and equipment rentals. It's one block east of I–25, one block north of Candelaria Road.

Gold's Gym (5001 Montgomery Blvd. NE, Suite 147, ☎ 505/881–8500) is a state-of-the-art fitness complex, part of the national chain. It offers free weights, a cardiovascular deck, aerobics, sportswear, and Proline supplements. Nonmembers pay $8 per day.

The facilities at **Liberty Gym** (2401 Jefferson St. NE, ☎ 505/884–8012), one of the largest body-building and fitness centers in the Southwest, include specialized machines (such as Stairmasters), free weights, personalized instruction, and nutritional counseling. The nonmembers' walk-in fee is $5.

Jogging

The **Albuquerque Parks and Recreation Department** maintains an extensive network of Designated Recreational Trails that joggers share with bicyclists, as follows:

Bear Canyon, a 1-mile trail along the Bear Arroyo, extends east from Eubank Boulevard to Juan Tabo Boulevard, passing through El Oso Grande Park.

Embudo, a 1½-mile trail, connects with the Las Montanas trail at Morris Street NE, then runs east along the Embudo Channel to Tramway Boulevard. A bicycle-pedestrian bridge at Tramway Boulevard links this with the Tramway Trail.

Jefferson-Osuna, a 4-mile trail, runs along the Bear Arroyo between Jefferson Street and Osuna Road NE.

Paseo del Bosque, a 5-mile trail, is parallel to the irrigation ditch on the east side of the Rio Grande. Trail users may enter at Candelaria, Campbell, and Mountain roads or at Central Avenue SW.

Paseo de las Montanas, a 4.2-mile trail, goes from east of Winrock at Pennsylvania Street to Tramway Boulevard NE.

Paseo de Noreste, a 6.13-mile asphalt trail, begins at Tucker Avenue (University of New Mexico campus) and ends at Sandia High School, Pennsylvania Street NE.

Pino, a 1½-mile trail, starts at Wyoming Boulevard near Harper Road at the Albuquerque Academy and proceeds west along the South Pino Channel to San Pedro Drive NE.

Tramway, a 4-mile trail, runs along the east side of Tramway Road from Montgomery Boulevard to I-40.

Swimming

The City of Albuquerque has a number of year-round pools that are open to both lap and recreational swimming. ☛ 37¢ children 6 mo–3 yrs, $1.05 children 4–12, $1.58 children 13–18, $1.84 adults, and 25¢ senior citizens. Special monthly and yearly rates are available.

Highland Pool (400 Jackson St. SE, ☎ 505/256–2096) is open for lap swimming (adults only) weekdays from 6 AM–8 AM and 11:30 AM–1 PM; recreational swimming hours are weekdays from 12:30–4:30 and 6:45–8.

Los Altos Pool (10100 Lomas Blvd. NE, ☎ 505/291–6290) has lap-swimming hours for adults only 6–9 AM and 5–6 PM weekdays, and recreational swimming hours weekdays 12:30–4:30 and 6–8.

Sandia Pool (7801 Candelaria Rd. NE, ☎ 505/291–6279) is open for lap swimming (adults only) weekdays 6–8 AM and 4:30–6 PM and for recreational swimming weekdays 12:30–4:30.

Valley Pool (1505 Candelaria Rd. NW, ☎ 505/761–4086) is reserved for lap swimming for adults only weekdays 6–8 AM and 5–6 PM; recreational swimming takes place Monday–Thursday noon–4 and 7–8:30, Friday noon–4 and 6–9, and weekends noon–5.

A number of public swimming pools are open only from June to mid-August (for schedule information, call 505/848–1381):

East San José (2015 Galena St. SE, ☎ 505/848–1396).
Eisenhower (11001 Camaro Rd. NE, ☎ 505/291–6292).
Montgomery (5301 Palo Duro Ave. NE, ☎ 505/888–8123).
Rio Grande (1410 Iron Ave. SW, ☎ 505/848–1397).
Sierra Vista (5001 Montaño Rd. NE, ☎ 505/897–4517).

Sunport (2033 Columbia Dr. SE, ☎ 505/848–1398).
West Mesa (6705 Fortuna Rd. NW, ☎ 505/836–0686).
Wilson (6000 Anderson Ave. SE, ☎ 505/256–2095).

Tennis

Albuquerque's wide-ranging network of public parks contains nearly three dozen public tennis facilities that generally have one to six courts. Lessons are available at some; others are lighted for night play (until 10 PM). For information call the Albuquerque Parks and Recreation Department (☎ 505/848–1381). In addition, the city maintains three tennis complexes:

Albuquerque Tennis Complex (1903 Stadium Blvd. SE, ☎ 505/848–1381) consists of 16 Laykold tennis courts and 4 racquetball/handball courts, which may be reserved by phone or in person; reservations are taken two days in advance at 10 AM. The rate is $2.10 per hour.

The **Jerry Cline Tennis Complex** (Louisiana Blvd. and Constitution Ave., ☎ 505/256–2032) has 12 Laykold courts, 3 of which are lighted. There is no charge, and no reservations are needed to play here.

Sierra Vista Tennis Complex (5001 Montano Rd. NW, ☎ 505/897–8819) consists of 10 tennis courts (2 Omni courts), 2 platform tennis courts, and a swimming-pool area. The reservation policy and charge for courts ($2.10 per hour) are the same as at the Albuquerque Tennis Complex. No racquetball facilities are available.

Along with the numerous tennis courts located in the city's various hotels and resorts (*see* Lodging, *below*), a number of private clubs have excellent facilities and generally allow guest privileges at a member's invitation or honor memberships from out-of-town clubs with reciprocal arrangements or equal status. Among these are the **Highpoint Racquet and Swim Club** (4300 Landau Dr. NE, ☎ 505/293–5820), **Tanoan Country Club** (10801 Academy Rd. NE, ☎ 505/822–0455), and the **Tennis Club of Albuquerque** (2901 Indian School Rd. NE, ☎ 505/262–1691).

Spectator Sports

The **Albuquerque Dukes** are the Triple-A farm team of the Los Angeles Dodgers and members of the Pacific Coast League; Orel Hershiser is a Dukes alumnus. Exciting professional baseball can be seen from April through September at the city-owned Albuquerque Sports Stadium, located at Stadium and University boulevards, the only stadium anywhere with a drive-in spectator area. ☛ Varies from $1 to $4. Call or write the Albuquerque Dukes (1601 Stadium Blvd. SE, Albuquerque 87125, ☎ 505/243–1791) for schedules and information.

The **University of New Mexico's** Lobo football and basketball games are also a major draw. The University Arena has a 17,000-seat capacity to accommodate the city's intensely loyal UNM basketball fans. Across the street is the 30,000-seat Lobo football stadium. For schedules and ticket information, call 505/277–2116.

Downs at Albuquerque is a glass-enclosed, climate-controlled racing facility located in the center of Albuquerque at the State Fairgrounds. Quarter-horse and Thoroughbred racing begins in January and runs through mid-June. General ☛ is free; preferred seating tickets range from $4 to $6. Parking is $2. Afternoon racing takes place on Friday, Saturday, Sunday, and holidays. Call 505/262–1188 for post times.

stigation t8

Ballooning

Mention hot-air ballooning to an enthusiast, and Albuquerque automatically comes to mind. The city's high altitude, few obstructions, and steady but manageable winds make it especially suitable. Albuquerque's long history of ballooning dates from 1882, when Professor Park A. Van Tassel, a saloon keeper, made the first balloon ascent at the Territorial Fair. Van Tassel's craft was destroyed during a subsequent flight, but that didn't dampen his enthusiasm. He bought another balloon; went on a world flight; and, during the trip, fell into the Pacific Ocean, where, it was rumored, he was eaten by sharks.

Since those colorful early beginnings, Albuquerque has become the hot-air-balloon capital of the world, partly because of the success of the annual **Albuquerque International Balloon Fiesta,** the first one of which took place in 1972, when 13 balloons participated. Today the nine-day event, held in early October, is the largest hot-air-balloon gathering in the world, attracting more than 600 registered hot-air balloons and entrants from as far away as Australia and Japan.

A special feature of the annual gathering is the "balloon glow," when hundreds of balloons are inflated after the sun sets. Propane burners send heat into the colorful envelopes, the balloons light up like giant light bulbs, and the magical glow can be seen for miles. The balloons remain grounded, or tethered; ballooning at night, when balloonists can't see telephone wires or other obstacles, is forbidden.

An estimated 1.5 million people attend the nine-day program, and thousands more glimpse the balloons as they float over Albuquerque's backyards, setting off a serenade of barking dogs. Most spectacular are the Saturday- and Sunday-morning ascensions on the opening and closing weekends of the fiesta. In the early hours of dawn 600 massive, candy-colored balloons are inflated and, shortly after, lift off, silently caressing the sky with fantasy and brilliance. It is one of New Mexico's biggest draws for out-of-state visitors and a delight for those who live here. For additional information, contact Albuquerque International Balloon Fiesta (8309 Washington Pl. NE, 87113, ☎ 505/821–1000).

DINING

Albuquerque loves to eat out. Many of the city's favorite dining spots specialize in northern New Mexican–style cooking, with flavorful Spanish recipes that have been handed down for generations. (*See* Pleasures and Pastimes *in* Chapter 1 for an explanation of New Mexican food terms.) French, Continental, Mediterranean, and Italian fare are also readily available, as are standard American favorites of seafood, steaks, and burgers. The clientele is a mix of locals and out-of-town visitors.

What to Wear

You can dress in most restaurants as casually as you like. Restaurants in the major business hotels tend to be a bit more formal, of course, but as the evening wears down, so do the restrictions.

CATEGORY	COST*
$$$	over $20
$$	$16–$20
$	under $16

per person, excluding drinks, service, and sales tax (5.8%)

120

Albuquerque Dining

$$$ **Casa Vieja.** Casa Vieja, in Corrales about 13 miles northwest of Albu-
★   querque, offers Continental dining in a charming 280-year-old adobe that
has a history almost as long as its menu. The oldest building in Corrales,
it was originally a homestead, then a church, the territorial governor's
home, and a military outpost; it became a restaurant in 1970. There are
two large dining rooms, a smaller one, and a patio for outdoor dining
in the summer. With beamed viga ceilings, regional paintings, Native Amer-
ican rugs on the walls, and handsome tinwork on the hand-carved doors,
it has a rich frontier flavor without straining to achieve it. Owner-chef
Jean Pierre Gozard specializes in French and northern Italian cuisine, with
wild game, quail, duck, and pheasant offered in season. ✗ *4541 Cor-
rales Rd.,* ☎ *505/898–7489. Reservations required. Jacket and tie re-
quired. AE, D, DC, MC, V. No lunch. Closed Mon.*

$$$ **High Noon Restaurant and Saloon.** In one of Old Town's original 200-
year-old adobe buildings, this restaurant was once a woodworking shop.
It now has fine dining in a Territorial setting, with viga ceilings, brick
floors, and handmade Southwestern tables and chairs. A skylight offers cool, defused lighting during the day and a glimpse of the sky at
night. Native American rugs and New Mexican art decorate the walls,
and antique pots rest on ledges and sills. White tablecloths and well-
appointed table settings create an upscale accent. A flamenco guitarist
plays here on weekends. Topping the menu selections are pepper steak,
oven-roasted rack of lamb with fresh herbs, and red trout dusted with
blue corn flour, panfried, and served with avocado margarita salsa. ✗
425 San Felipe Ave. NW, ☎ *505/765–1455. Reservations required. AE,
D, DC MC, V.*

$$$ **Monte Vista Fire Station.** This spacious, airy restaurant on Central Av-
★   enue was once an actual working fire station—it even has a brass
pole. The adobe-style building, built in 1936, was used as a fire sta-
tion until 1972; it's listed on Albuquerque's National Register of His-
toric Places. The new American menu includes a wide variety of
seafood, grilled meats and poultry, and pasta dishes; wild mushroom
ravioli or shrimp quesadilla with sun-dried tomatoes and Gorgonzola
cheese might top the ever-changing list of innovative appetizers pre-
pared by award-winning Chef Rosa Rajkovic. ✗ *3201 Central Ave.
NE,* ☎ *505/255–2424. AE, D, DC, MC, V. No lunch weekends.*

$$ **Antiquity Restaurant.** In the heart of Old Town, this secluded restaurant has adobe walls as old as time (thus the name). Two separate din-
ing areas face an open kitchen with a charcoal grill, where the chef
performs his wonders for all to see. The floors are brick, and local art
is featured on the walls, along with framed posters touting the glories
of Albuquerque, its balloon rallies and art festivals. The restaurant was
originally built as a honeymoon cottage, and the aura of romance remains. This Old Town favorite serves a great filet mignon, charcoal-
broiled chateaubriand, a Southwest pasta combination of linguine with
piñons and Brie, fresh seafood, veal, and excellent homemade desserts
in an intimate setting. ✗ *112 Romero St. NW,* ☎ *505/247–3545.
Reservations required. AE, D, DC, MC, V. No lunch. Closed Sun.*

$$ **Artichoke Cafe.** Excellent service and a variety of cuisines—new Amer-
★   ican, Italian, French—characterize this outstanding café, in a turn-of-
the-century brick building just east of downtown on Central Avenue.
Specialties include broiled salmon, fettuccine with smoked chicken
and duck in a marsala cream sauce, breast of chicken stuffed with bell
pepper and basil, and appetizers so wonderful you might want to com-
bine two or three into a meal. Founded in 1989 by Terry Keene (his
wife, Patricia, is the chef), the restaurant has received high local ac-
claim—thanks, in part, to dishes created with organically grown in-
gredients. The building is old, but the decor is uptown modern—soft

muted colors, a few plants, lots of art. Its one large dining room on three broad levels spills onto a small courtyard, where there are seven tables. Exhibited on the dining room walls, and replaced every two months, are the works of local artists, some established, others up-and-coming. All the paintings are for sale. ✕ *424 Central Ave. SE,* ☎ *505/ 243–0200. Reservations required. AE, DC, MC, V. Closed Sun.*

$$ **El Pinto.** This family-owned Mexican restaurant has been in business since 1962. It is in an adobe-style hacienda, with shade trees and a year-round heated dining patio (the largest in New Mexico). Specialties include *chile rellenos,* hot or mild chile from the southern New Mexico town of Hatch (known as the Chile Capital of the World), *sopa de pollo* (chicken soup), fajitas, tamales, and frijoles. There's a full bar and soft Mexican background music. ✕ *10500 4th St. NW,* ☎ *505/898–1771. AE, D, MC, V.*

$$ **La Crêpe Michel.** This French bistro is a pleasant alternative to the countless New Mexican restaurants in the Old Town area. The intimate yet rustic café is tucked into the Old Town Patio del Norte—a small nook of shops on the northeast side of the plaza—and is romantically Parisian, with two lovely patios, one enclosed, the other outdoors. The menu emphasizes an innovative assortment of chicken, beef, seafood, vegetarian, and dessert crepes, as well as classic French onion soup, escargot, and fresh-baked French bread. The only thing missing is the wine; the restaurant's proximity to Old Town's historic San Felipe de Neri Catholic Church prohibits it from having a liquor license. Given the restaurant's popularity, however, business doesn't seem affected by the absence of alcohol. ✕ *400 C-2 San Felipe St. NW, Patio del Norte,* ☎ *505/242–1251. Reservations required. MC, V. Closed Mon.*

$$ **La Placita.** Housed in a historic hacienda on Old Town Plaza, La Placita offers traditional New Mexican dishes, such as chiles rellenos, enchiladas, tacos, and sopaipillas, plus a wide selection of American entrées. The building dates from 1706. For years it housed Ambrosio Armijo's mercantile store, where ladies' lace gloves sold for 10¢ a pair and gents' linen underdrawers could be purchased for $1. The adobe walls are 3 feet thick in places. La Placita has six dining rooms, and since it's an art gallery as well, patrons dine surrounded by outstanding examples of Native American and Southwestern painting. ✕ *302 San Felipe Ave. NW,* ☎ *505/247–2204. AE, D, MC, V.*

$$ **Maria Teresa Restaurant & 1840 Bar.** This nationally preserved landmark in historic Old Town, next to the Sheraton, serves aged beef, seafood, poultry, and New Mexican specialties; recommended entrées include raspberry chicken (breast of chicken baked in a tangy raspberry sauce) and hearty lamb fajitas accompanied by a fresh lime margarita. The restored 1840s adobe, its 32-inch-thick brick adobe walls plastered with straw and more adobe, is entered through an attractive courtyard, a cool oasis even during the hottest days of summer. Maria Teresa's has early Spanish American furnishings—chests, carvings, and tables—Southwestern paintings, fireplaces, and walled gardens. In the summer, everyone wants to eat in the Plum Tree Courtyard. ✕ *618 Rio Grande Blvd. NW,* ☎ *505/242–3900. Reservations required. Jacket and tie advised. AE, DC, MC, V.*

$$ **Prairie Star.** The view from the patio of this sprawling 1940s adobe
★ hacienda is one of the city's best. Looking east toward Albuquerque's majestic Sandia Peak, this rural restaurant, located 15 miles north of Albuquerque in Bernalillo, is a favorite spot for sipping margaritas at sunset. The menu combines New American, Southwestern, and classical cuisine, including Truchas trout with piñon nuts, lightly breaded and fried green chile appetizers, and tender lamb loin. While the margaritas flow outdoors, diners inside are treated to classic New Mexi-

can decor in the 6,000-square-foot Mission-style home: Vigas and latillas accent dining room ceilings, while kiva-style fireplaces and bancos (small benches that gracefully emerge from the adobe walls) make the large spaces feel cozy. Homemade bread and desserts are fresh daily, and complimentary champagne comes with Sunday brunch. ✕ *255 Prairie Star Rd.,* ☎ *505/867–3327. Reservations required. AE, D, DC, MC, V.*

$$ Scalo Northern Italian Grill. Nob Hill trend-setters gather at this in-
★ formal eatery to experience the first-rate pasta, seafood, and meat en-trées. Most of the multilevel dining area looks onto an open kitchen, where wonders like *ravioli di magro al basilico* (ravioli filled with spinach and ricotta cheese), *salmon al pesto e pumnate* (salmon fillet with pesto and sun-dried tomato cream sauce), and *scaloppine con fungi al Madeira* (veal chop with wild mushrooms sautéed in Madeira wine) are created. The deep-dish pies are especially popular at lunchtime, and the homemade desserts are good anytime. The lively atmosphere is high-lighted by a full-service bar, which features fine Italian wines. ✕ *3500 Central Ave. SE, (within the Nob Hill Business Center),* ☎ *505/255–8781. Reservations required. AE, MC, V. No lunch weekends.*

$$ Smiroll's International Cuisine. This low-profile restaurant has a quaint
★ old-world setting and more veal on its menu than any restaurant in town. Diners at the "House of Veal," as it is commonly called, choose from veal scallopini, veal cordon bleu, veal Parmigiana, veal *piccata,* veal cutlet with lemon, and other veal specialties, all of which are equally delicious. But if veal isn't your thing, try the duck and Cornish game hens, or the lean and spicy homemade Italian sausage appetizer. The international menu is capped by an excellent selection of pasta, seafood, and fine wines. ✕ *108 Rio Grande Blvd. NW,* ☎ *505/242–9996. Reservations required. AE, D, DC, MC, V.*

$$ Stephen's. Readers of *Albuquerque Monthly* magazine have called
★ this the best place in the city to conduct a power lunch, but more than businesspeople come here for the solid Southwestern and new Amer-ican food. The pristine setting includes three different dining areas: a large Santa Fe–style room with a view of the open kitchen, an enclosed patio enveloped in lush greenery, and a formal dining room where an exposed brick wall dates to the Territorial-style building's 1915 ori-gins. The menu ranges from pasta to roast duckling and rack of lamb, from fine grilled fish to chicken and veal. Healthy eaters also enjoy the special spa menu, which offers dishes low in cholesterol, sodium, and calories. Service is excellent, as is the selection of more than 340 wines, supposedly the city's largest. ✕ *1311 Tijeras Ave. NW,* ☎ *505/842–1773. Reservations advised. AE, DC, MC, V.*

$ Il Vicino. This neighborhood pizzeria encourages adventurous pizza-
★ lovers to choose from among 25 gourmet toppings and to design their own pies. If you don't trust yourself to come up with a snazzy com-bination, just order any of the 12 house pizzas on the regular menu. The pizza rustica—a buttery cornmeal crust topped with roasted gar-lic, artichoke hearts, calamata olives, capers, fresh tomato sauce, oregano, and mozzarella—is pizza at its best, although every pie here is baked to excellence in a European-style wood-fired oven. Good sal-ads and pasta dishes round out the menu, and the lively Nob Hill lo-cation makes this a fine spot for people-watching. ✕ *3403 Central Ave. NE,* ☎ *505/266–7855. No reservations. MC, V.*

$ Nirvana Indian Cuisine. One of Nob Hill's only truly ethnic restaurants specializes in the vegetarian cuisine of South India. Though the cuisine of North India, which includes tangy curries and grilled meats, also is offered here, the focus is on cooking that is absent of all meats or ani-mal by-products. In lieu of that, whole or powdered rice and lentils are the basic ingredients in such specialties as the spicy *uppuma* (a blend of wheat, tomatoes, bell peppers, peas, mustard seed, cashew, onion, and crunchy fried lentils) or the huge *masala dosai* (a gram flour crepe stuffed with onions, tomatoes, nuts, and potatoes). All dishes are served with a yogurt-based soup or moist wheat flat breads with coconut-ginger chutney. Gray relief wall sculptures highlight pastel-colored walls to create a tasteful and relaxing dining experience. On Saturday nights, the house swells with authentic live Indian music and dance. ✕ *3523 Central Ave. NE,* ☎ *505/265-2172. AE, D, DC, MC, V.*

LODGING

As is typical of many large cities in the Southwest today, Albuquerque's hotels offer a comfortable mix of modern conveniences and Old West flavor. The city's accommodations range from budget motels to bed-and-breakfast inns to soaring hotel skyscrapers. All include much of the Southwest heritage in their decor and design. A waitress sitting down to chat with customers dining in a restaurant may be the stuff of TV sitcoms, but in the West—and cities come no more "Western" than Albuquerque—it really happens. This informality rubs off on guests as well. Ties come off, boots are pulled on, and the streets outside are littered with briefcases.

CATEGORY	COST*
$$$	over $100
$$	$65–$100
$	under $65

All prices are for a standard double room, excluding 5% room tax, 5.8% sales tax, and service charges.

Hotels

Around Albuquerque

$$$ **Albuquerque Hilton.** The charm and decor of the colorful Southwest—Native American rugs, arched doorways, and high ceilings—are blended with the sophistication and elegance of a contemporary hotel at the Albuquerque Hilton, located just 2 miles from downtown. The guest rooms are done in Southwestern pastels, with Santa Fe–style wooden furniture and bleached wood bedsteads; many have balconies. Original Native American and Western art is featured throughout, including numerous works by famed Taos painter R. C. Gorman. The elegant Ranchers Club restaurant has high beamed ceilings and a roaring fireplace over which a mounted buffalo head stares down benevolently. Its authentic grill room—you almost expect to find J. R. Ewing here—features prime meats and fresh seafood prepared over a selection of aromatic woods (patrons select the flavor—piñon, mesquite, and so on—themselves). The Casa Chaco, the hotel's other restaurant, serves typical coffee-shop breakfast and lunch fare but is transformed at night, when nouvelle Southwestern cuisine is served in considerably more elegant style: candlelit tables, waiters in tuxedos, crisp linens, and sparkling crystal. ⌂ *1901 University Blvd. NE, Box 25525, Albuquerque 87102,* ☎ *505/884–2500 or 800/274–6835,* ⊠ *505/889–9118. 264 rooms. Bar, café, dining room, indoor-outdoor pool, sauna, airport shuttle. AE, D, DC, MC, V.*

$$$ **Albuquerque Marriott.** This luxury property is located uptown at the junction of I–40 and Louisiana Boulevard, near some of the city's best shopping areas (Winrock and Coronado malls). Geared to the executive traveler with its special 28-room Concierge Level, complete with

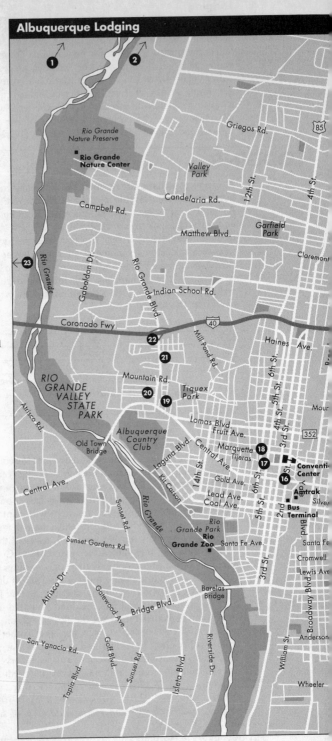

Albuquerque Lodging

Montano Rd.

Cliff's
Amusement
Park

Montgomery Blvd.

Edith Blvd.

425

Comanche Rd.

Montgomery
Park

Aztec

Ela
Park

Grisham
Park

Carlisle Blvd.

Candelaria Rd.

Princeton Dr.

Vassar Dr.

Richmond Dr.

Claremont Ave.

Adams St.

enaul Blvd.

Menaul Blvd.

40

Indian School Rd.

Odelia Rd.

Altura
Park

n Rd.

University Blvd.

Stanford

Girard Blvd.

Constitution

Washington

San Mateo Blvd.

San Pedro Blvd.

Pan American Fwy

Sigma Chi Rd.

Campus Blvd.

Lomas Blvd.

Roma Ave.

UNIVERSITY OF
NEW MEXICO

Solano

Grand Ave.

Central Ave.

Student
Union

Marquette

New Mexico
State
Fairgrounds

Coal Ave.

Silver Ave.

Central Ave.

Roosevelt
Park

Lead Ave.

Cornell

Wellesley

Coal Ave.

Coal Ave.

Garfield

Zuni Rd.

25

Sports
Stadium

Ridgecrest

Trumbull Ave.

UNIVERSITY OF
NEW MEXICO
(South Campus)

Burton
Park

Carlisle Blvd.

Girard

Kathryn Ave.

Ridgecrest Dr.

Louisiana Blvd.

Sunshine Terr. Ave.

University

Wellesley

N

Gibson Blvd.

TO ALBUQUERQUE
INTERNATIONAL
AIRPORT

TO KIRTLAND
AIR FORCE BASE

0   1 mile

0   1 km

faxes and computer hookups, it also has the vacationer in mind. The 17-story hotel with its elegantly decorated lobby (the glowing hues of the furnishings reflect the region's natural colors) has Southwestern touches throughout—kachina dolls, Native American art, and native pottery. It recently completed a $3.2 million renovation. Nicole's Restaurant is the hotel's upscale dining room, with soft lighting, pink napkins and tablecloths, and tableside service; Herbs & Roses, open for breakfast, lunch, and dinner, is more informal. Guest rooms feature walk-in closets, in-room movies, and modern furnishings, all in those pleasing Southwestern tones. The hotel has an exclusive concierge level with 28 rooms. ☒ *2101 Louisiana Blvd. NE, Albuquerque 87110,* ☎ *505/881–6800 or 800/228–9290,* ℻ *505/888–2982. 410 rooms. 2 restaurants, lobby lounge, indoor-outdoor pool, health club, gift shop, airport shuttle. AE, D, DC, MC, V.*

$$$ **Hyatt Regency Albuquerque.** Adjacent to the Albuquerque Convention
★ Center in the heart of downtown is the city's newest major hotel addition, and a beauty it is, with two soaring desert-colored towers climbing high above the city skyline. A private forest and a splashing fountain outside, a shopping promenade inside—it's all totally modern and luxurious. The spacious guest rooms are finished in contemporary Southwestern style with a mauve, burgundy, and tan color scheme and all the standard Hyatt amenities. The Presidential Suite has a canopy bed, as though Abe Lincoln himself might stop by. McGrath's, the hotel's award-winning restaurant, serves steaks, chops, chicken, and seafood in an intimate atmosphere of levels and alcoves, with rich-colored wood furnishing. It's open for breakfast, lunch, and dinner. ☒ *330 Tijeras Ave. NW, Albuquerque 87102,* ☎ *505/842–1234,* ℻ *505/766–6170. 395 rooms, 14 suites. Restaurant, 2 bars, pool, spa, health club. AE, D, DC, MC, V.*

$$$ **Ramada Hotel Classic.** Set in the heart of Albuquerque's uptown business and financial district, across from the Coronado Shopping Center, the state's largest, this modern, eight-story hotel has convention facilities and enough bars, restaurants, and space to keep all the delegates happy. Each of the hotel's recently refurbished, oversize guest rooms and suites is equipped with a refrigerator and boasts a grand view of the majestic Sandia Mountains or the desert West Mesa and the downtown skyline. Southwestern colors (mauve and light green) predominate in the rooms, complementing the Southwestern-style bedspreads and curtains. The bed lamps have pottery bases, and the ceiling lamps are brass. (One wonders why the featured artworks are primarily bland florals and European landscapes when so much good local art is available.) The Café Fennel is open for breakfast, lunch, and dinner, and the Classic Grille highlights grilled meat and seafood in a casual setting. ☒ *6815 Menaul Blvd. NE, Albuquerque 87110,* ☎ *505/881–0000,* ℻ *505/881–3736. 297 rooms. 2 restaurants, 2 bars, indoor pool, sauna, airport shuttle. AE, D, DC, MC, V.*

$$$ **Sheraton Old Town.** In the heart of Albuquerque's historical district, the Sheraton Old Town is a modern, 11-story structure that gracefully sits amid the region's 400 years of culture and history with no overly jarring effects. The guest rooms are large and modern, with tan desert-colored appointments and hand-wrought furnishings. The large bathrooms have vanities with lighted makeup mirrors. The Rio Grande Customs House Restaurant specializes in prime rib, steaks, seafood, and poultry, while the casual Café del Sol has a varied menu, with lots of Southwestern favorites for breakfast, lunch, and dinner. An extra bonus: The Albuquerque Museum and the New Mexico Museum of Natural History are both within walking distance. ☒ *800 Rio Grande Blvd. NW, Albuquerque 87104,* ☎ *505/843–6300 or 800/237–2133,*

FAX *505/842–9863. 190 rooms. 2 restaurants, 2 bars, pool, whirlpool, airport shuttle. AE, D, DC, MC, V.*

\$\$–\$\$\$ **La Posada de Albuquerque.** This historic, highly lauded hotel in the
★   heart of downtown Albuquerque oozes Southwestern charm, with its tiled lobby fountain, massive vigas, encircling balcony, fixtures of etched glass and tin, and Native American war-dance murals behind the reception desk. The guest rooms vary in size from small to spacious. Many have fireplaces; most are decorated throughout with Southwestern and Native American themes, from the designs on couches, slipcovers, and drapes to incidental pieces of Hopi pottery and R. C. Gorman prints on the walls. In 1939, Conrad Hilton opened the hotel, then called the Albuquerque Hilton, as his first lodging venture outside Texas; it was also the first air-conditioned building in New Mexico, Hilton's native state. The hotel mogul honeymooned here with his bride, Zsa Zsa Gabor. The 10-story La Posada has been carefully restored and is listed in the National Register of Historic Places. Its dining room, the popular Eulalia's Restaurant, features waiters and waitresses singing snippets from the latest Broadway hits. The cuisine is Continental, with veal, duck, filet mignon, and wonderful swordfish fajitas topping the list of specialties. There's live jazz and a good happy-hour buffet in the Lobby Lounge (*see* Nightlife, *below*). ⊡ *125 2nd St. NW, Albuquerque 87102,* ☎ *505/242–9090 or 800/777–5732,* FAX *505/242–8664. 114 rooms. Restaurant, bar, exercise room, airport shuttle. AE, D, DC, MC, V.*

\$\$ **Barcelona Court All-Suite Hotel.** This colorful, three-story hotel just off I–40 offers a touch of old Mexico with tile and wrought-iron decor. On the second floor is a large atrium fountain around which guests sip cocktails at sundown and enjoy complimentary breakfast. There is no restaurant on site, but lunch and dinner can be ordered via room service, with meals provided by the nearby **Cooperage Restaurant,** specializing in steaks and seafood. Each two-room suite has a galley kitchen with a wet bar and a microwave oven. Furnishings are contemporary, with Southwest flourishes and regional prints and posters—by Georgia O'Keeffe, R. C. Gorman, and company—on the walls. The hotel provides complimentary breakfast and cocktails. ⊡ *900 Louisiana Blvd. NE, Albuquerque 87110,* ☎ *505/255–5566 or 800/222–1122,* FAX *505/255–5566. 164 suites. 2 pools, sauna, airport shuttle. AE, D, DC, MC, V.*

\$\$ **Doubletree Hotel.** A two-story waterfall splashes down a marble backdrop in the lobby of this recently renovated, 15-story hotel. Convenient to the Albuquerque Convention Center and downtown, the hotel has comfortable guest rooms painted in pastels and appointed with custom-made Southwestern furnishings and regional art. A restaurant situated at the foot of the lobby's waterfall is called, appropriately, *La Cascada* (The Cascade). The restaurant serves good fresh seafood, soups, salads, and Southwestern specialties throughout the day in an airy, open atmosphere. Instead of mints, fresh-baked chocolate chip cookies await guests on the night of arrival. ⊡ *201 Marquette Ave. NW, Albuquerque 87102,* ☎ *505/247–3344,* FAX *505/247–7025, 294 rooms. Restaurant, bar, pool, exercise room, airport shuttle, Old Town shuttle. AE, D, DC, MC, V.*

\$ **Econolodge.** This clean, comfortable chain hotel features 48 rather ordinary rooms at budget rates. The Continental breakfast and airport shuttle are both complimentary. And the outdoor swimming pool is open during the warmer months. ⊡ *13211 Central Ave. NE, Albuquerque 87123,* ☎ *505/292–7600 or 800/424–4777,* FAX *505/298–4536. 48 rooms. Pool, airport shuttle. AE, D, DC, MC, V.*

$ **University Lodge.** Located in the middle of Nob Hill, six blocks east of the University of New Mexico, this small motel is average, but very affordable. The pastel rooms feature standard motel furnishings and are kept quite clean. Rooms equipped for travelers with disabilities are also available, and the Continental breakfast is free. ⚏ *3711 Central Ave. NE, Albuquerque 87108,* ☎ *505/266–7663. 52 rooms. Pool. AE, D, DC, MC, V.*

Airport

$$ **Best Western Fred Harvey Hotel.** Just 350 yards from the Albuquerque
★ International Airport, this 15-story hotel provides speedy access to your flight, day or night. The hotel was recently remodeled, and the rooms are standard, clean, and comfortable with a pastel color scheme and good lighting, large work desks, and leather chairs and ottomans. Dinner at Lil's, an intimate restaurant steeped in romantic Victorian-era appointments and ambience, is a highlight; the Continental menu includes Steak Oscar, a delectable steak topped with crab and bearnaise sauce. The seafood appetizer—shrimp, crab, scallops, and more served on a bed of ice—is a meal in itself. For less formal dining, visit the Harvey House, with a diverse American menu replete with a number of New Mexican red- or green-chile dishes. ⚏ *2910 Yale Blvd. SE, Albuquerque 87106,* ☎ *505/843–7000 or 800/227–1117,* ℻ *505/843–6307. 266 rooms. 2 restaurants, bar, pool, saunas, tennis court, exercise room, airport shuttle. AE, D, DC, MC, V.*

$$ **Courtyard by Marriott.** You don't have to be a businessperson to take advantage of the special corporate rates at this haven for working guests located ½ mile north of the Albuquerque International Airport, but a number of touches were created with the business traveler in mind. Rooms, done in blue and pink with Southwest-inspired paintings, have jacks for portable fax machines, large desks, and long telephone cords that reach the desks. The hotel lobby and hallways are appointed with cacti and couches with Native American–style designs. The casual Courtyard Cafe serves a number of spicy New Mexican dishes as well as pasta, chicken, burgers, and salads. ⚏ *1920 Yale Blvd. SE, Albuquerque 87106,* ☎ *505/843–6600 or 800/321–2211,* ℻ *505/843–8740. 136 rooms, 14 suites. Restaurant, indoor pool, spa, health club, airport shuttle. AE, D, DC, MC, V.*

$$ **Radisson Inn Albuquerque.** This newly renovated hotel just off I–25 provides fast access to all parts of the city and is just ¼-mile from the Albuquerque International Airport. A Southwestern Spanish flavor runs throughout the hotel, with arched balconies, tan desert colors, a year-round courtyard pool, and indoor and outdoor dining. The guest rooms are standard but comfortable. Diamondback's Café and Coyote's Cantina offer a Western setting and regional northern New Mexican cuisine including fajitas and enchiladas. No-smoking rooms are available, and pets are welcome. ⚏ *1901 University Blvd. SE, Albuquerque 87106,* ☎ *505/247–0512 or 800/333–3333,* ℻ *505/843–7148. 147 rooms, 1 suite. Restaurant, bar, no-smoking rooms, pool, sauna, spa, health club, racquetball, airport shuttle. AE, D, DC, MC, V.*

$ **Comfort Inn.** This hotel used to be a Texas Inn until it was renovated a few years ago, but the theme of the day here is still the Wild West. The saloon-like lobby has a dim, wooden interior with Western-style paintings and memorabilia. The rooms have standard but comfortable decor. While there's no restaurant on the premises, complimentary Continental breakfast is served each morning in the lobby, and a full-service restaurant and coffee shop is adjacent to the hotel. The Albuquerque International Airport is just a mile away. ⚏ *2300 Yale Blvd. SE, Albuquerque 87106,* ☎ *505/243–2244 or 800/221–2222,* ℻ *505/247–*

2925. *114 rooms. Pool, hot tub, sauna, airport shuttle. AE, D, DC, MC, V.*

Bed-and-Breakfasts

$$–$$$ **Casas de Suenos.** Long a historic gathering spot for artists, Casas de
★ Suenos—Houses of Dreams—provides a magical setting amid lush
English gardens and quiet patios. The 2-acre compound, adjacent to
Old Town on Rio Grande Boulevard SW, is made up of 17 attractively
decorated casitas that have beehive fireplaces, pigskin furniture,
bleached cattle skulls on the wall, regional paintings, and Native American rugs. Breakfasts start with decadent French toast or savory eggs,
a fruit platter, and a selection of fresh breads and muffins. A small gallery
has frequent exhibits by local artists. The inn's hallmark is its impeccable service; a concierge is on the premises to help you plan your stay.
⌂ *310 Rio Grande Blvd. SW, Albuquerque 87104,* ☏ *505/247–4560
or 800/242–8987,* ⅁ *505/842–8493. 3 rooms with bath, 14 suites.
AE, MC, V.*

$$ **Bottger Mansion.** The only bed-and-breakfast in Old Town, this pale
★ blue Victorian is listed on the National Register of Historic Places and
dates to 1912, when it was built by a German immigrant known sim-
ply as Mr. Bottger. Today, the Garcia family runs the mansion with its
three guest rooms draped in Victorian-era decor, each boasting origi-
nal tin ceilings and roomy brass beds. One room overlooks a patio gar-
den, another has its own private patio, and still another is highlighted
by a hand-painted mural created by a Bottger family member. The grassy
courtyard with marble patios provides a quiet escape from the Old Town
tourist frenzy. Homemade breakfasts of, for example, scrambled eggs
with green chile, or apricot French toast, as well as fresh fruit, coffee,
tea, and juice are served in the courtyard during the warmer months;
bizcochitos (the state's official shortbread-like cookies) are served as
evening snacks. Since Old Town is short on parking space, the outgo-
ing management picks up the tab for the parking lot across the street.
⌂ *110 San Felipe St. NW, Albuquerque 87104,* ☏ *505/243–3639. 3
rooms with bath. AE, MC, V.*

$$ **Casita Chamisa.** Set in a cottonwood-shaded valley in Los Ranchos,
this guest house is only about 15 minutes north of Old Town and 12
miles from the Albuquerque Airport. With just two bedrooms, the house
sleeps one to six and is rented to one party at a time. The furnishings
are Southwestern, with Native American blankets, pottery, and artifacts adding authenticity. Owners Kit and Arnold Sargeant opened their
guest house in 1974, the first bed-and-breakfast in Albuquerque. The
property is also an archaeological site, with remnants of a prehistoric
Native American dwelling still visible. Kit Sargeant, an archaeologist,
supervised the dig herself. Also for guests use, even at 2 AM if the urge
strikes, is an enclosed 15- by 33-foot swimming pool. The solar-heated
pool house has a hot tub and full bath. Breakfast is Country Continental, which translates into waffles, pancakes, and lots of seasonal
fruits (14 of Casita Chamisa's more than 200 trees are fruit bearing).
Arnold Sargeant is famous for his sourdough bread, "with a starter,"
he says, "that's 110 years old." ⌂ *850 Chamisal Rd. NW, Albuquerque 87107,* ☏ *505/897–4644. 2-bedroom guest house sleeps 1–
6. Pool, hot tub. AE, MC, V.*

$$ **Corrales Inn.** This Territorial adobe-style, solar-heated home located
14 miles north of Albuquerque in picturesque Corrales, was built to
serve as a bed-and-breakfast in 1987. Each of the guest rooms is theme
decorated—Oriental, Native American, Victorian, Corrales (South-
western), and Balloon (in honor of the hot-air-balloon festivals held

nearby). Rooms have individual temperature controls, as well as a sitting and dressing area. Full gourmet French country breakfasts—quiche, soufflés, omelets, crepes, croissants—are served in the guest rooms or in the inn's common room. Outside is a courtyard with a hot tub. ☎ *58 Perea Rd. (behind Plaza San Ysidro), Box 1361, Corrales 87048,* ☎ *505/897–4422. 6 rooms with bath. Hot tub. MC, V.*

$$ **Elaine's, A Bed and Breakfast.** This beautiful three-story log home, in
★ the evergreen folds of the Sandia Peaks, is tastefully furnished throughout with European antiques and a sprinkling of early regional pieces. The top two floors are for guest rooms, with balconies and big picture windows bringing the lush mountain views indoors. The third-floor room has cathedral ceilings and a brass bed, while the second-floor accommodations share a massive stone fireplace, as well as a bath. A well-stocked library and big fireplaces invite cerebral pursuits, and 4 acres of wooded grounds beckon just outside the back door. Full ham-and-egg–style breakfasts are served, with all the accompaniments. ☎ *72 Snowline Rd., Snowline Estate, Box 444, Cedar Crest 87008,* ☎ *505/281–2467 or 800/821–3092. 3 rooms, 2 with shared bath. No credit cards.*

$$ **Inn at Paradise.** On the first tee of the lush Paradise Hills Golf Club, 30 minutes from the airport, this upscale bed-and-breakfast resort is a golfer's dream: The 6,895 yards of bluegrass fairways and bent grass greens challenge players of all levels. The 16-suite hacienda sits atop the West Mesa and overlooks the lovely Rio Grande Valley, a perfect setting for either a business getaway or a romantic hideaway. Accommodations are clean and comfortable; the large rooms feature original art by local artists and craftspeople. Two suites have fireplaces, while a deluxe suite includes a fireplace, full kitchen, and a wet bar. Complimentary pastries, fruit, and coffee are delivered to your room in the morning, while other meals are served in the golf course club house. Relaxation is the theme here, whether it be in the form of a dip in the pool, an afternoon on the putting green, or sunset wine and cheese service on the veranda. Seasonal hot air balloon rides, on-site massage, and golf lessons are additional diversions. Some room rates include a daily round of golf with preferred tee times for guests. ☎ *10035 Country Club Lane NW, Albuquerque 87114,* ☎ *505/898–6161,* ℻ *505/898–9464. 16 rooms, 3 suites. Spa, 18-hole golf course, airport shuttle. AE, MC, V.*

$$ **Turquoise Inn Bed and Breakfast.** Nestled on 2¼ acres adjacent to Cibola National Forest (25 miles northeast of the Albuquerque Airport on the road to Sandia Crest), the Turquoise Inn Bed and Breakfast is surrounded by cedars, and ponderosa and piñon pines. The house was originally a four-bedroom private home that was remodeled and modified to become a bed-and-breakfast. One guest room, formerly the master bedroom, is furnished in Colonial antiques, with Southwestern touches. The large upstairs suite, with a private outside entrance, fireplace, and wet bar, showcases modern Scandinavian furnishings. A Continental breakfast served in the rooms helps guests get a good start on the day. ☎ *142 Sandia Crest Rd., Sandia Park 87047,* ☎ *505/281–4745. 1 room with bath, 1 suite. AE, D, MC, V.*

$$ **William E. Mauger Estate.** Centrally located downtown, 12 blocks from historic Old Town, this elegant 1897 Queen Anne residence offers comfortable accommodations. Four of the guest rooms are Victorian style, with either a brass bed, a cherry-wood sleigh bed, an iron bed, or a standard Victorian bed with a large, ornate headboard. The other two rooms are Art Deco in design, with tinted mirrors and fluted vases. Full breakfasts—egg dishes, home-baked pastries, juice, and coffee—are served in the guest rooms or in the downstairs parlor or common room. ☎ *701 Roma Ave. NW, Albuquerque 87102,* ☎ *505/242–8755. 8 rooms with bath, 1 suite. AE, D, DC, MC, V.*

$$ **Windmill Ranch Bed and Breakfast.** On the far west side of town in the heart of the bosque (4 miles west of I–40, Exit 155), this bed-and-breakfast has spectacular views of the Sandia Mountains. Guest rooms and public areas are furnished with antiques, including a player piano (with often-played tunes such as "Red River Valley"), a roller-type Edison, and a Victrola. (For the benefit of guests who are trying to sleep, not all of them get cranked up at the same time.) There's also a large-screen VCR with a film library of over 200 titles. The Windmill is only 100 yards from the Rio Grande, where ancient elms and cottonwoods grow in profusion. Paths along the river are ideal for biking, jogging, or walking. The 5,000-acre spread is a working ranch, so there are horses, ducks, and chickens scampering about. Freshly laid eggs are served for breakfast, with all the country trimmings. From the Windmill's balcony, visitors can overdose on scenery, watch the hot-air balloons glide by during seasonal balloon rallies, or just breathe the good air. ☎ *6400 Coors Blvd. NW, Albuquerque 87120, ☎ 505/898–6864. 4 rooms with bath, 2 with fireplaces. MC, V.*

Camping

Albuquerque KOA Central. This campground has full hookups, Kamping Kabins, a swimming pool and spa, hot showers, flush toilets, LP gas refills, and laundry facilities. There is also a shuttle between the campground, which is located within the city limits (Exit 166 off I–40), and Old Town. ☎ *12400 Skyline Rd., Albuquerque 87123, ☎ 505/296–2729. 200 sites, 101 full hookups. Water and electric hookup $21.95 per night, full hookup $23.95 per night. D, MC, V.*

KOA has another property in Albuquerque with similar services, the **Albuquerque North KOA** (555 S. Hill Rd. in Bernalillo, ☎ 505/867–5227).

Isleta Lakes and Recreation Area. This property, 15 minutes south of Albuquerque on I–25 (take Exit 215 to NM 47), has complete campground facilities and tent sites, and three fishing lakes. ☎ *Box 383, Isleta 87022, ☎ 505/877–0370. Over 100 tent sites. 40 RV hookups (water and electricity). Tent site $9 per night, RV site $12 per night. Showers and flush toilets in central bathhouse. MC, V.*

Turquoise Trail Campgrounds. This campground is in the Sandia Mountains, 15 minutes east of Albuquerque (east on I–40, Exit 175, 4 miles north on I–14). It has full hookups, hot showers, laundry, and a wooded tent area. ☎ *22 Calvary Rd., Cedar Crest 87008, ☎ 505/281–2005. Camping space for 2 is $10.50; a full hookup is $15.*

THE ARTS AND NIGHTLIFE

To find out what's on in town, check the Friday and Sunday editions of the *Albuquerque Journal,* and the Thursday edition of the *Albuquerque Tribune.*

The Arts

Dance
Sun Dance, Inc. (☎ 505/268–8756), presents an array of year-round dance performances, ranging from modern to flamenco to tap and ballet.

Music
The conductor of the **New Mexico Symphony Orchestra** (3301 Menaul NE, Suite 4, ☎ 505/881–8999), now in its 63rd year, swings a wide baton, with presentations of pops, Beethoven, and Handel's *Messiah* at Christmas. Performances are frequently scheduled under the stars

at the Rio Grande Zoo Bandshell and at Popejoy Hall on the University of New Mexico campus.

Opera

Albuquerque Civic Light Opera Association is one of the largest community-based producers of musical theater in the country. Its five annual productions are seen by a total audience of 75,000. Performances are held in the 2,000-seat Popejoy Hall at the University of New Mexico campus. For information or tickets, call the box office, ☎ 505/345–6577.

Theater

The KiMo Theater (423 Central Ave. NW; box office, ☎ 505/764–1700; business office, ☎ 505/848–1370), a 1927 movie palace on Central Avenue restored to its original design—Pueblo Deco–style architecture painted in bright colors—offers a varied program, everything from traveling road shows to local song-and-dance acts. **Rodey Theater** (☎ 505/277–4402), in the Fine Arts Center of the University of New Mexico, stages student and professional plays and dance performances throughout the year, including the acclaimed Summerfest Festival of New Plays and Flamenco Festival, held each summer. The **Albuquerque Little Theatre** (224 San Pasquale Ave. SW, ☎ 505/242–4750), a nonprofit community troupe, combines local volunteer talent with a staff of professionals to present an annual series of comedies, dramas, musicals, and mysteries of the highest caliber. The company theater, located across the street from historic Old Town, was built in 1936 and was designed by famed Southwestern architect John Gaw Meen. It contains an art gallery; a large, comfortable lobby; and a cocktail lounge. **La Compania de Teatro de Albuquerque** (518 1st St. NW, ☎ 505/242–7929), New Mexico's largest bilingual theater, performs classic and contemporary plays in English and Spanish during April, June, October, and December.

Nightlife

Bars and Lounges

The Dingo Bar (303 Gold Ave. SE, ☎ 505/243–0663) is a small downtown nightclub that draws big crowds with its live mix of jazz, blues, punk, pop, and world-beat dance offerings. The **El Rey Theatre** (624 Central Ave. SW, ☎ 505/243–7546) presents live blues, rock, alternative, jazz, metal, and country sounds in a renovated 1941 theater setting. **Fat Chance Bar and Grill** (2216 Central Ave. SE, ☎ 505/265–7531), across the street from the University of New Mexico, is a hangout for boisterous college students. It's got booths, a bar, tables, a dance floor, and live entertainment—from rock to reggae—Wednesday through Sunday nights.

Comedy Clubs

Laff's (3100 Juan Tabo Blvd. NE, ☎ 505/296–5653) is the place to go for live comedy in Albuquerque.

Country-and-Western Clubs

Caravan East (7605 Central Ave. NE, ☎ 505/265–7877) is a country-and-western nightclub offering free dance lessons and partners galore. Two live bands play nightly. There is a free buffet and half-price drinks during the 4:30–7 happy hour. **Midnight Rodeo** (4901 McLeod Rd. NE, ☎ 505/888–0100) is an enormous country-and-western complex, with a huge race-track-style dance floor, several bars, and even boutiques. The happy-hour buffet spread is incredible. The **Sundance Saloon** (12000 Candelaria Rd. NE, ☎ 505/296–6761) is another C&W favorite in Albuquerque.

Jazz Clubs
La Posada Lobby Lounge (La Posada de Albuquerque Hotel, ☎ 505/242–9090) has live weekend blues and jazz performances and a weekday happy-hour buffet that's very popular among the locals.

ALBUQUERQUE ESSENTIALS

Arriving and Departing

By Bus
Greyhound/Trailways and **Texas New Mexico & Oklahoma Coaches** offer comprehensive daily service into **Albuquerque's Transportation Center** (300 2nd St. SW, ☎ 505/243–4435 or 800/531–5332).

By Car
The main routes into Albuquerque are I–25 from points north and south and I–40 from points east and west.

By Plane
AIRPORT AND AIRLINES
Albuquerque International Airport (☎ 505/842–4366), 5 miles south of downtown Albuquerque, is the gateway to New Mexico. Car rentals, air taxis, and bus shuttles are readily available at the airport, which is 65 miles southwest of Santa Fe and 130 miles south of Taos.

Airlines serving Albuquerque International Airport are **America West** (☎ 800/235–9292), **American** (☎ 800/433–7300), **Continental** (☎ 800/525–0280), **Delta** (☎ 800/221–1212), **Mesa Air** (☎ 800/637–2247), **Southwest** (☎ 800/435–9792), **TWA** (☎ 800/221–2000), **United** (☎ 800/241–6522), and **USAir** (☎ 800/428–4322).

Air-shuttle service between Albuquerque and Santa Fe via **Mesa Airlines** operates four times a day; the flying time is approximately 25 minutes.

BETWEEN THE AIRPORT AND DOWNTOWN
The trip into town from the airport takes about 10–15 minutes, and there is a variety of ground transportation to choose from. Taxis, available at clearly marked stands, charge about $7 (plus 50¢ for each additional rider); *see* By Taxi, *below.* Sun Tran buses pick up at the sunburst signs every 30 minutes; the fare is 75¢; *see* By Bus, *below.* Most major hotels provide shuttle service to and from the airport, including Hilton, La Posada de Albuquerque, Marriott, Ramada, and Sheraton. If you like to go in high style, *see* By Limousine, *below.* For car-rental companies in New Mexico, *see* Car Rental in The Gold Guide.

By Train
Amtrak's (☎ 800/872–7245) *Southwest Chief* services Albuquerque daily from Los Angeles and Chicago. The Albuquerque Station, built by the Santa Fe Railroad in 1901 and famous for its grand Spanish-style architecture and graceful domes and archways, burned to the ground in January 1993. A temporary station (214 1st St. SW, ☎ 505/842–9650), literally in the former station's ashes, now services the line.

Getting Around

Unlike more compact Taos and Santa Fe, Albuquerque sprawls out in all directions, so you'll need transportation to get wherever you're going.

By Bus
The **Sun Tran** buses blanket the city with frequent connections (about every 30 minutes, less frequently in the more remote areas of the city and on weekends). The fare is 75¢. Bus stops are well marked with

the line's sunburst signs. For information, call 505/843–9200, or write Sun Tran (City of Albuquerque, 601 Yale SE, Albuquerque 87106).

By Limousine

Albuquerque has several limousine companies. Rates start at $35–$45 per hour for standard limousines and range up to $145 per hour for stretch limos comfortably seating 14; there is usually a two-hour minimum. Call for special airport shuttle rates. Companies include: **At Last, The Past,** Antique Limousine Service (☎ 505/298–9944), **Classic Limousine** (☎ 505/247–4000), **Dream Limousine** (☎ 505/884–6464), **Lucky's Limousine Service** (☎ 505/836–4035), **VIP Limousine Service** (☎ 505/883–4888).

By Taxi

Taxis are metered in Albuquerque, service is around the clock, and rates run about $2.90 for the first mile and $1.40 for each additional mile; each additional passenger is charged 50¢. Contact **Albuquerque Cab** (☎ 505/883–4888), **Yellow-Checker Cab** (☎ 505/243–7777), or **Yellow Cab** (☎ 505/247–8888) for service.

Opening and Closing Times

General business hours in Albuquerque are 9–5; most shops, galleries, and museums are open 10–5 or 6, with limited hours on weekends. Banking hours are weekdays 9–4, and, in some cases, Saturday 10–2.

Guided Tours

Orientation

Gray Line of Albuquerque offers several daily and seasonal tours (May–Oct.). Among them is a three-hour Albuquerque city tour, including the University of New Mexico campus, historic landmarks, and the Indian Pueblo Cultural Center. Other tours explore Old Town Albuquerque, Sandia Peak Aerial Tramway, and Santa Fe. Departure days and times depend on tour destination. For tour schedules, reservations, and information, call 505/242–3880 or 800/256–8991.

Special-Interest

Gray Line offers special tours to Acoma Indian Pueblo, the Anasazi cliff dwellings at Bandelier National Monument, and other Native American sites. Departure days and times vary depending on the destination.

International Universities (1101 Tijeras Ave. NW, ☎ 505/246–2233 or 800/547–5678) has fascinating educational seminars and excursions focusing on the culture and history of New Mexico, including Indian Pueblos, Santa Fe, and the Turquoise Trail. Customized group planning is available.

There are also many operators offering early morning **hot-air balloon tours** of Albuquerque (*see* Ballooning in Sports and the Outdoors, *above*).

Walking

The **Albuquerque Museum** (☎ 505/243–7255) leads hour-long historical walks through **Old Town** at 11 AM Tuesday–Sunday. There is no charge for the tour, which is available on a first-come basis and meets in the lobby of the Albuquerque Museum before setting out for Old Town. Tours do not run in winter.

A 30-minute walking tour of the **University of New Mexico's** campus, available through the Public Affairs office (☎ 505/277–5813), emphasizes the university's cohesive Pueblo-style architecture. Designed for small groups, the tour has no set time and is available only on request. **Student Outreach** (☎ 505/277–5161) offers daily campus tours (9 AM and 1:30 PM), designed primarily for prospective students.

Important Addresses and Numbers

Emergencies
Fire, medical, or police (☎ 911; police nonemergency ☎ 505/768–1986).

Hospital emergency rooms. University Hospital (2211 Lomas NE, ☎ 505/843–2411), Presbyterian Hospital (1100 Central Ave. SE, ☎ 505/841–1234). Call either for locations of Urgent Care Centers around the city.

Dentist referrals (☎ 505/292–2620).

Late-Night Pharmacies
Walgreens offers a 24-hour prescription-refill service at two locations (2950 Central Ave. SE, ☎ 505/262–1743, and 5001 Montgomery NE, ☎ 505/881–5050).

Visitor Information
The **Albuquerque Convention and Visitors Bureau** (Springer Bldg., 121 Tijeras Ave. NE, Box 26866, Albuquerque 87125, ☎ 505/243–3696 or 800/284–2282) publishes a variety of informative materials, including quarterly calendars of events and brochures describing local and out-of-town driving tours. A tape-recorded bulletin on current local events in Albuquerque can be reached after 5 PM on weekdays and all day Saturday and Sunday by phoning 505/243–3696 or 800/284–2282; the same numbers can be used to request an information packet. The bureau also maintains an information center on the lower level of the airport at the bottom of the escalator; it is open daily from 9:30 to 8.

Other Numbers
Time and temperature (☎ 505/247–1611).

Road conditions (☎ 505/827–5213 or 800/432–4269).

5 Carlsbad and Southern New Mexico

CARLSBAD CAVERNS NATIONAL PARK, in the southeastern part of the state, contains one of the largest
and most spectacular cave systems in the world. As
such, it is the area's main lure, but the town of Carlsbad and such nearby
attractions as Living Desert State Park are also well worth visiting. About
3½ hours northwest of Carlsbad are the historic towns of Lincoln
County and the striking White Sands National Monument, which
make an interesting one- to two-day excursion from Carlsbad.

EXPLORING CARLSBAD

Carlsbad Caverns National Park

The huge, subterranean chambers, fantastic rock formations, and delicate mineral sculptures of Carlsbad Caverns National Park draw
about three quarters of a million people each year to a remote corner
of southeast New Mexico. Although the park is in the Chihuahuan
Desert, near the rugged canyons and peaks of the Guadalupe mountain range and the piñon and ponderosa pines of Lincoln National Forest, the most spectacular sights here are all below the earth's surface,
with such evocative names as the Green Lake Room, the King's Palace,
the Devil's Den, the Sequoia Room, the Hooded Klansman, the China
Wall, and Iceberg Rock.

This cave system, hundreds of millions of years in the making, is one
of the largest and most impressive in the world, but it was discovered
relatively recently. Pictographs near the cave entrance tell us that pre-
Columbian Native Americans took shelter in Carlsbad Caverns more
than 1,000 years ago, but archaeologists doubt that they ventured in
very far; access to the depths was limited and the tribe may have believed that the dwellings of the dead lay below.

It wasn't until the 19th century that nearby settlers, curious about the
huge groups of bats they saw in the area, rediscovered the caves. They
were mined for bat guano (dung), which was used as fertilizer, for a
number of years, but no one was interested in the caves for any other
reason until the early 20th century, when one of the guano miners, Jim
White, began exploring and told people about this amazing underground
universe.

White brought a photographer, Ray Davis, to bear witness to his ex-
travagant claims for the place. Displayed in the nearby town of Carlsbad in 1915, Davis's black-and-white pictures astounded people and
started a rush of interest in the caverns. White turned tour operator,
taking people down 170 feet in a bucket left over from the days of mining bat guano and lighting their way with kerosene lamps.

Washington got wind of this natural wonder in the early 1920s, and
in 1923 inspector Robert Holley was dispatched by the U.S. Department of Interior to investigate. His report was instrumental in getting
Carlsbad Caverns declared a national monument later that year by President Calvin Coolidge. The area was designated a national park in 1930.

The newest discovery in Carlsbad Caverns National Park is Lechugilla
Cave, the deepest limestone cave in the United States. Scientists began
mapping the cave network a few years ago, and although they've discovered 80½ miles of caverns extending to a depth of 1,566 feet, there
remains more to explore. Recently, a team of NASA scientists and re-

The Carlsbad Region

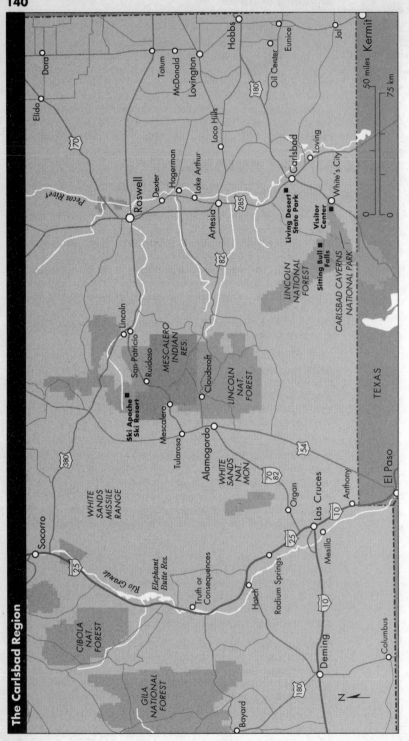

Dora
Elida
Tatum
McDonald
Lovington
Hobbs
Eunice
Oil Center
Jal
Kermit

70

Pecos River

Roswell
Dexter
Hagerman
Lake Arthur
Loco Hills
Carlsbad
Loving
White's City

180

285

Artesia

82

Living Desert State Park
Visitor Center
Sitting Bull Falls
LINCOLN NATIONAL FOREST
CARLSBAD CAVERNS NATIONAL PARK

Lincoln
San Patricio
Ruidoso
MESCALERO INDIAN RES.
Cloudcroft
LINCOLN NAT. FOREST

Ski Apache Ski Resort

Mescalero
Tularosa
Alamogordo
WHITE SANDS NAT. MON.

TEXAS

54

380

WHITE SANDS MISSILE RANGE

70
82

Organ
Las Cruces
Anthony
El Paso

Socorro

25

Rio Grande

Elephant Butte Res.

Truth or Consequences

10

Radium Springs
Mesilla

CIBOLA NAT. FOREST

Hatch

10

GILA NATIONAL FOREST

Deming

180

Bayard

Columbus

N

50 miles
75 km

searchers descended into the precipitous passages to search for microorganisms that could shed light on the kind of life that may exist or may have existed on Mars. The bacteria in the cave derive energy from sulfur, believed to be one of the two main ingredients of Martian soil. The cave is not yet open to the public (because of its dangerous terrain and scientific value), but there is an exhibit on it in the visitor center as well as a video, *The Spirit of Exploration* (for sale at the park bookstore), that describes the history of Lechuguilla Cave and the other caves in the park. Of the 77 caves in the park, only two, Carlsbad Cavern and Slaughter Canyon Cave, are open to the public.

Carlsbad Caverns owes its existence as much to slow drips and accretions as to cataclysmic events. Its origins go back some 250 million years, when Capitan Reef, 400 miles long, formed around the edge of the warm, shallow sea that once covered this region. The sea evaporated and the reef was buried until a few million years ago, when a combination of erosion and convulsions that also created the Guadalupe Mountains brought parts of it back above ground. Rainwater seeping down through the reef's cracks gradually enlarged them into cavities, which eventually collapsed, forming huge rooms. Over millennia, evaporated limestone deposited on the ceilings grew into great hanging stalactites, which in turn dripped the crystals that over time rose into massive stalagmites and other, more delicate formations—cave pearls, draperies, popcorn, and lily pads.

Whether you take the long route or the elevator shortcut, the trek through Carlsbad Cavern is long, and you may find yourself getting a bit disoriented. The sheer vastness of the interior is overwhelming, and the proportions seem to change as one goes along. In places where pools of water have formed beside the walkway, reflections and reality merge; you may have to pause for a moment to regain your equilibrium.

Although you may be tempted to touch the cave's walls and jutting rock formations, heed the ranger's warning against doing so. Oil from the human hand forms a type of waterproofing that inhibits the natural water seepage. One or two people pawing at the rocks wouldn't make much of a difference, but thousands tour the cavern daily. Visitors are also warned not to leave the guided pathways. They're not told, however, that if they wander astray, silent alarms will quickly summon park rangers. The interior of Carlsbad Cavern is well lighted, but many people seem more concerned about where they're stepping than with what's ahead and make most of the trip looking down at their feet.

There are two self-guided routes into Carlsbad Cavern: **Natural Entrance Route** and **The Big Room Route.** If you take the former, you'll proceed on foot along the paved walkway that winds down into the caverns' depths for about 1 mile, passing through a series of underground rooms and descending slowly to a depth of about 750 feet. It takes about one hour to complete; the trail can be slick in parts and the grades are fairly steep, so be prepared for a strenuous hike. The Big Room Route is less difficult. You take a high-speed elevator from the visitor center down 750 feet to an underground lunchroom, and begin your exploration there. This route also takes about an hour to walk and covers a distance of 1 mile. (The elevator makes a portion of the main cavern accessible to visitors using wheelchairs.) In both cases, you'll visit the Big Room, so called because it's large enough to hold 14 Houston Astrodomes; one corner could contain the White House. The highest ceiling reaches 256 feet. *The Natural Entrance Route: open June–Aug., daily 8:30–5; Sept.–May, daily 8:30–3:30. The Big Room Route: open June–Aug., daily 8:30–3:30; Sept.–May, 8:30–2.*

A third option for exploring the caverns is the **King's Palace Tour,** a ranger-led tour that takes visitors through the King's Palace, the Queen's Chamber, the Papoose Room, and the Green Lake Room. These areas used to be a part of the self-guided tours, but because this route passes very close to many rock formations there was a problem with breakage and vandalism. The Park Service estimated it was losing some 2,000 rock formations per year, and the new tour is an attempt to preserve the integrity of the caverns. The tour covers about 1 mile over fairly level trails and takes about 1½ hours to complete. *Tour hours: June–Aug., daily and hourly 9–3:00; Sept.–May, daily: 9, 11, 1, and 3.*

The temperature inside Carlsbad Cavern remains at a constant 56°F, and it's damp, so a sweater or warm clothes are recommended. So are comfortable shoes with rubber soles—because of the moisture, the underground walkways are slippery. But the cavern is well lighted and numerous park rangers are stationed about to offer assistance and information. Tours on portable CD players with headphones are available. As you walk through various sections of the caverns, infrared beams trigger descriptions stored on the CD. Visitors may use the keyboard on the CD players to request more detailed information (a CD stores roughly 75 hours worth of information). At press time (summer 1995), the CD tour cost $1.50.

Apart from the cave itself, one of the great attractions at Carlsbad Cavern is the **nightly bat flights.** Each evening between late-May and mid-October at about sunset, bats by the tens of thousands exit from the natural entrance of the cavern and go flying about the countryside scouting for flying insects. They consume the insects in flight, collectively more than three tons of yummy bugs per night. (No scientist has yet figured out how a bat hanging upside down in a dark cave knows when the sun has set outside.) Because bats are among the most maligned and misunderstood creatures, park rangers give informative talks about them each evening prior to the exodus, at about 7. The time of the bat flights varies over the course of the season, so ranger lectures are flexible as well; the time is usually posted, but if not, check at the visitor center. Lectures are suspended during the winter months, when the bats leave for Mexico.

Slaughter Canyon Cave, 25 miles from the main cavern, is much less accessible. You'll have to provide your own transportation to get there, and reservations (☎ 505/785–2232) are required at least a day in advance; during the busy summer months, two weeks in advance are recommended. The last few miles of the roadway there is gravel, and the mouth of the cave is a half-mile climb up a 500-foot rise. Give yourself plenty of time to complete the drive and the climb to the cave, so you don't arrive late for the tour. The tour is offered June–August twice daily, at 9 and 12:30; September–May on weekends, at 10 and 1.

Millions of years old, Slaughter Canyon Cave was discovered by Tom Tucker, a local goatherd, in 1937. Guided tours have been available only during the past few years. The cave consists primarily of a single corridor, 1,140 feet long, with numerous side passages. The total extent of the surveyed passage is 1¾ miles, and the lowest point is 250 feet below the surface. Outstanding formations are the Christmas Tree, the Monarch, the Hooded Klansman, the Tear Drop, and the China Wall. Rangers lead groups of 25 on a two-hour lantern tour. Children under 6 aren't permitted. The cave temperature is a constant 62°F, and the humidity is a clammy 90%. You'll need to bring along your own flashlight, hiking boots or good walking shoes (sneakers aren't recommended), and drinking water. Photographs are permitted, but no tripod setups are allowed, since the group moves along at a relatively brisk pace and you *really* wouldn't want to be left behind. Unless you're in great physical shape, with a long attention span, Slaughter Cave may be more cave peeping than you bargained for.

While you're exploring Carlsbad Cavern, you can pretty much set your own pace, either walking, which takes about three hours, or using the elevators up and down, for a total of perhaps 1½ hours. Add another hour or two if you have lunch at the cavern and peruse the museum exhibits and the gift and book shops. That means a half day would certainly cover all the highlights. Then you can relax and enjoy the natural wonders of the park itself. Box lunches are available at the caverns' underground lunchroom, so you may want to have lunch at **Rattlesnake Springs.** (Don't let the name scare you; no one's seen a rattlesnake there in years.) A pleasant picnic area, with shade trees, grass, picnic tables, water, grills, and toilets, it's also a favorite spot for bird-watchers. Located near the Black River, Rattlesnake Springs was a source of water for Native Americans hundreds of years ago. Army troops exploring the area used it as well, and today it's the main source of water for all the park facilities.

Another option is to take the scenic 9½-mile **Walnut Canyon Drive.** This loop begins a half mile from the visitor center and travels along the top of the ridge to the edge of Rattlesnake Canyon and back down through upper Walnut Canyon to the main entrance road. It's a one-way gravel road, and the backcountry scenery is stunning; go late in the afternoon or early in the morning to enjoy the full spectrum of changing light and dancing colors. There's also a self-guided **Desert Nature Walk,** about a half-mile long, which begins near the cavern's entrance. Experienced hikers might enjoy taking advantage of more than 50 miles of primitive trails that meander through the backcountry. On the other hand, if all or any of that sounds like a bit more of the Great Outdoors than you care to experience in one day, you could head into the town of Carlsbad and enjoy any number of the attractions there. *Carlsbad Caverns National Park, 3225 National Parks Hwy., Carlsbad 88220,* ☎ *505/785–2232. Cavern* ☛ *Natural Entrance and Big Room Route: $5 adults, $3 children 6–15, children 5 and under free for entry into the cavern, $2.50 Golden Age Passport carriers; King's Palace Tour: In addition to the general entrance fee to cavern, $5 adults, $2.50 children 6–15, children under 6 free, $2.50 Golden Age Passport carriers; Slaughter Canyon Cave: $8 adults, $4 children 6–15 and Golden Age Passport carriers, children under 6 not permitted; fees for periodic, special guided trips into other undeveloped caves cost $12 adults, $6 children ages 6–15 and Golden Age Passport carriers, children under 6 not permitted.* ☉ *June–Aug., daily 8–7; Sept.–May, daily 8–5:30. For tour reservations, call 505/785–2232, ext.429, 8:30–4:30 mountain time. The Golden Age Passport is issued for a processing fee of $10 to any U.S. citizen who presents an ID that shows that they are age 62 or older. It is good for discounts at any of the U.S. federal recreation sites, including campgrounds and is valid for life. You can apply for the passport at the Carlsbad Caverns Visitor Center. Facilities at Carlsbad include a kennel, bookstore, gift shop, and 2 restaurants, 1 above ground and another 750 feet below.*

Carlsbad and Environs

With the world-famous caverns nearby, the town of **Carlsbad** is among the most popular tourist destinations in New Mexico. Originally named Eddy after pioneer cattleman Charles B. Eddy, the town's name was changed to Carlsbad in 1889 because its spring-water mineral content was discovered to be similar to that found in Karlsbad, Bohemia, a famous health spa. Situated along the Pecos River, which affords it 27 miles of beaches and picturesque pathways, Carlsbad is an attractive town of 30,000 that seems pleasantly suspended between the past and the present. Only a block from the river, its Territorial town square encircles a pueblo-style country courthouse designed by the famed New Mexican architect John Gaw Meem, who also designed many of the buildings on the University of New Mexico campus in Albuquerque. Surprisingly for a city its size, Carlsbad has 30 parks, more than any other city in New Mexico. It also has more than its share of hokey attractions—miniature train rides, riverboat paddle wheelers, an amusement village with carnival thrill rides—but somehow it all seems to work.

Carlsbad Museum and Arts Center, on the town square, contains the bones of prehistoric animals that once roamed the region—mammoths, camels, and ancient horses. It also has pioneer Apache relics, Pueblo pottery, Native American art, early cowboy memorabilia, and remains of meteorites. The prize, however, is the McAdoo Collection, with its excellent sculptures by Frederic Remington and Charles Russell's paintings of the Old West, as well as works by painters of the Taos Society of Artists. The museum also has changing monthly shows featuring the work of local as well as nationally known artists. *418 W. Fox St., Carlsbad, ☎ 505/887–0276. ☛ Free. ☉ Mon.–Sat. 10–5; closed Sun.*

Living Desert State Park, atop Ocotillo Hills, about 1½ miles northwest of Carlsbad (off U.S. 285; look for the signs), contains an impressive collection of plants and animals native to the Chihuahuan Desert, which extends north from Mexico into southwestern Texas and southeastern New Mexico. Like many deserts, it's surprisingly rich in animal and plant life, as the park reveals. The Desert Arboretum has hundreds of exotic cacti and succulents. The Living Desert Zoo, more a reserve than a traditional zoo, is home to mountain lions, deer, elk, wolves, buffalo, rattlesnakes, and other indigenous species. The park has numerous shaded rest areas, rest rooms, and water fountains. *Living Desert State Park, Carlsbad, ☎ 505/887–5516. ☛ $3, children 6 and under free. ☉ Memorial Day weekend–Labor Day weekend, daily 8–8; the rest of the year, 9–5 . Tours are self-guided, and you must begin them at least 1½ hours before closing.*

Million Dollar Museum, 20 miles southeast of Carlsbad in the desert resort town of White's City (take U.S. 62/180 to White's City, then head west on NM 7), has 11 big rooms on two levels filled with Early American memorabilia and artifacts—antique dolls and dollhouses, guns and rifles, music boxes, old cars, and a 6,000-year-old mummified Native American. There's an arcade and shooting gallery next door. *21 Carlsbad Caverns Hwy., White's City, ☎ 505/785–2291. ☛ $2.50 adults, $2 senior citizens, $1.50 children 6–12, children under 6 free. ☉ Mid-May–mid-Sept., daily 7–8; mid-Sept.–mid-Mar., 7–6.*

SPORTS AND THE OUTDOORS

Bird-watching

From turkey vultures to golden eagles, more than 200 species of birds have been identified in Carlsbad Caverns National Park. The best place to go birding in the park, if not the entire state, is Rattlesnake Springs, a desert oasis (*see* Carlsbad Caverns National Park in Exploring

Carlsbad, *above*). Ask for a checklist at the visitor center, and then start checking: red-tailed hawk, red-winged blackbird, white-throated swift, northern flicker, pygmy nuthatches, yellow-billed cuckoo, roadrunner, mallard, American coot, green-winged and blue-winged teal—over 200 in all.

Hiking

More than 50 miles of trails provide access to the 46,000 acres of scenic desert, plunging canyons, steep rocky ridges, and mountain wilderness of Carlsbad Caverns National Park. An hour's drive to the southwest is the rugged 76,293-acre Guadalupe Mountains National Park, containing eight of Texas's highest peaks.

Black walnut, oak, desert willow, and hackberry proliferate along the canyons' bottoms. The ridges and walls of the canyons contain a variety of desert plants—yucca, agave, sotol, sticklike branches of ocotillo, and clusters of sparse desert grass. Higher up, piñon, juniper, ponderosa pine, and Douglas fir dominate. Animals that scamper about or roam the area at a more leisurely pace include raccoon, skunk, rabbit, fox, gopher, wood rat, mouse, porcupine, mule deer, coyote, and the ever-elusive badger, bobcat, and mountain lion. There are plenty of snakes in the area, but because they're both nocturnal and shy, visitors rarely see them.

Backcountry hiking in Carlsbad Caverns National Park can be exhilarating—the desert terrain is stark and awesome—but few trails are marked as in other national parks, and there is no water. A topographical map, available at the visitor center, will be helpful in defining some of the old ranch trails. Permits aren't required, except for overnight backpacking expeditions, but all hikers are requested to register at the information desk at the visitor center. Bring plenty of water. No pets or guns are permitted. The following is a sampling of some of the most interesting and accessible trails.

Guadalupe Ridge Trail, also known as the Jeep Road, starts at Walnut Canyon Loop Road and covers 13 miles, mostly along ridge tops, to Putnam Cabin. The 2,000-foot ascent is a gradual climb to the highest point in the park.

The Guano Trail, a little more than 3½ miles, was originally the truck and wagon route that miners used to transport guano from Carlsbad Caverns to White's City. The trail starts from the Bat Flight Amphitheater and affords good views on what is mostly flat terrain.

Take the short (¼-mile) **Rattlesnake Canyon Overlook Trail** to get superlative views of Rattlesnake Canyon. You can pick it up along the Walnut Canyon Drive (*see* Carlsbad Caverns National Park in Exploring Carlsbad, *above*), a few hundred yards north of the Rattlesnake Canyon Trailhead.

Rattlesnake Canyon Trail covers close to 3 miles and descends from 4,570 to 3,900 feet as it goes down into the canyon. This trail, which is well defined and marked with rock cairns, starts from the Walnut Canyon Drive.

Yucca Canyon Trail, about 6 miles long, begins at the mouth of Yucca Canyon and climbs up to the junction of Double Canyon Trail (the elevation ranges from 4,300 to 6,150 ft); at the top of the ridge, a level, well-marked route offers wonderful views of the Guadalupe escarpment. Much of the trail leads through a lovely forested area.

DINING

Lunches can be purchased at the Carlsbad Caverns National Park's unique restaurant, located 750 feet underground, or at the full-service restaurant on the surface. There are numerous eating places in White's City and Carlsbad as well. You can dress casual.

CATEGORY	COST*
$$$	over $25
$$	$10–25
$	under $10

*per person, excluding drinks, service, and tax (5.8%)

Carlsbad

$$ **Lucy's.** This is a family-owned (Lucy and Justo Yanez) oasis of great Mexican food. It was recently remodeled in Southwestern decor. Alas, a large-screen TV blares accompaniment to meals, which are served in the restaurant and, when it gets crowded, the adjoining lounge. But the food is fresh and fabulous. When the waitress asks you "smoking or nonsmoking?" she's not referring to your nicotine habit but to the degree of fire you want in your food. All the New Mexican standards are available, along with some not-so-standard items, such as *chapa* chicken *chacos* (chicken tacos with guacamole) and Tucson-style chimichangas (chicken, beef, or brisket with chile, cheeses, and special seasonings). ✗ 701 S. Canal St., ☎ 505/887–7714. No reservations. AE, D, DC, MC, V.

$ **Cortez Cafe.** This charming family-owned Mexican restaurant, with an all-brick interior and photo murals of Old Mexico, has been in business for more than half a century. Most people choose the all-you-can-eat option: For $8 you can fill up on almost anything on the menu. Try the combination plate, fajitas (tortillas stuffed with sizzling chunks of beef or pork), or sour-cream enchiladas. ✗ 506 S. Canal St., ☎ 505/885–4747. No credit cards.

White's City

$$ **The Velvet Garter Restaurant and Saloon.** Come here for steak, chicken, catfish, shrimp, and Mexican food in a whoopee Wild West atmosphere, with bawdy paintings on the wall, the Carlsbad Caverns in stained glass, and rinky-dink background music. Food prices are old style, too—a 12-ounce rib-eye steak costs $12.95—but a shot of tequila in the saloon will set you back $3.50. ✗ 26 Carlsbad Caverns Hwy., White's City, ☎ 505/785–2291. No reservations. AE, D, DC, MC, V.

$ **Fast Jack's.** This fast-food favorite shares an adobe-style building with the Velvet Garter Restaurant and Saloon. Seated at one of the booths or at the counter, you can order great burgers; 32 flavors of homemade ice cream; and freshly baked pies, along with standard breakfast, lunch, and dinner fare, including Mexican specialties and some seafood selections. This is a good spot to chow down a hearty breakfast before heading off into the caverns. Owner Jack White, whose grandfather founded White's City, graduated from Stanford with a degree in electrical engineering. He makes sure the bank of video games and souvenir token slot machines are all in good working order. ✗ 26 Carlsbad Caverns Hwy., White's City, ☎ 505/785–2291. No reservations. No credit cards.

LODGING

Since tourism is a major industry in Carlsbad, the area offers a wide choice of motels and other services. Most of them are strung out along the highway going to the caverns, appropriately called National Parks Highway. At the turnoff from the highway to the caverns, White's City is a honky-tonk tourist complex, with three motels, a tent and RV campground, restaurants, a post office, souvenir shops, a small amusement park and museum, a miniature golf course, and a saloon.

CATEGORY	COST*
$$$	$100–$150
$$	$65–$100
$	under $65

All prices are for a standard double room, excluding 5.8% tax.

Hotels and Motels

Carlsbad

$$ **Holiday Inn Carlsbad Downtown.** The city's newest hotel is the old Carls-
★ bad Inn, the two-story structure at the corner of Canal and Lea streets, totally revamped and renamed. The rugs, the paintings, and the soft desert colors in the guest rooms all harmonize with the Territorial New Mexican decor, a combination of regional and European styles. The hotel's Phenix (*sic*) restaurant is a grill room and pub; Ventanas ("Windows"), its gourmet restaurant, serves Italian cuisine. Kids under 9 stay and play free. ☎ *601 S. Canal St., Carlsbad 88220, ☎ 505/885–8500 or 800/742–9586, FAX 505/887–5999. 100 rooms. 2 restaurants, bar, pool, hot tub, playground, laundry service. AE, D, DC, MC, V.*

$ **Best Western Motel Stevens.** An old favorite, both locally and with tour groups, this is a reliable, well-operated place. The guest rooms feature bright desert colors, mirrored vanities, and modern furnishings; some have kitchenettes, some have private patios, some have both. Buildings are scattered over a landscaped area covering more than a city block. The motel's Flume Room, an elegant local favorite dining spot, features steaks, prime rib, and table-side service. There's also a coffee shop offering regional and Mexican specialties. The hotel is owned by Carlsbad's ex-mayor, Bob Forrest, but even knowing him won't get you a table at its Silver Spur bar and lounge on Saturday night when the Chaparrals are playing. ☎ *1829 S. Canal St., Box 580, Carlsbad 88220, ☎ 505/887–2851 or 800/730–2851 for reservations, FAX 505/887–6338. 202 rooms. Restaurant, bar, pool, wading pool, playground, coin laundry. AE, D, DC, MC, V.*

$ **Carlsbad Travelodge South.** This three-story motel, 2 miles from the airport and one block from the Convention Center in Carlsbad, has rooms decorated in cheerful Southwestern tones, although the furnishings are generic. Each paying adult gets a complimentary full breakfast. There is no restaurant on the premises, but Jerry's, in the immediate vicinity, serves fast food fare 24 hours a day. ☎ *3817 National Parks Hwy., Carlsbad 88220, ☎ 505/887–8888 or 800/255–3050 for reservations, FAX 505/885–0126. 60 rooms. Pool, hot tub. AE, D, DC, MC, V.*

$ **Continental Inn.** South of Carlsbad, on National Parks Highway, the Continental Inn is about 30 minutes from Carlsbad Caverns. It has simple rooms with matching curtains and bedspreads in colorful Southwestern patterns. The small grounds are pretty and well kept. While there is no restaurant on the grounds, Jerry's, which offers fast-food fare 24 hours a day, is within walking distance. ☎ *3820 National Parks Hwy., Carlsbad 88220, ☎ 505/887–0341, FAX 505/885–1186. 57 rooms, 3 suites. Pool, airport shuttle. AE, D, DC, MC, V.*

$ **Quality Inn.** Located 1 mile from the airport, this two-story, stone-faced property encloses a landscaped patio with a pool and a sun deck about as large as an aircraft hangar. Rooms are comfortable, with undistinguished modern furnishings and one king-size or two double beds with bright Native American–design bedspreads. The Cafe in the Park serves breakfast and lunch, and the Chaparral Grill Room, a more formal dining room, is open for dinner. Scott's Archery Range is next door. ☎ *3706 National Parks Hwy., Carlsbad 88220,* ☎ *505/887–2861 or 800/321– 2861,* FAX *505/887–2861. 124 rooms. 2 restaurants, bar, pool, hot tub, shop, laundry service, airport shuttle. AE, D, DC, MC, V.*

$ **Stagecoach Inn.** This family-style motor inn is close to many of the major Carlsbad attractions and offers basic rooms at affordable rates. There's a tree-shaded park withplayground and picnic area. ☎ *1819 S. Canal St., Carlsbad 88220,* ☎ *and fax 505/887–1148. 57 rooms. Restaurant, pool, wading pool, hot tub, laundry service. AE, D, DC, MC, V.*

White's City

$$ **Best Western Cavern Inn.** This two-story motor inn with Southwestern-style rooms is run in conjunction with the neighboring Best Western Guadalupe Inn, sharing the same pools and restaurants. The hotel offers the closest accommodations to Carlsbad Caverns and is an immediate neighbor of the popular Velvet Garter Restaurant (*see* Dining, *above*). It's a pleasant, friendly place, determined to help you have a good time. Lots of tour groups are booked here, as well as families. ☎ *17 Carlsbad Caverns Hwy., White's City 88268,* ☎ *505/785–2291 or 800/CAVERNS,* FAX *505/785–2283. 62 rooms. (Guadalupe Inn has 44 rooms.) Café, 2 pools, spa, playground. AE, D, DC, MC, V.*

Camping

Backcountry camping is by permit only in Carlsbad Caverns National Park; free permits can be obtained at the visitor center, where you can also pick up a map of areas closed to camping. You'll need to hike to campsites, which may not be seen from established roadways. There are no vehicle or RV camping areas in the park.

Nearby Brantley Lake State Park, the newest state park in New Mexico, and Lincoln National Forest both have camping facilities. In addition, a number of commercial sites are available at White's City, 7 miles northeast of the Caverns, and in Carlsbad, 27 miles northeast.

Brantley Lake State Park. Twelve miles north of Carlsbad via Highway 285, this facility has a playground, boat ramps, picnic areas, grills, bathhouse with running water and flush toilets, overnight camping spaces, and a visitor center. Fishing (bass, trout, and crappie), boating, and other water sports are offered. ☎ *Box 2288, Carlsbad 88221,* ☎ *505/457–2384. 52 water and electric hookups, dump station. Primitive-area camping (no immediate facilities) $6 per night, developed-area camping (with facilities) $7 per night, hookup sites $11 per night. No reservations. No credit cards.*

Carlsbad Kampgrounds. This shaded, full-service campground has level gravel sites, trees, year-round grass for tenters, a swimming pool, laundry, public phone and phone hookups, hot showers, flush toilets, a grocery store, grills, and sewage disposal. A professional RV service is located next door. ☎ *4301 National Parks Hwy., Carlsbad 88220,* ☎ *505/885–6333. 170 sites, 46 full hookups, 68 water and electric. $16.50 for full-service RV site, $12 for tent sites. 10% discounts for AAA and AARP. Reservations advised during summer months. D, MC, V.*

Park Entrance RV Park. In the heart of White's City, 7 miles from Carlsbad Caverns, this popular RV park offers natural desert sites with canopied shaded tables. Included are flush toilets, hot showers, sewage disposal, gasoline, grocery store, grills, parking control gates, and nearby recreational facilities (recreation hall, arcade, playground, tennis court, and two heated swimming pools). ⌂ *17 Carlsbad Caverns Hwy. (Box 128), White's City 88268,* ☎ *505/785–2291 or 800/228–3767 for reservations. 150 sites. 60 full hookups, 48 pull-throughs. $14 per vehicle. Reservations advised in summer. AE, D, MC, V.*

Windmill RV Park. Facilities for swimming, hot showers, and flush toilets, are available at this RV park located on National Parks Highway (accessed by NM 180/62 South). ⌂ *3624 National Parks Hwy., Carlsbad 88220,* ☎ *505/885–9761. 61 RV sites, water, flush toilets, hot showers. $6 for tent sites, $11 full hookup (cable TV $1 extra). AE, D, MC, V.*

NIGHTLIFE

Carlsbad Caverns closes at 7 PM during the summer, 5:30 PM during the winter; between late-May and mid-October you can hang around until sunset to watch thousands of bats leave the caves en masse to forage for food (*see* Carlsbad Caverns National Park in Exploring Carlsbad, *above*). For more conventional types of nighttime activities, you're pretty much limited to the Carlsbad lounge circuit. You can dance to country-and-western music at the **Silver Spur Lounge** in the Best Western Motel Stevens (☎ 505/887–2851), where live bands play Monday–Saturday 9 PM–1:30 AM. (If you want to start early, happy hour is 2–7 PM.) The **Quality Inn's lounge** (☎ 505/887–2861) has a big-screen TV and a jukebox. It's open Monday–Saturday from 4 PM until around midnight. Also operating during those hours is **My Way Lounge** (203 S. Central St., ☎ 505/887–0212), a popular place for shooting pool, playing video games, and (you guessed it) dancing to live country-and-western music; bands play from around 9 PM until 2 AM on Friday and Saturday only.

EXCURSION TO LINCOLN COUNTY AND WHITE SANDS NATIONAL MONUMENT

This tour takes you through pine-covered mountains to four of southern New Mexico's most interesting spots. It's possible to see them all in one day, but getting to them from Carlsbad takes about four hours by car. It is probably a good idea to plan on spending a night in the area (*see* Lodging, *below*) so that you can avoid driving the eight-hour round-trip in one day. We've arranged the tour to start in Ruidoso, which makes a good base from which to explore the region.

Exploring Lincoln County

Ruidoso

Sprawled at the base of the Sierra Blanca Peak on the eastern slopes of the pine-covered Sacramento Mountains, midway between Alamogordo and Roswell, Ruidoso is a sophisticated year-round resort that retains, at least for the time being, its rustic small-town charm. Summer visitors arrive from all over the Southwest to fill the cabins and hotels and to fish and swim in swift-moving streams and deep blue lakes. In winter, the Mescalero Apache–run ski area, Ski Apache (*see below*), makes Ruidoso a major area ski resort. A convention center has just opened, and there's talk of building a resort hotel and performing-arts center there amid the snowy peaks, mountain streams, colorful village shops, and pine-shaded trails. At first glance, the town itself isn't much to look at. But though its business district is little longer than a shoestring, it supports a surfeit of interesting shops, antiques stores, bars, and restaurants.

Ruidoso (which means "noisy" in Spanish) has an official population of only 4,800, but it's no one-horse town. Not by a long shot. Each summer, it becomes the epicenter of American quarter-horse racing, thanks to the fabulous **Ruidoso Downs,** self-proclaimed Home of the World's Richest Horse Races and the first stop on this tour, right on Highway 70 East. On Labor Day, it is the site of the All-American Quarter Horse Futurity, with a total purse of as much as $2.5 million, more than $1 million of it going to the winner alone. Purses for other quarter-horse and Thoroughbred events throughout the season (May through Labor Day) are almost as spectacular.

Ruidoso's role as a big-money racing center came about quite naturally. The breeding and racing of horses is one of New Mexico's oldest enterprises. Among the Spanish who explored the region, horsemen were the aristocrats. In the more recent past, Ruidoso attracted freewheeling Texans, Oklahomans, and New Mexicans willing to bet on anything. While spending their summers in the cool New Mexico mountains, they were entertained by ranchers who would race their most spirited horses in the cornfields and meadows. The visitors wagered, often cleaning out their bank accounts to bet on horses. The purses got bigger and bigger, and Ruidoso Downs emerged.

In operation since 1947, the track has changed ownership numerous times. Current owner R. D. Hubbard purchased it in 1988 and immediately began a $3 million renovation; betting windows, concession stands, and rest rooms, as well as barns and the stable area, were remodeled. Chairman and chief executive of AFG Industries, the second-largest glass manufacturer in the United States, Hubbard has infused considerable money in Ruidoso. Another of his investments is the new state-of-the-art **Ruidoso Downs Sports Theater,** a half mile east of the track, just off Highway 70 (look for the signs), which features year-round pari-mutuel racing plus other sports events on large-screen TV sets. *Hwy. 70, Box 449, Ruidoso Downs, 88346,* ☎ *505/378–4431 or 378–4410.* ☛ *Open seating free, reserved seating $2.50, grandstand $3.50–$5. Theater* ☛ *Free. Parking: $3. Racing May 9–July 1, Thurs.–Sun.; July 1–Labor Day, Thurs.–Mon. Post time is 1 PM (earlier on Labor Day).*

Ruidoso's newest showcase, opened in May 1992 in a newly renovated 40,000-square-foot building about a half mile east of the track, is the **Museum of the Horse,** built to house the Anne C. Stradling Museum of the Horse Collection, consisting of over 10,000 pieces related to the horse—paintings, drawings, and bronzes by master artists; saddles from Mexico and China and those used by the Pony Express; carriages and wagons; a 400-year-old oxcart; and memorabilia from Teddy Roosevelt, Frederic Remington, and the DuPont family. Some items date from Roman times, and there's a chariot bit from ancient Greece. This museum is also a Hubbard undertaking. Long a fixture of Patagonia, Arizona, the massive collection was given to Hubbard when its founder, Anne Stradling, became too ill to care for it properly (she died in 1992 at age 78). Hubbard promised to keep the collection intact and to display it under Stradling's name. *Hwy. 70 E, Box 1679, Ruidoso Downs 88346;* ☎ *505/378–4809 or 505/378–4142.* ☛ *$4 adults, $3 senior citizens, $2.50 children 5–18, children under 5 free.* ☉ *May 1–Labor Day, daily 9–5:30; rest of year, daily 10–5.*

Bordering Ruidoso to the west, about a 15-minute drive from the racetrack, is the **Mescalero Apache Indian Reservation,** home to more than 2,500 Mescalero Apaches, most of whom work in the lumber and fishing industries. The famous **Inn of the Mountain Gods** (*see* Lodging, *below*), the most elegant resort in the state, is Apache-owned and -operated. Other sights on the reservation include a **general store,** a **trading post,** and a **museum,** which has clothing and crafts displays, a 12-minute video about life on the reservation, and regular talks about the history and culture of the Mescalero Apaches. There are also campsites (with hookups at Silver and Eagle lakes only) and picnic areas. Ritual dances are occasionally performed for the public, the most colorful during the annual Fourth of July celebrations. The reservation's **Ski Apache** area on nearby Sierra Blanca (11,400 ft) has fine powder skiing from Thanksgiving until mid-April, or longer if the snows persist. *Tribal Office, Hwy. 70, Box 227, Mescalero 88340,* ☎ *505/671– 4494; for Ski Apache, Box 220, Ruidoso 88345,* ☎ *505/336–4357.* ☛ *To the reservation and tribal museum (open weekdays 8–4:30) is free; daily lift tickets for Ski Apache are $35 ($99 for three-day passes).*

San Patricio

Twenty miles east of Ruidoso on U.S. 70 is San Patricio. Caught in the right light at the right time of day, the tiny village, nestled in the Hondo Valley where the Ruidoso River glistens silver in the sun, is hauntingly beautiful. The all-white **church of San Patricio,** with its meager bell tower hardly scraping the sky, is the first thing to catch your eye. The peaceful valley is filled with horse ranches, orchards, and herds of sheep. In the fall, roadside fruit stands sell apples, jugs of sweet cider, and strings of bright red chiles. Small wonder that the area has long appealed to artists.

The **Hurd-La Rinconada Gallery,** on the Sentinel Ranch, is part of the sprawling art compound belonging to one of America's leading art dynasties. Showcased in the unique adobe gallery is the work of the late Peter Hurd, who gained world recognition as a regional landscape painter and portraitist—and won perhaps even more fame for a portrait commissioned by President Lyndon B. Johnson who, unhappy with the results, refused to hang it in the White House. Also on display are the works of Hurd's elderly widow, Henriette Wyeth Hurd (Andrew Wyeth's sister), and their son, artist Michael Hurd. Paintings by Andrew Wyeth and his father, N. C. Wyeth, round out the impressive presentation. Signed reproductions as well as some original paintings are for sale. Bring your checkbook. *U.S. 70, mile marker 281,* ☎ *505/653– 4331.* ☛ *Free.* ☉ *Mon.–Sat. 9–5, Sun. 10–4.*

Adjacent to the Hurds' Sentinel Ranch—just turn right at the polo field and keep going—is **Fort Meigs Gallery,** designer John Meigs's lifetime collection of just about everything collectible. Meigs was a longtime friend of the Hurds as well as of other notable artists, such as Georgia O'Keeffe. Displayed in his 22-room mansion are paintings, graphics, antiques, photographs, Oriental scrolls, Chinese ceramics, a Ferris wheel made of toothpicks, furniture, coffins, an embroidery by D. H. Lawrence, a bedspread from a Juárez bordello, religious carvings, and an entire library of 40,000 books. In frail health, Meigs has decided to put his collection up for sale, piece by piece, but he appears to be in no particular hurry to part with anything. *U.S. 70, mile marker 281;* ☎ *505/653– 4320.* ☛ *Free.* ☉ *Daily 10–6; call ahead to confirm hours.*

Lincoln

It may not be as well known as Tombstone, Arizona, or Deadwood, South Dakota, but Lincoln, 10 miles east of San Patricio on U.S. 70, ranks right up there with the toughest of the tough old towns of the Old West. It was just over a century ago that the violent Lincoln County Wars took place, as two opposing factions clashed over lucrative government contracts to feed the army and the Native Americans on reservations in the area. The bloody confrontation lasted a full year. One of the more infamous figures to emerge from it was a short, slight, sallow young man with buckteeth, startling blue eyes, and curly reddish-brown hair. His name was Billy the Kid.

The role of Billy—born William H. Bonney—in the Lincoln County Wars is not quite clear. He was a ranch hand for John Tunstall and already enjoyed a modest reputation as a gunman when he surfaced in Lincoln County in the mid-1870s. But apparently during the last four years of his life, spent mostly in and around Lincoln, his guns hardly had time to cool. He is said to have killed 21 men, including Lincoln's sheriff William Brady; it was for Brady's murder that he was convicted in 1881 and sentenced to hang. But Billy managed to elude the gallows.

On April 28 of that year, though manacled and shackled, Billy made a daring escape from the old Lincoln County Courthouse (*see below*), killing two guards. The first, James W. Bell, was shot on the courthouse steps and managed to stumble into the backyard before he died. The other, Robert W. Ollinger, came running from the dining room of the nearby Wortley Hotel when he heard the shots. Billy gunned him down from the second-floor window. Today, stone markers designate the places where they fell. Three months later, a posse led by Sheriff Pat Garrett tracked Billy down at the home of a friend in Old Fort Sumner, surprised him in the dark, and finished him off with two clean shots. One of the West's most notorious gunmen, and ultimately one of its best-known folk legends, was dead at 21.

Surprisingly little has changed since the Lincoln County War. The town's only street (Hwy. 380) is lined with adobe homes and buildings dating from its historic, tumultuous past. After undergoing extensive restoration in recent years, Lincoln has emerged as one of New Mexico's premier tourist attractions. Settled during the early 1850s, the town was originally called La Placita ("village square" in Spanish); today it is a National Historic Landmark and still a living, if small, community with a population of 60. Several historic structures, including the Tunstall Store Museum and the Lincoln County Courthouse Museum (*see below*), are operated by New Mexico State Monuments, part of the Museum of New Mexico.

A visit might best begin at the **Historical Center,** at the eastern end of town, where a 10-minute slide show introduces Lincoln's attractions. Exhibits here are devoted to Billy the Kid, the Lincoln County Wars, cowboys, Apaches, and Buffalo Soldiers (black horse troops of the 9th and 10th Cavalry), with guides and attendants dressed in period costumes. The center and a well-stocked museum store are operated by the Lincoln County Heritage Trust (☎ 505/653–4025).

Just west of the Historical Center are the **Tunstall Store Museum** (505/653–4372), which still contains much of its original stock dating back to the 1800s, the **Dr. Woods House** (505/653–4529), a fine example of a typical late 19th-century Southwestern adobe home belonging to the wealthy, and the **Lincoln County Courthouse Museum** (505/653–4372), housed in the two-story building from which Billy the Kid made his daring escape. For a free copy of the detailed **Billy the Kid Country** brochure, contact the New Mexico Department of Tourism (491 Old Santa Fe Trail, Lamy Bldg., Room 751, Santa Fe 87503, ☎ 800/545–2040).

Historical Center and County Courthouse Museum open May–Sept., daily 9–6, Oct.–Apr., daily 9–5; Tunstall Store Museum open May–Sept., daily 9–6; Dr. Woods House open May–mid-June, daily 9–5; mid-June–Sept., daily 10–6. General ☛ pass to all sites: May–Sept., $4.50; Oct.–Apr., $2.25; children under 16 free.

White Sands National Monument

Heading back south on U.S. 70 past Ruidoso, 15 miles southwest of Alamogordo, you come to **White Sands National Monument,** a scene out of the *Arabian Nights,* with shifting sand dunes 60 feet high. White Sands encompasses 145,344 acres, the largest deposit of gypsum sand in the world (the sand on most beaches is silica; gypsum is used for making plaster of paris); it is one of the few landforms that is recognizable from space. The **Visitor Center** here has a museum display relating to the dunes and how they were formed. There's also an information desk, a bookstore, and a snack bar. From here, a 16-mile round-trip takes you into the eerie wonderland of gleaming white sand. Who can resist climbing to the top of the dunes for a photograph, then tumbling down, wading knee-deep in the gypsum crystals? Visitors are cautioned, however, not to tunnel into the sand dunes; in loose sand, tunnels can easily collapse and cause suffocation. When you want to explore on foot, follow the **Big Dune Trail,** a mile-long, self-guided nature trail; a sign in the parking lot marks the beginning of the trail. Written information about the plants and animals you may encounter is available free at the visitor center. A picnic area has shaded tables and grills. Backcountry campsites are available by permit, obtainable at the visitor center; camping is free, but facilities are primitive—there aren't any.

Not surprisingly, White Sands has been used for many TV commercials and numerous Hollywood films, the most recent being *White Sands,* an espionage thriller starring Willem Dafoe and Mickey Rourke. Surrounded on three sides by the White Sands Missile Range and on the fourth by Holloman Air Force Base, the park occasionally delays its early morning openings as a safety precaution when missile tests are being conducted overhead. Once a month between May and October, White Sands celebrates the full moon by remaining open until 11 PM, allowing visitors to experience the eerie lunar light. *Box 1086, Holloman AFB 88330, ☎ 505/479–6124. ⊙ Daily 7 AM to 30 min past sunset. ☛ $2 per person on foot and on motorcycle, or $4 per car.*

Dining and Lodging

Ruidoso

DINING

$$$ **La Lorraine.** Classic French cuisine, such as chateaubriand, beef bourguignon, and sausage-stuffed quail, is served amid elegant colonial French surroundings. In summer, you can dine outdoors on the patio amid cages of exotic Amazonian birds. ✕ *2523 Sudderth Dr., ☎ 505/257–2954. Reservations advised. Jacket advised. AE, MC, V. No lunch Sun.*

$$–$$$ **Dan-Li-Ka.** This is the dining room at the popular Inn of the Mountain Gods resort on the Mescalero Apache Reservation, just southwest of Ruidoso. Dan-Li-Ka, which means "good food" in Apache, occupies one large room with wooden chairs and tables, and knockout views of Mescalero Lake and mountains cloaked in ponderosa pine. The extensive menu includes Spanish, Native American, and regional New Mexican specialties: Texas chicken strips, mountain trout, burgers topped with green chiles and jalapeño jack cheese, Apache fry bread, and classic Reuben sandwiches for lunch; fresh game, sautéed red

trout, sirloin steaks, and prime rib for dinner. ✕ *Inn of the Mountain Gods, Mescalero Apache Reservation,* ☎ *505/257–5315. Reservations advised for dinner. AE, D, DC, MC, V.*

$$–$$$ **Inncredible Restaurant and Saloon.** This rustic Western spot has been a local favorite for 30 years for lobster dinners, prime rib, and filet mignon. There's a lounge and an atrium for dining under the stars. ✕ *Hwy. 48 N at Alto Village,* ☎ *505/336–4312. Reservations advised for dinner. AE, D, MC, V.*

$–$$ **Cattle Baron Steak House.** This cozy lounge and steak house offers daily cut steaks, prime rib, and seafood in three separate dining rooms filled with tables and booths. Fireplaces add Western warmth, and large picture windows provide stunning mountain views. A skylit lounge at one end is bright and airy. On Sunday, there are all-you-can-eat ribs and "peel your own shrimp" specials in addition to the always-colossal salad bar. ✕ *657 Sudderth Dr.,* ☎ *505/257–9355. Reservations advised. AE, D, DC, MC, V.*

LODGING

★   **Inn of the Mountain Gods.** The Mescalero Apaches own and operate
$$$ this spectacular year-round resort on the banks of the Mescalero Lake, about 3 miles southwest of Ruidoso. The rooms are large and handsomely furnished with Western and Native American flourishes; each has a balcony. The inn has its own minicasino with poker and lotto machines, and part of the front reception desk has been given over to the sale of pull-tab gambling tickets, which seems to draw a steady line of players all day long. The resort's 18-hole golf course was designed by Ted Robinson, who also created the famous courses at the Acapulco Princess and at California's Tamarisk. ⌨ *Carrizon Canyon Rd., Box 269, Mescalero 88340,* ☎ *505/257–5141 or 800/ 545–6040,* ⅏ *505/257–6173. 250 rooms with bath. Restaurant, bar, pool, hot tub, 18-hole golf course, tennis court, archery, fishing, casino. AE, D, DC, MC, V.*

$$$ **The Lodge.** This burly Victorian lodge some 40 miles south of Ruidoso was built in 1899 by the Alamagordo and Sacramento Mountain Railway to house its workers. A stuffed bear stands snarling in the mammoth lobby, and a long-horned eland stares down from above a copper-sheathed fireplace. The rooms are decorated with chenille bedspreads, period antiques, flocked wallpaper in pastel shades, ceiling fans, and, in many cases, four-poster beds. Rebecca's, the hotel restaurant, is named after a brazen resident ghost who is rumored to have appeared naked in guests' bathtubs. (Breakfast at Rebecca's is included in the room rate.) The lodge complex also includes the Lodge Pavilion, a rustic 11-room B&B. ⌨ *1 Corona Pl., Box 497, Cloudcroft 88317,* ☎ *505/682– 2566 or 800/395–6343,* ⅏ *505/682–2715. 60 rooms. Restaurant, bar, pool, sauna, spa. AE, D, DC, MC, V.*

$$ **Best Western Swiss Chalet Inn.** The closest hotel to Ski Apache, this two-story hilltop chalet fills up quickly in winter but is popular in the summer as well. The hotel sprawls out along the contours of the hill, with its restaurant and lounge at one end and meeting facilities at the other. The rooms are what you'd expect in a chain hotel—large, nondescript, and furnished in contemporary style, but they do have steam saunas. ⌨ *1451 Mechem Dr. (Hwy. 48), Box 795, Ruidoso 88345,* ☎ *505/258– 3333 or 800/47–SWISS,* ⅏ *505/258–5325. 82 rooms with bath. Restaurant, bar, indoor pool, hot tub, spa. AE, D, DC, MC, V.*

$$ **Shadow Mountain Lodge.** The Ruidoso River flows by just across the street from this small L-shape hotel in the historic Upper Canyon. Fieldstone fireplaces in each room add to the lodge's alpine ambience; rooms also come equipped with California king-size beds and kitchen facilities. A veranda runs along the front of the hotel, with grills out-side for marshmallow or hot-dog toasting. ⊞ *107 Main Rd., Box 1427, Ruidoso 88345,* ☎ *505/257–4886 or 800/441–4331,* ⬛ *505/257– 2000. 19 suites. AE, D, DC, MC, V.*

San Patricio

LODGING

$$$ **Hurd Ranch Guest Homes.** These two adobe casitas on the Sentinel Ranch, adjacent to the Hurd Gallery, opened recently—becoming the sole members of San Patricio's lodging scene. Stylishly decorated with paintings, sculptures, and Native American artifacts, and with mod-ern and Western furnishings, the casitas are an outgrowth of guest houses that artist Michael Hurd made available to friends and portrait sub-jects who needed accommodations while their commissions were being completed. Both casitas have washing machines and dryers, and fully equipped kitchens, although there are three restaurants relatively close by—the Silver Dollar (☎ 505/653–4425), a turn-of-the-century dance pavilion and concert hall in Tinnie; and Rene's (☎ 505/653–4101) and Burrito Express (☎ 505/653–4202) in Hondo. A new casita named after actress Helen Hayes, a family friend and frequent visitor, was com-pleted in the spring of 1995. A wing of the Hurd gallery with apart-ment facilities may also be rented. The area offers plenty to do if you're adventurous and ready to do some exploring. ⊞ *U.S. 70, Box 100, San Patricio 88348,* ☎ *505/653–4331,* ⬛ *505/653–4218. 2 ca-sitas with bath, gallery wing with bath. MC, V.*

Lincoln

DINING

$ **The Stagecoach Cafe.** Centered in the midst of Lincoln's many historic buildings and just across the street from the now-defunct Worley Hotel, The Stagecoach Cafe was built in 1858. Its low ceilings, fire-place, and archival photos of the town's more notorious inhabitants give the café a cozy feel. The food is fairly nondescript New Mexican fare (e.g., enchiladas, burritos, chile rellenos). ☉ Tues.–Thurs. 8–3, Fri.–Sat. 8–6. ✗ *Hwy. 380,* ☎ *505/653–4524. No reservations. No credit cards.*

LODGING

$$ **Casa de Patrón.** This attractive bed-and-breakfast on Lincoln's main street is in a historic adobe—once the home of Juan Patron, an early settler and father of three who was gunned down at age 29 in the vi-olence that swept Lincoln County. The main house has high viga ceil-ings and Mexican tile baths. Owners Jeremy and Cleis Jordan also offer two small adobe casitas decorated with traditional New Mexican fla-vor, cathedral ceilings, vigas, and portals. All rooms are furnished with antiques and collectibles. Full country breakfasts are served in the main house, Continental breakfasts in the casitas. ⊞ *Hwy. 380, Box 27, Lincoln 88338,* ☎ *505/653–4676 or 653–1500,* ⬛ *505/653–4671. 3 rooms in the main house, 2 casitas (1 with a 2-bedroom suite) with bath. MC, V.*

$$ **The Ellis Store & Co. Bed and Breakfast.** This B&B has a rich history dating back to 1850, when it was a modest, two-room adobe in terri-tory where the Mescalero Indians still posed a threat to settlers. Dur-ing the Lincoln County War Billy the Kid was kept here under protective custody pending his trial, and guests can even rent the room where he slept. Owners David and Jinny Vigil have eight rooms for rent: four in the main house, which are decorated mainly with antiques, and four back in the Mill House, which is ideally suited for family stays, as it has a large common room on the second floor. Jinny cooks gourmet six-course meals in the evening (by reservation only) which guests can enjoy in a spacious dining room filled with firelight that reflects off the dark wood paneling. There is also fishing in the river behind the house. ⬚ *Hwy. 380, mile marker 98, Box 15, Lincoln, NM 88338,* ☎ *505/653–4609 or 800/653–5460,* ⬚ *505/653–4610. 2 double rooms with shared bath, 2 double rooms with bath, 4 double rooms with shared bath in Mill House. D, MC, V.*

Capitán

DINING

$$ **Hotel Chango.** Despite its name, this is not a hotel, it's a restaurant that serves up some of the best food in the area. The owner, Jerrold Flores, is continually experimenting with new dishes, including such specialties as chicken with lime and tequila sauce which he complements with a wide variety of wines. And the experimentation doesn't stop there— every year Jerrold heads for Central America to buy antiques and artwork, which he uses to redecorate the warm, brown stucco confines of the restaurant. All of these items are for sale, so in addition to a meal, you can order almost anything you see on a wall, including some of his own artwork. ✕ *103 S. Lincoln St. at the intersection of Hwy. 380 and Hwy. 48,* ☎ *505/354–4213. Reservations required. No credit cards. Closed Sun.–Tues.*

Lincoln County Essentials

Getting There

Ruidoso, the starting point of this excursion, is 170 miles north of Carlsbad Caverns via U.S. 285 to Roswell, and then U.S. 70 to Ruidoso.

Visitor Information

Ruidoso Valley Chamber of Commerce–Convention and Visitors Bureau (720 Sudderth Dr., Box 698, Ruidoso 88345, ☎ 800/253–2255 or 505/ 257–7395) has free brochures, maps, booklets, and other information, and is the main source of information about San Patricio.

To find out about Lincoln, contact **Lincoln County Heritage Trust,** Box 98, Lincoln 88338, ☎ 505/653–4025, and **Lincoln State Monument,** Box 36, Lincoln 88338, ☎ 505/653–4372, or write **Lincoln County Historical Society,** Box 91, Lincoln 88338.

The information desk at the **Visitor Center** of the White Sands National Monument (Box 1086, Holloman AFB 88330, ☎ 505/479–6124) provides general information and free maps and pamphlets.

CARLSBAD ESSENTIALS

Arriving and Departing

By Bus

TNM&O Greyhound (☎ 505/887–1108) provides transcontinental bus service and connects Carlsbad and White's City. **Silver Stage** (☎ 800/ 522–0162) offers van service to Carlsbad Caverns National Park from any point on the Carlsbad–El Paso route. The round-trip fare from Carlsbad is $16; make reservations one day in advance.

By Car

Driving south from Albuquerque on I–25 for about 77 miles, exit on U.S. 380 East and continue for 165 miles to Roswell. There switch to U.S. 285 and continue directly to Carlsbad, about 75 miles from Roswell (a total of 320 miles from Albuquerque). The drive is a bit monotonous, with dry rolling hills and nothing to see but brown wooden road signs heralding "Carlsbad Caverns" along the way. From El Paso, Texas, going east on U.S. 180, the distance to Carlsbad is 167 miles. From Pecos, Carlsbad can be reached via U.S. 285 (off I–10 at Van Horn).

By Plane

The **Albuquerque International Airport,** 380 miles north of Carlsbad, is the gateway to New Mexico and is served by most major airlines (*see* Air Travel in Important Contacts A to Z). Air-shuttle service via **Mesa Airlines** (☎ 800/637–2247 or, in Carlsbad, 505/885–0245) connects four times daily during the week, and twice daily on weekends, to and from Cavern City Air Terminal in Carlsbad. Flying time aboard the nine-passenger Cessna Caravan is about 90 minutes. The fare ranges from $109 (for a 21-day advance purchase that is nonrefundable and nonchangeable, and requires a Saturday layover) to $230 (for an unrestricted ticket requiring no advance purchase) round-trip. The one-way fare is between $115 and $139 depending on time of year and advance purchase discounts. Interline buses at Albuquerque International Airport connect Mesa Airlines with all Albuquerque connections.

For Carlsbad car rental, go to **Hertz Car Rental** (☎ 505/887–1500) at Cavern City Air Terminal. Taxi transfers from the Carlsbad airport are available via **Cavern City Cab Company** (☎ 505/887–0994).

Guided Tours

While explorations of the main cavern are designed to be self-guided, park rangers frequently conduct guided tours during the low-visitation winter months when the crowds are more manageable.

Pets

Not even leashed pets are allowed into the cavern, and park rangers advise that animals not be left in parked cars, even with the windows open. Suffocating heat can build up quickly in the desert. Clean, air-conditioned kennels are available at the visitor center. Inquire at the gift shop. The cost is $5 for the duration of the tour, usually four hours.

Important Addresses and Numbers

Visitor Information

Carlsbad Caverns National Park (3225 National Parks Hwy., Carlsbad 88220, ☎ 505/785–2232 or 505/785–2251 for 24-hour recorded information).

Carlsbad Chamber of Commerce (302 S. Canal St., Box 910, Carlsbad 88220, ☎ 505/887–6516 or 800/221–1224).

Living Desert State Park (Box 100, Carlsbad 88221, ☎ 505/887–5516).

A Note of Caution

Be aware that motor homes and RVs are frequently the targets of thieves in national parks and forests. Don't leave vehicle doors unlocked or windows open. And don't leave behind valuables, such as cameras and traveler's checks, whether hidden under seats or in blankets or towels; they're the first places thieves will look. The visitor center has safe coin-operated lockers. If you are the victim of a crime or see someone tampering with a car, call the park rangers (☎ 505/785–2232) or the Eddy County sheriff (☎ 505/887–7551).

6 Pueblos of the Rio Grande

TRAVELING ACROSS COUNTRY, one is immediately impressed with the many recently built forts, Native American villages, and trading posts that dot the landscape everywhere from New Jersey to Cleveland. In some places, Native Americans in jeans and sports jackets sign in for work in the morning, change into tribal regalia, and then spend the rest of the day making pots and baskets and performing dances and other ancient rituals for the entertainment of tourists. Such places may be sincere in their efforts to portray Native American life and culture, but they often come across as inane and theatrical. But not so in the West, where reservations are perhaps the only places left where traditional Native American culture and skills are retained with a sense of dignity and pride. Descendants of the highly civilized Anasazi, the Pueblo peoples of northern New Mexico in particular, continue to preserve their customs amid a changing world. Each pueblo has its own personality, history, and specialties in art and design.

Before venturing off to visit the pueblos, you'd do well to visit the striking **Indian Pueblo Cultural Center** in Albuquerque (*see* Important Addresses and Numbers, *below*), which exhibits and sells the best of arts and crafts from all the New Mexico pueblos; coming here will help you decide which of the pueblos to visit. Native American ceremonial dances are held during summer weekends, and photography is allowed (photographing Indian rituals is generally not allowed at any of the individual pueblos).

Fall, when the pueblos celebrate the harvest with special ceremonies, dances, and sacred rituals, is the best time to visit. The air is fragrant with curling piñon smoke. Clusters of *ristras* (red chiles) decorate many homes, with the chiles destined to add their distinct flavor to stews and sauces throughout the year. Drums throb with insistent cadence. Dancers adorn themselves with some of the most beautiful turquoise and jewelry seen anywhere. The atmosphere is lighthearted, evocative of a country fair: Excited children laugh and scamper, and wives chuckle and gossip, conversing in Tewa, Keresan, Tiwa—tongues both strange and fascinating to outsiders.

Admission is free to all pueblos in this chapter unless otherwise indicated. Donations, however, are always welcome.

For locations of the pueblos listed below, see the map of New Mexico at the front of this book.

PUEBLOS NEAR SANTA FE

The pueblos around Santa Fe, the state capital, are more infused with Spanish culture than are the pueblos in other areas. Pueblo dwellers here also have the keenest business sense when dealing with the sale of handicrafts and art and with matters touristic.

Cochiti Pueblo

The Cochiti Pueblo is known for its excellent crafts and jewelry, storyteller pottery figures, leather, beadwork, and drums. The latter play a significant role in Cochiti ceremonials on the July 14 feast day in honor of San Buenaventura. Most of the people of the pueblo work in Santa Fe or Albuquerque, but enough members of the tribe continue to work as farmers and artists to maintain the tribal traditions and culture. The late Helen Cordero, inspired by her grandfather's storytelling tradition, began making distinctive storyteller pottery figures in 1964; now her daughter-in-law, Mary Trujillo, is one of many tribal pottery artists who continue the tradition by creating charming images of children piled on a storyteller's lap, listening in awe and wonder to spellbinding tales of the past. The pueblo is located on the west bank of the Rio Grande near recreational facilities at Cochiti Lake (about 45 minutes from Santa Fe, west of I–25) that are administered by the U.S. Army Corps of Engineers. These include picnic tables, boat ramps and rentals, RV hookups, and a beach for swimming. *Box 70, Cochiti Pueblo 87072, ☎ 505/465–2244. ⊙ Daily 8–5. Still and video cameras, video and tape recorders, and sketching materials prohibited.*

Jemez Pueblo

This pueblo, located in the red sandstone canyon of the Jemez River, west of Santa Fe (northwest of Bernalillo, off NM 44), is noted for its polychrome pottery and fine baskets made from yucca leaves. After Pecos Pueblo was abandoned in the 1830s, Jemez was the only Towa-speaking pueblo remaining in the state. The Smithsonian Institution turned over 86 sacred objects to Jemez Pueblo officials in November 1993, the largest collection ever returned to an Indian tribe by a U.S. museum. The items, however, are not on display. The Jemez Reservation, encompassing 88,000 acres, contains two recreational sites, Holy Ghost Springs and Dragonfly Lakes, on NM 4 near the pueblo. Fishing licenses for both areas can be acquired from the Jemez game warden for $2–$5 per day, depending on the season. Hunting permits are also available. The village may hold little of interest for the casual visitor as the pueblo is open to the public only on its major feast days, August 2 (in honor of Our Lady of the Angels) and November 12 (for San Diego). However, the beautiful San Diego de Jemez Mission at the Jemez State Monument, 13 miles north, is a popular attraction. The great stone mission church was founded in the early 1600s by Fray Gerónimo Zárate Salmerón. *Box 143, Jemez Springs 87025, ☎ 505/ 834–7359 pueblo; 505/829–3530 state monument. Photography, sketching, and recording are prohibited at the pueblo, but are permitted at Jemez State Monument.*

Nambe Pueblo

It is here at the Nambe Pueblo, 15 miles northeast of Santa Fe (via U.S. 84/285; take a right at NM 4, then look for signs), that the famous Nambe cooking pots are made of golden micaceous clay. This ceramic work, along with other outstanding pottery pieces, woven belts, silver jewelry, and beadwork, may be purchased at the pueblo's crafts center. Recreational facilities open to the public here include trout fishing, camping, hiking, and picnicking at nearby Nambe Falls and Lake. Contemporary new buildings have replaced the original pueblo and mission church, but the landscape and the stunning views of the Sangre de Cristo Mountains remain unchanged. The pueblo holds ceremonial dances on July 4 (the Nambe Falls Ceremonial) and on October 4, the feast day of St. Francis of Assisi. *Rte. 1, Box 117-BB, Santa Fe 87501, ☎ 505/455–2036. ⊙ Daily 8–5. Fishing is allowed for a fee Mar.–Nov., and permits are available for picnicking, camping, and boating. Photo permits may be purchased as well. Fees are $5 for still cameras, $15 for video recorders and movie cameras.*

Pojoaque Pueblo

Drawing visitors from nearby Santa Fe (it's 15 miles north, just off U.S. 84/285), the Pojoaque Pueblo attracts Los Alamos and Espanola residents, too. It has more than 25 businesses aimed at the tourist trade, including a visitor center, tourist information office, tribal-owned supermarket, mobile-home park, a bingo and video gaming center, and shops offering an extensive selection of northern New Mexican pottery and other traditional arts and crafts for sale. Tribal enterprises, conducted primarily along a commercial strip fronting U.S. 84/285, have made the Pojoaque Pueblo one of the more prosperous in northern New Mexico. However, it has no definable village as such and has virtually ceased to exist as a viable community. Of the original settlement, only low mounds scattered in fields and among houses remain. A smallpox epidemic in 1890 nearly wiped out the entire tribe, but its numbers have increased considerably since then, and prospered. The pueblo celebrates its feast day on December 12 in honor of Our Lady of Guadalupe. On the first Saturday in August, Pojoaque hosts the Plaza Fiesta, a multicultural celebration that features Native American, Western, and international folk dancing, as well as food and hot-air balloon rides. *Rte. 71, Box 21, Santa Fe 87501,* ☎ *505/455–2278.* ☉ *Daily 8–5. Sketching and still and video cameras are not allowed.*

San Ildefonso Pueblo

This was the home of the most famous of all pueblo potters, Maria Martinez, whose work is now on permanent display in the Millicent Rogers Museum in Taos (*see* Tour 4 *in* Chapter 3) as well as in other museums throughout the Southwest. She created exquisite designs in red and black pottery from the 1920s to the 1980s. The San Ildefonso Pueblo has long been known for its outstanding pottery and boasts a number of highly acclaimed potters as well as other artists and craftspeople, many of whom open their homes to prospective buyers. There are also several trading posts on the pueblo, a visitor center, and a museum where much of Maria Martinez's work can be seen. Fishing is permitted in a nearby pond. San Ildefonso is one of the more active pueblos in retaining its ceremonial dances and customs. Its feast day is celebrated on January 23, when unforgettable Buffalo, Deer, and Comanche dances are performed throughout the day. *Rte. 5, Box 315-A, Santa Fe 87501,* ☎ *505/455–3549 or 505/455–2273.* ☉ *Daily 8–5. Cameras are not permitted at any of the ceremonial dances but may be used at other times with a permit. Fees are $5 for still cameras, $25 for video recorders, and $15 for sketching.*

Santa Clara Pueblo

The Santa Clara Pueblo, located just off NM 30, southwest of Espanola, is the home of the beautiful Puye Cliff Dwellings, which rise above it, and of Santa Clara Canyon with its four ponds, miles of stream fishing, picnicking, and camping facilities. Most of the traditional tribal dwellings have been demolished and replaced by more conventional houses. Santa Clara remains famous nonetheless for its shiny red-and-black engraved pottery and for its myriad well-known painters and sculptors; visitors who knock on the doors with signs announcing pottery will be invited inside to meet the artists. The population of the pueblo is about 2,000. Self-guided and guided tours are offered to Puye Cliff Dwellings, Santa Clara's ancestral home, which are topped by the ruins of a 740-room pueblo. The feast day of St. Clare is celebrated on August 12. *Box 580, Espanola 87532,* ☎ *505/753–7326.* ☉ *Daily*

8–4:30. Permits for the use of trails, camping, and picnic areas, as well as for fishing in trout ponds, are available at the sites. Fees are $5 for photography and video cameras.

Tesuque Pueblo

The Tesuque Pueblo, 10 miles north of Santa Fe along U.S. 84/285, is the home of one of the smallest Tiwa-speaking tribes. Because of its proximity to Santa Fe, it was one of the first pueblos to establish contact with the Spanish and eventually became one of their most vicious foes. Built around the year 1250, it has maintained its identity well and is today one of the oldest and most traditional of the pueblos—listed on the National Register of Historic Places—but unfortunately it's perhaps better known for its bingo parlor than for its arts and crafts. The pueblo has no crafts shops or trading posts, and most sales are made from private homes. The tribe operates an RV park and general store, among other businesses. Tesuque Farms grows food without the use of pesticides. The pueblo's lands are some of the most beautiful for horseback riding, camping, and fishing, with the majestic Sangre de Cristo Mountains rising in the distance. Wind-eroded sandstone formations, such as nearby Camel Rock, form the "badlands" north of the pueblo. Tesuque celebrates its feast day on November 12 in honor of San Diego with ceremonial dances. It's the one time of the year during which the pueblo seems to open its arms and its doors to visitors (bingo players don't have access to most of Tesuque). For directions and information, stop by the administrative office. *Rte. 11, Box 1, Santa Fe 87501,* ☎ *505/983–2667. Cameras, recorders, and sketch pads not allowed during ceremonial dances (and there's not much to photograph otherwise). Tesuque Pueblo bingo begins at 5 nightly, with the early-bird special at 6:30 and the main series beginning at 7. For bingo information, call 505/984–8414.*

PUEBLOS NEAR TAOS

The famous Taos Pueblo, unchanged over the centuries, is the personification of classic Pueblo Native American culture. It and the other northern pueblos near Taos offer first-rate recreational facilities as well as a glimpse into the past.

Picuris Pueblo

The Picuris (Keresan for "those who paint") Native Americans once lived in large six- and seven-story dwellings similar to those still standing at the Taos Pueblo, but they were abandoned in the wake of 18th-century Pueblo uprisings. Relatively isolated—off NM 68, between Espanola and Taos, Picuris is surrounded by the timberland of the Carson National Forest—and is one of the smallest pueblos in New Mexico. A multipurpose building on the grounds contains the Hidden Valley Restaurant (American and Native American food) and a convenience store, the Picuris Market. There's also a museum where samples of mica-flecked pottery and other crafts can be seen and purchased. Guided tours are conducted to recently excavated areas of the pueblo. Fishing, picnicking, and camping are permitted at nearby trout-stocked Pu-Na and Tu-Tah lakes. (Fishing and overnight camping permits can be obtained at the Picuris Market.) The 270-member, Tiwa-speaking Picuris tribe governs itself as a separate tribal nation and has no treaties with any foreign country, including the United States. The tribe also owns controlling interest in the Hotel Santa Fe in Santa Fe. The pueblo's patron saint, San Lorenzo, is honored on August 10. *Box 487, Penasco*

*87553, ☎ 505/587–2957. Fees are charged for guided tours to the ruins,
as well as for sketching, video and still cameras.* ⊙ *Daily, hours vary.*

San Juan Pueblo

Site of the first regional Spanish settlement in 1598 (the first capital
of *Nueva España,* New Spain), the San Juan Pueblo is situated on the
confluence of the Chama River and the Rio Grande, 5 miles north of
Espanola on NM 68. Headquarters of the Eight Northern Indian
Pueblo Council, it has a beautiful arts center called Oke-Oweenge
Arts and Crafts Cooperative where beadwork, jewelry, baskets, textiles, and the pueblo's special thick-walled red-and-black pottery can
be purchased. One of the more picturesque of the pueblos along the
Rio Grande and the largest of the Tewa-speaking pueblos, it has two
handsome kivas and a New England–style church. The pueblo also conducts public bingo games, and its Tewa Restaurant, near the center of
the old village, serves fine Native American specialties. The pueblo has
fishing ponds open in the spring and summer, with permits available
on the sites. Its feast days are June 23–24. At Christmas, the San Juan
dancers perform the Matachines dance, a colorful adaptation of a
Spanish morality play based on the Spanish conquest of the Aztec Em-
pire. *Box 1099, San Juan 87566, ☎ 505/852–4400.* ⊙ *8–5 daily. No
video cameras, tape recording, or sketching allowed. Still cameras are
allowed by permit ($5 per camera), which can be bought weekdays from
8 to 4:30 at the San Juan Pueblo tribal office (behind the post office).*

Taos Pueblo

The Taos-Tiwa Native Americans have lived in the Taos Pueblo for almost 1,000 years. It is the largest existing multistory pueblo structure
in the United States and has become Taos's number-one tourist attraction.
For full coverage, *see* Exploring Taos *in* Chapter 3.

PUEBLOS NEAR ALBUQUERQUE

Sports enthusiasts from Albuquerque regularly escape the confines of
urban life to fish in the well-stocked lakes and reservoirs of the nearby
pueblos. The legendary Acoma "Sky City" Pueblo, probably the most
spectacular of the pueblo communities, is a short drive from the city.

Acoma Pueblo

Situated atop a 367-foot mesa that rises abruptly from the valley floor,
Acoma Pueblo deserves its name, Sky City. The pueblo was built more
than a thousand years before the Spanish conquistadores discovered
it while searching for the Seven Cities of Cibola. Captain Hernando
de Alvarado of Coronado's Expedition of 1540, the first European to
see Acoma, reported that he had "found a rock with a village on top,
the strongest position ever seen in the world." However, the Acomas
were defeated by a force sent by Governor Don Juan Onate in January
of 1599. A smaller contingent of Spanish soldiers, led by Onate's
nephew, Don Juan de Zaldívar, had been attacked by the Acomas. Only
a few soldiers escaped; the rest were killed. A larger force of 70 men
laid siege to the village for three days before they successfully conquered
it. Then in 1629, Fray Juan Ramírez became Acoma's first permanent
missionary. Father Ramírez built the incredible mission church of San
Esteban del Rey at Sky City, with walls 60 feet high and 10 feet thick,
between 1629 and 1641. By 1699, the Acomas had formally accepted
the Spanish monks and their bearded Christ. Today, the pueblo is still

inhabited, although its onetime population of 6,000 has dwindled to a mere 50 who live in the village without electricity or running water. (Acoma people from neighboring Acomita, Anzac, and McCarty's return to their ancestral home during feast days and celebrations, the most important of which is on September 2.) Actually a series of terraced adobe pueblos, dominated by the massive mission church of San Esteban del Rey (its 40-foot ceiling vigas were hauled up the mesa from mountains 30 miles away on the backs of 17th-century pueblo men), Acoma Pueblo is by far the most spectacular of the pueblo communities. Although a widened road takes you there today, the pueblo was originally accessible only by a narrow path carved into the face of the rock; food and water had to be hauled up the sides of the cliffs. The Acoma Native Americans are known for their fine, thin-walled pottery, characterized by "Op Art" patterns and Mimbres (small animal and godlike figures) designs. The 70-acre village, about 60 miles west of Albuquerque (12 miles off I–40), may be visited by guided tours only. A shuttle bus leaves every hour from the visitor center just below the mesa and drives to the top, where the tours are conducted on foot. At the visitor center there is also a museum, a restaurant, and a crafts shop. Nearby is the ubiquitous bingo hall. *Acoma Tourist Center, Box 309, Acoma 87034,* ☎ *800/747–0181.* ☛ *$6 adults, $5 senior citizens, $4 children 6–18.* ☉ *Spring and summer, daily 8–7, tours daily 8–6; fall and winter, daily 8–4:30, tours daily 8–3:30. There is a $5 charge per camera for still photos. Movie and video cameras are prohibited.*

Isleta Pueblo

The original pueblo was abandoned during the Pueblo Revolt in 1680, when many of the Tiwa-speaking Isleta Native Americans fled to Hopi; they returned and built a new village in 1693, which stands where it did then, 13 miles south of Albuquerque off I–25. Isleta, Spanish for "little island," now consists of several communities spread out across the reservation, the largest of which is Shiawiba to the west of the Rio Grande. Visitors will find a bingo hall on the reservation, as well as picnicking and camping facilities and fishing at the Isleta Lakes and Recreation Area (*see* Camping *in* Chapter 4). Polychrome pottery with red-and-black designs on a white background is the specialty here. The pueblo celebrates its feast days on August 28 and September 4, both in honor of St. Augustine. *Box 1270, Isleta 87022,* ☎ *505/869–3111.* ☉ *Year-round. Cameras permitted (no permit necessary). Camping, fishing, and picnicking permits available at Isleta Lakes.*

Laguna Pueblo

The Laguna Pueblo, 46 miles west of Albuquerque on old Route 66, consists of six scattered villages: the stunning white facade of St. Joseph of the Lake Mission Church, visible from I–40, is a landmark at Old Laguna. It is one of the youngest and largest of the New Mexican pueblos, and one of the most enterprising, with such businesses as Laguna Industries (manufacturer of U.S. Army communications shelters). A large uranium field located on Laguna lands provided mining jobs for many of its members for years and is now the site of ongoing restoration through the Laguna Reclamation Project. The 1970s brought about a resurgence of interest in traditional crafts, so an abundance of fine pottery, decorated in geometric designs, is to be found in the area. The pueblo celebrates many feast days and dances (March 19, San José feast day; September 8, Virgin Mary feast day; October 17, Sts. Margaret and Mary feast day), since each of the six villages hosts its own ceremony, but all join at Old Laguna on September 19 to honor St. Joseph with Buffalo, Corn, and Eagle dances and a fair. Permits for fishing the pueblo's Paguate Reservoir can be obtained in Paguate village. *Box 194, Laguna Pueblo 87026, ☎ 505/552–6654 or 505/243–7616. ☼ Daily 8–5. Photography regulations vary in each village; contact the governor's office (☎ 505/552–6654) for information.*

San Felipe Pueblo

San Felipe is one of the most traditional and conservative of the pueblo communities. Ceremonial dances are performed several times a year; the most notable is the Green Corn Dance on May 1, celebrating the feast of St. Philip, the pueblo's patron saint. Wearing symbolic costumes, hundreds of men, women, and children participate in the singing and dancing rituals that continue throughout the day. The plaza on the pueblo has been worn deep, like a rounded-out bowl, 3 feet below the surface of the surrounding ground, by years of dancing feet. A recent revival in beadwork and pottery has spawned a growing number of pueblo artists. San Felipe is located off I–25, between Albuquerque and Santa Fe, about 10 miles north of Bernalillo. *Box 4339, San Felipe Pueblo 87001, ☎ 505/867–3381. ☼ Daily 9–6 except special feast days; closed days of religious celebrations. Cameras, sketching, and recording are prohibited.*

Sandia Pueblo

The Sandia Pueblo was one of the pueblos that Francisco Coronado visited in 1540. It had been occupied since AD 1300; today, it has a population of 318 and covers 22,884 acres. The people have maintained their traditional lifestyle, their ceremonials and dances. Agriculture provides one strong source of income; others include the leasing of land for Albuquerque's aerial tramway; bingo (the tribal bingo hall is open 24 hours a day, seven days a week); and the operation of fishing, boating, and picnicking facilities at Sandia Lakes. Although this is one the more industrious of the Rio Grande Pueblos, its residents are particularly well versed in traditional arts and crafts (most of the sold at its Bien Mur Indian Market Center on I–25 come from pueblos and reservations). In fairness, the Sandia Pueblo does a variety of small, rough pottery pieces and some flat, t paintings. The pueblo's original Tiwa Indian name was *N* ing "a dusty place." Coronado, the first European to vis Spanish name *Sandía* (watermelon) for the bright-red w of the surrounding mountains at sunset. The pueblo' St. Anthony, whose feast day is June 13—a day on ally, mothers bring their unmarried daughters to he will find husbands for them. (It's also the day festival, the San Antonio Corn Dance.) The pue north of Albuquerque. *Box 6008, Bernalill 3317. ☼ Daily 8–5. Cameras, sketching, a*

Santa Ana Pueblo

Tribal lands of the Santa Ana Pueblo Bernalillo on NM 44, have been rede creating two distinct pueblos: the t ness pueblo. Except for ceremoni appears to be empty most of the houses off the grounds. Howev sion on Santa Ana feast day, Craftspeople of the pueblo bands, paintings, and pottery, all of which can be purchased through the pueblo's Ta-Ma-Ya Cooperative Association (open Tues. and Thurs. 10–4:30 and noon–4 on Sun.). The business pueblo has the attractive 27-hole Valle Grande Golf Course that opened in 1990 and a Las Vegas–style casino that opened in 1993. The business pueblo is open year-round, but since the traditional pueblo is not always open to visitors, check with the tribal governor's office before making the trip. *2 Dove Rd., Bernalillo 87004, ☎ 505/867–3301. Traditional pueblo: Village is open only for ceremonial dances on Jan. 1 and 6, Easter Day, June 24 and 29, July 25 and 26, Dec. 25–28. Still and video cameras; video and tape recorders; and sketching materials prohibited. Business pueblo: Golf course, restaurant, casino open year-round.*

Santo Domingo Pueblo

The Santo Domingo Pueblo operates a small Indian Arts and Crafts Center, where its outstanding *heishi* (shell) jewelry is sold, along with other traditional arts and crafts. Sales are also made from stands along the road, leading into the pueblo, which is located off I–25 at the Santo Domingo exit between Albuquerque and Santa Fe. Long a farming community, the Santo Domingo Pueblo is now developing commercial property along the interstate. It is the Santo Domingo Native Americans who are most often seen selling their wares beneath the portal of the Palace of the Governors on the Santa Fe Plaza, and the pueblo's annual three-day Labor Day Arts and Crafts Fair has artists and visitors out in full force. The August 4th Corn Dance is one of the most colorful and dramatic of all the pueblo ceremonial dances. Held in honor of St. Dominic, the pueblo's patron saint, the dance attracts more than 2,000 Native American dancers, clowns, singers, and drummers. *Box 99, Santo Domingo 87052, ☎ 505/465–2214. ☉ Daily sunrise–sunset. Donations are encouraged. Still and video cameras, video and tape recorders, and sketching materials prohibited.*

...blo has existed at its present site, 17 miles northwest of ...44, since the early 1300s; it was once one of the largest ...blos, boasting eight plazas and 6,000 residents. ... on the New Mexican flag was adopted from ... population is now 700. The Zia bird and ...eblo trademarks and often adorn the fine ... by the skillful Zia potters. The tribe's ...roducing outstanding watercolors that ...orn Dance is held on August 15, the ...ing Our Lady of the Assumption. Per- ...t 2 miles west of the pueblo, may be ... Square Dr., Zia Pueblo, San Ysidro ...ily 8–5. Still and video cameras, ...hing materials prohibited.*

photography but require a permit, which usually costs about $5 for a still camera and up to $35 for the privilege of setting up an easel and painting all day. Be sure to ask permission before photographing anyone in the pueblos; it's also customary to give the subject a dollar or two for agreeing to be photographed. Native American law prevails on the pueblos, and violations of photography regulations could result in confiscation of cameras. Restrictions for the various pueblos are noted in the individual descriptions below.

Possessing or using drugs and/or alcohol on Native American land is forbidden.

Ritual dances often have serious religious significance and should be respected as such. Silence is mandatory. That means no questions about ceremonies or dances while they're being performed. Don't walk across the dance plaza during a performance, and don't applaud afterward.

Kiva and ceremonial rooms are restricted to pueblo members only.

Cemeteries are sacred. They're off limits to all visitors and should never be photographed.

Unless pueblo dwellings are clearly marked as shops, don't wander or peek inside. Remember, these are private homes.

Many of the pueblo buildings are hundreds of years old. Don't try to scale adobe walls or climb on top of buildings, or you may come tumbling down.

Don't litter. Nature is sacred on the pueblos, and defacing of land can be a serious offense.

Important Addresses and Numbers

The **Indian Pueblo Cultural Center** (2401 12th St. NW, Albuquerque 87104, ☏ 505/843–7270) is the best source of information on New Mexico's Native Americans.

The detailed *New Mexico Vacation Guide,* available free from the **New Mexico Department of Tourism** (Lamy Bldg., 491 Old Santa Fe Trail, Santa Fe 87503, ☏ 505/827–7400 or 800/545–2040), includes an informative section on the state's pueblos.

7 Portraits of New Mexico

NEW MEXICO

SUPERFICIALLY, THE WORLD has become small and known. Poor little globe of earth, the tourists trot round you as easily as they trot round the Bois or round Central Park. There is no mystery left, we've been there, we've seen it, we know all about it. We've done the globe, and the globe is done.

This is quite true, superficially. On the superficies, horizontally, we've been everywhere and done everything, we know all about it. Yet the more we know, superficially, the less we penetrate, vertically. It's all very well skimming across the surface of the ocean, and saying you know all about the sea. There still remain the terrifying underdeeps, of which we have utterly no experience.

The same is true of land travel. We skim along, we get there, we see it all, we've done it all. And as a rule, we never once go through the curious film which railroads, ships, motor-cars, and hotels stretch over the surface of the whole earth. Peking is just the same as New York, with a few different things to look at; rather more Chinese about, etc. Poor creatures that we are, we crave for experience, yet we are like flies that crawl on the pure and transparent mucous-paper in which the world like a bon-bon is wrapped so carefully that we can never get at it, though we see it there all the time as we move about it, apparently in contact, yet actually as far removed as if it were the moon.

As a matter of fact, our great-grandfathers, who never went anywhere, in actuality had more experience of the world than we have, who have seen everything. When they listened to a lecture with lantern-slides, they really held their breath before the unknown, as they sat in the village school-room. We, bowling along in a rickshaw in Ceylon, say to ourselves: "It's very much what you'd expect." We really know it all.

We are mistaken. The know-it-all state of mind is just the result of being outside the mucous-paper wrapping of civilization. Underneath is everything we don't know and are afraid of knowing.

I realized this with shattering force when I went to New Mexico.

New Mexico, one of the United States, part of the U.S.A. New Mexico, the picturesque reservation and playground of the eastern states, very romantic, old Spanish, Red Indian, desert mesas, pueblos, cowboys, penitentes, all that film-stuff. Very nice, the great South-West; put on a sombrero and knot a red kerchief round your neck to go out in the great free spaces!

That is New Mexico wrapped in the absolutely hygienic and shiny mucous-paper of our trite civilization. That is the New Mexico known to most of the Americans who know it at all. But break through the shiny sterilized wrapping and actually *touch* the country, and you will never be the same again.

I THINK NEW MEXICO was the greatest experience from the outside world that I have ever had. It certainly changed me forever. Curious as it may sound, it was New Mexico that liberated me from the present era of civilization, the great era of material and mechanical development. Months spent in holy Kandy, in Ceylon, the holy of holies of Southern Buddhism, had not touched the great psyche of materialism and idealism that dominated me. And years, even in the exquisite beauty of Sicily, right among the old Greek paganism that still lives there, had not shattered the essential Christianity on which my character was established. Australia was a sort of dream or trance, like being under a spell, the self remaining unchanged, so long as the trance did not last too long. Tahiti, in a mere

This essay is taken from *Phoenix: The Posthumous Papers of D. H. Lawrence*. Lawrence visited New Mexico with his wife, Frieda, in the early 1920s as part of an extended tour of Europe, Mexico, and the American Southwest. The couple lived on a ranch north of Taos, where Lawrence continued to write.

glimpse, repelled me; and so did California, after a stay of a few weeks. There seemed a strange brutality in the spirit of the western coast, and I felt: O, let me get away!

But the moment I saw the brilliant, proud morning shine high up over the deserts of Santa Fe, something stood still in my soul, and I started to attend. There was a certain magnificence in the high-up day, a certain eagle-like royalty, so different from the equally pure, equally pristine and lovely morning of Australia, which is so soft, so utterly pure in its softness, and betrayed by green parrot flying. But in the lovely morning of Australia one went into a dream. In the magnificent fierce morning of New Mexico one sprang awake, a new part of the soul woke up suddenly, and the old world gave way to a new.

There are all kinds of beauty in the world, thank God, though ugliness is homogeneous. How lovely is Sicily, with Calabria across the sea like an opal and Etna with her snow in a world above and beyond! How lovely is Tuscany, with little red tulips wild among the corn: or bluebells at dusk in England, or mimosa in clouds of pure yellow among the grey-green dun foliage of Australia, under a soft, blue, unbreathed sky! But for a *greatness* of beauty I have never experienced anything like New Mexico. All those mornings when I went with a hoe along the ditch to the Cañon, at the ranch, and stood in the fierce, proud silence of the Rockies, on their foothills, to look far over the desert to the blue mountains away in Arizona, blue as chalcedony, with the sage-brush desert sweeping grey-blue in between, dotted with tiny cube-crystals of houses, the vast amphitheatre of lofty, indomitable desert, sweeping round to the ponderous Sangre de Cristo mountains on the east, and coming up flush at the pine-dotted foot-hills of the Rockies! What splendor! Only the tawny eagle could really sail out into the splendor of it all. Leo Stein once wrote to me: It is the most aesthetically-satisfying landscape I know. To me it was much more than that. It had a splendid silent terror and a vast far-and-wide magnificence that made it way beyond mere aesthetic appreciation. Never is the light more pure and overweening than there, arching with a royalty almost cruel over the hollow, uptilted world. For it is curious that the land that has produced modern political democracy at its highest pitch should give one the greatest sense of overweening, terrible proudness and mercilessness: but so beautiful, God! so beautiful! Those who have spent morning after morning alone there pitched among the pines above the great proud world of desert will know, almost unbearably how beautiful it is, how clear and unquestioned is the might of the day. Just day itself is tremendous there. It is so easy to understand that the Aztecs gave hearts of men to the sun. For the sun is not merely hot or scorching, not at all. It is of a brilliant and unchallengeable purity and haughty serenity that would make one sacrifice the heart to it. Ah, yes, in New Mexico the heart is sacrificed to the sun and the human being is left stark, heartless, but undauntedly religious.

AND THAT WAS the second revelation out there. I had looked over all the world for something that would strike *me* as religious. The simple piety of some English people, the semi-pagan mystery of some Catholics in southern Italy, the intensity of some Bavarian peasants, the semi-ecstasy of Buddhists or Brahmins: all this had seemed religious all right, as far as the parties concerned were involved, but it didn't involve me. I looked on at the religiousness from the outside. For it is still harder to feel religion at will than to love at will.

I had seen what I felt was a hint of wild religion in the so-called devil dances of a group of naked villagers from the far-remote jungle in Ceylon, dancing at midnight under the torches, glittering wet with sweat on their dark bodies as if they had been gilded, at the celebration of the Pera-hera, in Kandy, given to the Prince of Wales. And the utter dark absorption of these naked men, as they danced with their knees wide apart, suddenly affected me with a *sense* of religion. I *felt* religion for a moment. For religion is an experience, an uncontrollable sensual experience, even more so than love: I use sensual to mean an experience deep down in the senses, inexplicable and inscrutable.

But this experience was fleeting, gone in the curious turmoil of the Pera-hera, and I had no permanent feeling of religion till I came to New Mexico and penetrated into the old human race experience there. It is curious that it should be in America, of all places, that a European should really experience religion, after touching the old Mediterranean and the East. . . . A vast old religion that once swayed the earth lingers in unbroken practice there in New Mexico—older, perhaps, than anything in the world save Australian aboriginal taboo and totem, and that is not yet religion.

You can feel it, the atmosphere of it, around the pueblos. Not, of course, when the place is crowded with sight-seers and motor-cars. But go to Taos pueblo on some brilliant snowy morning and see the white figure on the roof, or come riding through at dusk on some windy evening, when the black skirts of the silent women blow around the white wide boots, and you will feel the old, old root of human consciousness still reaching down to depths we know nothing of: and of which, only too often, we are jealous. It seems it will not be long before the pueblos are uprooted.

BUT NEVER SHALL I FORGET watching the dancers, the men with the fox-skin swaying down from their buttocks, file out at San Geronimo, and the women with seed rattles following. The long, streaming, glistening black hair of the men. Even in ancient Crete long hair was sacred in a man, as it is still in the Indians. Never shall I forget the utter absorption of the dance, so quiet, so steadily, timelessly rhythmic, and silent, with the ceaseless downtread, always to the earth's centre, the very reverse of the upflow of Dionysiac or Christian ecstasy. Never shall I forget the deep singing of the men at the drum, swelling and sinking, the deepest sound I have heard in all my life, deeper than thunder, deeper than the sound of the Pacific Ocean, deeper than the roar of a deep waterfall: the wonderful deep sound of men calling to the unspeakable depths.

Never shall I forget coming into the little pueblo of San Filipi one sunny morning in spring, unexpectedly, when bloom was on the trees in the perfect little pueblo more old, more utterly peaceful and idyllic than anything in Theocritus, and seeing a little casual dance. Not impressive as a spectacle, only, to me, profoundly moving because of the truly terrifying religious absorption of it.

Never shall I forget the Christmas dances at Taos, twilight, snow, the darkness coming over the great wintry mountains and the lonely pueblo, then suddenly, again, like dark calling to dark, the deep Indian cluster-singing around the drum, wild and awful, suddenly arousing on the last dusk as the procession starts. And then the bonfires leaping suddenly in pure spurts of high flame, columns of sudden flame forming an alley for the procession. . . . Never shall I forget the Indian races, when the young men, even the boys, run naked, smeared with white earth and stuck with bits of eagle fluff for the swiftness of the heavens, and the old men brush them with eagle feathers, to give them power. And they run in the strange hurling fashion of the primitive world, hurled forward, not making speed deliberately. And the race is not for victory. It is not a contest. There is no competition. It is a great cumulative effort. The tribe this day is adding up its male energy and exerting it to the utmost—for what? To get power, to get strength: to come, by sheer cumulative, hurling effort of the bodies of men, into contact with the great cosmic source of vitality that gives strength, power, energy to the men who can grasp it, energy for the zeal of attainment.

It was a vast old religion, greater than anything we know: more starkly and nakedly religious. There is no God, no conception of a god. All is god. But it is not the pantheism we are accustomed to, which expresses itself as "God is everywhere, God is in everything." In the oldest religion, everything was alive, not supernaturally but naturally alive. There were only deeper and deeper streams of life, vibrations of life more and more vast. So rocks were alive, but a mountain had a deeper, vaster life than a rock, and it was much harder for a man to bring his spirit, or his energy, into contact with the life of the mountain, and so draw strength from the mountain, as from a great standing well of life, than it was to come into contact with the rock. And he had to put forth a great religious effort. For the whole life-effort of man was to get his life into direct contact with the elemental life of the cosmos, mountain-life, cloud-life, thunder-life, air-life, earth-life, sun-life. To come into immediate *felt* contact, and so derive energy, power, and a dark sort of joy. This effort into sheer naked contact, *without an intermediary or mediator,* is the root meaning of religion, and at the sacred races the runners hurled themselves in a terrible cumulative effort, through the air, to come at last into naked contact with the very life of air, which is the life of the clouds, and so of the rain.

It was a vast and pure religion, without idols or images, even mental ones. It is the oldest religion, a cosmic religion the same for all peoples, not broken up into specific gods or saviours or systems. It is the religion that precedes the god-concept, and is therefore greater and deeper than any god-religion.

And it lingers still, for a little while in New Mexico: but long enough to have been a revelation to me. And the Indian, however objectionable he may be on occasion, has still some of the strange beauty and pathos of the religion that brought him forth and is now shedding him away into oblivion. When Trinidad, the Indian boy, and I planted corn at the ranch, my soul paused to see his brown hands softly moving the earth over the maize in pure ritual. He was back in his old religious self, and the ages stood still. Ten minutes later he was making a fool of himself with the horses. Horses were never part of the Indian's religious life, never would be. He hasn't a tithe of feeling for them that he has for a bear, for example. So horses don't like Indians.

But there it is: the newest democracy ousting the oldest religion! And once the oldest religion is ousted, one feels the democracy and all its paraphernalia will collapse, and the oldest religion, which comes down to us from man's pre-war days, will start again. The skyscraper will scatter on the winds like thistledown, and the genuine America, the America of New Mexico, will start on its course again. This is an interregnum.

By D. H. Lawrence

MORE PORTRAITS

General Interest

A list of classic books on New Mexico would include *Death Comes for the Archbishop,* by Willa Cather, a novel based on the life of Archbishop Jean Baptiste Lamy, who built, among other churches, the St. Francis Cathedral in Santa Fe. *Great River,* by Paul Horgan; *The Wind Leaves No Shadow,* by Ruth Laughlin; *Miracle Hill,* by Barney Mitchell; *Navajos Have Five Fingers,* by T. D. Allen; *Santa Fe,* by Oliver La Farge; *New Mexico,* by Jack Schaefer; and *Moon Over Adobe,* by Dorothy Pillsbury, are all good choices as well. *Lautrec,* by Norman Zollinger, is an entertaining mystery set in Albuquerque. Zollinger, who owns the Little Professor Book Center on Lomas Boulevard NE, in Albuquerque, also wrote *Riders to Cibola,* which chronicles the conquistadors' search for the legendary Seven Cities of Gold. Albuquerque author Tony Hillerman received an Edgar Allan Poe Award from the Mystery Writers of America in 1974 for his book *Dance Hall of the Dead. The Wood Carvers of Cordova, New Mexico,* by Charles L. Briggs, is a prize-winning study of the making and selling of religious images in a northern New Mexico village. *Eliot Porter's Southwest* is the famed photographer's poetic view of the Southwest, much of it focused around his Tesuque, New Mexico, home. *An Illustrated History of New Mexico* is by Thomas E. Chavez, director of the Palace of the Governors in Santa Fe, who uses quotes to underscore his visual chronicle of New Mexican history.

Native American Lore and Pueblo Life

The Man Who Killed the Deer, by Frank Waters, is a classic of Pueblo life. *Masked Gods,* by the same author, has a following that reaches cult proportions. J. J. Brody's profusely illustrated book *Anasazi and Pueblo Painting* is an indispensable volume for art historians and students of Southwestern culture. *Mornings in Mexico,* by D. H. Lawrence, contains a number of essays pertaining to Taos and the Pueblo ritual dances. *Pueblo Style and Regional Architecture,* edited by Nicholas C. Markovich, Wolfgang F. E. Preiser, and Fred G. Strum, covers the evolution of architecture in the Southwest, with particular emphasis on New Mexico. *Pueblos: Prehistoric Indian Cultures of the Southwest,* by Sylvio Acatos, with photos by Maximilien Bruggman, is a portrait of the peace-loving people who carved out a civilization in the region. *Nacimientos: Nativity Scenes by Southwest Indian Artists,* by Guy and Doris Monthan, offers photographs and descriptions of ceramic Nativity scenes produced by Pueblo Native Americans.

New Mexican Personalities

Billy the Kid: A Short and Violent Life, by Robert M. Utley, a noted historian, is considered the definitive work on the notorious outlaw. *The Life of D. H. Lawrence,* by Keith Sagar, published in 1980, is a good biography of the world-renowned author so strongly associated with (and buried in) New Mexico. Taos is also Georgia O'Keeffe country, and there is a wealth of books about the artist. Among the best is *Georgia O'Keeffe: Arts and Letters,* published by the New York Graphic Society in conjunction with a retrospective of her work at the National Gallery of Art, Washington, D.C. Also worthy of note is the reissue of the coffee-table book, *Georgia O'Keeffe,* with text by the artist herself. *Portrait of an Artist: A Biography of Georgia O'Keeffe,* by Laurie Lisle, spans the artist's life and career. *Georgia O'Keeffe: Some Memories of Drawings,* edited by Doris Bry, is a collection of the artist's major 1915–1963 drawings, with comments on each.

Albuquerque, Santa Fe, and Taos

Albuquerque—A Narrative History, by Marc Simmons, is a fascinating look at the city's birth and development. *The Wingspread Collectors Guide to Santa Fe and Taos* and *The Wingspread Collectors Guide to Albuquerque and Corrales* (Wingspread, Box 13566-T, Albuquerque 87192) provide high-quality reproductions and useful information about art galleries, art, and crafts of the region; they also include listings of museums, hotels, restaurants, and historic sites. *Taos: A Pictorial History,* by John Sherman, contains numerous black-and-white historical photographs of the major characters, events, and structures that formed the backbone of Taos, as well as of Native Americans, Hispanics, and Anglo immigrants, with accompanying text.

For information about bed-and-breakfasts in the area, consult *Fodor's The Southwest's Best Bed and Breakfasts.*

Videos

Northern New Mexico has provided memorable scenic backdrops for several feature films, particularly Westerns. *Silverado* (1985) and *Wyatt Earp* (1994) are Westerns that were photographed in the Santa Fe vicinity. For television, two mini-series based on popular Larry McMurtry novels with Old West settings, *Lonesome Dove* (1989) and *Buffalo Girls* (1995), were shot near Santa Fe. *The Milagro Beanfield War* (1988), directed by Robert Redford, based on the novel by Taos author John Nichols, was photographed in Truchas, on the High Road to Taos. Other popular movies using Santa Fe area locations include *Late for Dinner* (1991) and *The Cowboy Way* (1994).

The Albuquerque area appears in director Oliver Stone's *Natural Born Killers* (1994). Southern New Mexico provides settings for *Young Guns* (1988), *Gas, Food, Lodging* (1992), *White Sands* (1992), and *Mad Love* (1995). Other movies photographed around New Mexico include *The Cowboys* (1972), starring John Wayne; *Outrageous Fortune* (1987), with Bette Midler and Shelley Long; *Powwow Highway* (1985); and *City Slickers* (1991), starring Billy Crystal.

INDEX

✕ = restaurant, ▥ = hotel

NOTES

NOTES

NOTES

NOTES

NOTES

NOTES

NOTES

Your guide to a picture-perfect vacation

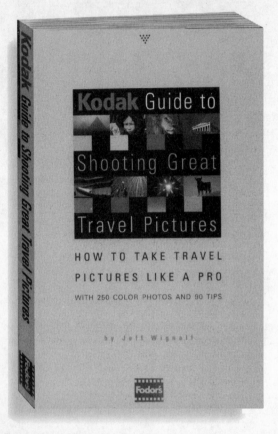

Kodak and Fodor's join together to create the guide that travelers everywhere have been asking for—one that covers the terms and techniques, the equipment and etiquette for taking first-rate travel photographs.

The most authoritative and up-to-date book of its kind, **The Kodak Guide to Shooting Great Travel Pictures** includes over 200 color photographs and spreads on 100 points of photography important to travelers, such as landscape basics, under sea shots, wildlife, city street, close-ups, photographing in museums and more.

$16.50   ($22.95 Canada)

At bookstores everywhere, or call 1-800-533-6478.

Escape to ancient cities and

journey to   *exotic islands with*

CNN Travel Guide, a wealth of valuable advice. Host

Valerie Voss will take you to

all of your favorite destinations,

including those off the beaten

path. Tune-in to your passport to the world.

CNN TRAVEL GUIDE
SATURDAY 12:30 PMET   SUNDAY 4:30 PMET

CNN®

Fodor's Travel Publications

Available at bookstores everywhere, or call 1–800–533–6478, 24 hours a day.

Gold Guides

U.S.

Alaska	Florida	New Orleans	Santa Fe, Taos, Albuquerque
Arizona	Hawaii	New York City	Seattle & Vancouver
Boston	Las Vegas, Reno, Tahoe	Pacific North Coast	The South
California	Los Angeles	Philadelphia & the Pennsylvania Dutch Country	U.S. & British Virgin Islands
Cape Cod, Martha's Vineyard, Nantucket	Maine, Vermont, New Hampshire	The Rockies	USA
The Carolinas & the Georgia Coast	Maui	San Diego	Virginia & Maryland
Chicago	Miami & the Keys	San Francisco	Waikiki
Colorado	New England		Washington, D.C.

Foreign

Australia & New Zealand	Europe	Madrid & Barcelona	Provence & the Riviera
Austria	Florence, Tuscany & Umbria	Mexico	Scandinavia
The Bahamas	France	Montréal & Québec City	Scotland
Bermuda	Germany	Moscow, St. Petersburg, Kiev	Singapore
Budapest	Great Britain	The Netherlands, Belgium & Luxembourg	South America
Canada	Greece		Southeast Asia
Cancún, Cozumel, Yucatán Peninsula	Hong Kong	New Zealand	Spain
Caribbean	India	Norway	Sweden
China	Ireland	Nova Scotia, New Brunswick, Prince Edward Island	Switzerland
Costa Rica, Belize, Guatemala	Israel		Thailand
The Czech Republic & Slovakia	Italy	Paris	Tokyo
	Japan	Portugal	Toronto
Eastern Europe	Kenya & Tanzania		Turkey
Egypt	Korea		Vienna & the Danube
	London		

Fodor's Special-Interest Guides

Branson	Fodor's London Companion	Kodak Guide to Shooting Great Travel Pictures	Walt Disney World for Adults
Caribbean Ports of Call	France by Train	Shadow Traffic's New York Shortcuts and Traffic Tips	Where Should We Take the Kids? California
The Complete Guide to America's National Parks	Halliday's New England Food Explorer	Sunday in New York	Where Should We Take the Kids? Northeast
Condé Nast Traveler Caribbean Resort and Cruise Ship Finder	Healthy Escapes	Sunday in San Francisco	
	Italy by Train	Walt Disney World, Universal Studios and Orlando	
Cruises and Ports of Call			

Special Series

Affordables
Caribbean
Europe
Florida
France
Germany
Great Britain
Italy
London
Paris

Fodor's Bed & Breakfasts and Country Inns
America's Best B&Bs
California's Best B&Bs
Canada's Great Country Inns
Cottages, B&Bs and Country Inns of England and Wales
The Mid-Atlantic's Best B&Bs
New England's Best B&Bs
The Pacific Northwest's Best B&Bs
The South's Best B&Bs
The Southwest's Best B&Bs
The Upper Great Lakes' Best B&Bs

The Berkeley Guides
California
Central America
Eastern Europe
Europe
France
Germany & Austria
Great Britain & Ireland
Italy
London
Mexico

Pacific Northwest & Alaska
Paris
San Francisco

Compass American Guides
Arizona
Chicago
Colorado
Hawaii
Hollywood
Las Vegas
Maine
Manhattan
Montana
New Mexico
New Orleans
Oregon
San Francisco
South Carolina
South Dakota
Texas
Utah
Virginia
Washington
Wine Country
Wisconsin
Wyoming

Fodor's Español
California
Caribe Occidental
Caribe Oriental
Gran Bretaña
Londres
Mexico
Nueva York
Paris

Fodor's Exploring Guides
Australia
Boston & New England
Britain

California
Caribbean
China
Florence & Tuscany
Florida
France
Germany
Ireland
Italy
London
Mexico
Moscow & St. Petersburg
New York City
Paris
Prague
Provence
Rome
San Francisco
Scotland
Singapore & Malaysia
Spain
Thailand
Turkey
Venice

Fodor's Flashmaps
Boston
New York
San Francisco
Washington, D.C.

Fodor's Pocket Guides
Acapulco
Atlanta
Barbados
Jamaica
London
New York City
Paris
Prague
Puerto Rico

Rome
San Francisco
Washington, D.C.

Rivages Guides
Bed and Breakfasts of Character and Charm in France
Hotels and Country Inns of Character and Charm in France
Hotels and Country Inns of Character and Charm in Italy

Short Escapes
Country Getaways in Britain
Country Getaways in France
Country Getaways Near New York City

Fodor's Sports
Golf Digest's Best Places to Play
Skiing USA
USA Today The Complete Four Sport Stadium Guide

Fodor's Vacation Planners
Great American Learning Vacations
Great American Sports & Adventure Vacations
Great American Vacations
National Parks and Seashores of the East
National Parks of the West

Before Catching Your Flight, Catch Up With Your World.

Fueled by the global resources of CNN and available in major airports across America, CNN Airport Network provides a live source  of current domestic and  international news, sports, business, weather and lifestyle programming. Plus two daily Fodor's features for the facts you need: "Travel Fact," a useful and creative mix of travel trivia; and "What's Happening," a comprehensive round-up of upcoming events in major cities around the world.

With CNN Airport Network, you'll never be out of the loop.

HERE'S YOUR OWN PERSONAL VIEW OF THE WORLD.

Here's the easiest way to get up-to-the-minute, objective, personalized information about what's going on in the city you'll be visiting—before you leave on your trip! Unique information you could get only if you knew someone personally in each of 160 destinations around the world. Everything from special places to dine to local events only a local would know about.

It's all yours—in your Travel Update from Worldview, the leading provider of time-sensitive destination information.

Review the following order form and fill it out by indicating your destination(s)

and travel dates and by checking off up to eight interest categories. Then mail or fax your order form to us, or call your order in. (We're here to help you 24 hours a day.)

Within 48 hours of receiving your order, we'll mail your convenient, pocket-sized custom guide to you, packed with information to make your travel more fun and interesting. And if you're in a hurry, we can even fax it.

Have a great trip with your Fodor's Worldview Travel Update!

Fodor's WORLDVIEW TRAVEL UPDATE

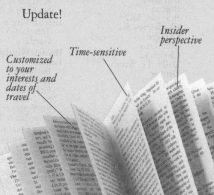

Insider perspective

Time-sensitive

Customized to your interests and dates of travel

DESTINATIONS

Worldview covers more than 160 destinations worldwide. Choose the
destination(s) that match your itinerary from the list below:

Europe
Amsterdam
Athens
Barcelona
Berlin
Brussels
Budapest
Copenhagen
Dublin
Edinburgh
Florence
Frankfurt
French Riviera
Geneva
Glasgow
Lausanne
Lisbon
London
Madrid
Milan
Moscow
Munich
Oslo
Paris
Prague
Provence
Rome
Salzburg
Seville
St. Petersburg
Stockholm
Venice
Vienna
Zurich

**United States
(Mainland)**
Albuquerque
Atlanta
Atlantic City
Baltimore
Boston
Branson, MO
Charleston, SC
Chicago
Cincinnati
Cleveland
Dallas/Ft. Worth
Denver
Detroit
Houston
Indianapolis
Kansas City
Las Vegas
Los Angeles
Memphis
Miami
Milwaukee
Minneapolis/St. Paul
Nashville
New Orleans
New York City
Orlando
Palm Springs
Philadelphia
Phoenix
Pittsburgh

Portland
Reno/Lake Tahoe
St. Louis
Salt Lake City
San Antonio
San Diego
San Francisco
Santa Fe
Seattle
Tampa
Washington, DC

Alaska
Alaskan Destinations

Hawaii
Honolulu
Island of Hawaii
Kauai
Maui

Canada
Quebec City
Montreal
Ottawa
Toronto
Vancouver

Bahamas
Abaco
Eleuthera/
  Harbour Island
Exuma
Freeport
Nassau &
  Paradise Island

Bermuda
Bermuda Countryside
Hamilton

**British Leeward
Islands**
Anguilla
Antigua & Barbuda
St. Kitts & Nevis

British Virgin Islands
Tortola & Virgin
Gorda

**British Windward
Islands**
Barbados
Dominica
Grenada
St. Lucia
St. Vincent
Trinidad & Tobago

Cayman Islands
The Caymans

Dominican Republic
Santo Domingo

Dutch Leeward Islands
Aruba
Bonaire
Curacao

**Dutch Windward
Island**
St. Maarten/St. Martin

French West Indies
Guadeloupe
Martinique
St. Barthelemy

Jamaica
Kingston
Montego Bay
Negril
Ocho Rios

Puerto Rico
Ponce
San Juan

Turks & Caicos
Grand Turk/
  Providenciales

U.S. Virgin Islands
St. Croix
St. John
St. Thomas

Mexico
Acapulco
Cancun & Isla Mujeres
Cozumel
Guadalajara
Ixtapa & Zihuatanejo
Los Cabos
Mazatlan
Mexico City
Monterrey
Oaxaca
Puerto Vallarta

South/Central America
Buenos Aires
Caracas
Rio de Janeiro
San Jose, Costa Rica
Sao Paulo

Middle East
Istanbul
Jerusalem

**Australia & New
Zealand**
Auckland
Melbourne
South Island
Sydney

China
Beijing
Guangzhou
Shanghai

Japan
Kyoto
Nagoya
Osaka
Tokyo
Yokohama

Pacific Rim/Other
Bali
Bangkok
Hong Kong & Macau
Manila
Seoul
Singapore
Taipei

INTERESTS

For your personalized Travel Update, choose the eight (8) categories you're most interested in from the following list:

1.	Business Services	Fax & Overnight Mail, Computer Rentals, Protocol, Secretarial, Messenger, Translation Services
	Dining	
2.	All-Day Dining	Breakfast & Brunch, Cafes & Tea Rooms, Late-Night Dining
3.	Local Cuisine	Every Price Range — from Budget Restaurants to the Special Splurge
4.	European Cuisine	Continental, French, Italian
5.	Asian Cuisine	Chinese, Far Eastern, Japanese, Other
6.	Americas Cuisine	American, Mexican & Latin
7.	Nightlife	Bars, Dance Clubs, Casinos, Comedy Clubs, Ethnic, Pubs & Beer Halls
8.	Entertainment	Theater — Comedy, Drama, Musicals, Dance, Ticket Agencies
9.	Music	Classical, Opera, Traditional & Ethnic, Jazz & Blues, Pop, Rock
10.	Children's Activites	Events, Attractions
11.	Tours	Local Tours, Day Trips, Overnight Excursions
12.	Exhibitions, Festivals & Shows	Antiques & Flower, History & Cultural, Art Exhibitions, Fairs & Craft Shows, Music & Art Festivals
13.	Shopping	Districts & Malls, Markets, Regional Specialties
14.	Fitness	Bicycling, Health Clubs, Hiking, Jogging
15.	Recreational Sports	Boating/Sailing, Fishing, Golf, Skiing, Snorkeling/Scuba, Tennis/Racket
16.	Spectator Sports	Auto Racing, Baseball, Basketball, Golf, Football, Horse Racing, Ice Hockey, Soccer
17.	Event Highlights	The best of what's happening during the dates of your trip.
18.	Sightseeing	Sights, Buildings, Monuments
19.	Museums	Art, Cultural
20.	Transportation	Taxis, Car Rentals, Airports, Public Transportation
21.	General Info	Overview, Holidays, Currency, Tourist Info

Please note that content will vary by season, destination, and length of stay.

Name _____

Address _____

City _____ State Country _____ ZIP

Tel # ( ) ___ - ___ Fax # ( ) ___ - ___

Title of this Fodor's guide: _____

Store and location where guide was purchased: _____

INDICATE YOUR DESTINATIONS/DATES: You can order up to three (3) destinations from the previous page. Fill in your arrival and departure dates for each destination. **Your Travel Update itinerary (all destinations selected) cannot exceed 30 days from beginning to end.**

		Month	Day	Month	Day
(Sample) **LONDON**	From:	**6** /	**21**	To: **6** /	**30**
1	From:	/		To:	/
2	From:	/		To:	/
3	From:	/		To:	/

CHOOSE YOUR INTERESTS: Select up to eight (8) categories from the list of interest categories shown on the previous page and circle the numbers below:

1 2 3 4 5 6 7 8 9 10 11 12 13 14 15 16 17 18 19 20 21

CHOOSE WHEN YOU WANT YOUR TRAVEL UPDATE DELIVERED (Check one):
❑ Please send my Travel Update immediately.
❑ Please hold my order until a few weeks before my trip to include the most up-to-date information.
Completed orders will be sent within 48 hours. Allow 7–10 days for U.S. mail delivery.

ADD UP YOUR ORDER HERE. SPECIAL OFFER FOR FODOR'S PURCHASERS ONLY!

	Suggested Retail Price	Your Price	This Order
First destination ordered	$ 9.95	$ 7.95	$ 7.95
Second destination (if applicable)	$ 6.95	$ 4.95	+
Third destination (if applicable)	$ 6.95	$ 4.95	+

DELIVERY CHARGE (Check one and enter amount below)

	Within U.S. & Canada	Outside U.S. & Canada
First Class Mail	❑ $2.50	❑ $5.00
FAX	❑ $5.00	❑ $10.00
Priority Delivery	❑ $15.00	❑ $27.00

ENTER DELIVERY CHARGE FROM ABOVE: + _____

TOTAL: $ _____

METHOD OF PAYMENT IN U.S. FUNDS ONLY (Check one):
❑ AmEx ❑ MC ❑ Visa ❑ Discover ❑ Personal Check (U. S. & Canada only)
❑ Money Order/International Money Order

Make check or money order payable to: Fodor's Worldview Travel Update

Credit Card __/__/__/__/__/__/__/__/__/__/__/__/__/__/ **Expiration Date:__/__**

Authorized Signature _____

SEND THIS COMPLETED FORM WITH PAYMENT TO:
Fodor's Worldview Travel Update, 114 Sansome Street, Suite 700, San Francisco, CA 94104

OR CALL OR FAX US 24-HOURS A DAY
Telephone **1-800-799-9609** • Fax **1-800-799-9619** (From within the U.S. & Canada)
(Outside the U.S. & Canada: Telephone 415-616-9988 • Fax 415-616-9989)

(Please have this guide in front of you when you call so we can verify purchase.)
Code: FTG   Offer valid until 12/31/97